DOCTOR FATE

THE BLOOD PRICE

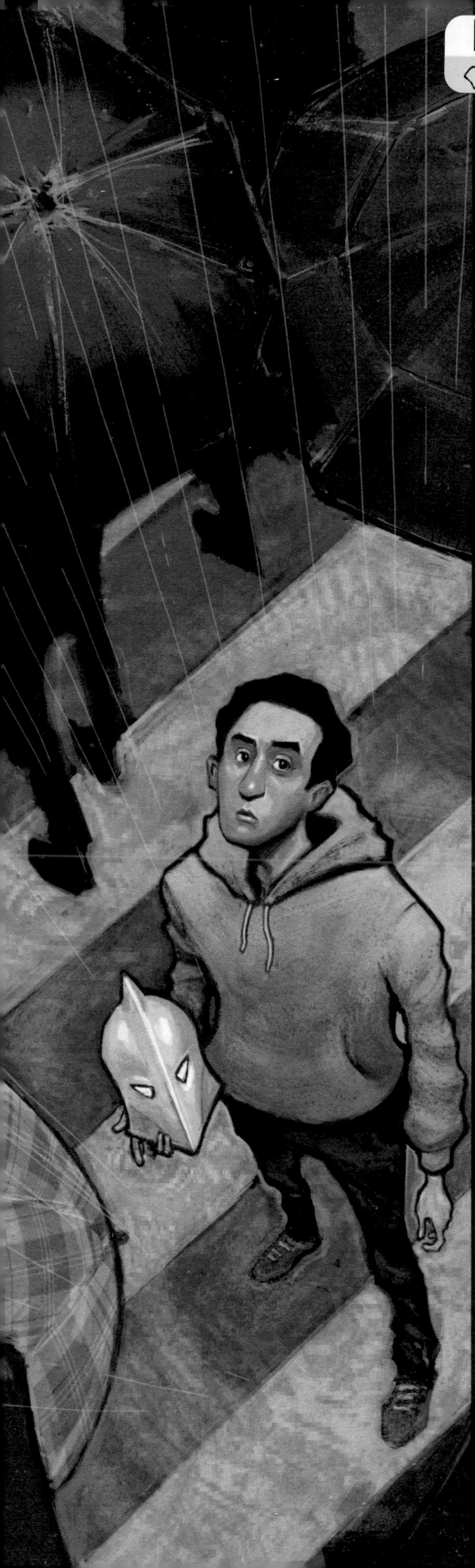

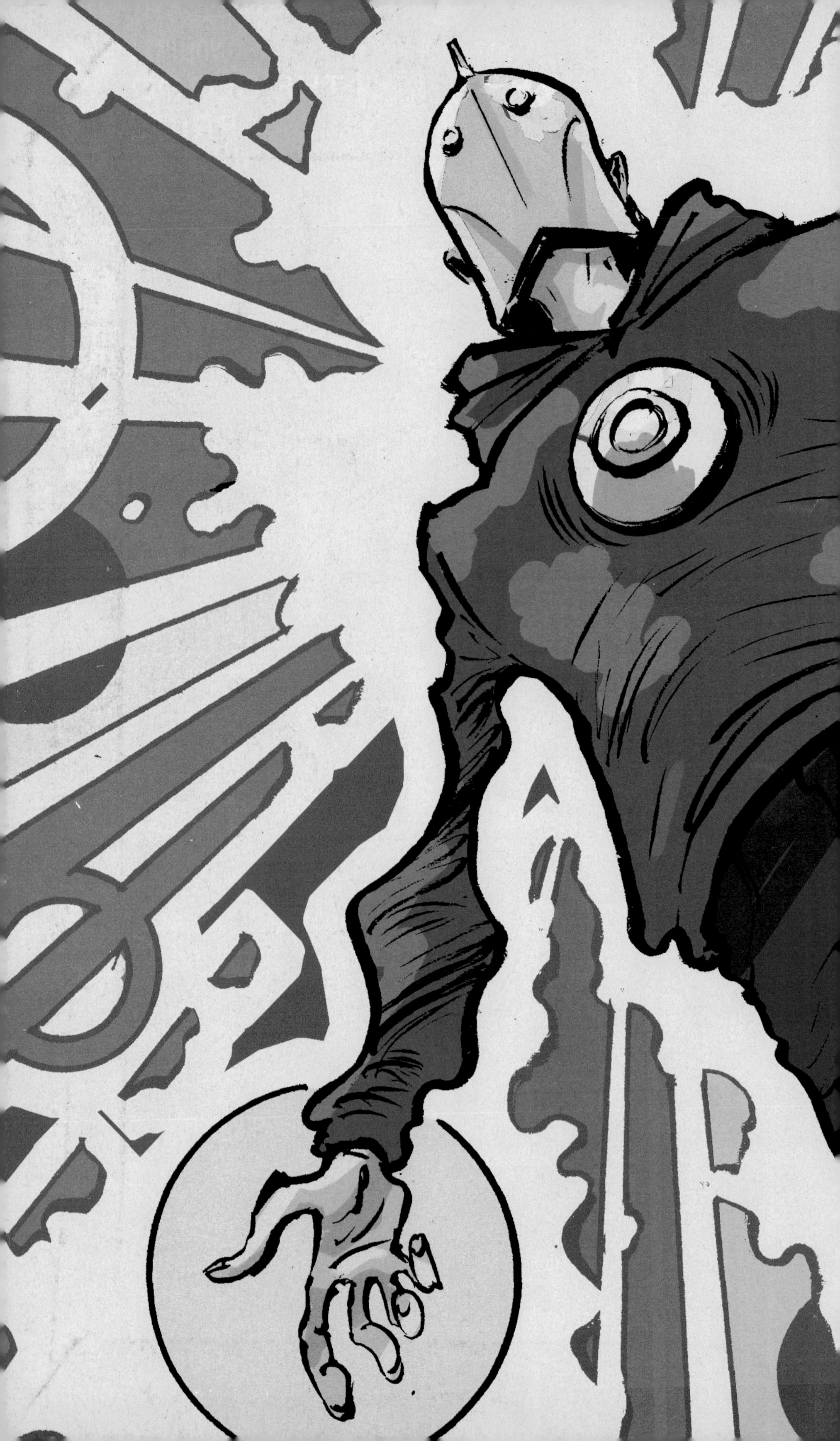

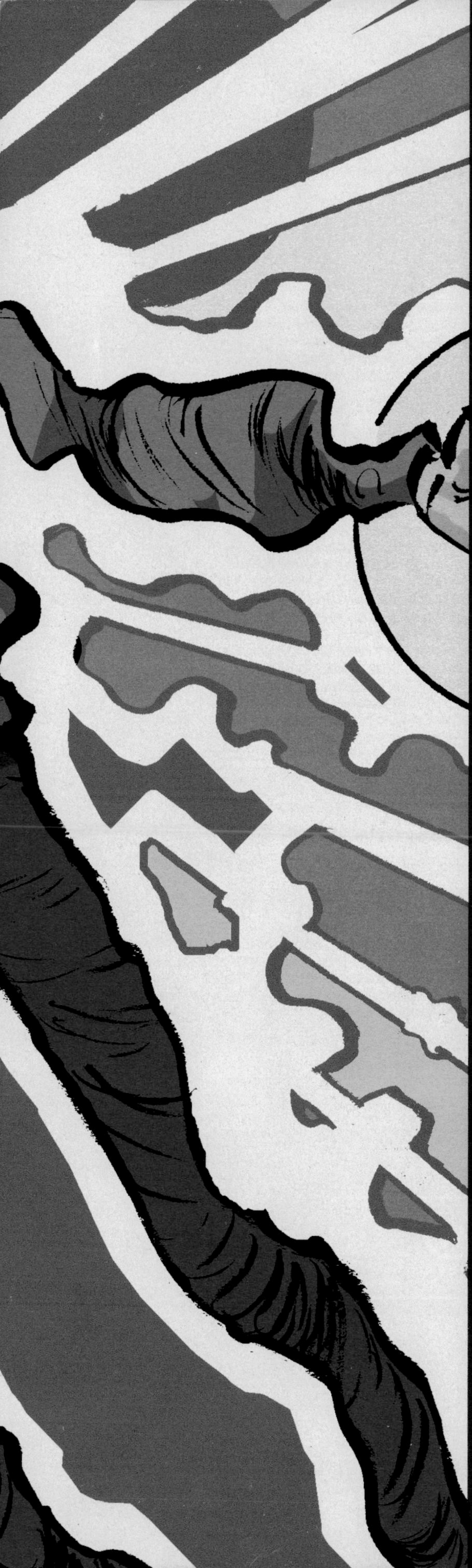

DOCTOR FATE

VOLUME 1
THE BLOOD PRICE

WRITTEN BY
PAUL LEVITZ

ART BY
SONNY LIEW

COLOR BY
LEE LOUGHRIDGE
SONNY LIEW

LETTERS BY
NICK J. NAPOLITANO
STEVE WANDS

COLLECTION COVER ART BY
SONNY LIEW

ANDY KHOURI Editor – Original Series
AMEDEO TURTURRO Assistant Editor – Original Series
JEB WOODARD Group Editor – Collected Editions
LIZ ERICKSON Editor – Collected Edition
STEVE COOK Design Director – Books
DAMIAN RYLAND Publication Design

BOB HARRAS Senior VP – Editor-in-Chief, DC Comics

DIANE NELSON President
DAN DIDIO and JIM LEE Co-Publishers
GEOFF JOHNS Chief Creative Officer
AMIT DESAI Senior VP – Marketing & Global Franchise Management
NAIRI GARDINER Senior VP – Finance
SAM ADES VP – Digital Marketing
BOBBIE CHASE VP – Talent Development
MARK CHIARELLO Senior VP – Art, Design & Collected Editions
JOHN CUNNINGHAM VP – Content Strategy
ANNE DEPIES VP – Strategy Planning & Reporting
DON FALLETTI VP – Manufacturing Operations
LAWRENCE GANEM VP – Editorial Administration & Talent Relations
ALISON GILL Senior VP – Manufacturing & Operations
HANK KANALZ Senior VP – Editorial Strategy & Administration
JAY KOGAN VP – Legal Affairs
DEREK MADDALENA Senior VP – Sales & Business Development
JACK MAHAN VP – Business Affairs
DAN MIRON VP – Sales Planning & Trade Development
NICK NAPOLITANO VP – Manufacturing Administration
CAROL ROEDER VP – Marketing
EDDIE SCANNELL VP – Mass Account & Digital Sales
COURTNEY SIMMONS Senior VP – Publicity & Communications
JIM (SKI) SOKOLOWSKI VP – Comic Book Specialty & Newsstand Sales
SANDY YI Senior VP – Global Franchise Management

DOCTOR FATE VOLUME 1: THE BLOOD PRICE

DC Comics, 2900 West Alameda Ave., Burbank, CA 91505
Printed by RR Donnelley, Salem, VA, USA. 2/19/16. First Printing.
ISBN: 978-1-4012-6121-4

Library of Congress Cataloging-in-Publication Data is available.

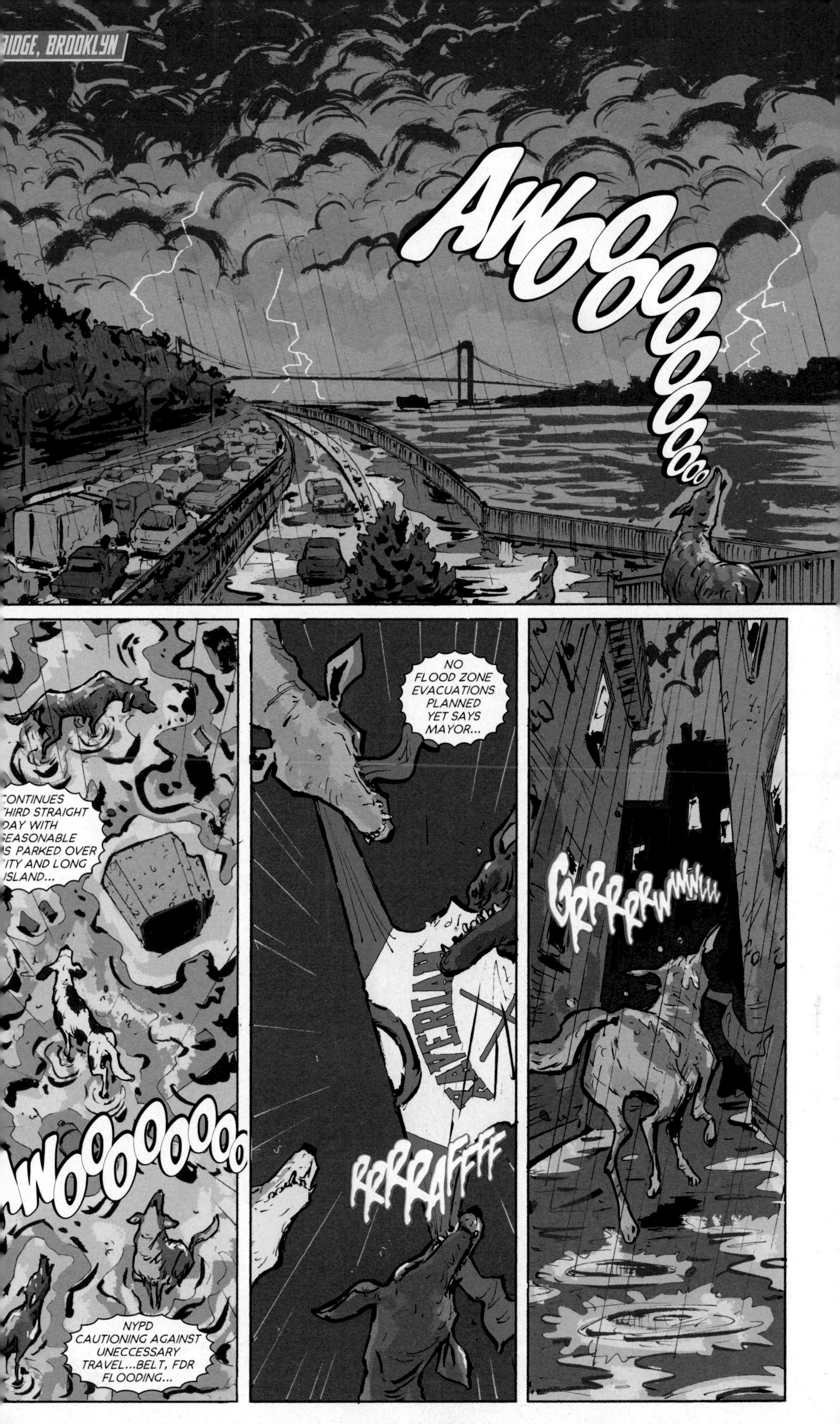

RIDGE, BROOKLYN
AWOOOOOOOOOOOO
ONTINUES THIRD STRAIGHT DAY WITH EASONABLE S PARKED OVER ITY AND LONG ISLAND...
AWOOOOOOOOO
NYPD CAUTIONING AGAINST UNECCESSARY TRAVEL...BELT, FDR FLOODING...
NO FLOOD ZONE EVACUATIONS PLANNED YET SAYS MAYOR...
RRRRAFFFF
GRRRRRWWWLLL

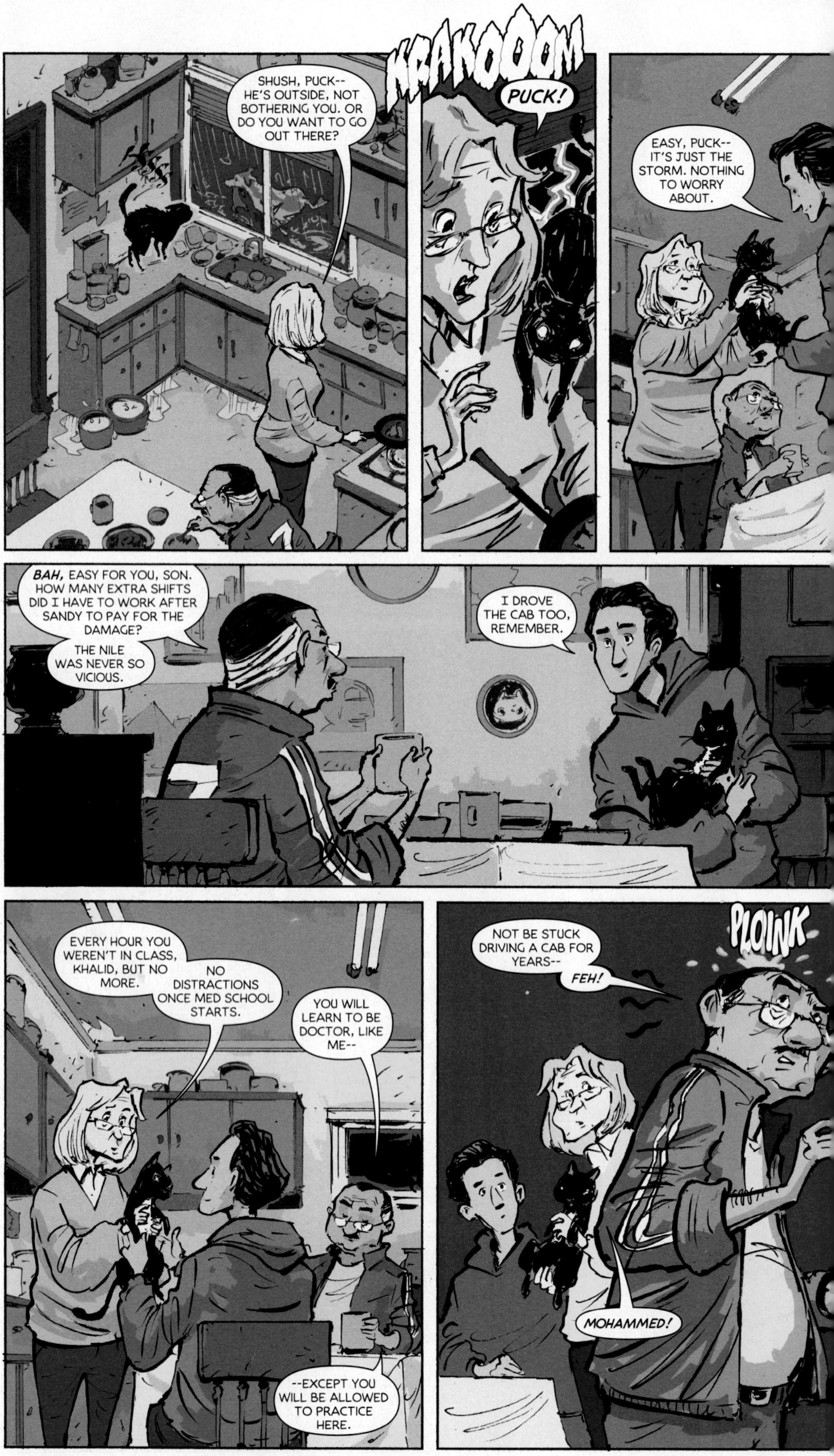
SHUSH, PUCK-- HE'S OUTSIDE, NOT BOTHERING YOU. OR DO YOU WANT TO GO OUT THERE?
KRAKOOOM
PUCK!
EASY, PUCK-- IT'S JUST THE STORM. NOTHING TO WORRY ABOUT.
BAH, EASY FOR YOU, SON. HOW MANY EXTRA SHIFTS DID I HAVE TO WORK AFTER SANDY TO PAY FOR THE DAMAGE?
THE NILE WAS NEVER SO VICIOUS.
I DROVE THE CAB TOO, REMEMBER.
EVERY HOUR YOU WEREN'T IN CLASS, KHALID, BUT NO MORE.
NO DISTRACTIONS ONCE MED SCHOOL STARTS.
YOU WILL LEARN TO BE DOCTOR, LIKE ME--
--EXCEPT YOU WILL BE ALLOWED TO PRACTICE HERE.
PLOINK
NOT BE STUCK DRIVING A CAB FOR YEARS-- FEH!
MOHAMMED!

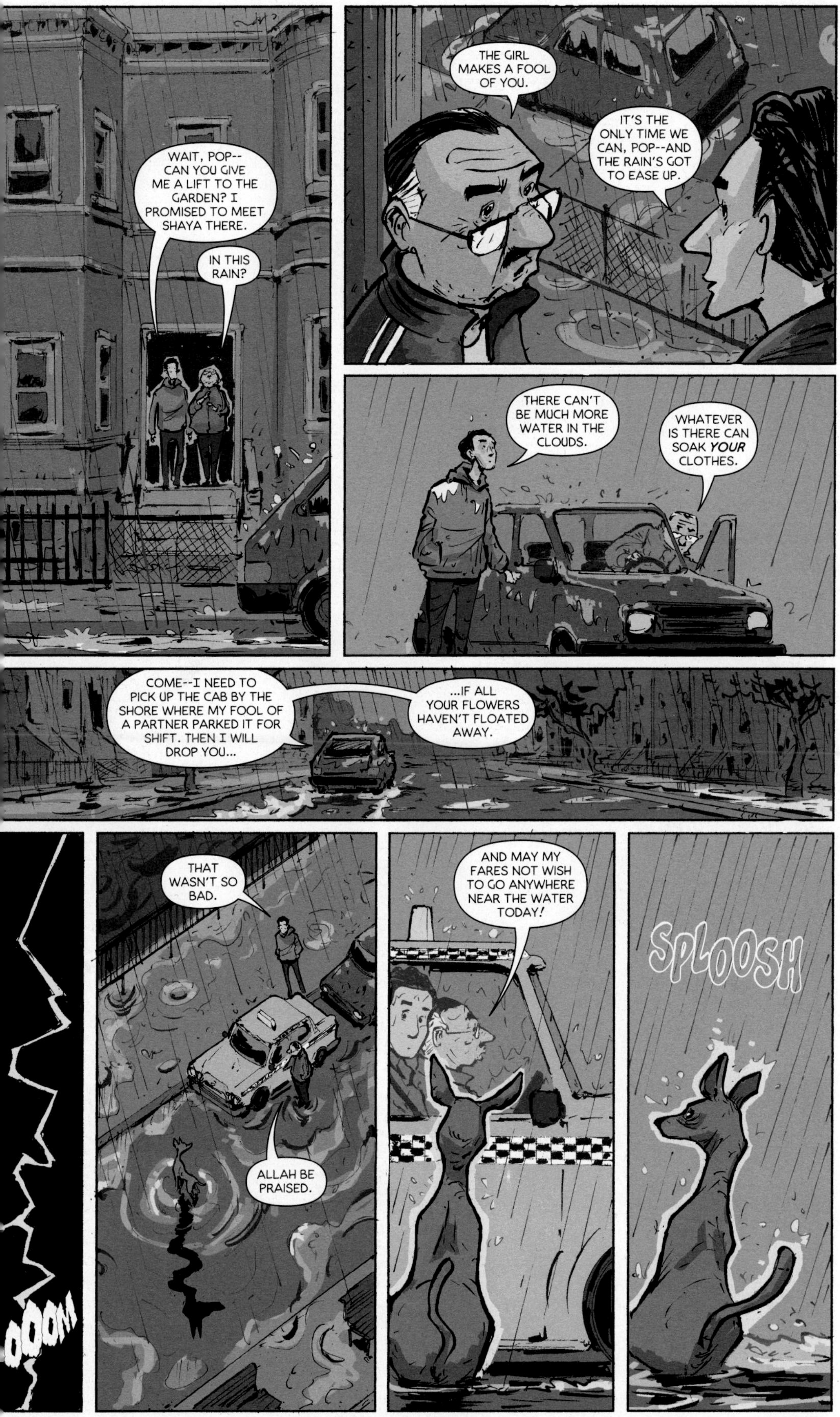

WAIT, POP-- CAN YOU GIVE ME A LIFT TO THE GARDEN? I PROMISED TO MEET SHAYA THERE.
IN THIS RAIN?
THE GIRL MAKES A FOOL OF YOU.
IT'S THE ONLY TIME WE CAN, POP--AND THE RAIN'S GOT TO EASE UP.
THERE CAN'T BE MUCH MORE WATER IN THE CLOUDS.
WHATEVER IS THERE CAN SOAK ***YOUR*** CLOTHES.
COME--I NEED TO PICK UP THE CAB BY THE SHORE WHERE MY FOOL OF A PARTNER PARKED IT FOR SHIFT. THEN I WILL DROP YOU...
...IF ALL YOUR FLOWERS HAVEN'T FLOATED AWAY.
OOOM
THAT WASN'T SO BAD.
ALLAH BE PRAISED.
AND MAY MY FARES NOT WISH TO GO ANYWHERE NEAR THE WATER TODAY!
SPLOOSH

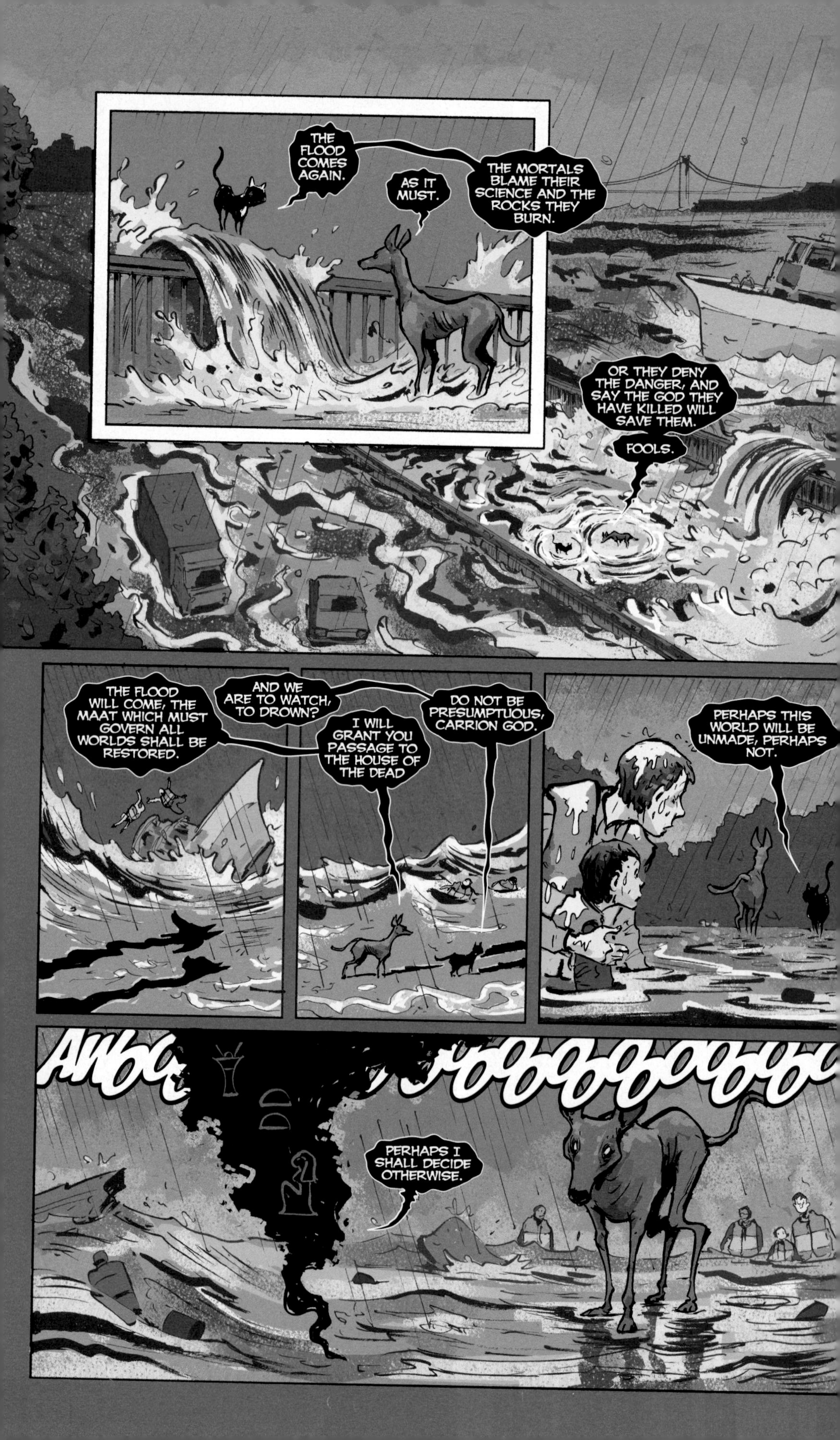
THE FLOOD COMES AGAIN.
AS IT MUST.
THE MORTALS BLAME THEIR SCIENCE AND THE ROCKS THEY BURN.
OR THEY DENY THE DANGER, AND SAY THE GOD THEY HAVE KILLED WILL SAVE THEM.
FOOLS.
THE FLOOD WILL COME, THE MAAT WHICH MUST GOVERN ALL WORLDS SHALL BE RESTORED.
AND WE ARE TO WATCH, TO DROWN?
I WILL GRANT YOU PASSAGE TO THE HOUSE OF THE DEAD
DO NOT BE PRESUMPTUOUS, CARRION GOD.
PERHAPS THIS WORLD WILL BE UNMADE, PERHAPS NOT.
AWOOOOOOOOOOOO
PERHAPS I SHALL DECIDE OTHERWISE.

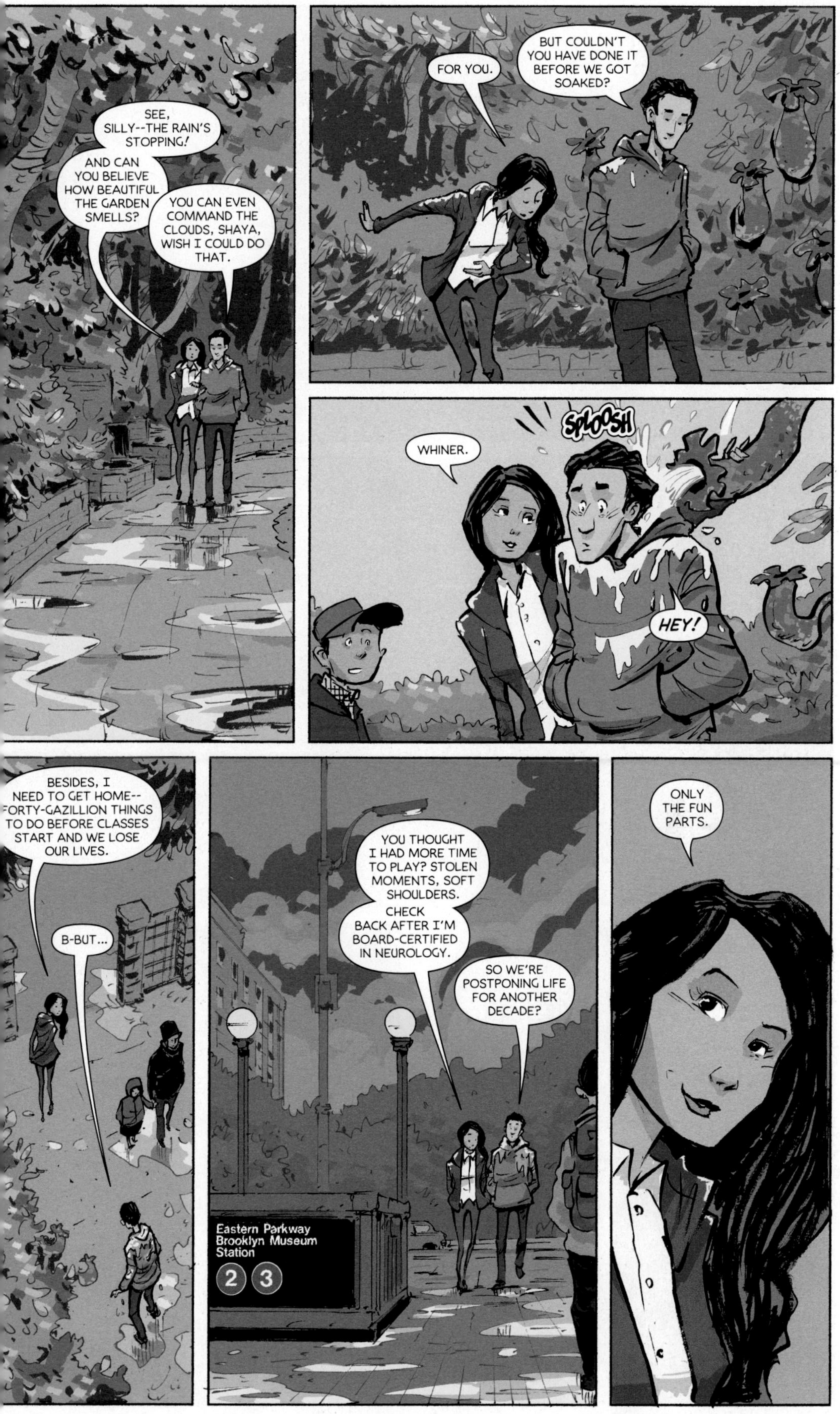
SEE, SILLY--THE RAIN'S STOPPING!
AND CAN YOU BELIEVE HOW BEAUTIFUL THE GARDEN SMELLS?
YOU CAN EVEN COMMAND THE CLOUDS, SHAYA, WISH I COULD DO THAT.
FOR YOU.
BUT COULDN'T YOU HAVE DONE IT BEFORE WE GOT SOAKED?
SPLOOSH
WHINER.
HEY!
BESIDES, I NEED TO GET HOME--FORTY-GAZILLION THINGS TO DO BEFORE CLASSES START AND WE LOSE OUR LIVES.
B-BUT...
YOU THOUGHT I HAD MORE TIME TO PLAY? STOLEN MOMENTS, SOFT SHOULDERS.
CHECK BACK AFTER I'M BOARD-CERTIFIED IN NEUROLOGY.
SO WE'RE POSTPONING LIFE FOR ANOTHER DECADE?
Eastern Parkway Brooklyn Museum Station
2 3
ONLY THE FUN PARTS.

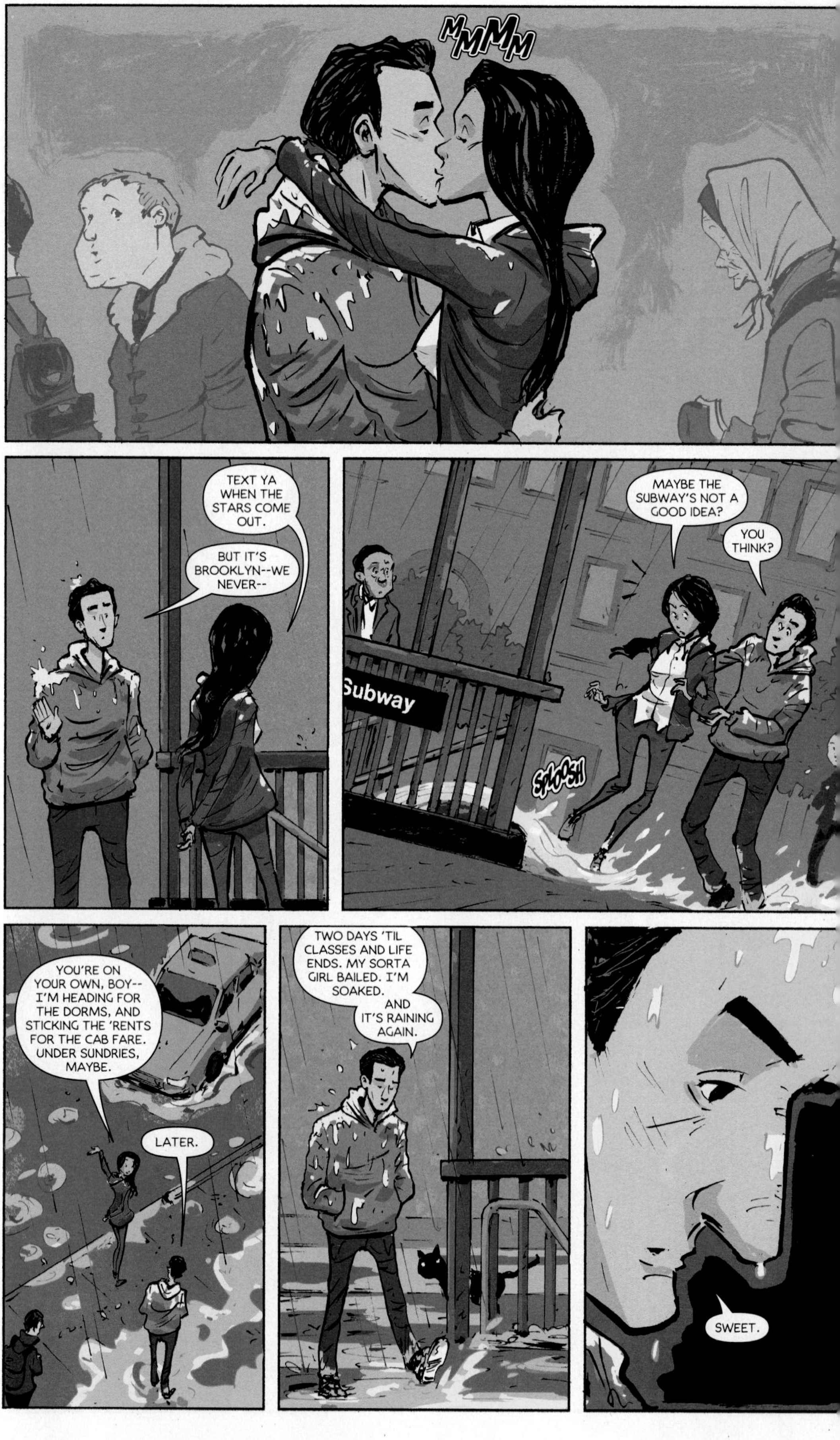
MMMM
TEXT YA WHEN THE STARS COME OUT.
BUT IT'S BROOKLYN--WE NEVER--
MAYBE THE SUBWAY'S NOT A GOOD IDEA?
YOU THINK?
Subway
SPLOOSH
YOU'RE ON YOUR OWN, BOY-- I'M HEADING FOR THE DORMS, AND STICKING THE 'RENTS FOR THE CAB FARE. UNDER SUNDRIES, MAYBE.
LATER.
TWO DAYS 'TIL CLASSES AND LIFE ENDS. MY SORTA GIRL BAILED. I'M SOAKED.
AND IT'S RAINING AGAIN.
SWEET.

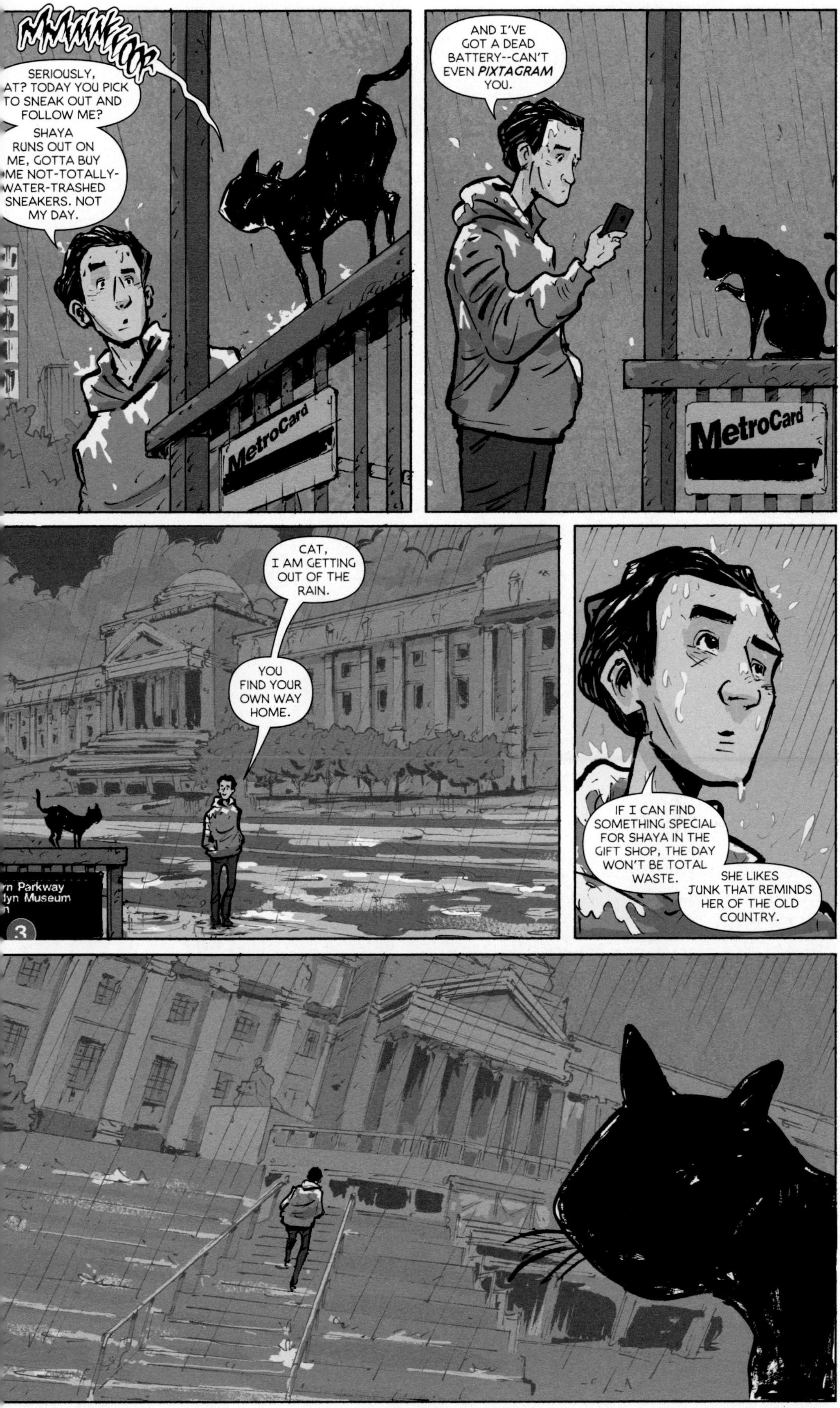
MMMMRROOR
SERIOUSLY, AT? TODAY YOU PICK TO SNEAK OUT AND FOLLOW ME?
SHAYA RUNS OUT ON ME, GOTTA BUY ME NOT-TOTALLY-WATER-TRASHED SNEAKERS. NOT MY DAY.
MetroCard
AND I'VE GOT A DEAD BATTERY--CAN'T EVEN *PIXTAGRAM* YOU.
MetroCard
CAT, I AM GETTING OUT OF THE RAIN.
YOU FIND YOUR OWN WAY HOME.
rn Parkway
lyn Museum
3
IF I CAN FIND SOMETHING SPECIAL FOR SHAYA IN THE GIFT SHOP, THE DAY WON'T BE TOTAL WASTE.
SHE LIKES JUNK THAT REMINDS HER OF THE OLD COUNTRY.

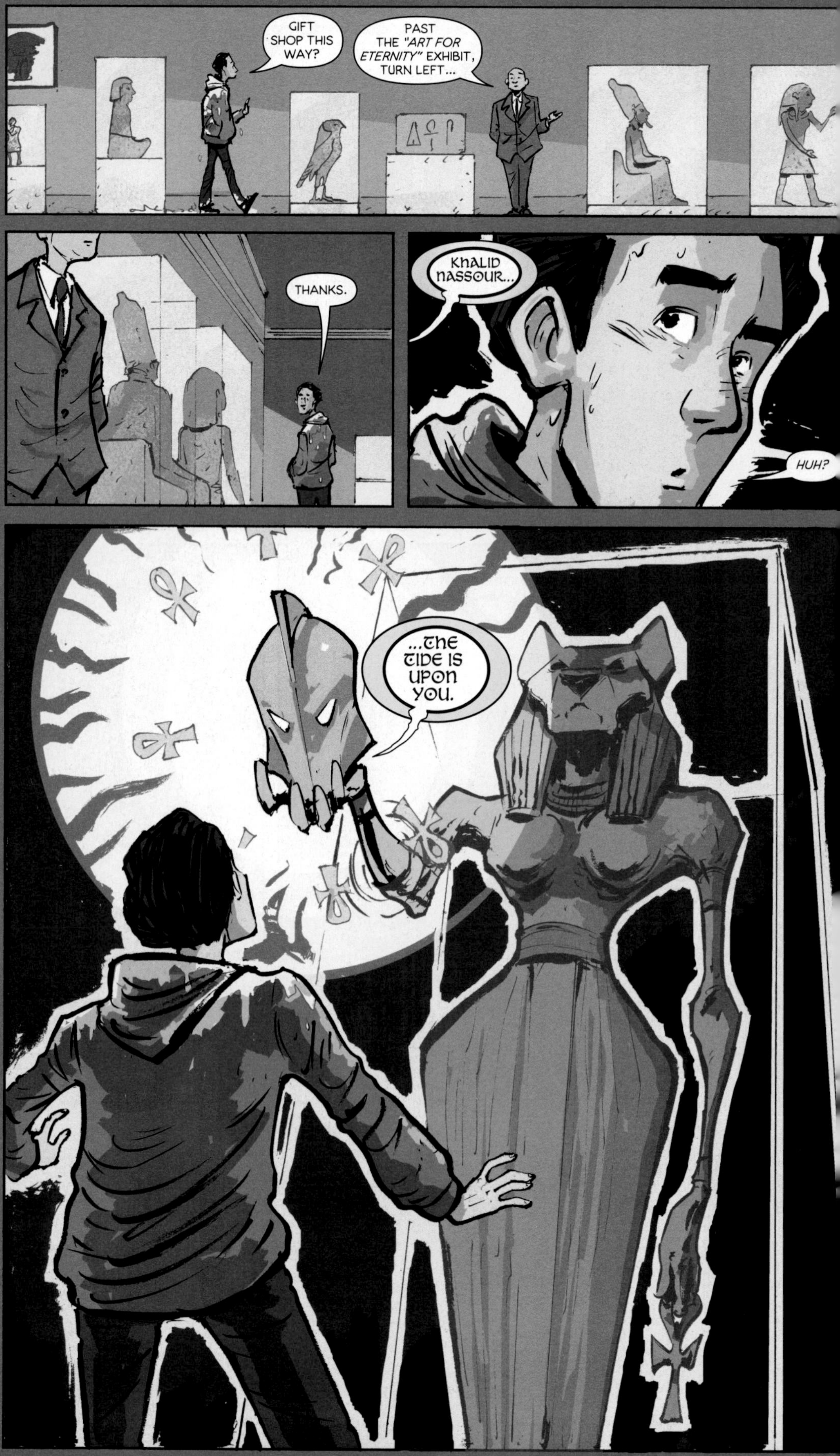
GIFT SHOP THIS WAY?
PAST THE "ART FOR ETERNITY" EXHIBIT, TURN LEFT...
THANKS.
KHALID NASSOUR...
HUH?
...THE TIDE IS UPON YOU.

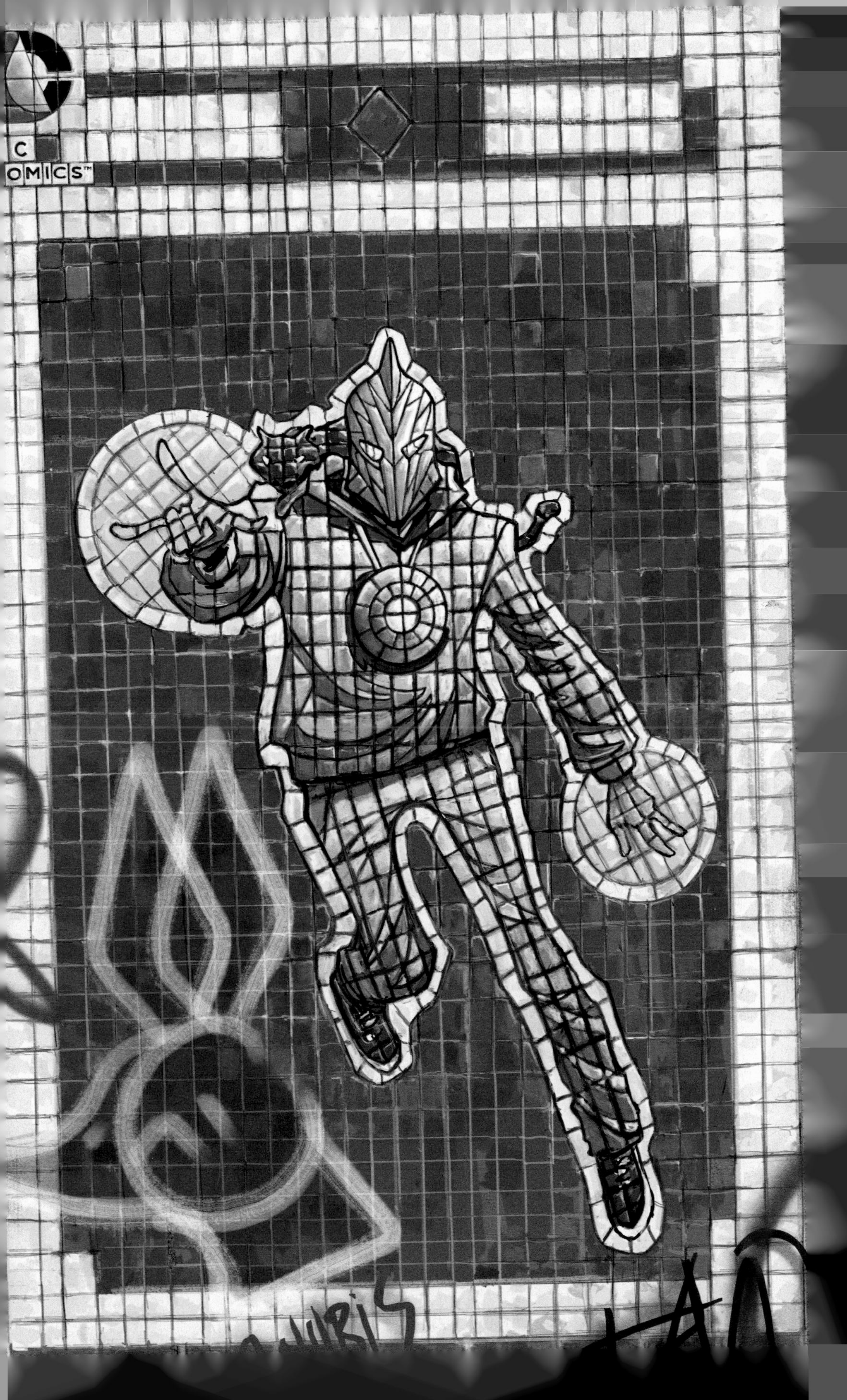
C
OMICS™

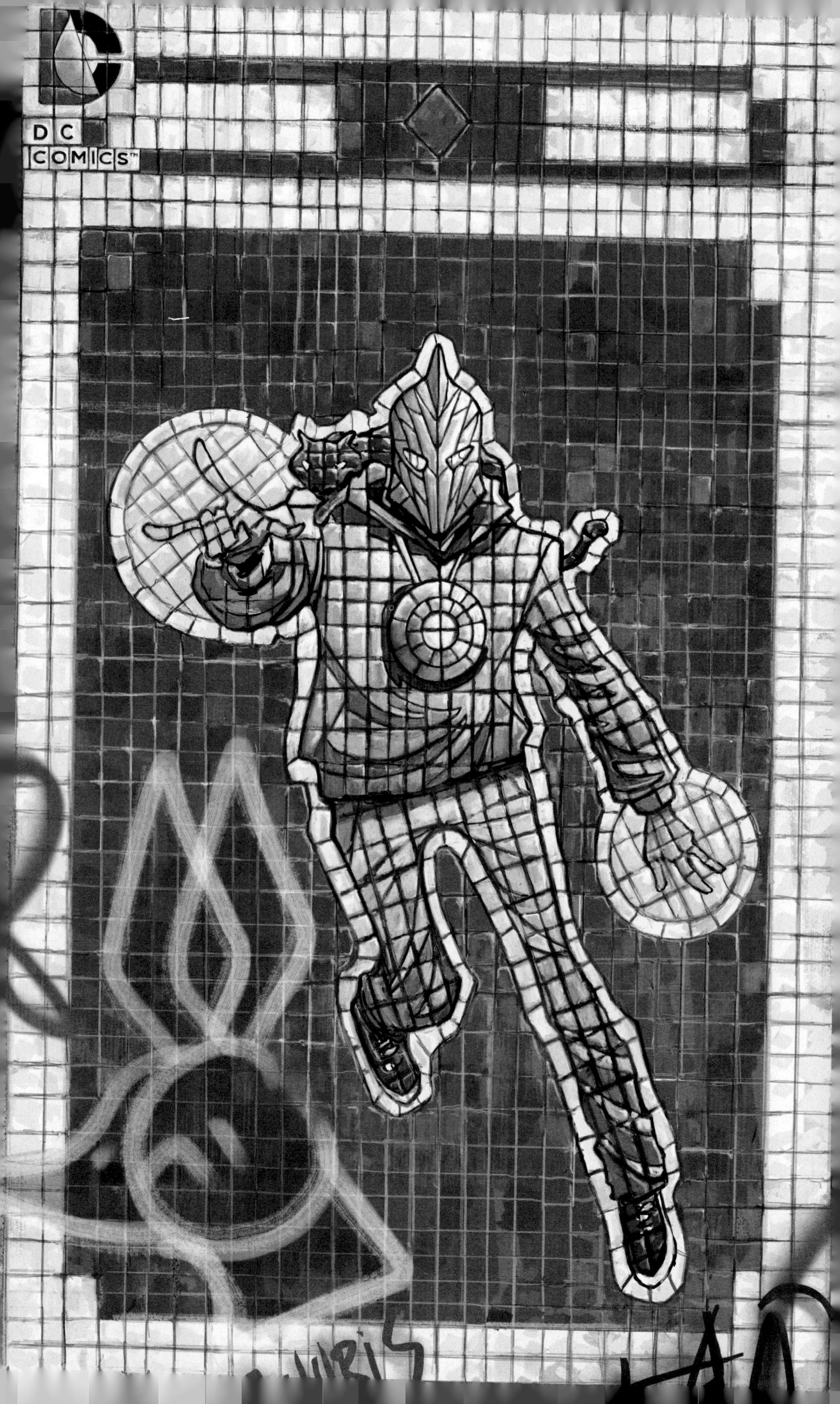
DC
COMICS™

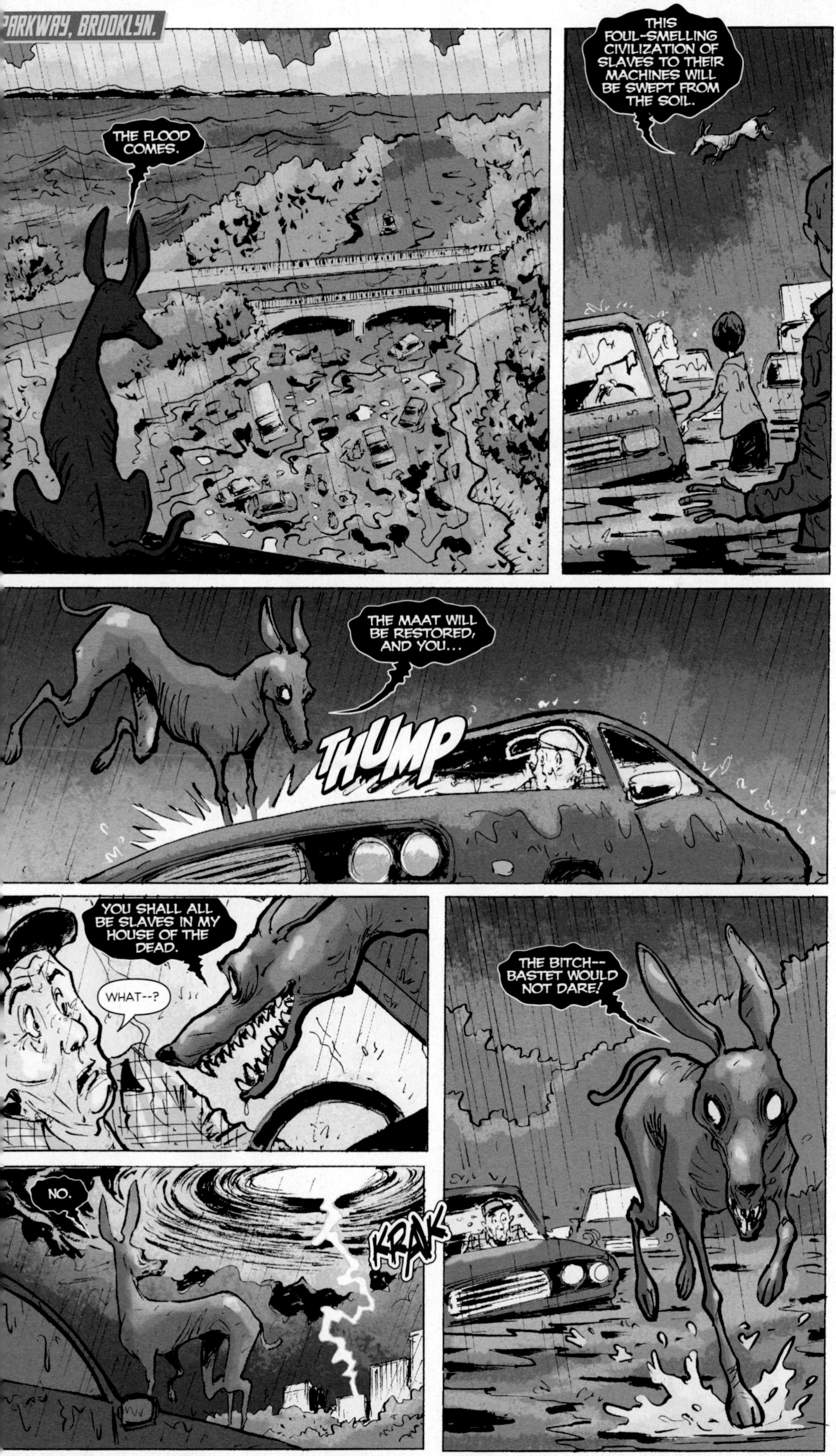
PARKWAY, BROOKLYN.
THE FLOOD COMES.
THIS FOUL-SMELLING CIVILIZATION OF SLAVES TO THEIR MACHINES WILL BE SWEPT FROM THE SOIL.
THE MAAT WILL BE RESTORED, AND YOU...
THUMP
YOU SHALL ALL BE SLAVES IN MY HOUSE OF THE DEAD.
WHAT--?
NO.
KRAK
THE BITCH-- BASTET WOULD NOT DARE!

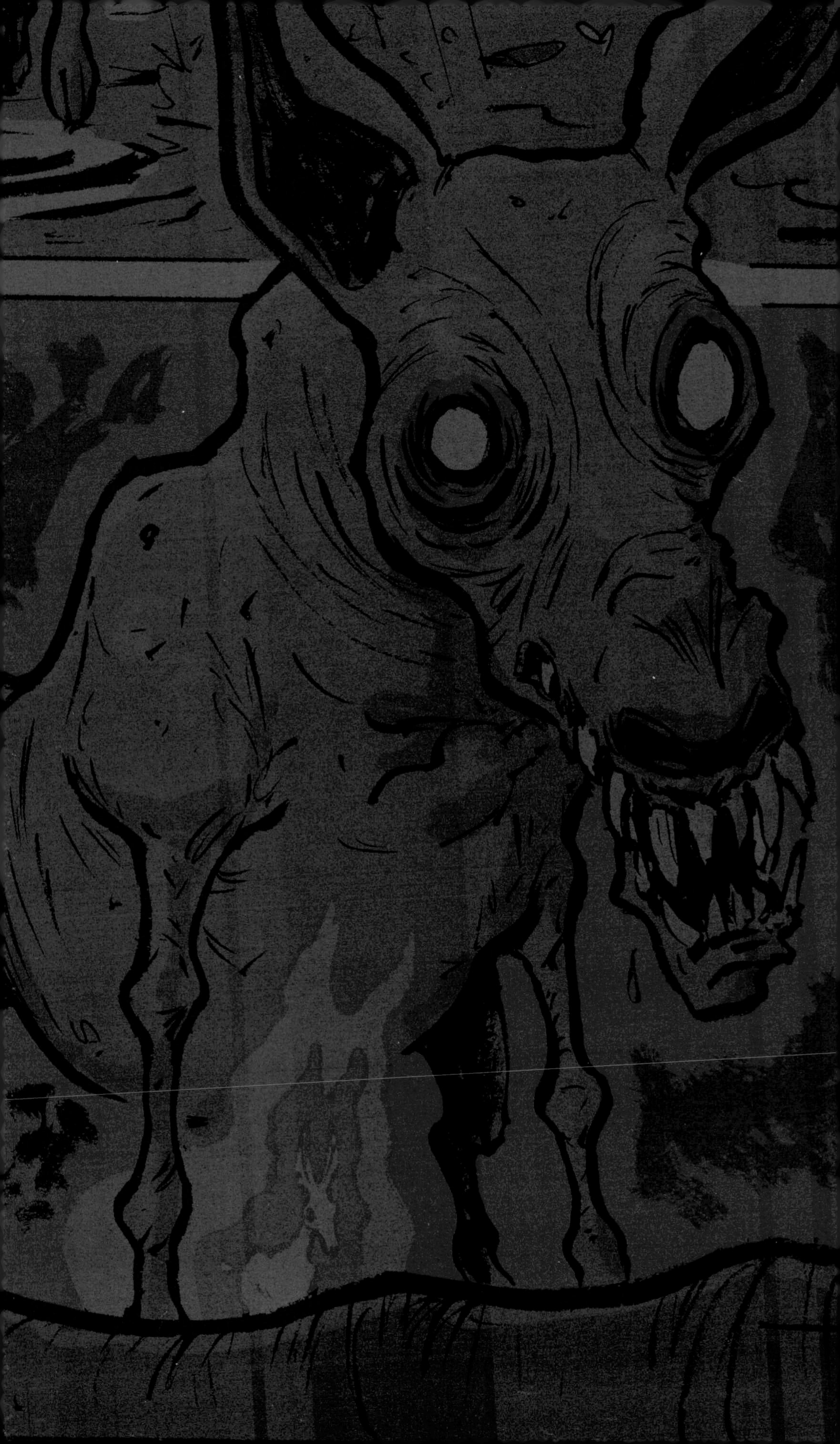

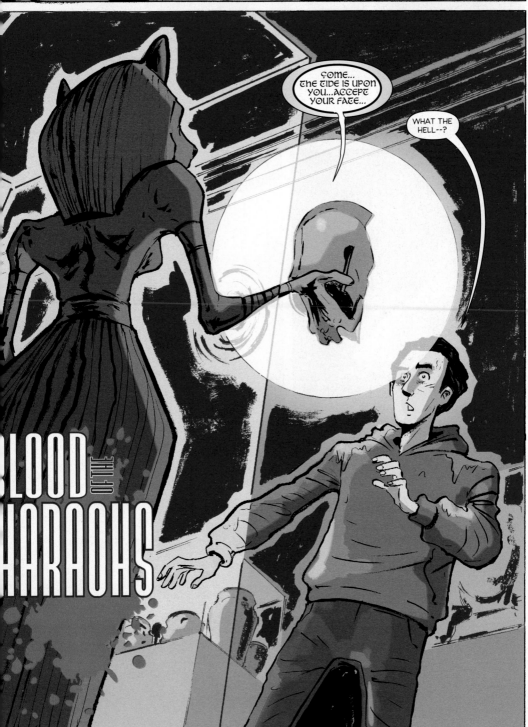

KHALID... COME TO ME...

COME... THE TIDE IS UPON YOU...ACCEPT YOUR FATE...

WHAT THE HELL--?

BLOOD OF THE PHARAOHS

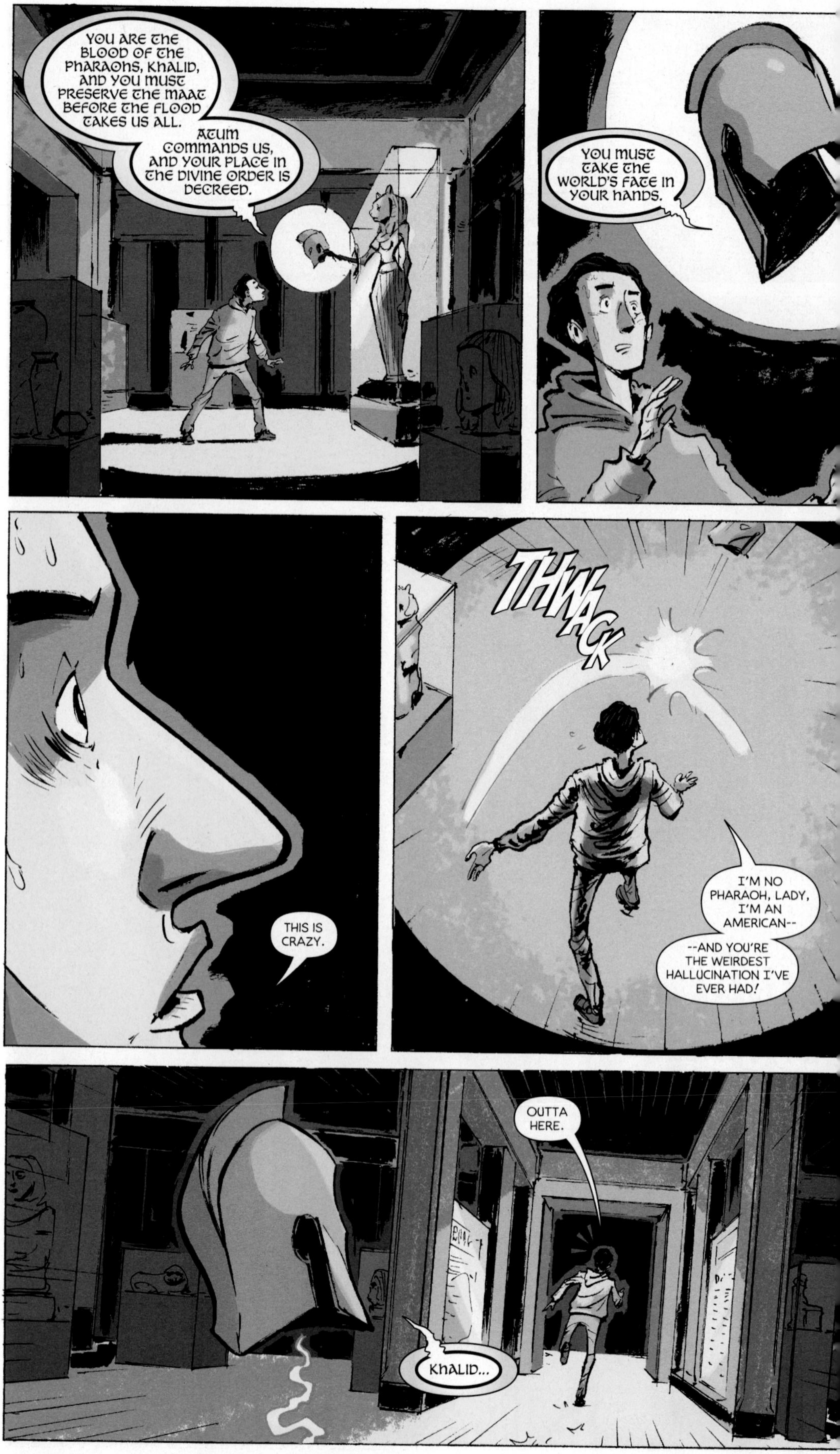
YOU ARE THE BLOOD OF THE PHARAOHS, KHALID, AND YOU MUST PRESERVE THE MAAT BEFORE THE FLOOD TAKES US ALL.
ATUM COMMANDS US, AND YOUR PLACE IN THE DIVINE ORDER IS DECREED.
YOU MUST TAKE THE WORLD'S FATE IN YOUR HANDS.
THIS IS CRAZY.
THWACK
I'M NO PHARAOH, LADY, I'M AN AMERICAN--
--AND YOU'RE THE WEIRDEST HALLUCINATION I'VE EVER HAD!
OUTTA HERE.
KHALID...

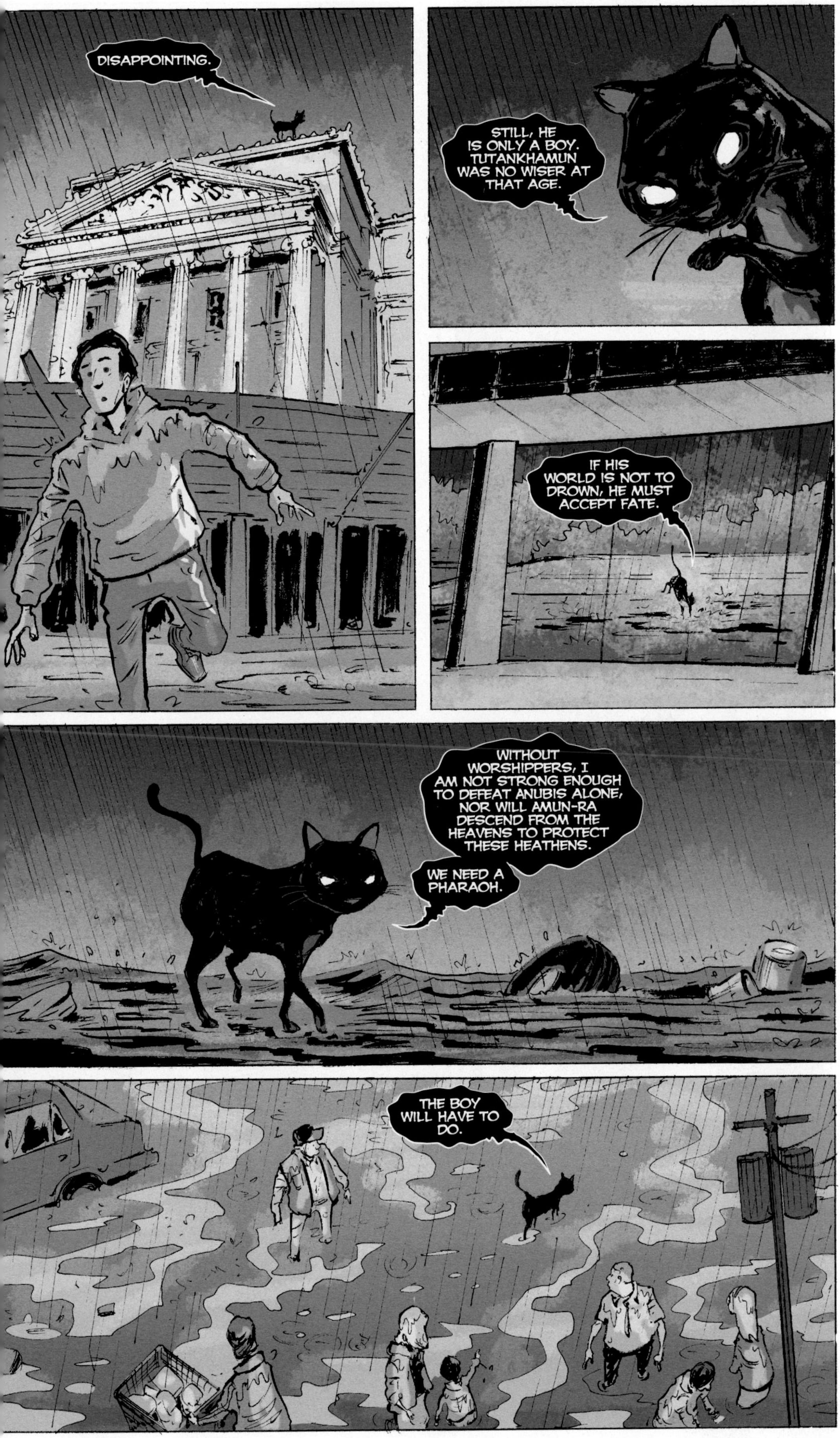
DISAPPOINTING.
STILL, HE IS ONLY A BOY. TUTANKHAMUN WAS NO WISER AT THAT AGE.
IF HIS WORLD IS NOT TO DROWN, HE MUST ACCEPT FATE.
WITHOUT WORSHIPPERS, I AM NOT STRONG ENOUGH TO DEFEAT ANUBIS ALONE, NOR WILL AMUN-RA DESCEND FROM THE HEAVENS TO PROTECT THESE HEATHENS.
WE NEED A PHARAOH.
THE BOY WILL HAVE TO DO.

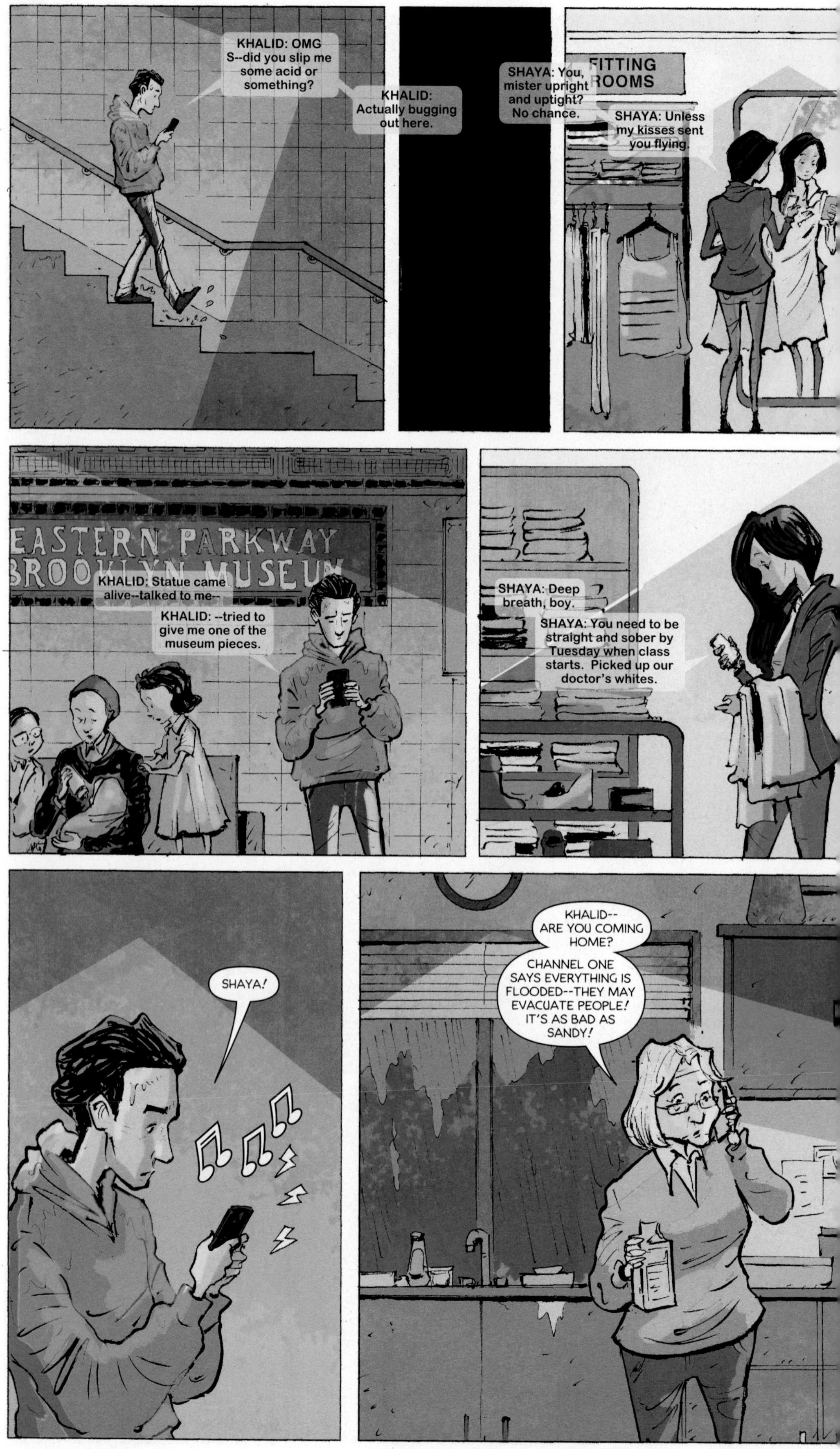
KHALID: OMG S--did you slip me some acid or something?
KHALID: Actually bugging out here.
SHAYA: You, mister upright and uptight? No chance.
FITTING ROOMS
SHAYA: Unless my kisses sent you flying.
EASTERN PARKWAY BROOKLYN MUSEUM
KHALID: Statue came alive--talked to me--
KHALID: --tried to give me one of the museum pieces.
SHAYA: Deep breath, boy.
SHAYA: You need to be straight and sober by Tuesday when class starts. Picked up our doctor's whites.
SHAYA!
KHALID-- ARE YOU COMING HOME?
CHANNEL ONE SAYS EVERYTHING IS FLOODED--THEY MAY EVACUATE PEOPLE! IT'S AS BAD AS SANDY!

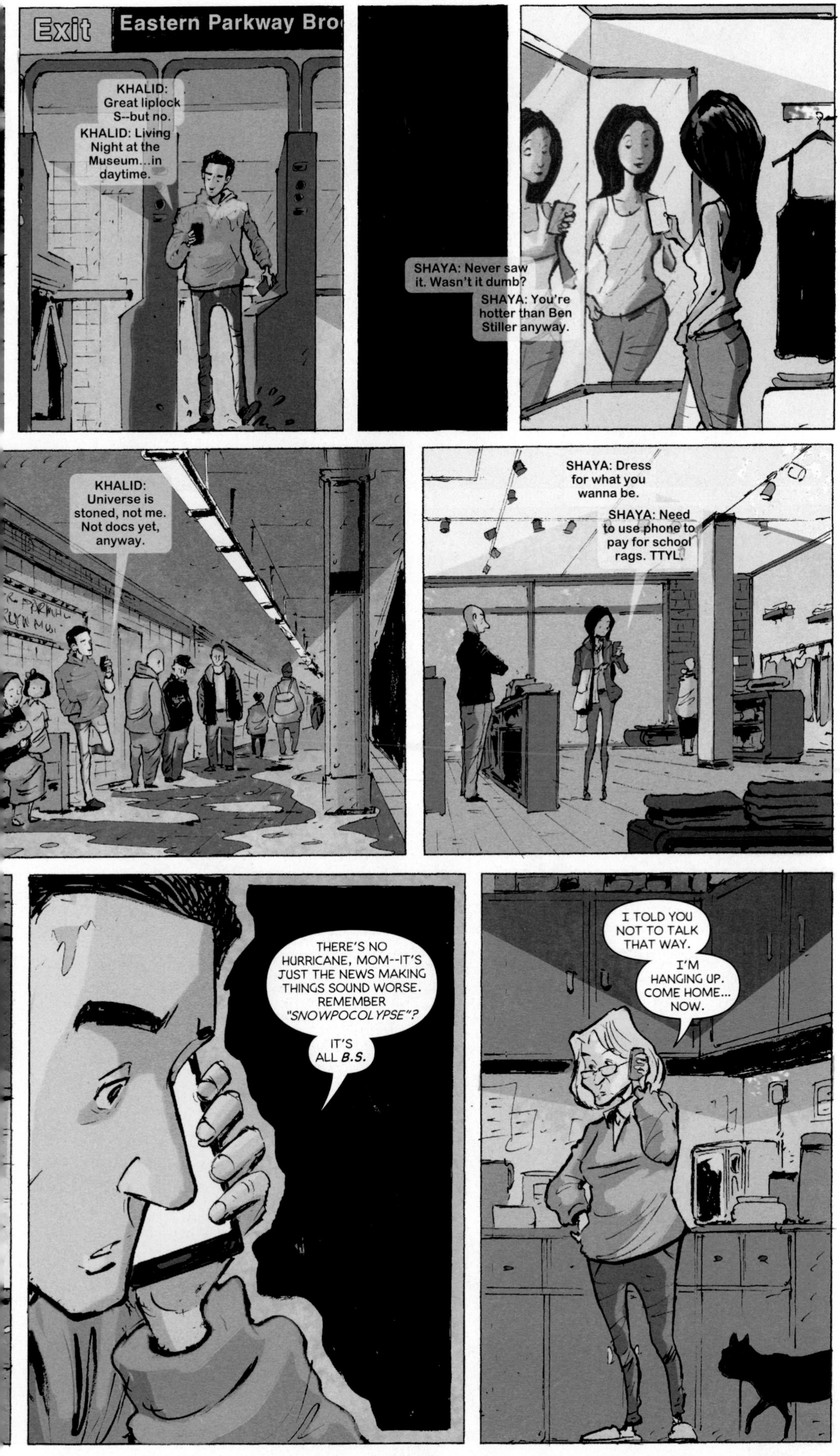
Exit
Eastern Parkway Bro
KHALID: Great liplock S--but no.
KHALID: Living Night at the Museum...in daytime.
SHAYA: Never saw it. Wasn't it dumb?
SHAYA: You're hotter than Ben Stiller anyway.
KHALID: Universe is stoned, not me. Not docs yet, anyway.
SHAYA: Dress for what you wanna be.
SHAYA: Need to use phone to pay for school rags. TTYL.
THERE'S NO HURRICANE, MOM--IT'S JUST THE NEWS MAKING THINGS SOUND WORSE. REMEMBER *"SNOWPOCOLYPSE"*?
IT'S ALL ***B.S.***
I TOLD YOU NOT TO TALK THAT WAY.
I'M HANGING UP. COME HOME... NOW.

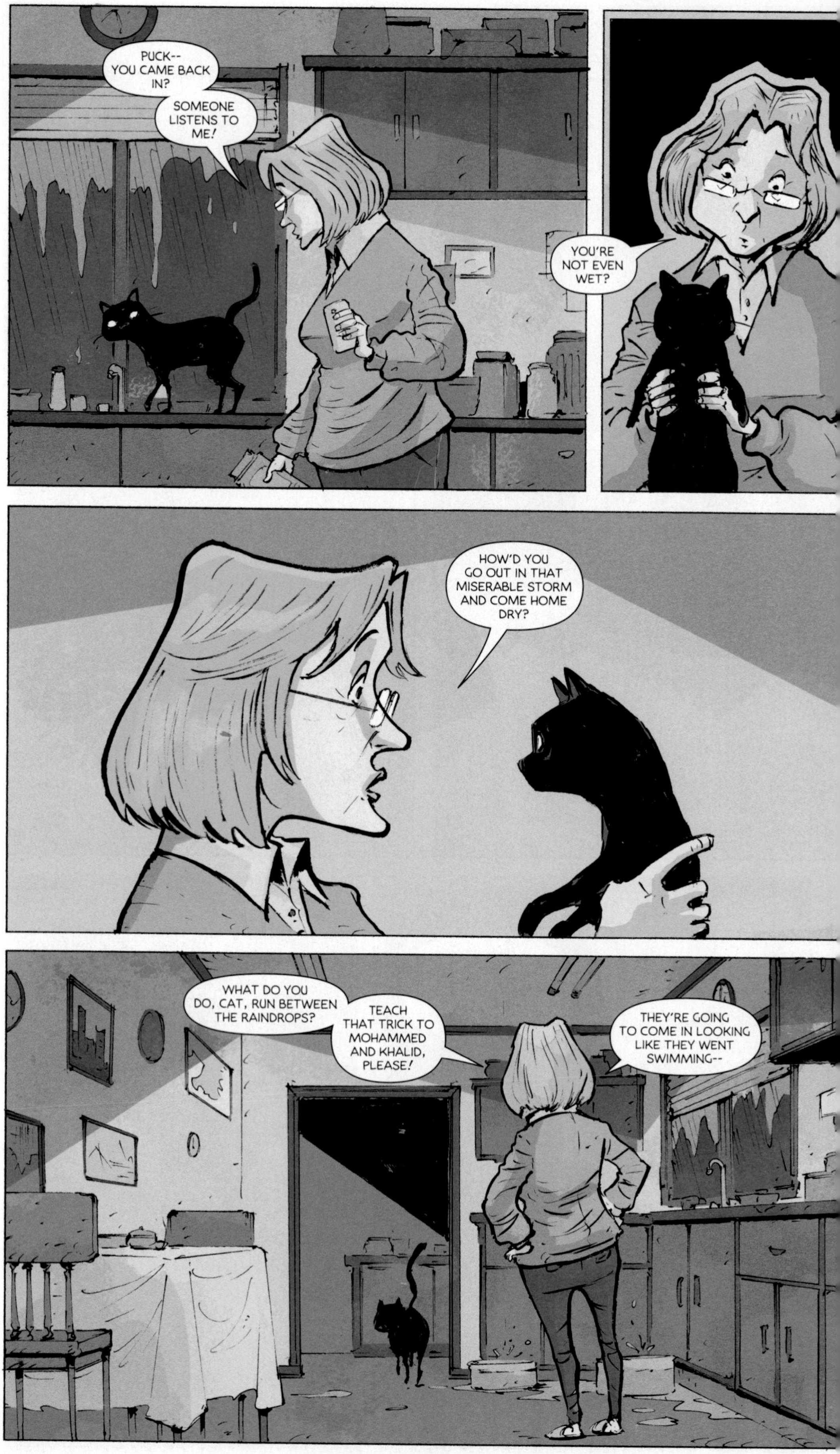
PUCK--
YOU CAME BACK IN?
SOMEONE LISTENS TO ME!
YOU'RE NOT EVEN WET?
HOW'D YOU GO OUT IN THAT MISERABLE STORM AND COME HOME DRY?
WHAT DO YOU DO, CAT, RUN BETWEEN THE RAINDROPS?
TEACH THAT TRICK TO MOHAMMED AND KHALID, PLEASE!
THEY'RE GOING TO COME IN LOOKING LIKE THEY WENT SWIMMING--

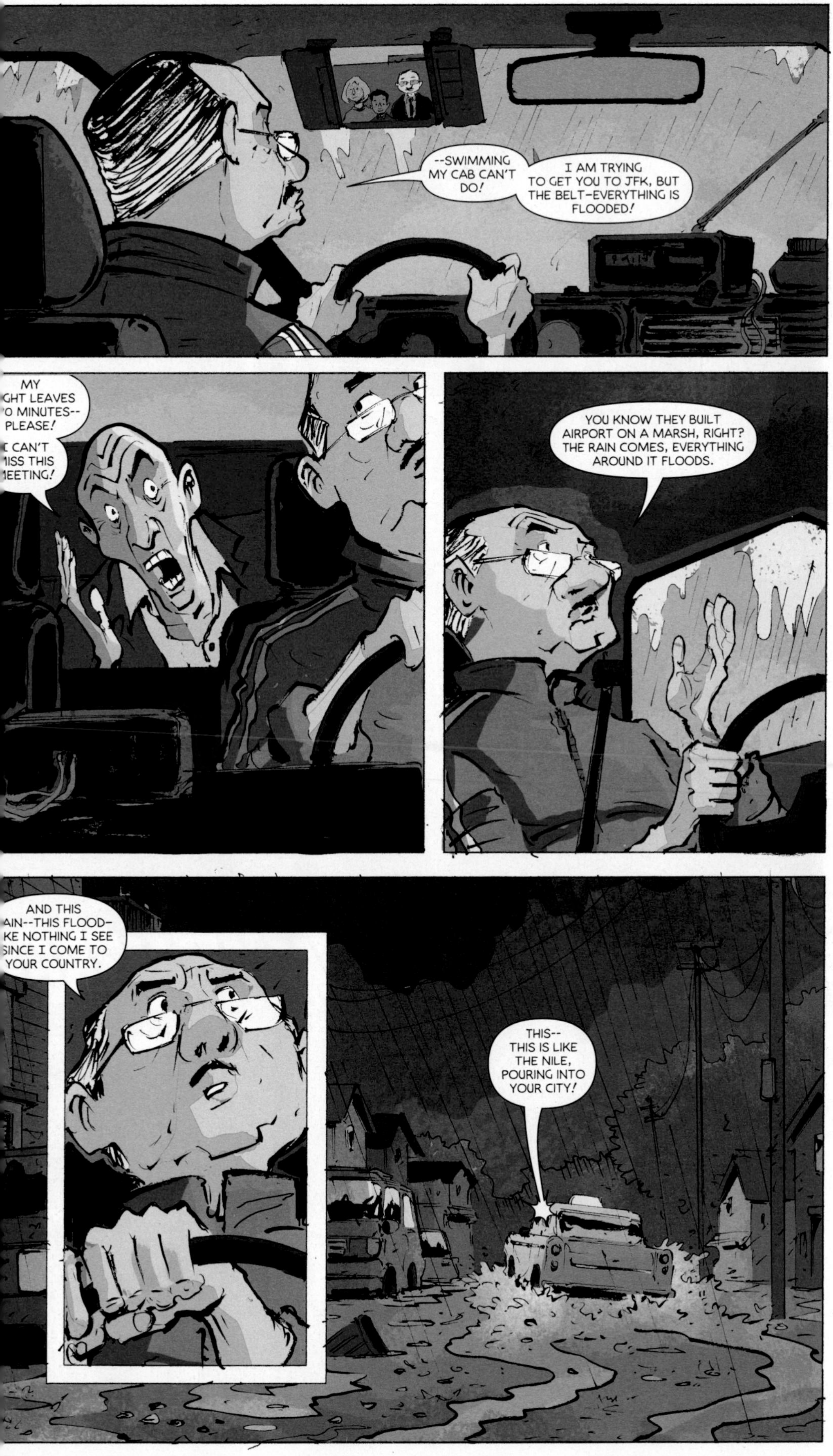
--SWIMMING MY CAB CAN'T DO!
I AM TRYING TO GET YOU TO JFK, BUT THE BELT--EVERYTHING IS FLOODED!
MY GHT LEAVES O MINUTES-- PLEASE!
I CAN'T ISS THIS EETING!
YOU KNOW THEY BUILT AIRPORT ON A MARSH, RIGHT? THE RAIN COMES, EVERYTHING AROUND IT FLOODS.
AND THIS AIN--THIS FLOOD-KE NOTHING I SEE SINCE I COME TO YOUR COUNTRY.
THIS-- THIS IS LIKE THE NILE, POURING INTO YOUR CITY!

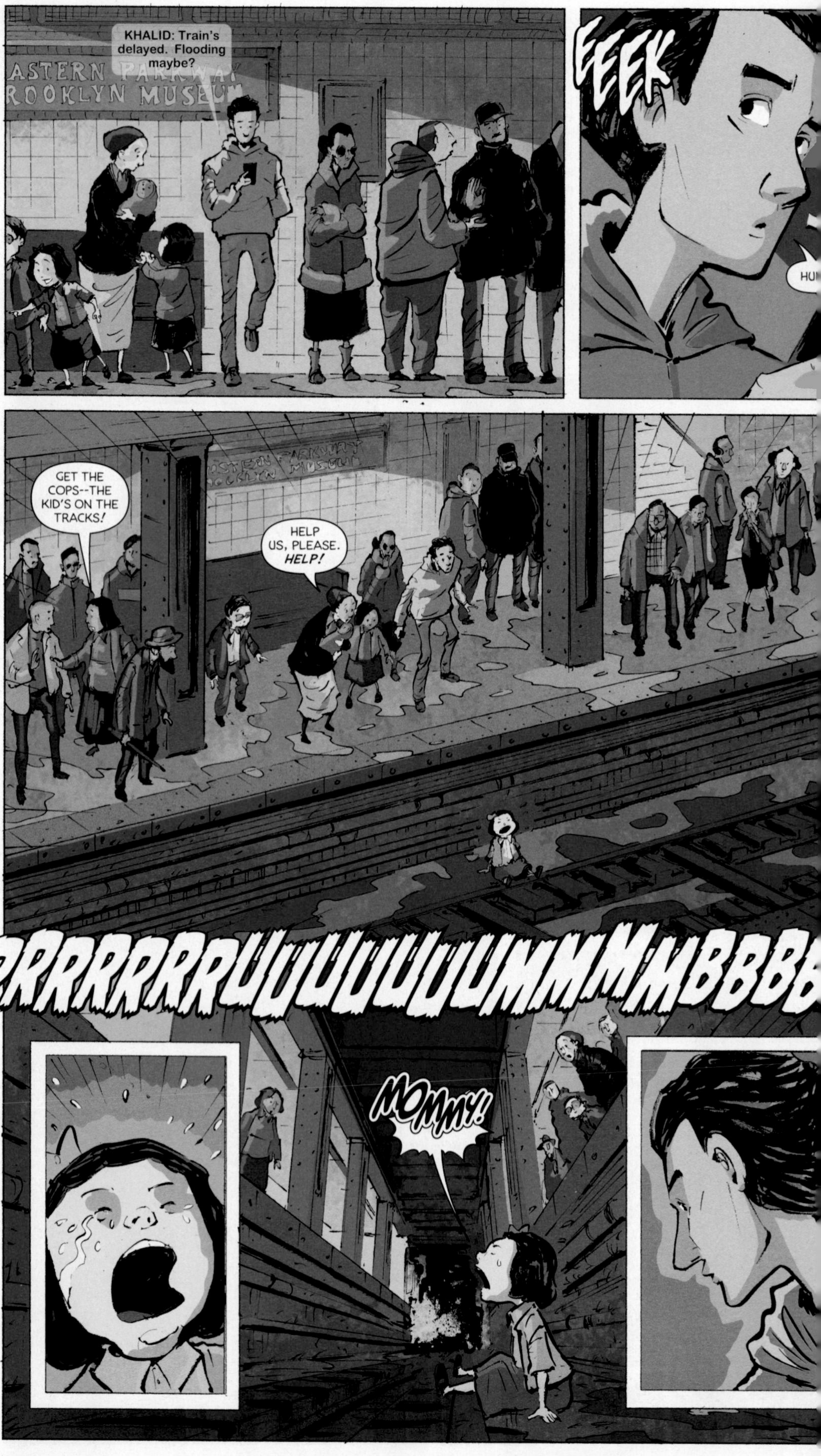
KHALID: Train's delayed. Flooding maybe?
ASTERN PARKWAY
ROOKLYN MUSEUM
EEEK
HU
GET THE COPS--THE KID'S ON THE TRACKS!
HELP US, PLEASE. *HELP!*
RRRRRRRRUUUUUUUUMMMMBBBB
MOMMY!

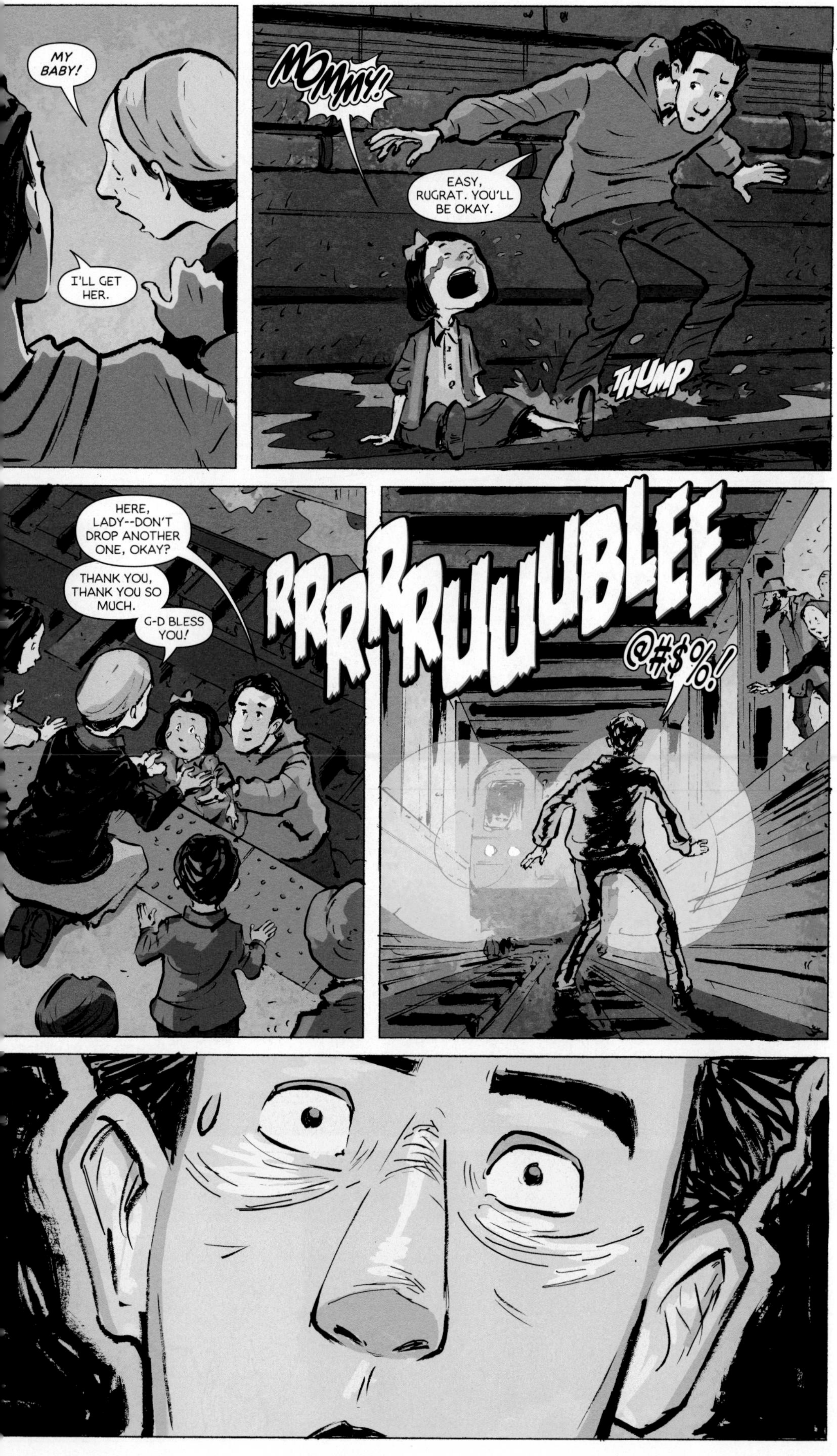
MY BABY!
I'LL GET HER.
MOMMY!
EASY, RUGRAT. YOU'LL BE OKAY.
THUMP
HERE, LADY--DON'T DROP ANOTHER ONE, OKAY?
THANK YOU, THANK YOU SO MUCH.
G-D BLESS YOU!
RRRRRUUUBLEE
@#$%!

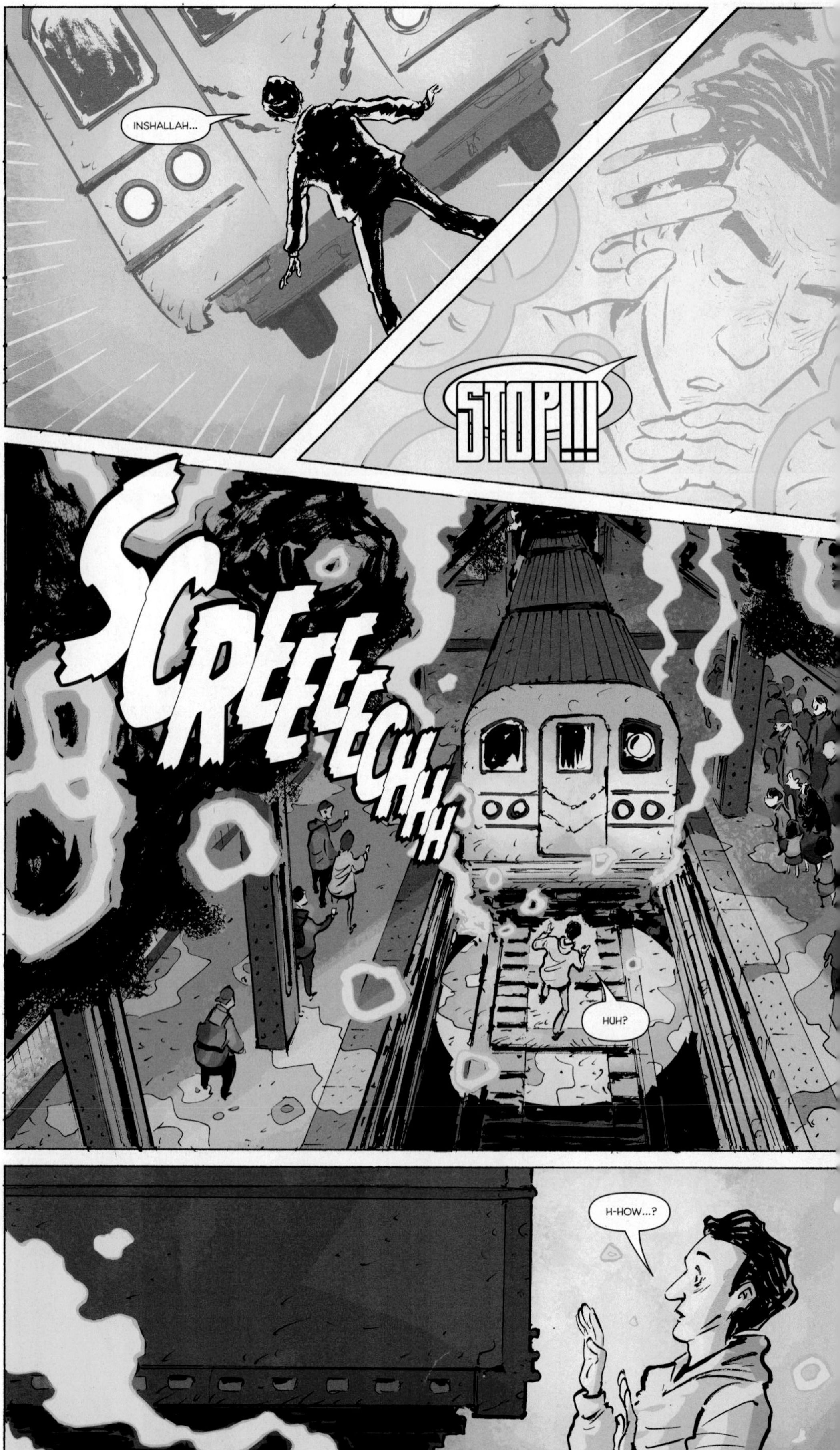
INSHALLAH...
STOP!!!
SCREEEECHHH
HUH?
H-HOW...?

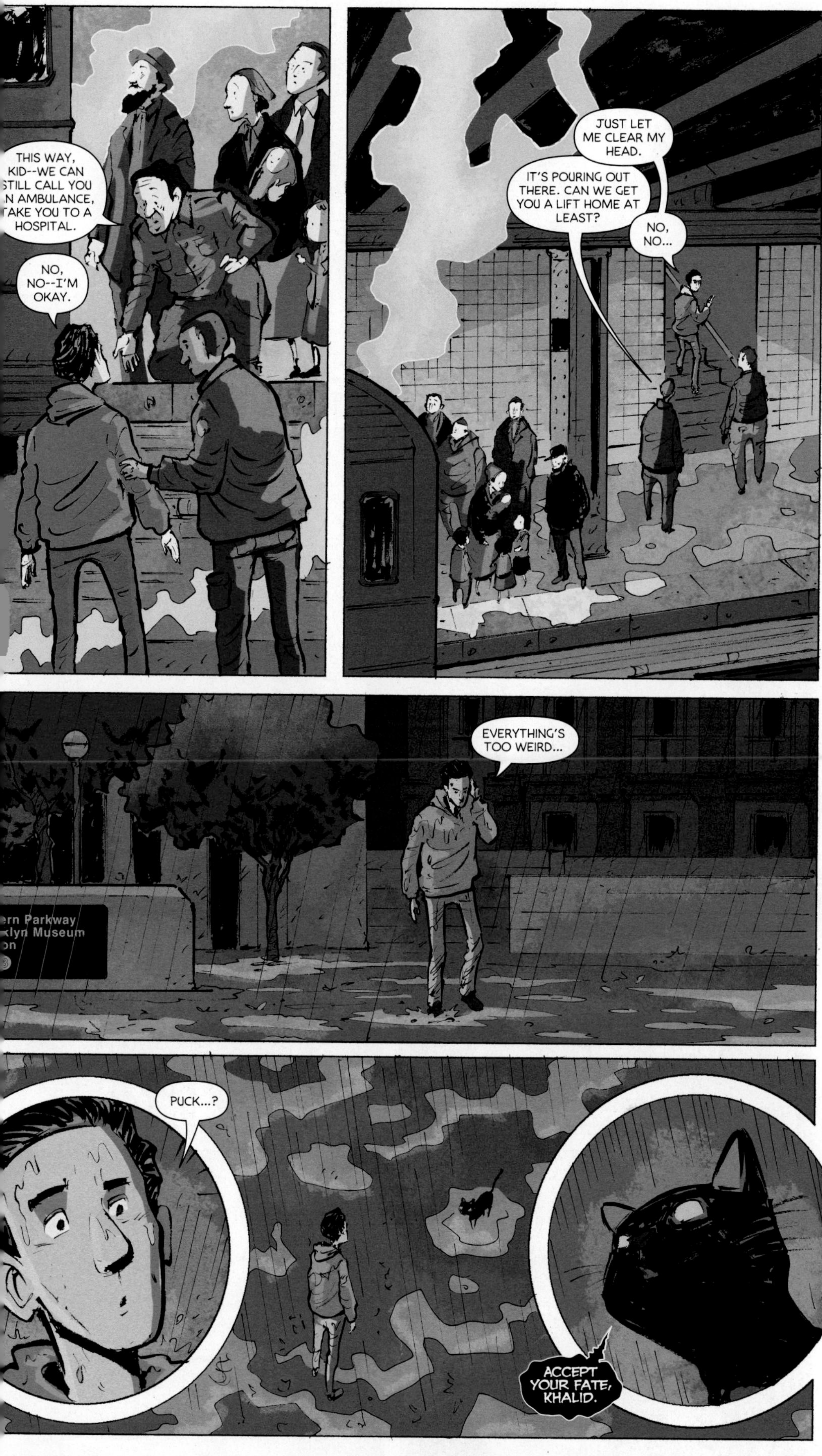
THIS WAY, KID--WE CAN STILL CALL YOU N AMBULANCE, TAKE YOU TO A HOSPITAL.
NO, NO--I'M OKAY.
JUST LET ME CLEAR MY HEAD.
IT'S POURING OUT THERE. CAN WE GET YOU A LIFT HOME AT LEAST?
NO, NO...
ern Parkway
klyn Museum
on
EVERYTHING'S TOO WEIRD...
PUCK...?
ACCEPT YOUR FATE, KHALID.

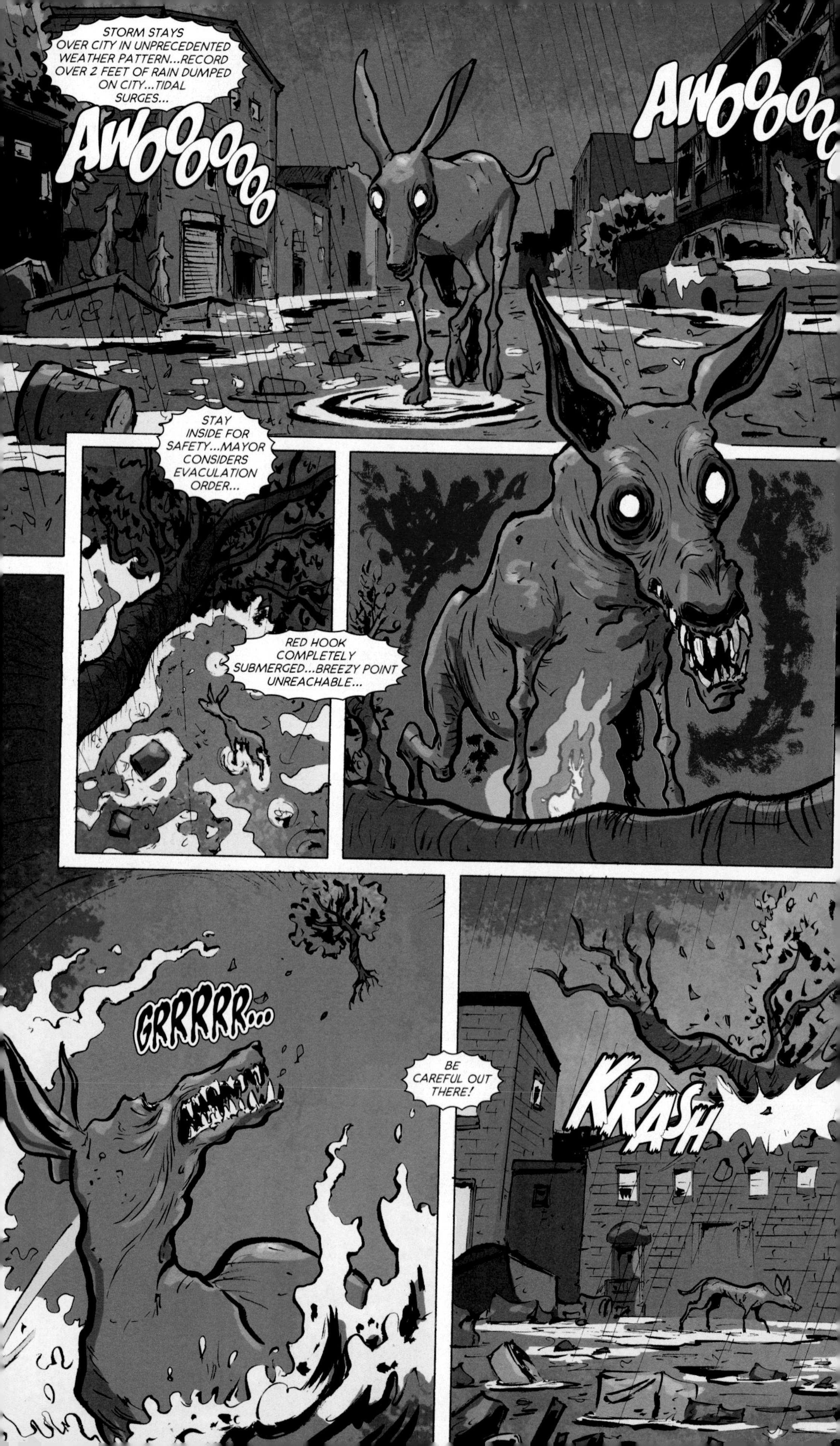
STORM STAYS OVER CITY IN UNPRECEDENTED WEATHER PATTERN...RECORD OVER 2 FEET OF RAIN DUMPED ON CITY...TIDAL SURGES...
AWOOOOOOO
AWOOOOOO
STAY INSIDE FOR SAFETY...MAYOR CONSIDERS EVACUATION ORDER...
RED HOOK COMPLETELY SUBMERGED...BREEZY POINT UNREACHABLE...
GRRRRR...
BE CAREFUL OUT THERE!
KRASH

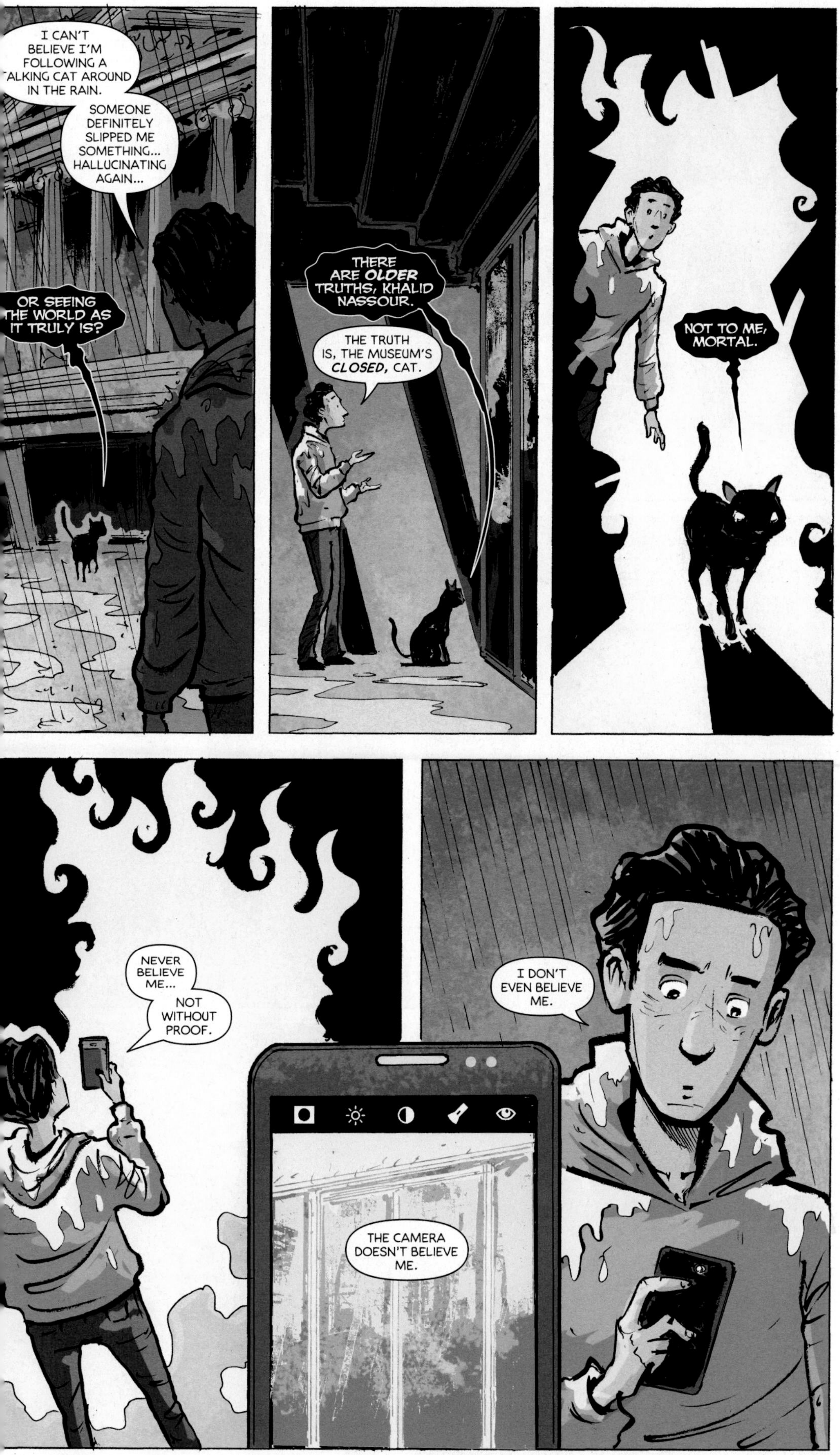
I CAN'T BELIEVE I'M FOLLOWING A TALKING CAT AROUND IN THE RAIN.
SOMEONE DEFINITELY SLIPPED ME SOMETHING... HALLUCINATING AGAIN...
OR SEEING THE WORLD AS IT TRULY IS?
THERE ARE OLDER TRUTHS, KHALID NASSOUR.
THE TRUTH IS, THE MUSEUM'S CLOSED, CAT.
NOT TO ME, MORTAL.
NEVER BELIEVE ME...
NOT WITHOUT PROOF.
THE CAMERA DOESN'T BELIEVE ME.
I DON'T EVEN BELIEVE ME.

BELIEVE ME, CHILD OF THE BLOOD.

I HAVE WATCHED OVER YOU AND WAITED FOR THIS MOMENT. ANUBIS SEEKS TO USE THE FLOODS TO CLEANSE THE EARTH, AND RESTORE THE MAAT--THE ORDER OF THINGS--TO WHAT SUITS THE JACKAL.

ATUM REQUIRES YOU TO OPPOSE ANUBIS AND HEAL YOUR WORLD.

WHY ME?

I'M A KID-- FRESH OUT OF COLLEGE ABOUT TO START MED SCHOOL--I CAN'T HEAL A STUBBED TOE.

FATE SUMMONS YOU.

AS YOU FOUND COURAGE TO SAVE THAT CHILD, YOU SHALL FIND THE WILL TO SAVE THE WORLD YOU LOVE.

TAKE THE MASK OF THOTH AND SIT IN JUDGMENT. SEE THE PLANES BEYOND AND WIELD THE POWER AWAKENING IN YOUR SOUL.

I AM AN OLD GOD, AND NO LONGER LOVED... MY TIME HERE WANES... YOU MUST PRESERVE THE MAAT AS YOU WISH, HEALER.

TAKE YOUR FATE...

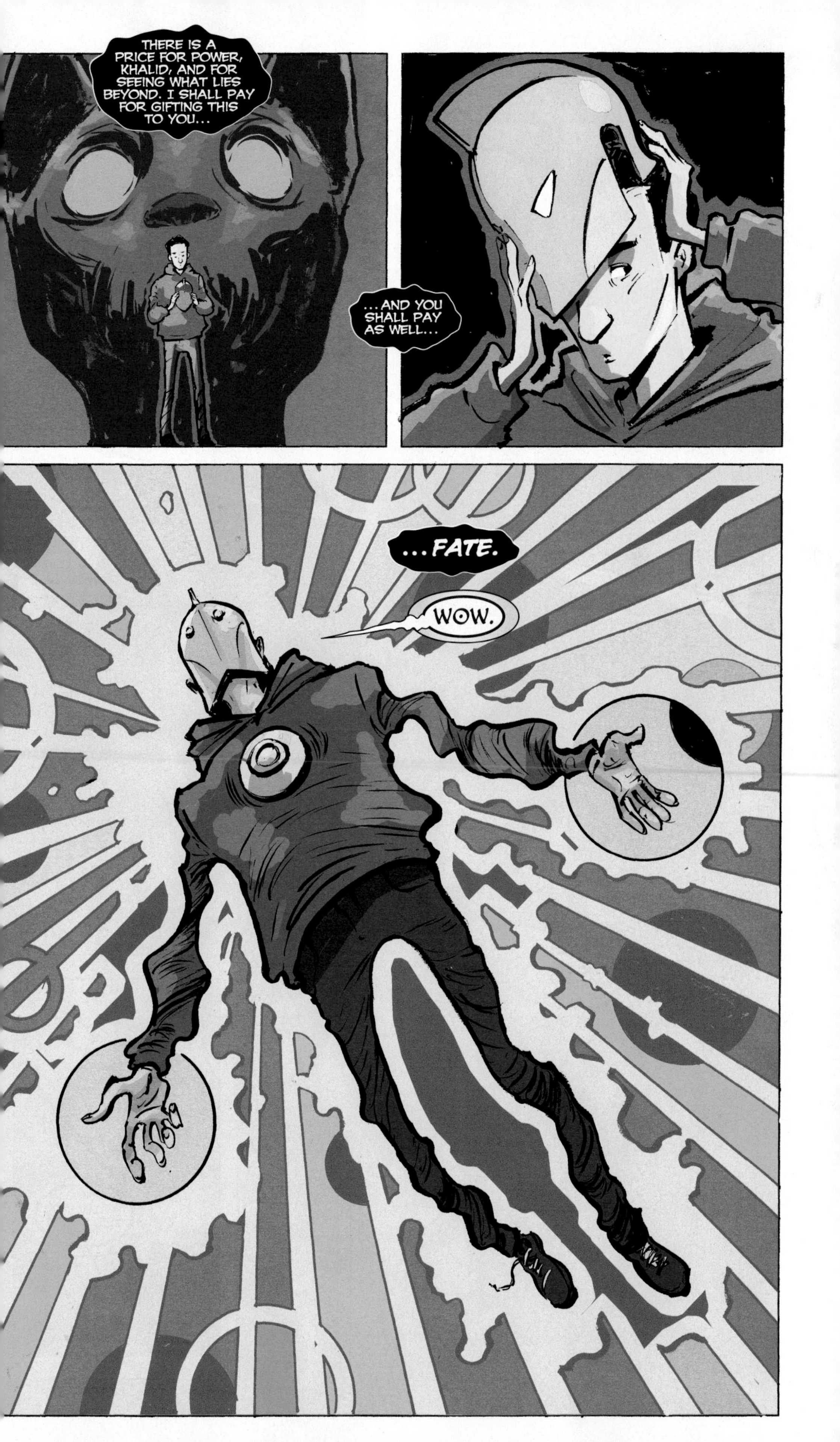
THERE IS A PRICE FOR POWER, KHALID, AND FOR SEEING WHAT LIES BEYOND. I SHALL PAY FOR GIFTING THIS TO YOU...
...AND YOU SHALL PAY AS WELL...
...FATE.
WOW.

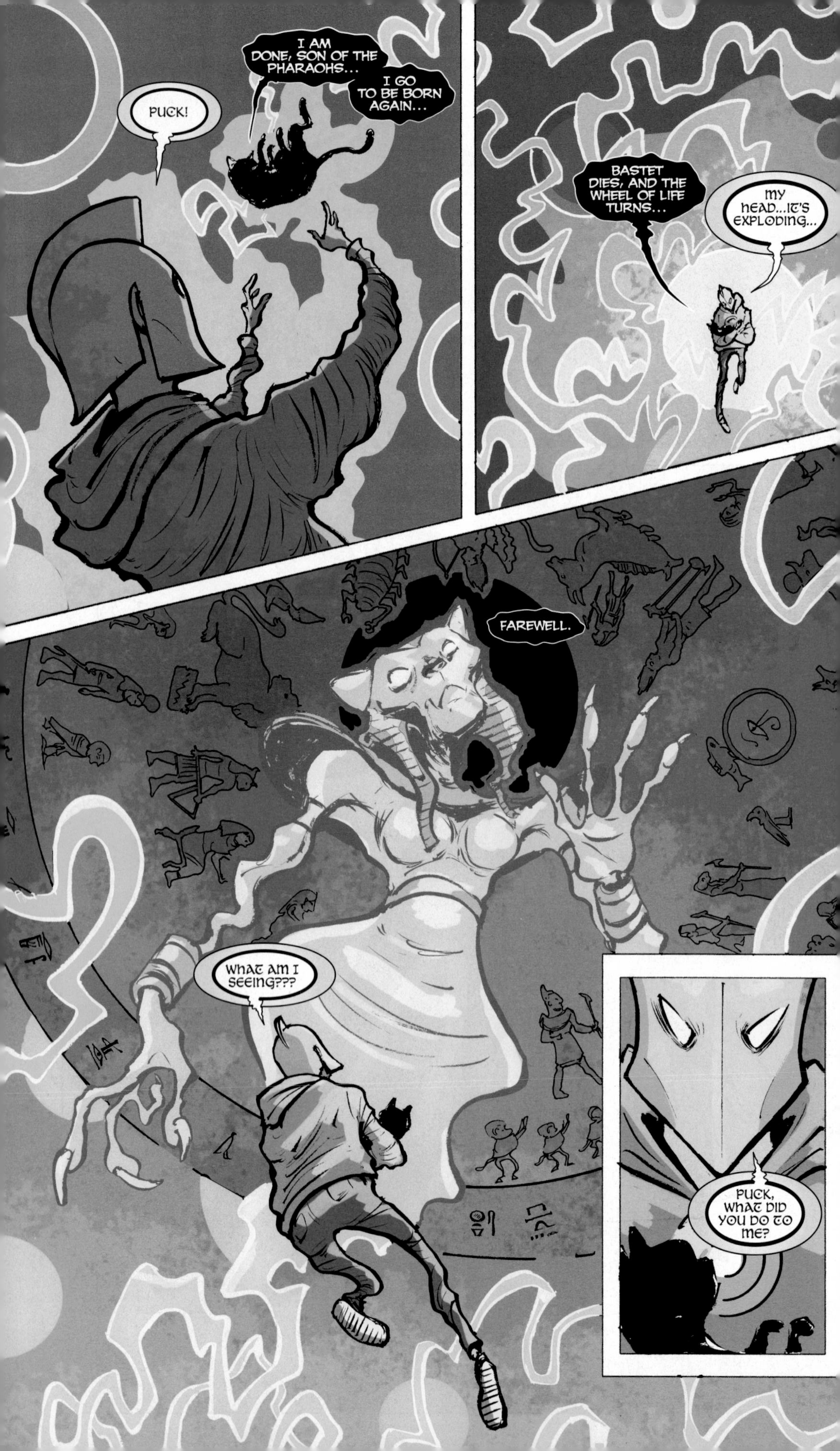
PUCK!
I AM DONE, SON OF THE PHARAOHS...
I GO TO BE BORN AGAIN...
BASTET DIES, AND THE WHEEL OF LIFE TURNS...
MY HEAD...IT'S EXPLODING...
FAREWELL.
WHAT AM I SEEING???
PUCK, WHAT DID YOU DO TO ME?

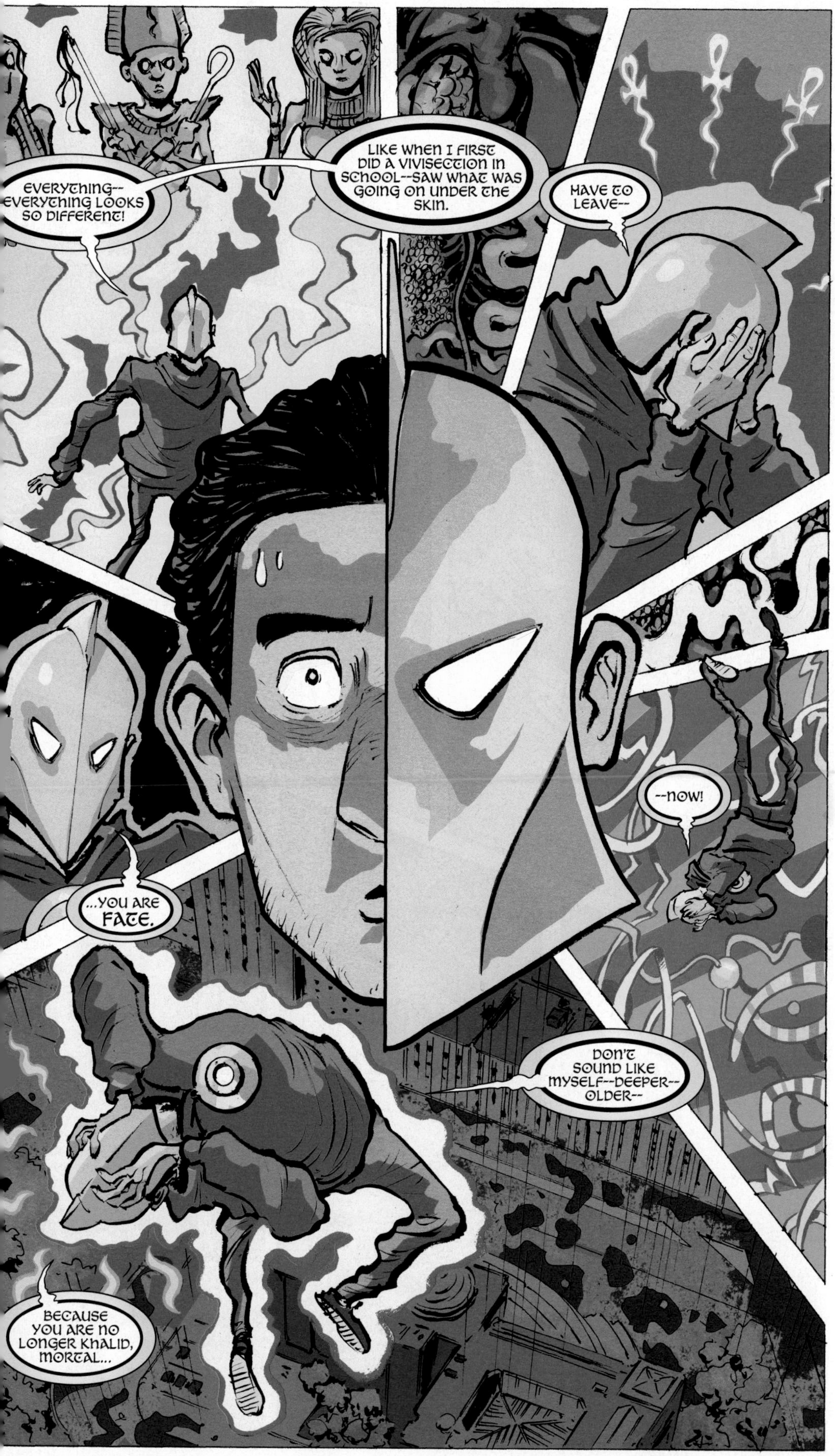

EVERYTHING--EVERYTHING LOOKS SO DIFFERENT!
LIKE WHEN I FIRST DID A VIVISECTION IN SCHOOL--SAW WHAT WAS GOING ON UNDER THE SKIN.
HAVE TO LEAVE--
--NOW!
...YOU ARE FATE.
DON'T SOUND LIKE MYSELF--DEEPER--OLDER--
BECAUSE YOU ARE NO LONGER KHALID, MORTAL...

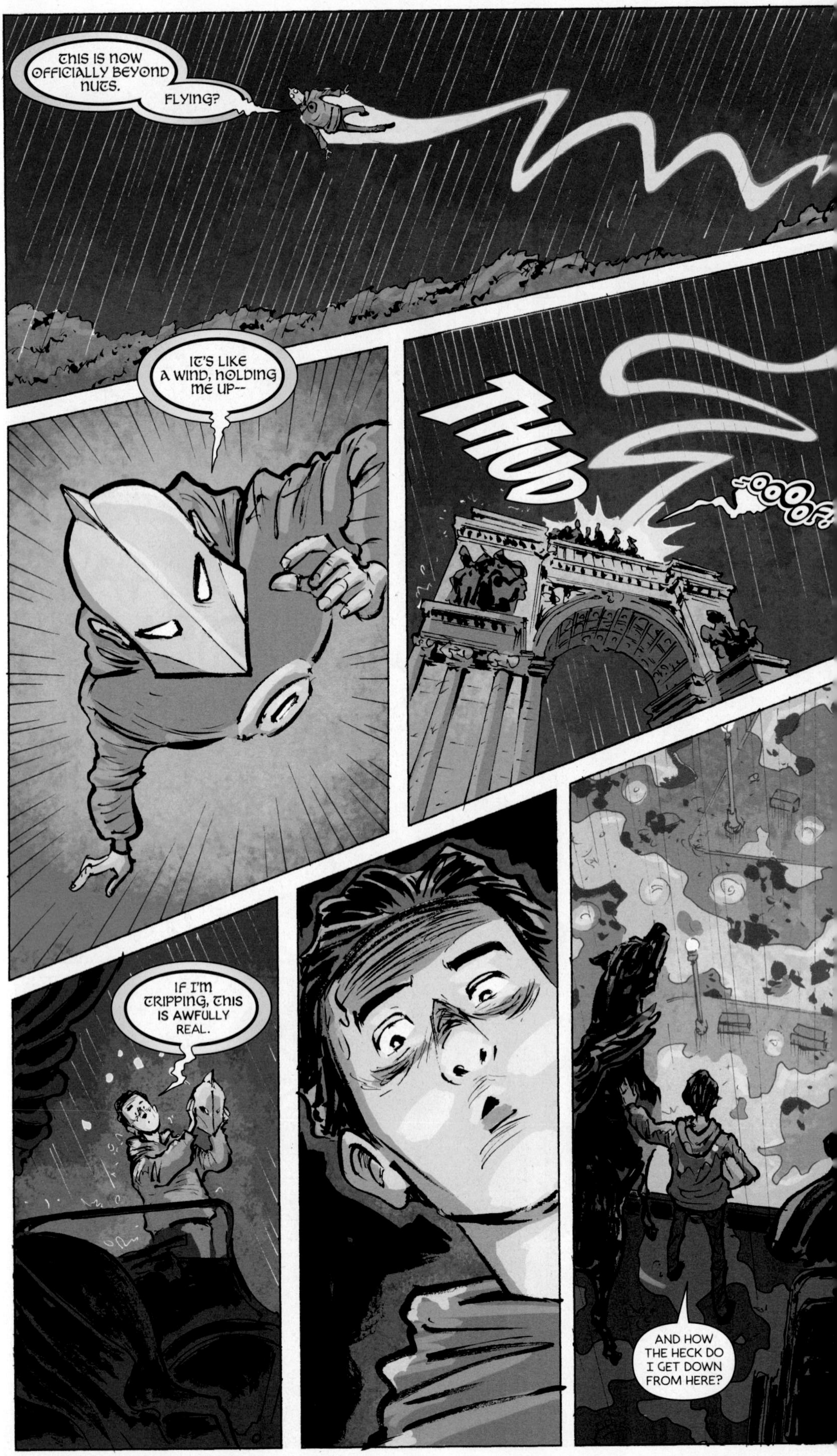
THIS IS NOW OFFICIALLY BEYOND NUTS.
FLYING?
IT'S LIKE A WIND, HOLDING ME UP--
THUD
-OOOOF!
IF I'M TRIPPING, THIS IS AWFULLY REAL.
AND HOW THE HECK DO I GET DOWN FROM HERE?

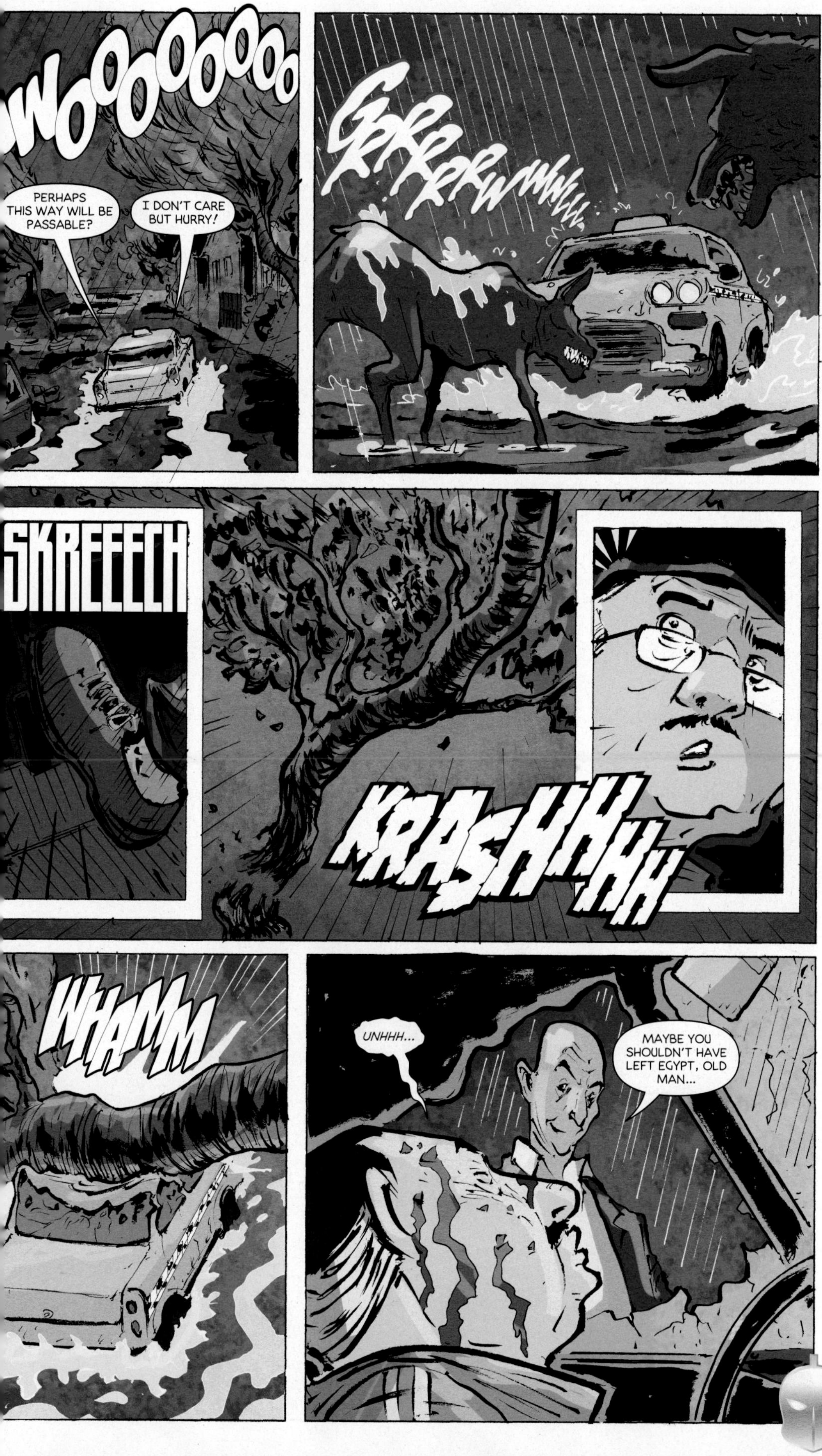
WOOOOOOOO
PERHAPS THIS WAY WILL BE PASSABLE?
I DON'T CARE BUT HURRY!
GRRRRRWWLLLL
SKREEECH
KRASHHHHH
WHAMM
UNHHH...
MAYBE YOU SHOULDN'T HAVE LEFT EGYPT, OLD MAN...

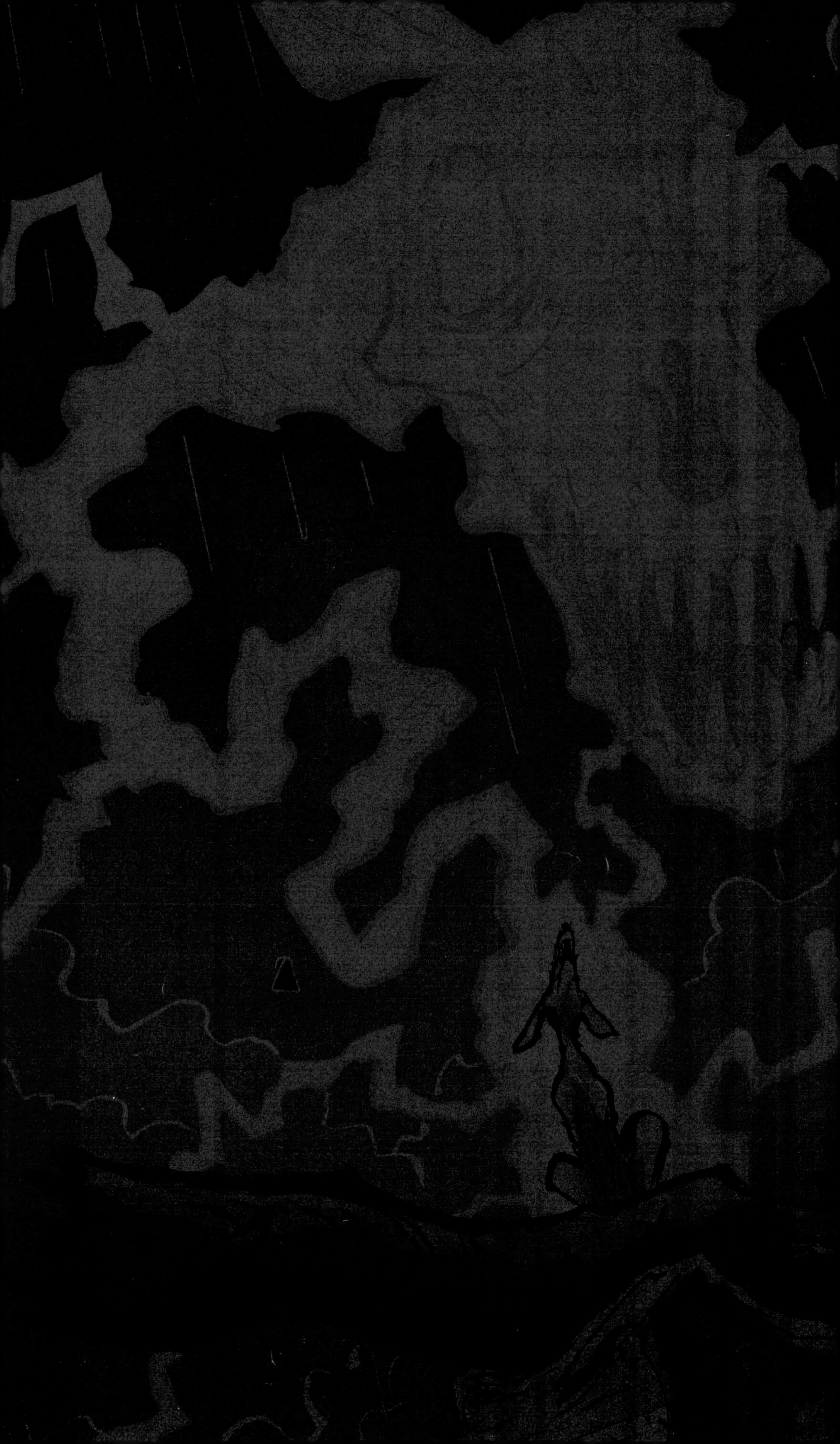

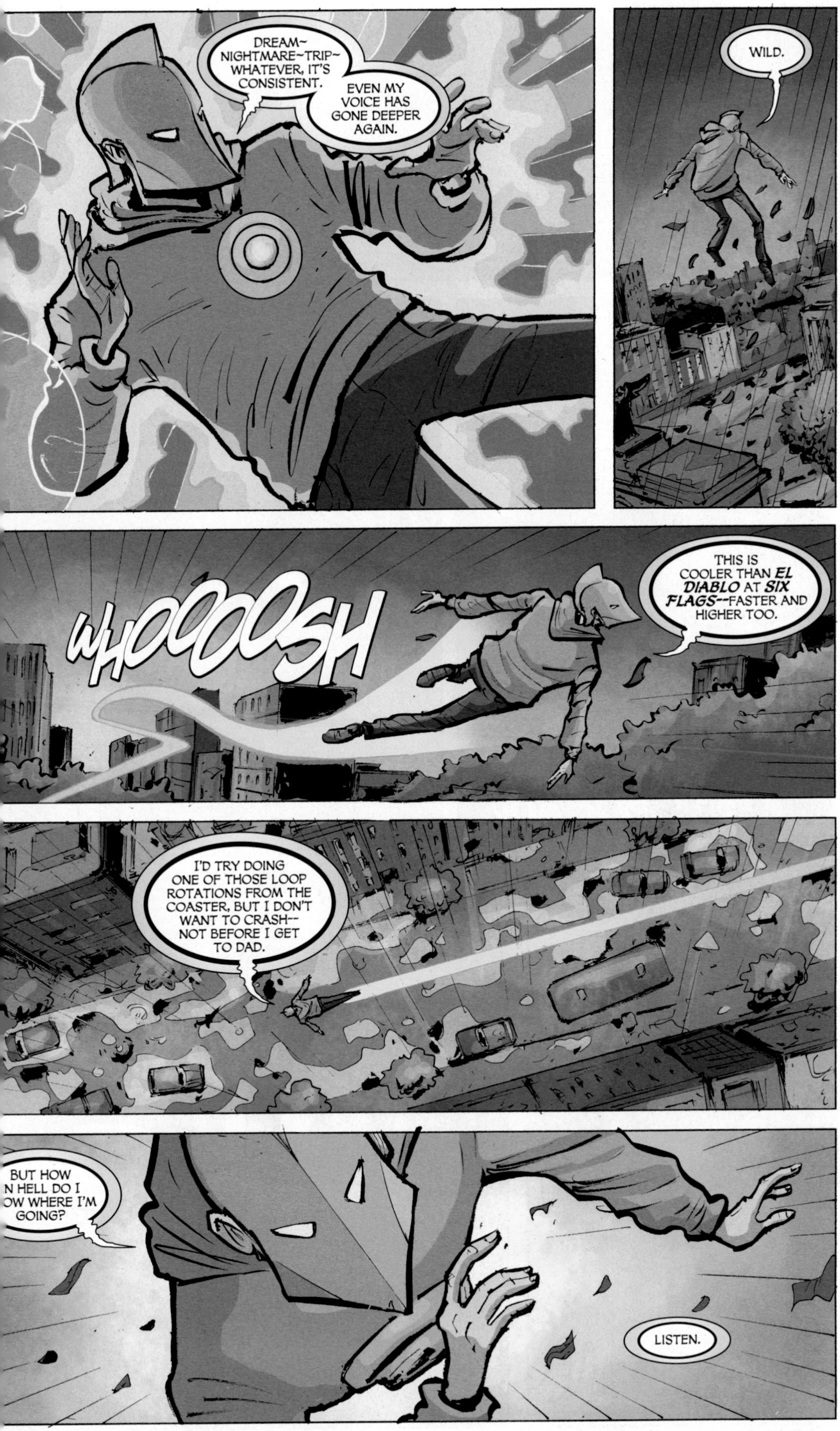

DREAM~ NIGHTMARE~TRIP~ WHATEVER, IT'S CONSISTENT.
EVEN MY VOICE HAS GONE DEEPER AGAIN.
WILD.
WHOOOOOSH
THIS IS COOLER THAN *EL DIABLO* AT *SIX FLAGS*--FASTER AND HIGHER TOO.
I'D TRY DOING ONE OF THOSE LOOP ROTATIONS FROM THE COASTER, BUT I DON'T WANT TO CRASH-- NOT BEFORE I GET TO DAD.
BUT HOW N HELL DO I OW WHERE I'M GOING?
LISTEN.

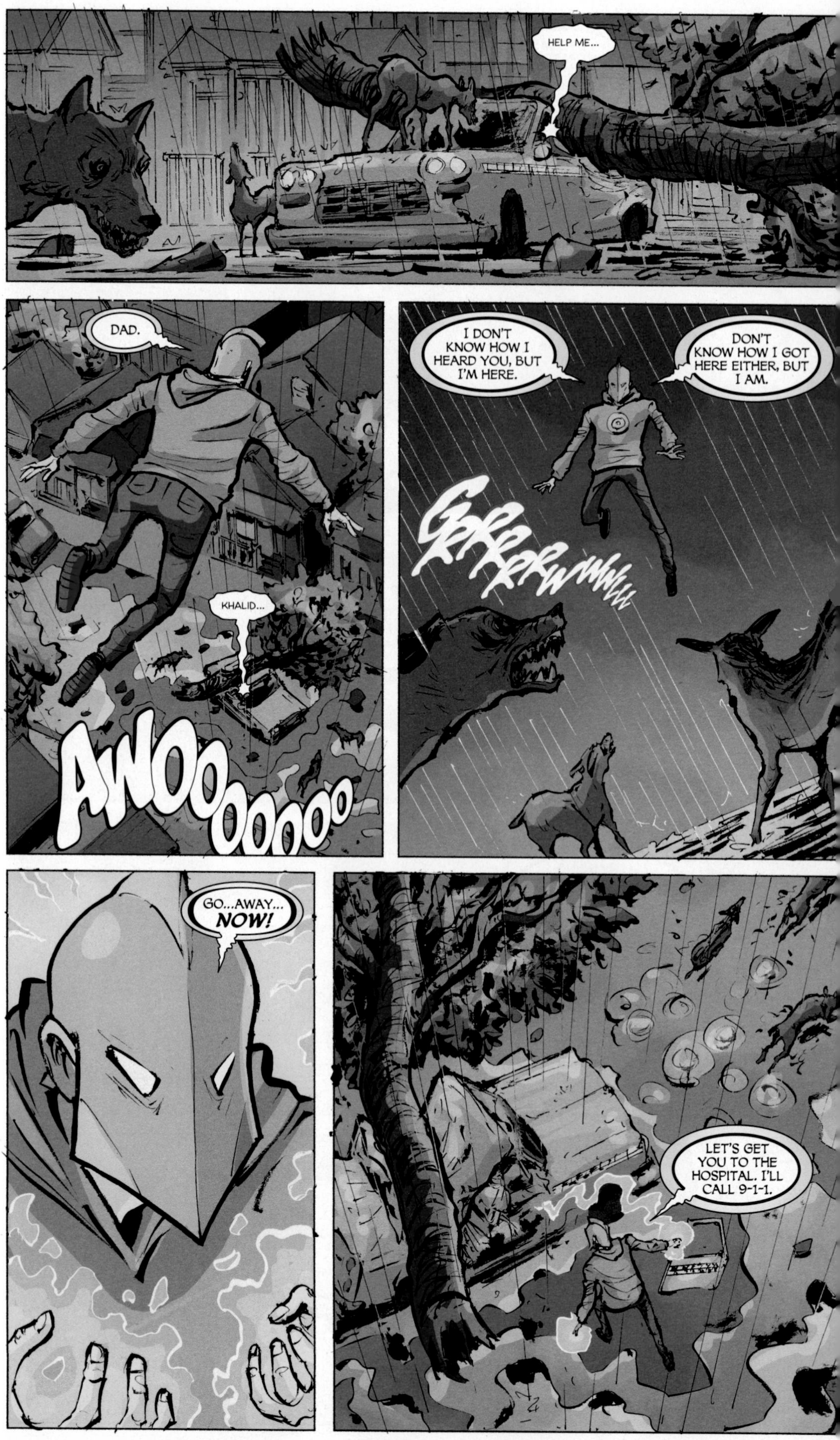
HELP ME...
DAD.
KHALID...
AWOOOOOOO
I DON'T KNOW HOW I HEARD YOU, BUT I'M HERE.
DON'T KNOW HOW I GOT HERE EITHER, BUT I AM.
GRRRRRWWWLLL
GO...AWAY... NOW!
LET'S GET YOU TO THE HOSPITAL. I'LL CALL 9-1-1.

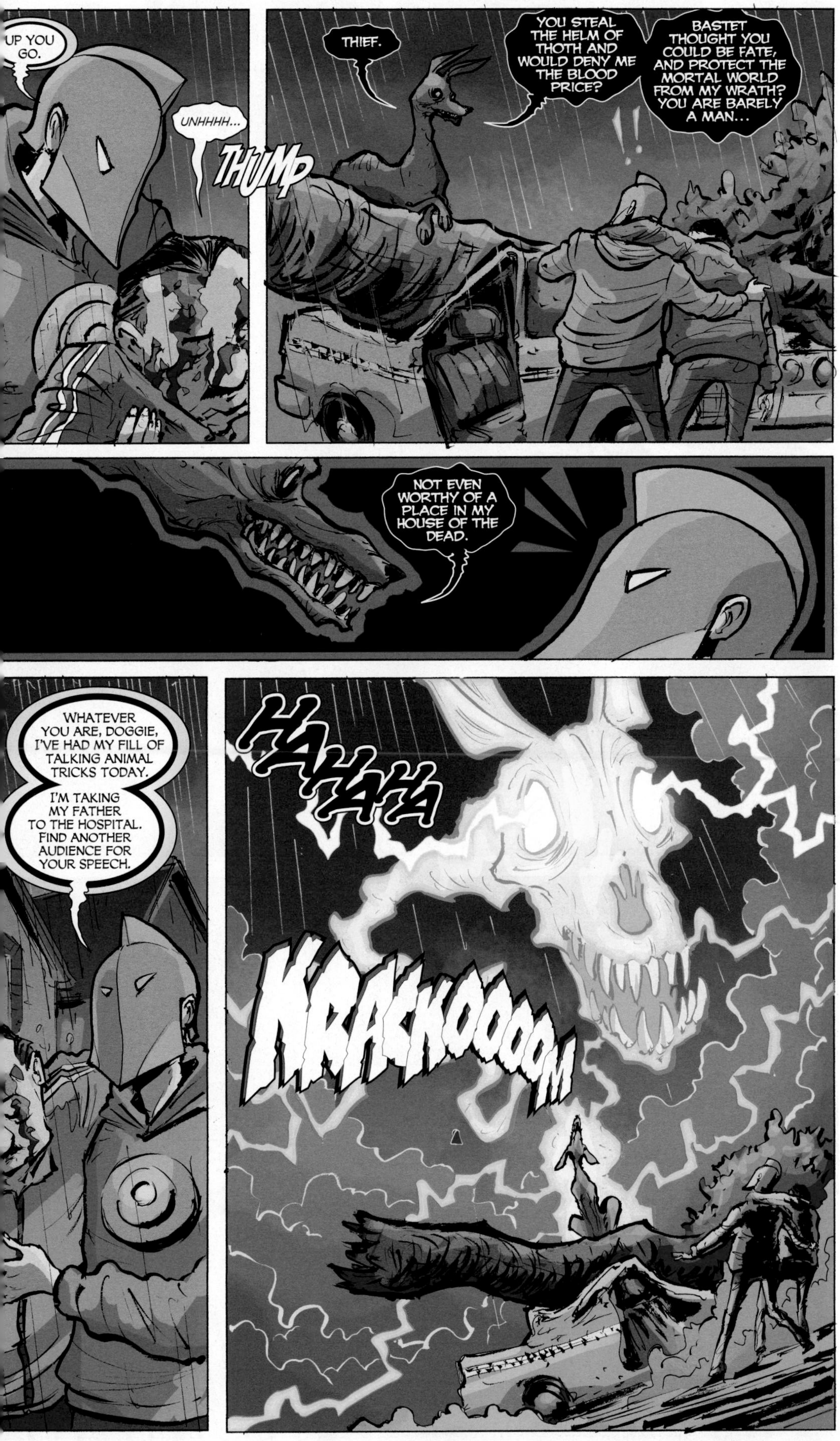
UP YOU GO.
UNHHHH...
THUMP
THIEF.
YOU STEAL THE HELM OF THOTH AND WOULD DENY ME THE BLOOD PRICE?
!!
BASTET THOUGHT YOU COULD BE FATE, AND PROTECT THE MORTAL WORLD FROM MY WRATH? YOU ARE BARELY A MAN...
NOT EVEN WORTHY OF A PLACE IN MY HOUSE OF THE DEAD.
WHATEVER YOU ARE, DOGGIE, I'VE HAD MY FILL OF TALKING ANIMAL TRICKS TODAY.
I'M TAKING MY FATHER TO THE HOSPITAL. FIND ANOTHER AUDIENCE FOR YOUR SPEECH.
HAHAHA
KRACKOOOOM

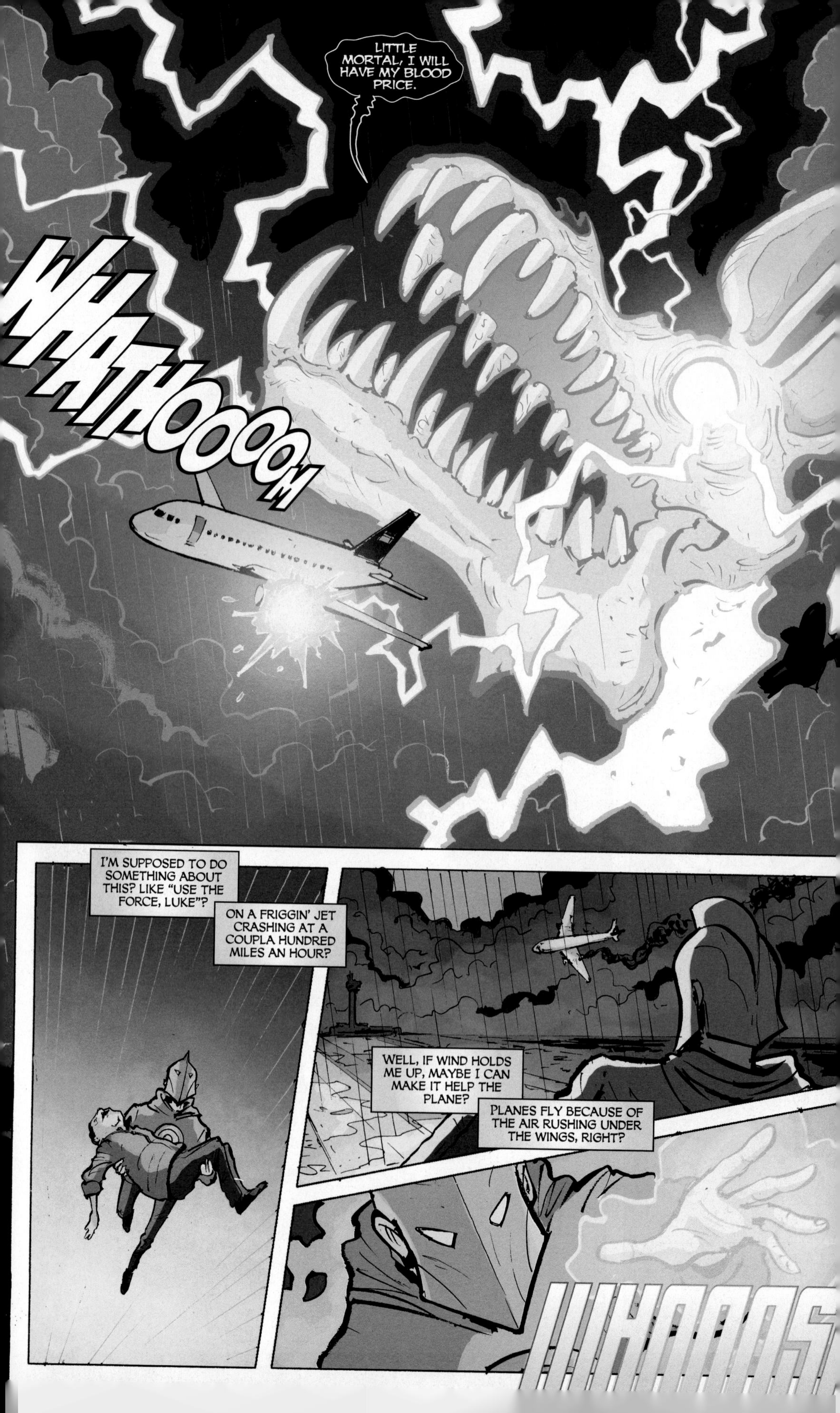
LITTLE MORTAL, I WILL HAVE MY BLOOD PRICE.
WHATHOOOOOM
I'M SUPPOSED TO DO SOMETHING ABOUT THIS? LIKE "USE THE FORCE, LUKE"?
ON A FRIGGIN' JET CRASHING AT A COUPLA HUNDRED MILES AN HOUR?
WELL, IF WIND HOLDS ME UP, MAYBE I CAN MAKE IT HELP THE PLANE?
PLANES FLY BECAUSE OF THE AIR RUSHING UNDER THE WINGS, RIGHT?
WHOOOSH

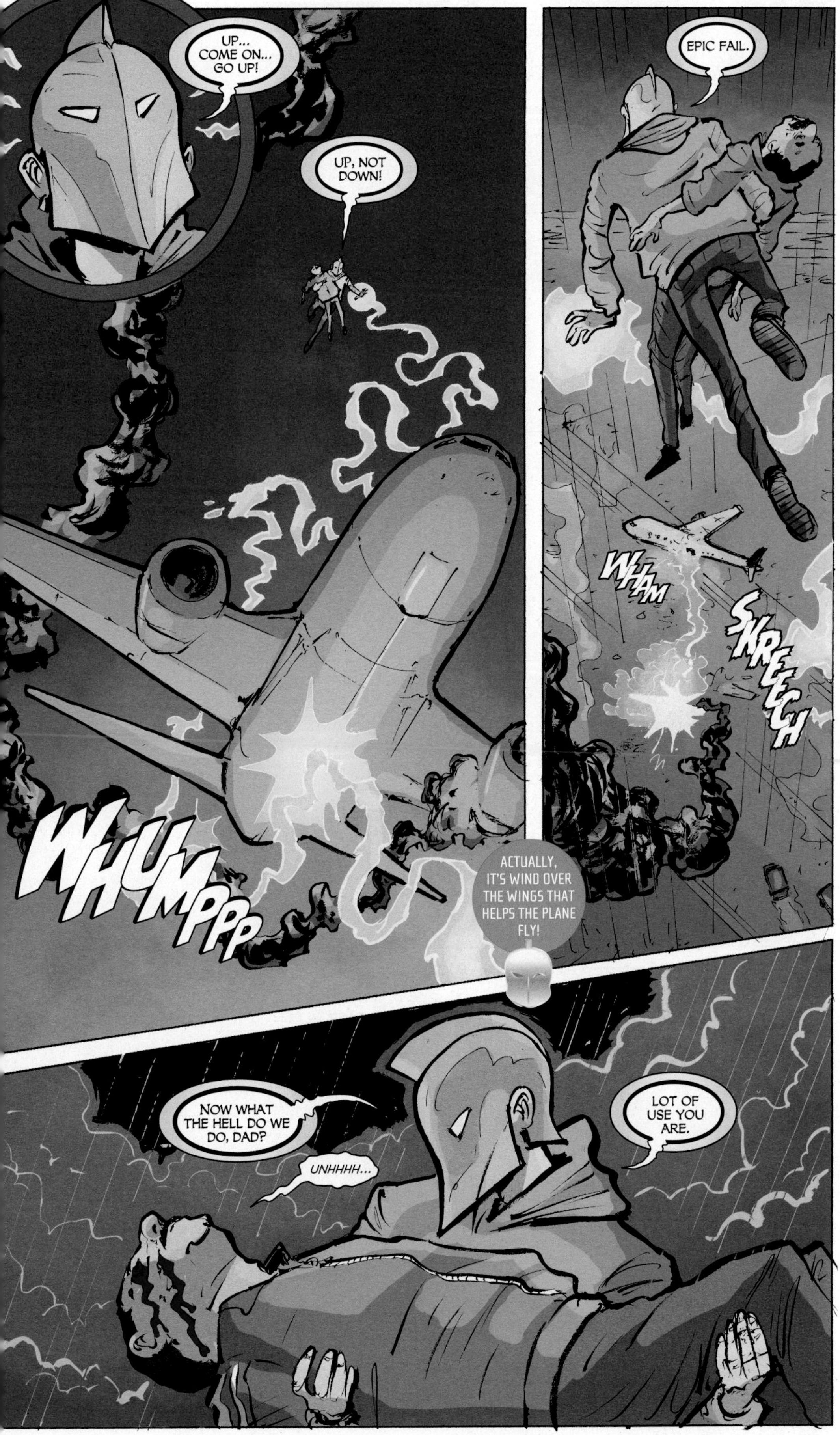
UP... COME ON... GO UP!
UP, NOT DOWN!
EPIC FAIL.
WHAM
SKREECH
WHUMPPP
ACTUALLY, IT'S WIND OVER THE WINGS THAT HELPS THE PLANE FLY!
NOW WHAT THE HELL DO WE DO, DAD?
UNHHHH...
LOT OF USE YOU ARE.

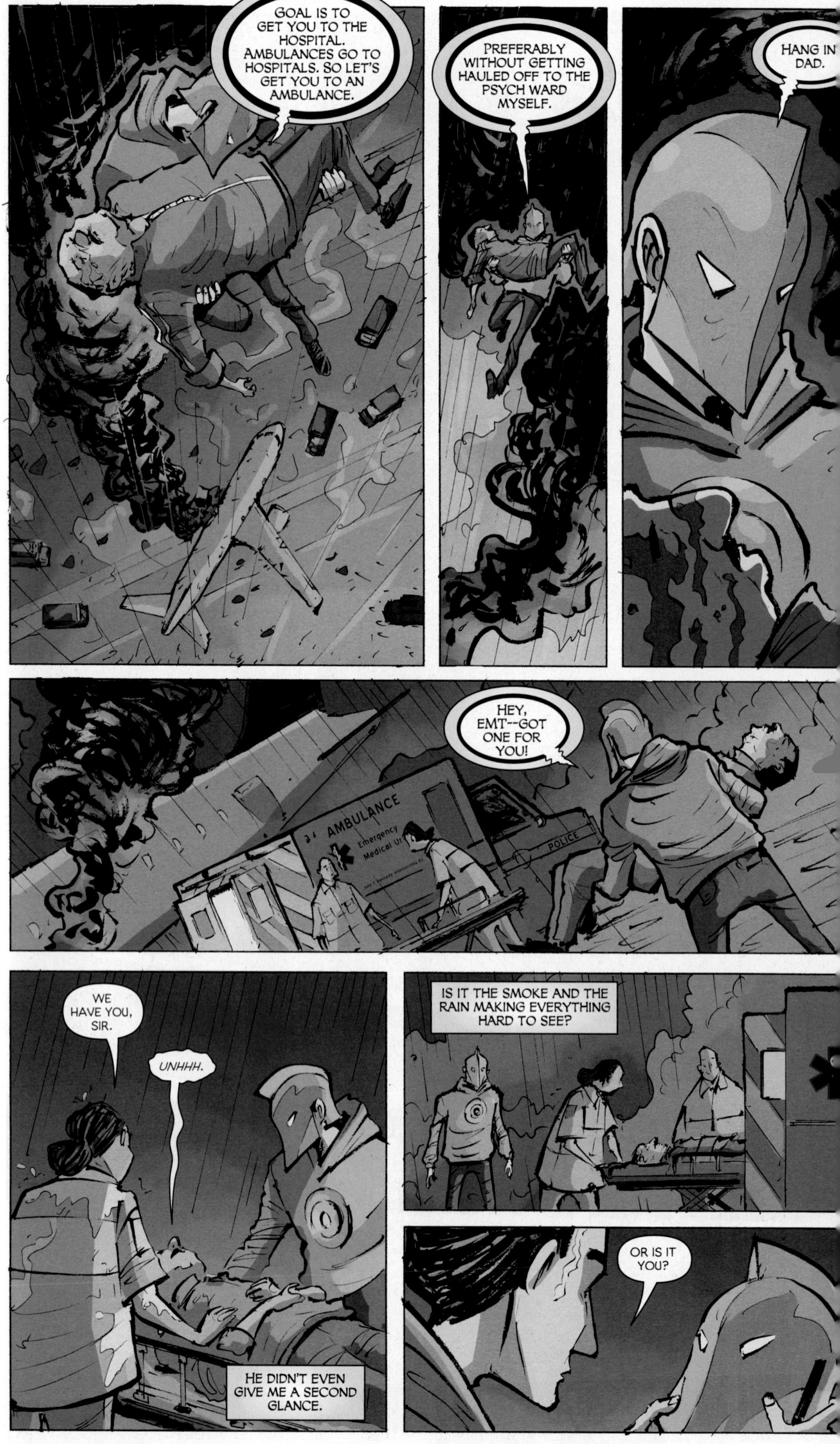

GOAL IS TO GET YOU TO THE HOSPITAL. AMBULANCES GO TO HOSPITALS. SO LET'S GET YOU TO AN AMBULANCE.
PREFERABLY WITHOUT GETTING HAULED OFF TO THE PSYCH WARD MYSELF.
HANG IN DAD.
HEY, EMT--GOT ONE FOR YOU!
AMBULANCE
Emergency Medical
POLICE
WE HAVE YOU, SIR.
UNHHH.
HE DIDN'T EVEN GIVE ME A SECOND GLANCE.
IS IT THE SMOKE AND THE RAIN MAKING EVERYTHING HARD TO SEE?
OR IS IT YOU?

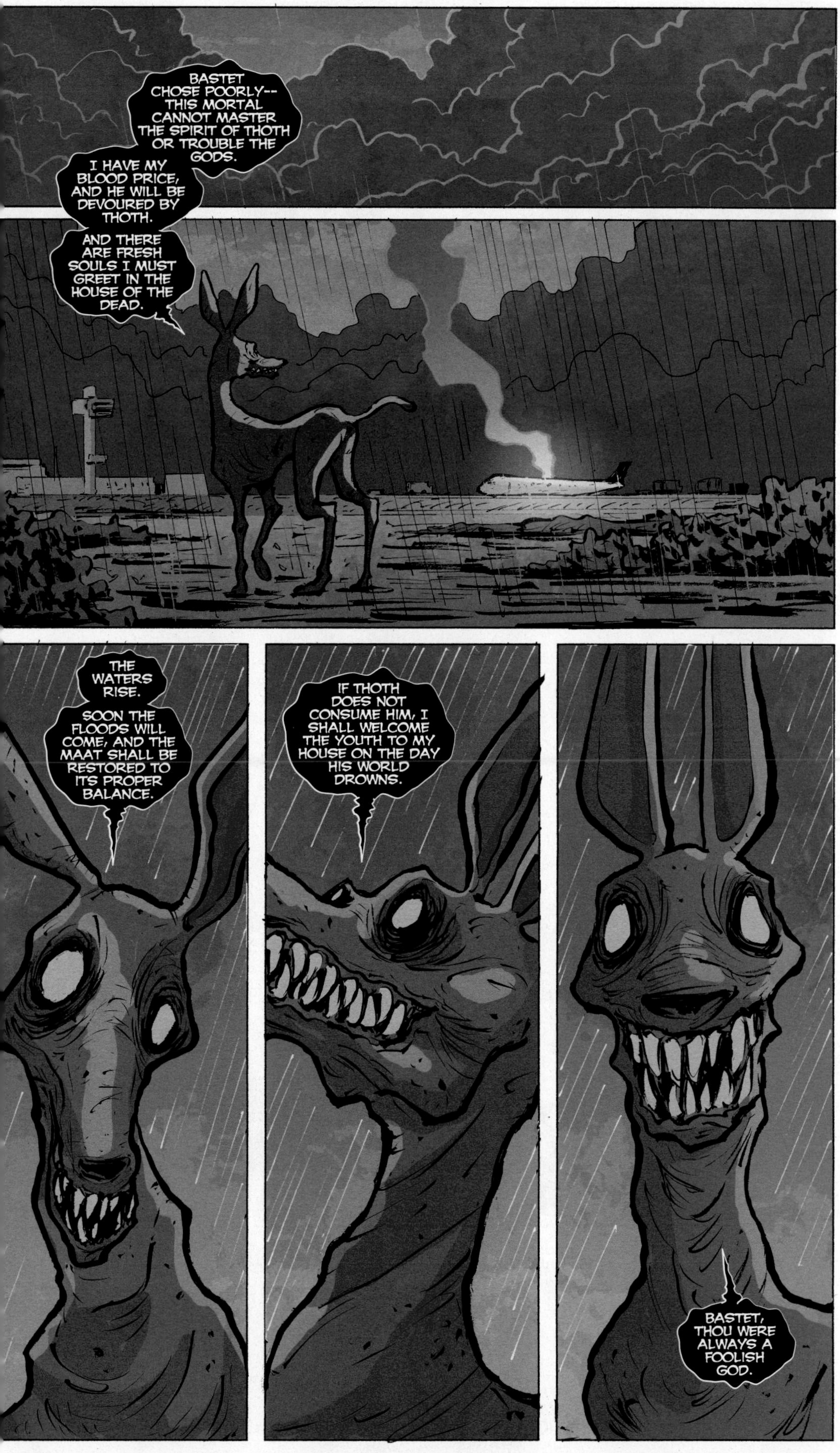
BASTET CHOSE POORLY-- THIS MORTAL CANNOT MASTER THE SPIRIT OF THOTH OR TROUBLE THE GODS.
I HAVE MY BLOOD PRICE, AND HE WILL BE DEVOURED BY THOTH.
AND THERE ARE FRESH SOULS I MUST GREET IN THE HOUSE OF THE DEAD.
THE WATERS RISE.
SOON THE FLOODS WILL COME, AND THE MAAT SHALL BE RESTORED TO ITS PROPER BALANCE.
IF THOTH DOES NOT CONSUME HIM, I SHALL WELCOME THE YOUTH TO MY HOUSE ON THE DAY HIS WORLD DROWNS.
BASTET, THOU WERE ALWAYS A FOOLISH GOD.

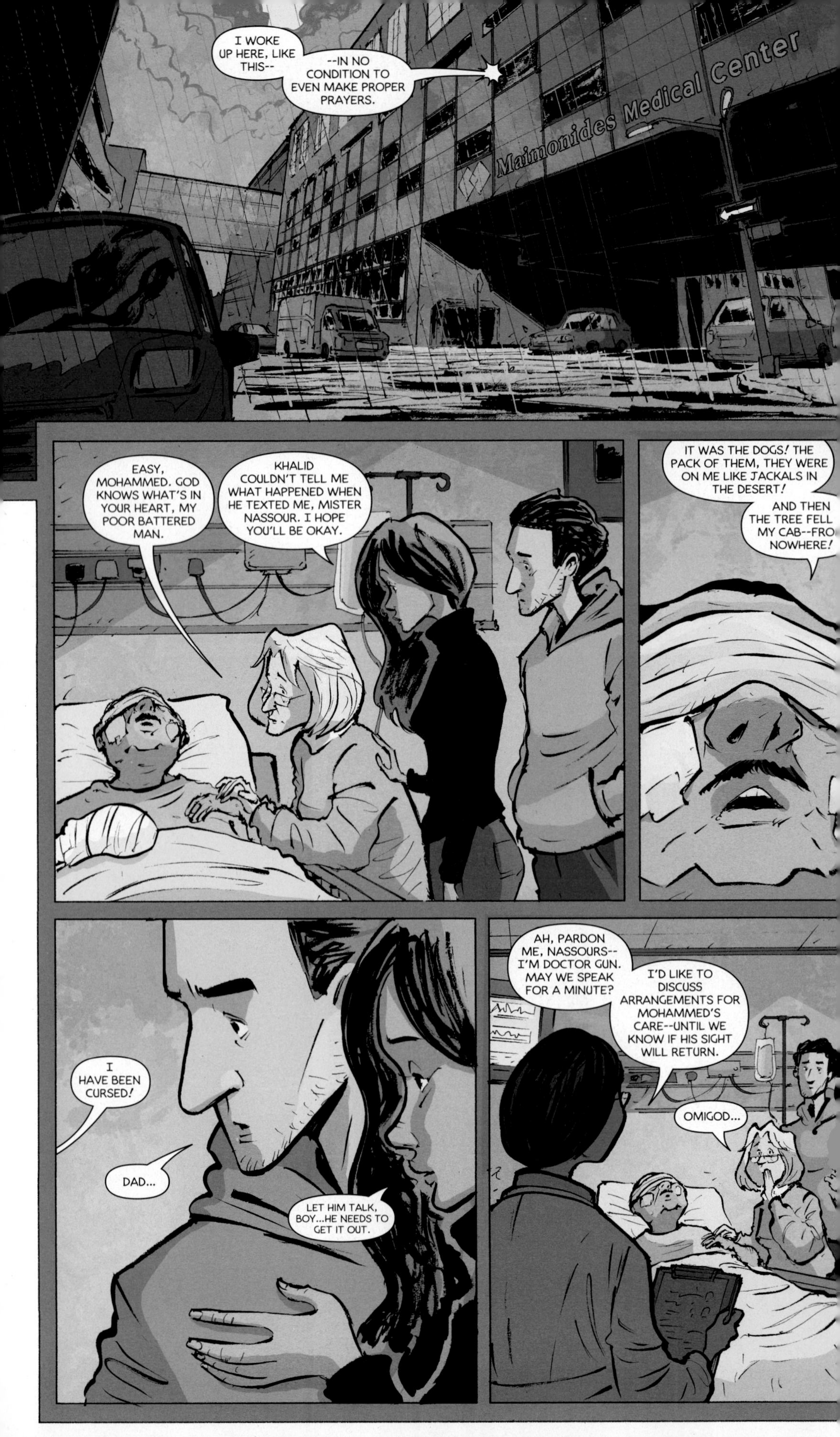
I WOKE UP HERE, LIKE THIS--
--IN NO CONDITION TO EVEN MAKE PROPER PRAYERS.
Maimonides Medical Center
EASY, MOHAMMED. GOD KNOWS WHAT'S IN YOUR HEART, MY POOR BATTERED MAN.
KHALID COULDN'T TELL ME WHAT HAPPENED WHEN HE TEXTED ME, MISTER NASSOUR. I HOPE YOU'LL BE OKAY.
IT WAS THE DOGS! THE PACK OF THEM, THEY WERE ON ME LIKE JACKALS IN THE DESERT!
AND THEN THE TREE FELL MY CAB--FRO NOWHERE!
I HAVE BEEN CURSED!
DAD...
LET HIM TALK, BOY...HE NEEDS TO GET IT OUT.
AH, PARDON ME, NASSOURS-- I'M DOCTOR GUN. MAY WE SPEAK FOR A MINUTE?
I'D LIKE TO DISCUSS ARRANGEMENTS FOR MOHAMMED'S CARE--UNTIL WE KNOW IF HIS SIGHT WILL RETURN.
OMIGOD...

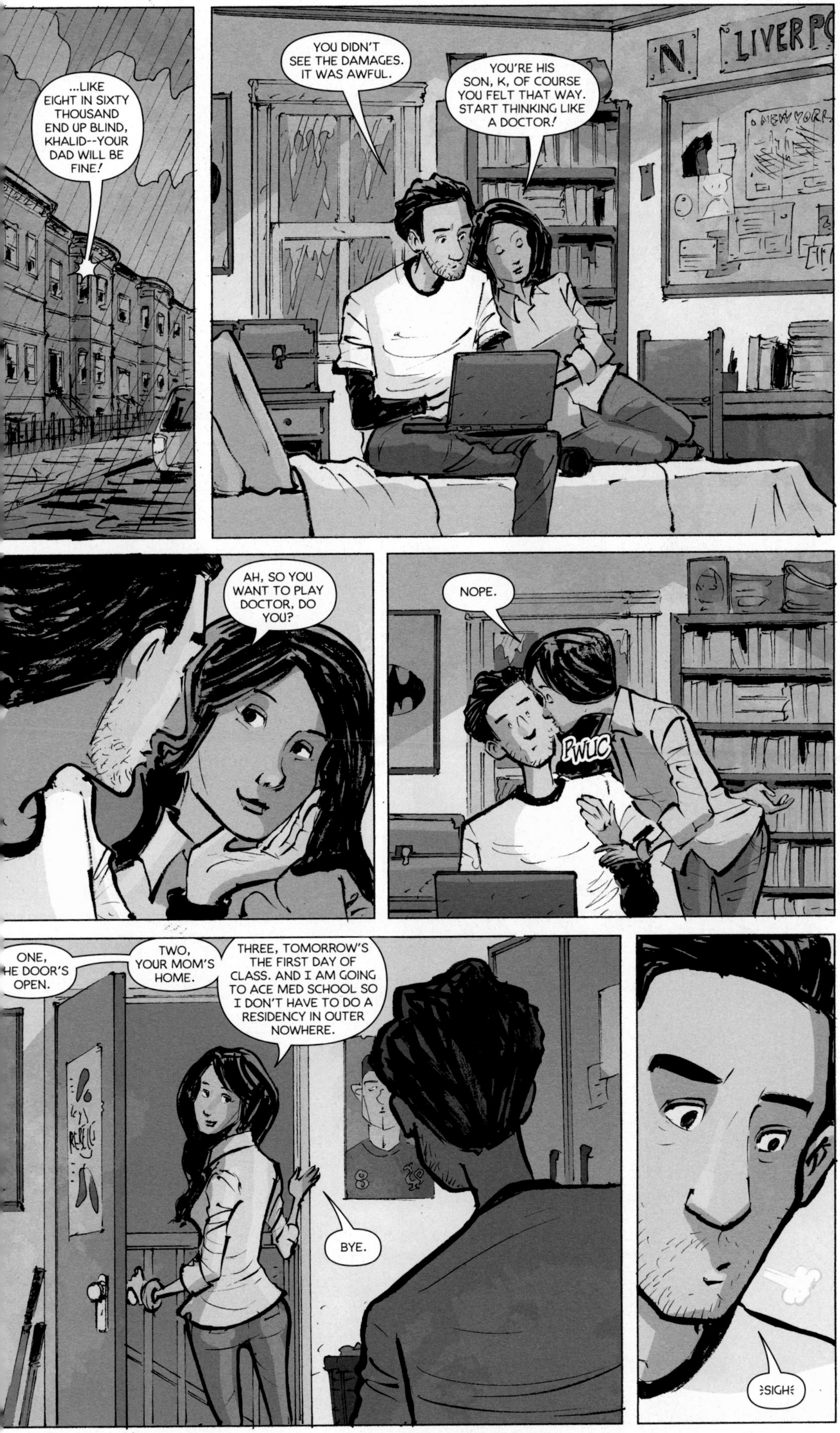
...LIKE EIGHT IN SIXTY THOUSAND END UP BLIND, KHALID--YOUR DAD WILL BE FINE!
YOU DIDN'T SEE THE DAMAGES. IT WAS AWFUL.
YOU'RE HIS SON, K, OF COURSE YOU FELT THAT WAY. START THINKING LIKE A DOCTOR!
N
LIVERPO
AH, SO YOU WANT TO PLAY DOCTOR, DO YOU?
NOPE.
PWUC
ONE, THE DOOR'S OPEN.
TWO, YOUR MOM'S HOME.
THREE, TOMORROW'S THE FIRST DAY OF CLASS. AND I AM GOING TO ACE MED SCHOOL SO I DON'T HAVE TO DO A RESIDENCY IN OUTER NOWHERE.
BYE.
SIGH

THUNK

HUH?

REALLY...?

WOULD YOU STOP THAT?!

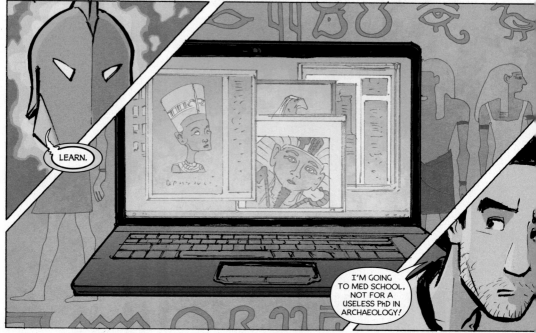

LEARN.

I'M GOING TO MED SCHOOL, NOT FOR A USELESS PhD IN ARCHAEOLOGY!

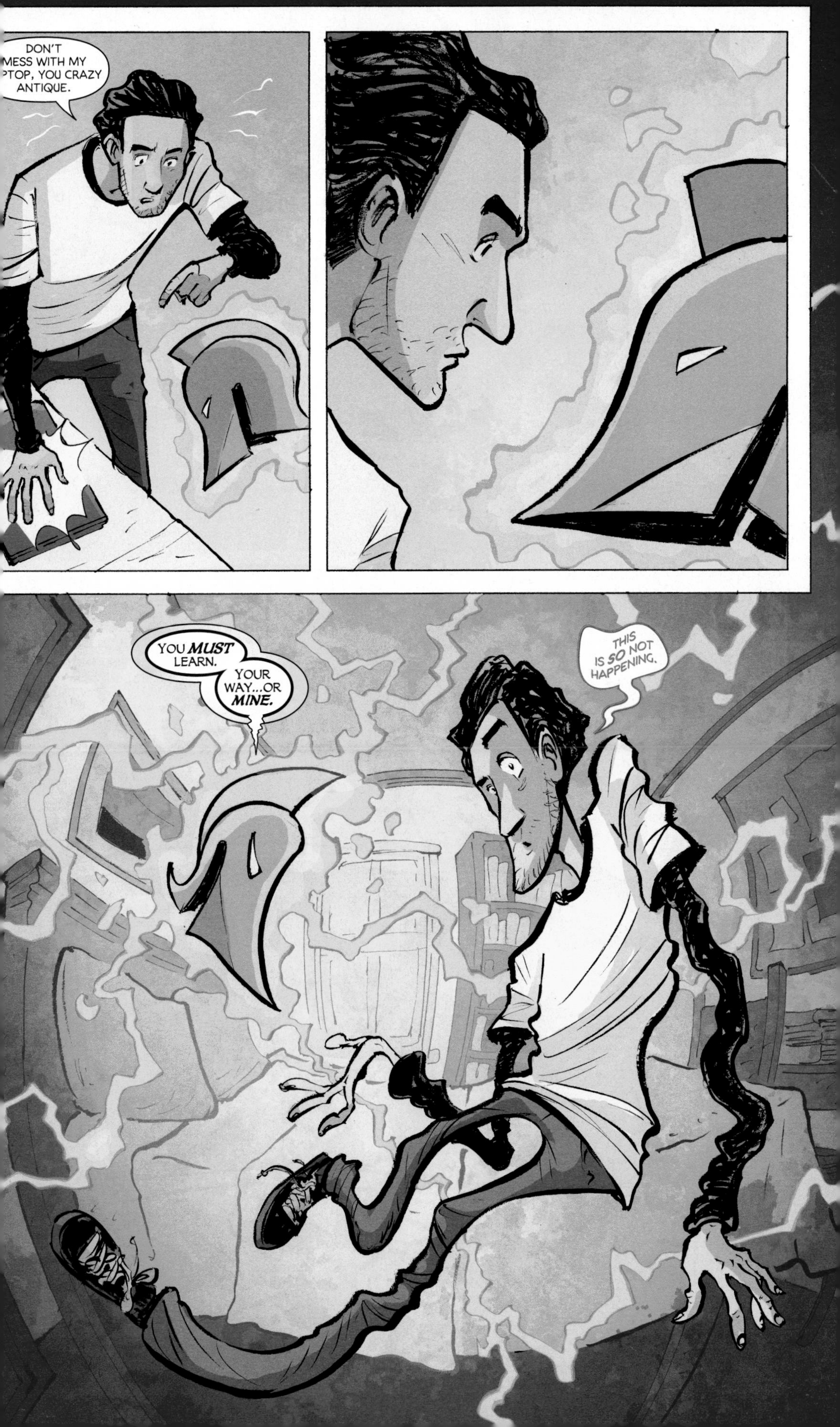
DON'T MESS WITH MY PTOP, YOU CRAZY ANTIQUE.
YOU *MUST* LEARN.
YOUR WAY...OR *MINE.*
THIS IS *SO* NOT HAPPENING.

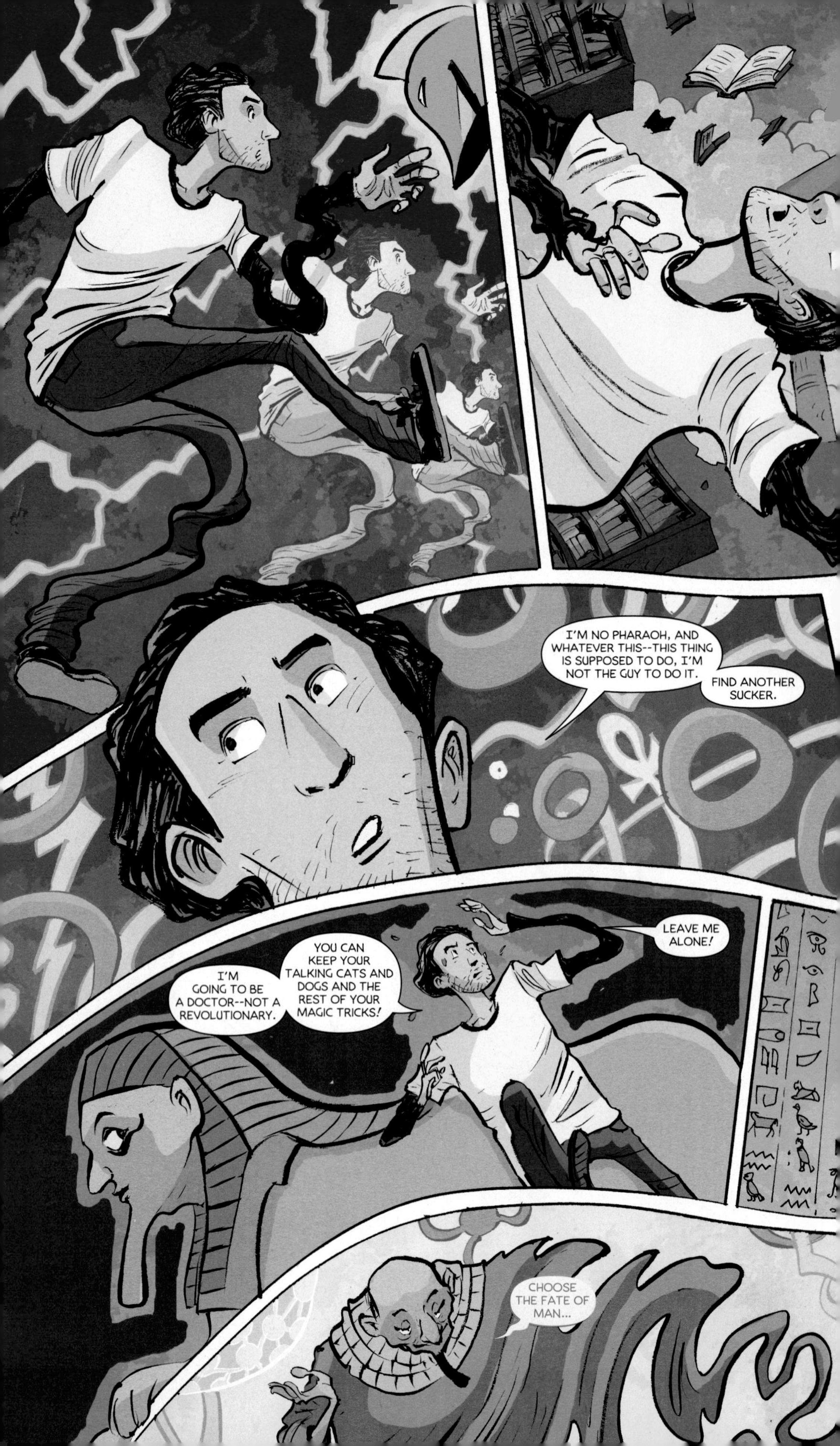
I'M NO PHARAOH, AND WHATEVER THIS--THIS THING IS SUPPOSED TO DO, I'M NOT THE GUY TO DO IT.
FIND ANOTHER SUCKER.
LEAVE ME ALONE!
YOU CAN KEEP YOUR TALKING CATS AND DOGS AND THE REST OF YOUR MAGIC TRICKS!
I'M GOING TO BE A DOCTOR--NOT A REVOLUTIONARY.
CHOOSE THE FATE OF MAN...

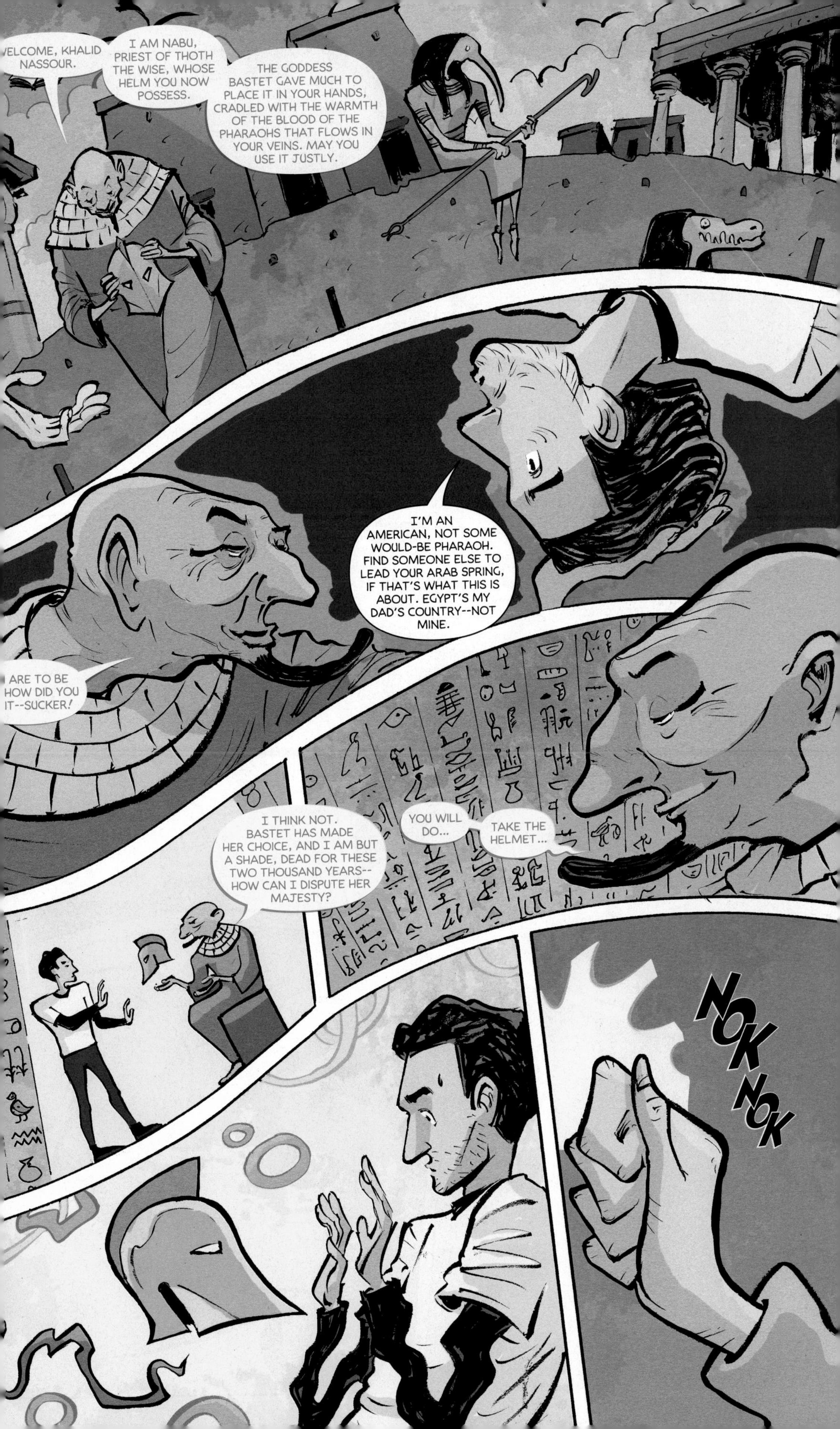
WELCOME, KHALID NASSOUR.
I AM NABU, PRIEST OF THOTH THE WISE, WHOSE HELM YOU NOW POSSESS.
THE GODDESS BASTET GAVE MUCH TO PLACE IT IN YOUR HANDS, CRADLED WITH THE WARMTH OF THE BLOOD OF THE PHARAOHS THAT FLOWS IN YOUR VEINS. MAY YOU USE IT JUSTLY.
I'M AN AMERICAN, NOT SOME WOULD-BE PHARAOH. FIND SOMEONE ELSE TO LEAD YOUR ARAB SPRING, IF THAT'S WHAT THIS IS ABOUT. EGYPT'S MY DAD'S COUNTRY--NOT MINE.
ARE TO BE HOW DID YOU IT--SUCKER!
I THINK NOT. BASTET HAS MADE HER CHOICE, AND I AM BUT A SHADE, DEAD FOR THESE TWO THOUSAND YEARS-- HOW CAN I DISPUTE HER MAJESTY?
YOU WILL DO...
TAKE THE HELMET...
NOK NOK

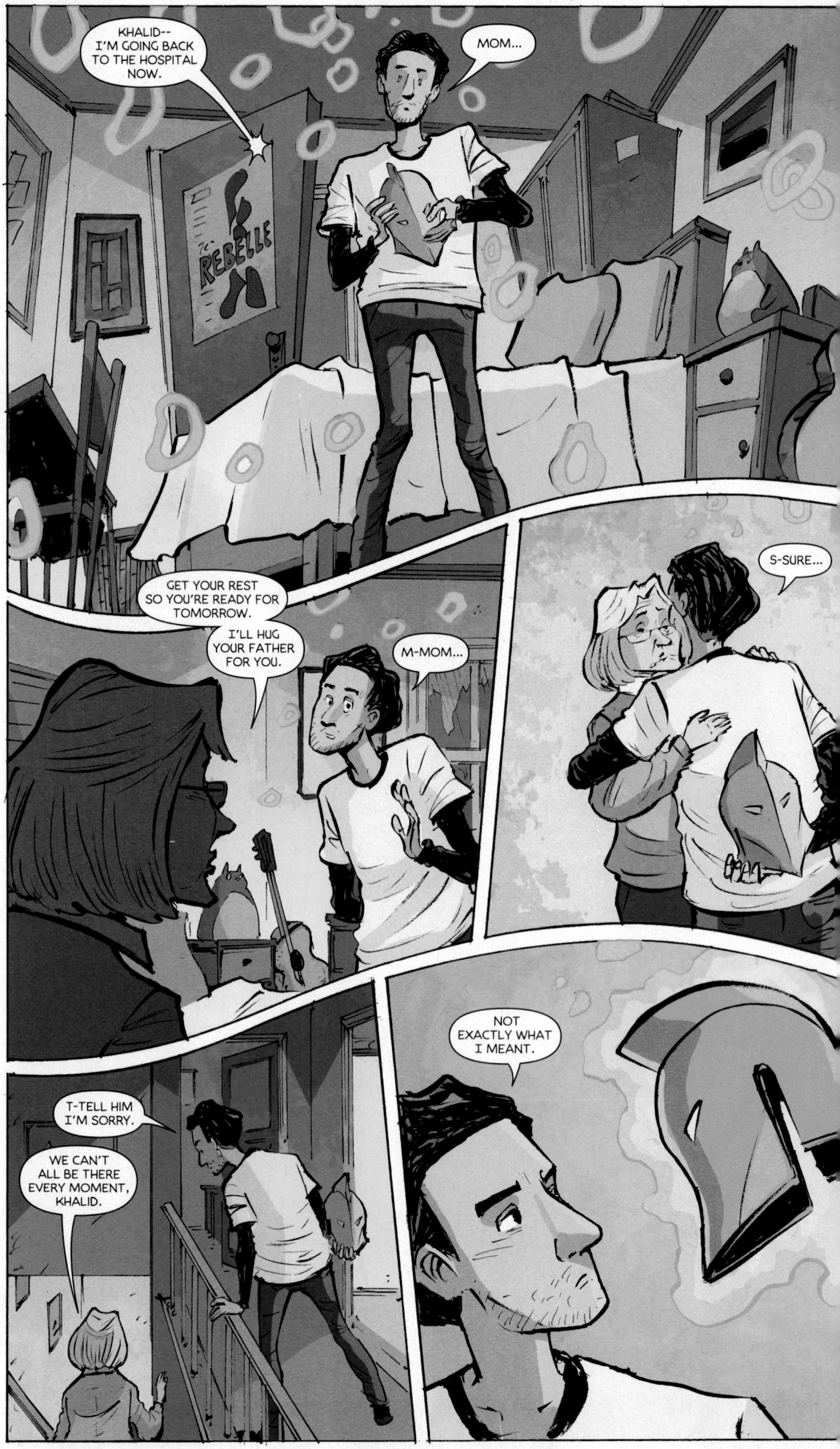
KHALID-- I'M GOING BACK TO THE HOSPITAL NOW.
MOM...
GET YOUR REST SO YOU'RE READY FOR TOMORROW.
I'LL HUG YOUR FATHER FOR YOU.
M-MOM...
S-SURE...
T-TELL HIM I'M SORRY.
WE CAN'T ALL BE THERE EVERY MOMENT, KHALID.
NOT EXACTLY WHAT I MEANT.

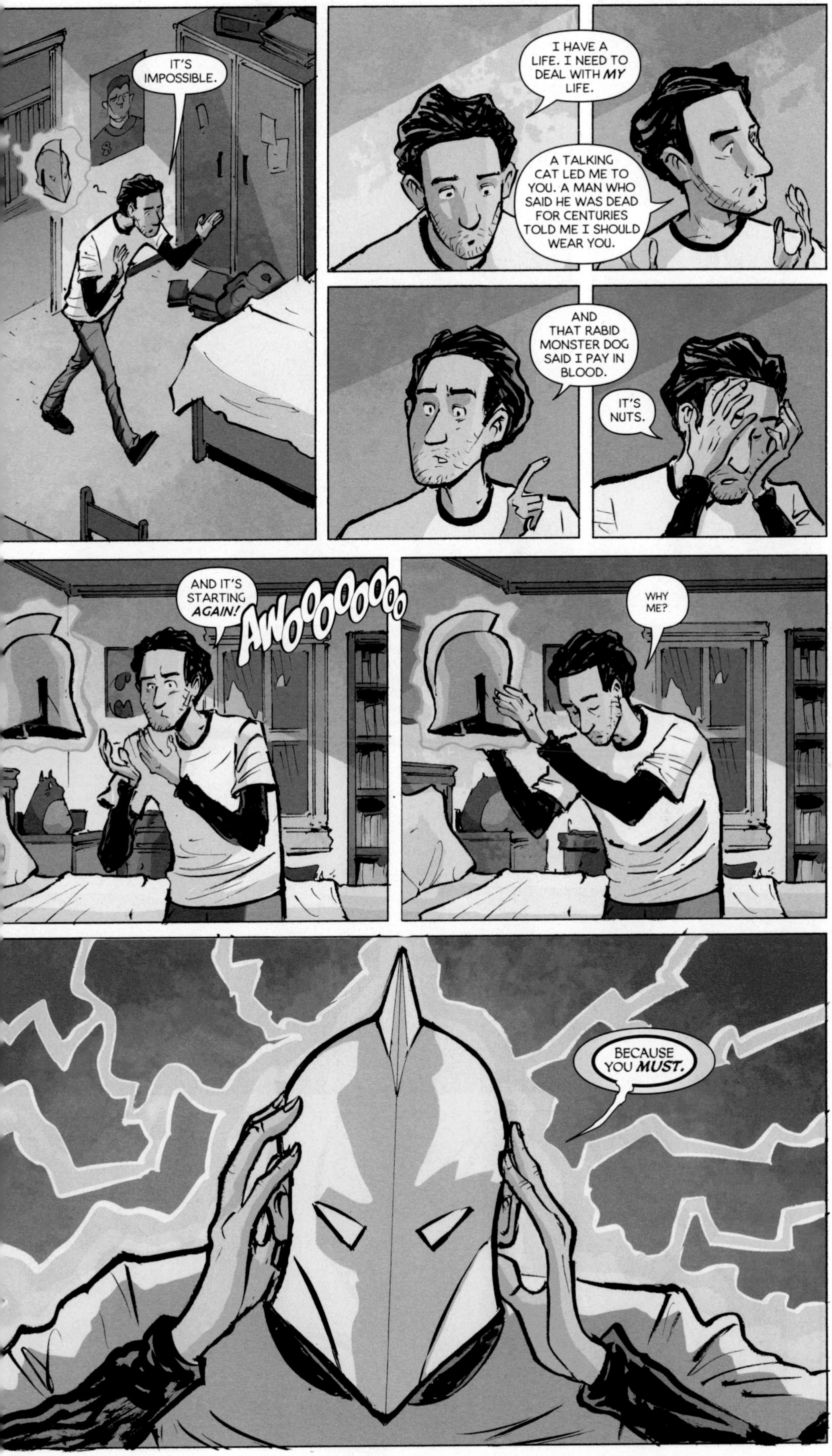
IT'S IMPOSSIBLE.
I HAVE A LIFE. I NEED TO DEAL WITH MY LIFE.
A TALKING CAT LED ME TO YOU. A MAN WHO SAID HE WAS DEAD FOR CENTURIES TOLD ME I SHOULD WEAR YOU.
AND THAT RABID MONSTER DOG SAID I PAY IN BLOOD.
IT'S NUTS.
AND IT'S STARTING AGAIN!
AWOOOOOOOO
WHY ME?
BECAUSE YOU MUST.

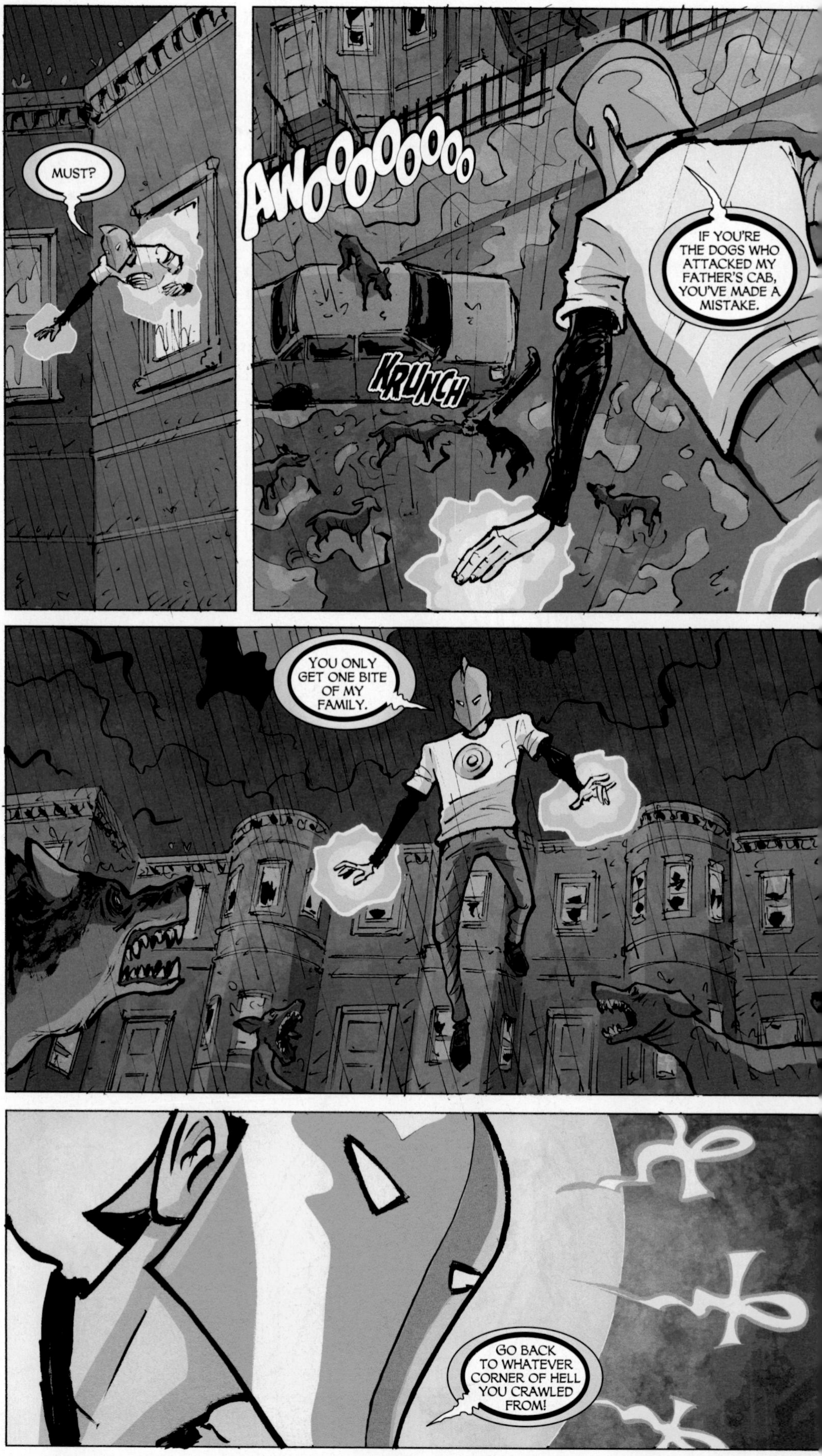
MUST?
AWOOOOOOOO
KRUNCH
IF YOU'RE THE DOGS WHO ATTACKED MY FATHER'S CAB, YOU'VE MADE A MISTAKE.
YOU ONLY GET ONE BITE OF MY FAMILY.
GO BACK TO WHATEVER CORNER OF HELL YOU CRAWLED FROM!

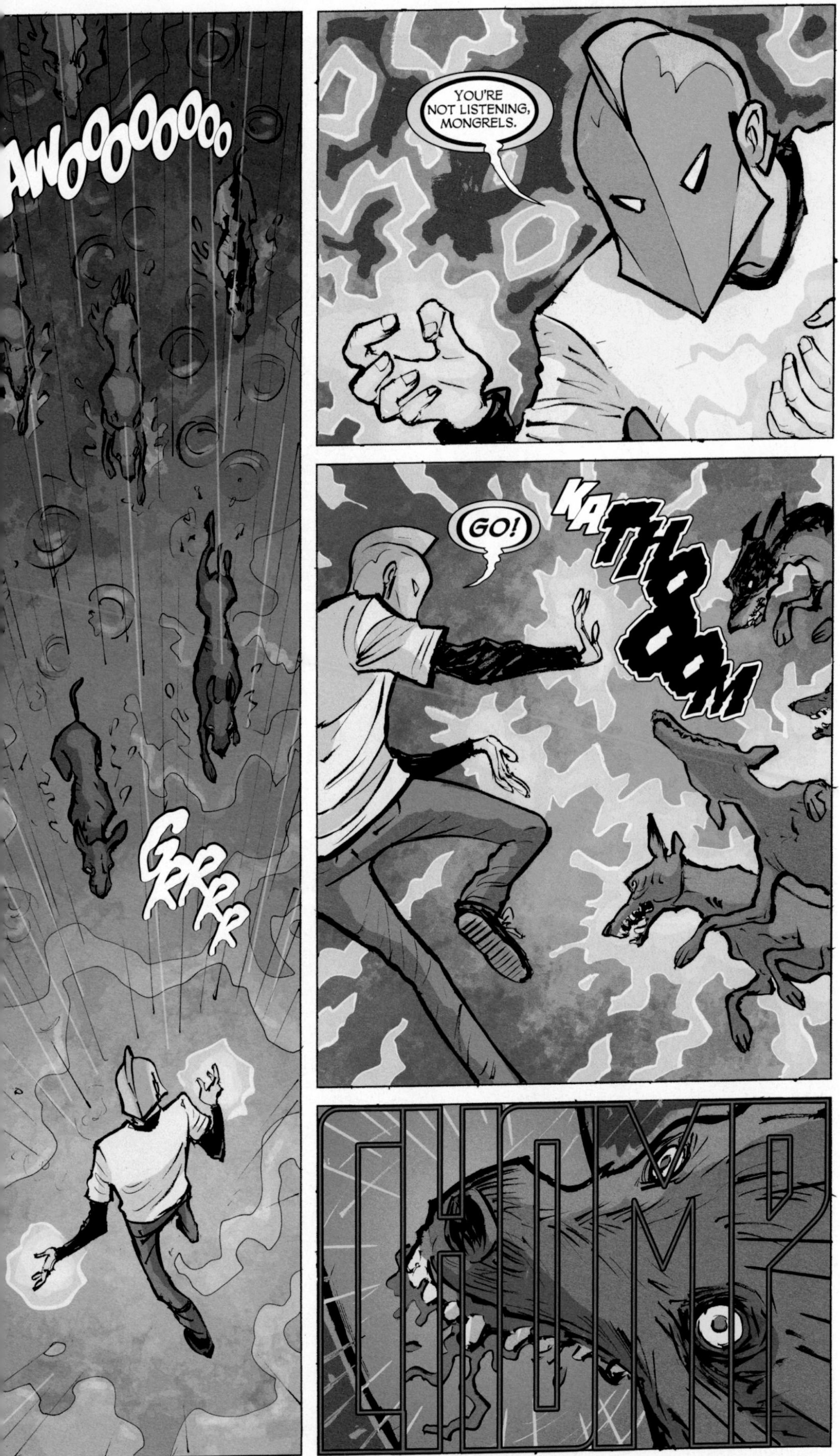
AWOOOOOOOO
GRRRR
YOU'RE NOT LISTENING, MONGRELS.
GO!
KATHOOM
CHOMP

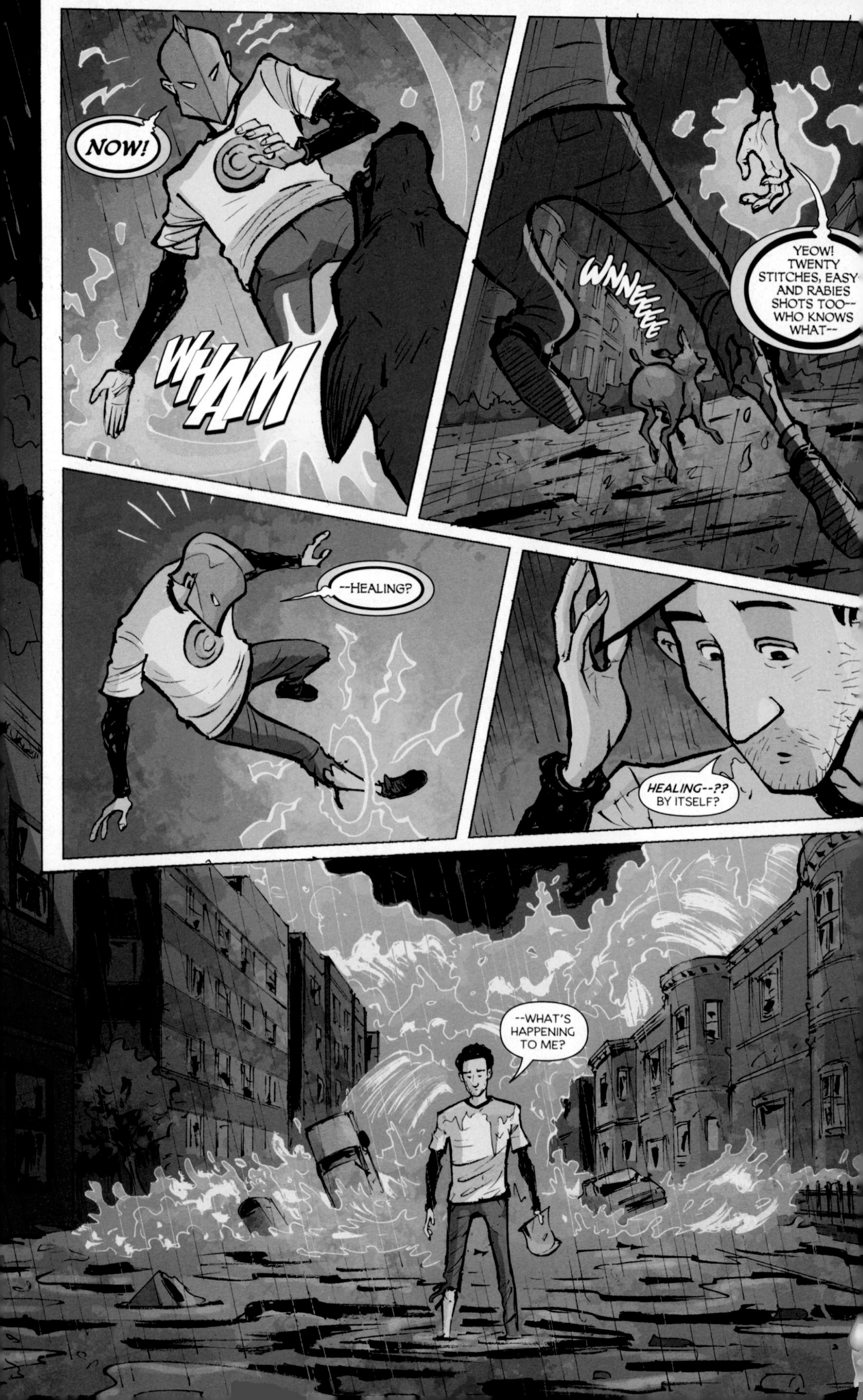
NOW!
WHAM
WNNEEEE
YEOW! TWENTY STITCHES, EASY AND RABIES SHOTS TOO-- WHO KNOWS WHAT--
--HEALING?
HEALING--?? BY ITSELF?
--WHAT'S HAPPENING TO ME?

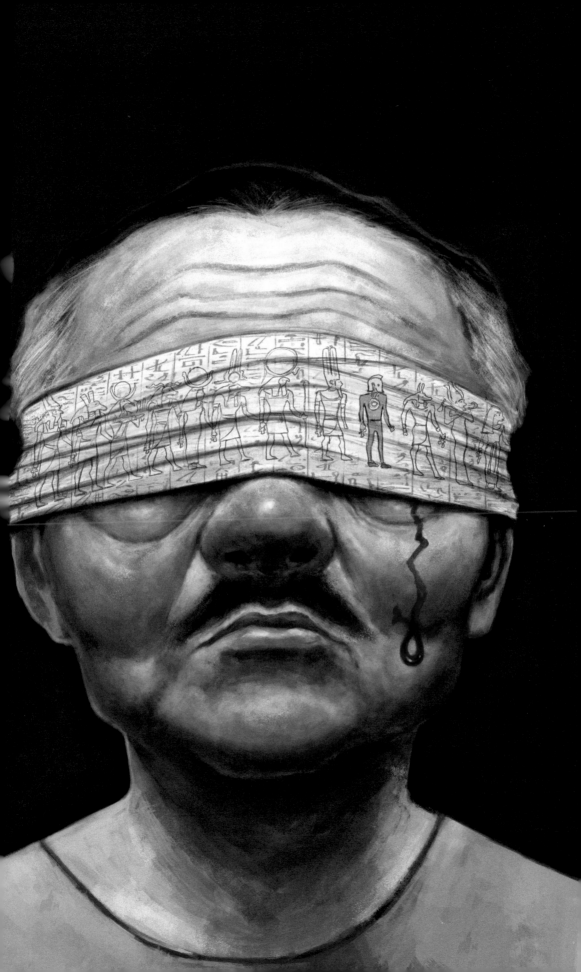

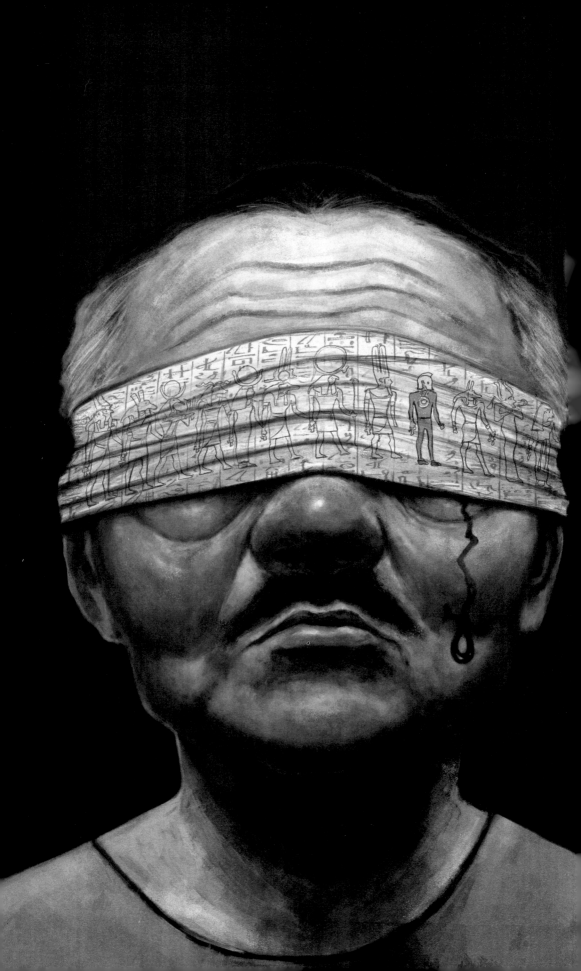

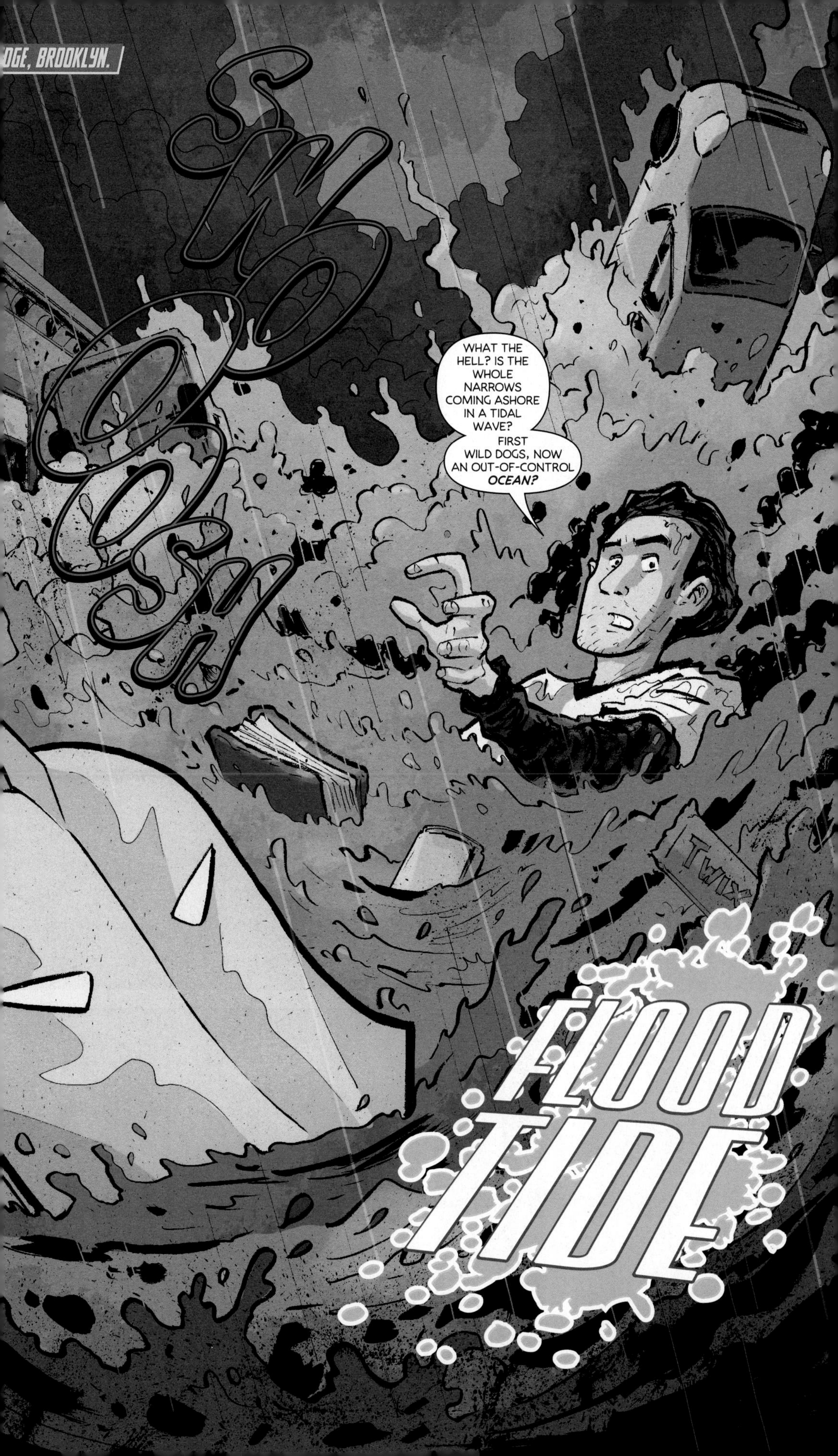

DGE, BROOKLYN.
SWOOSH
WHAT THE HELL? IS THE WHOLE NARROWS COMING ASHORE IN A TIDAL WAVE?
FIRST WILD DOGS, NOW AN OUT-OF-CONTROL *OCEAN?*
TWIX
FLOOD TIDE

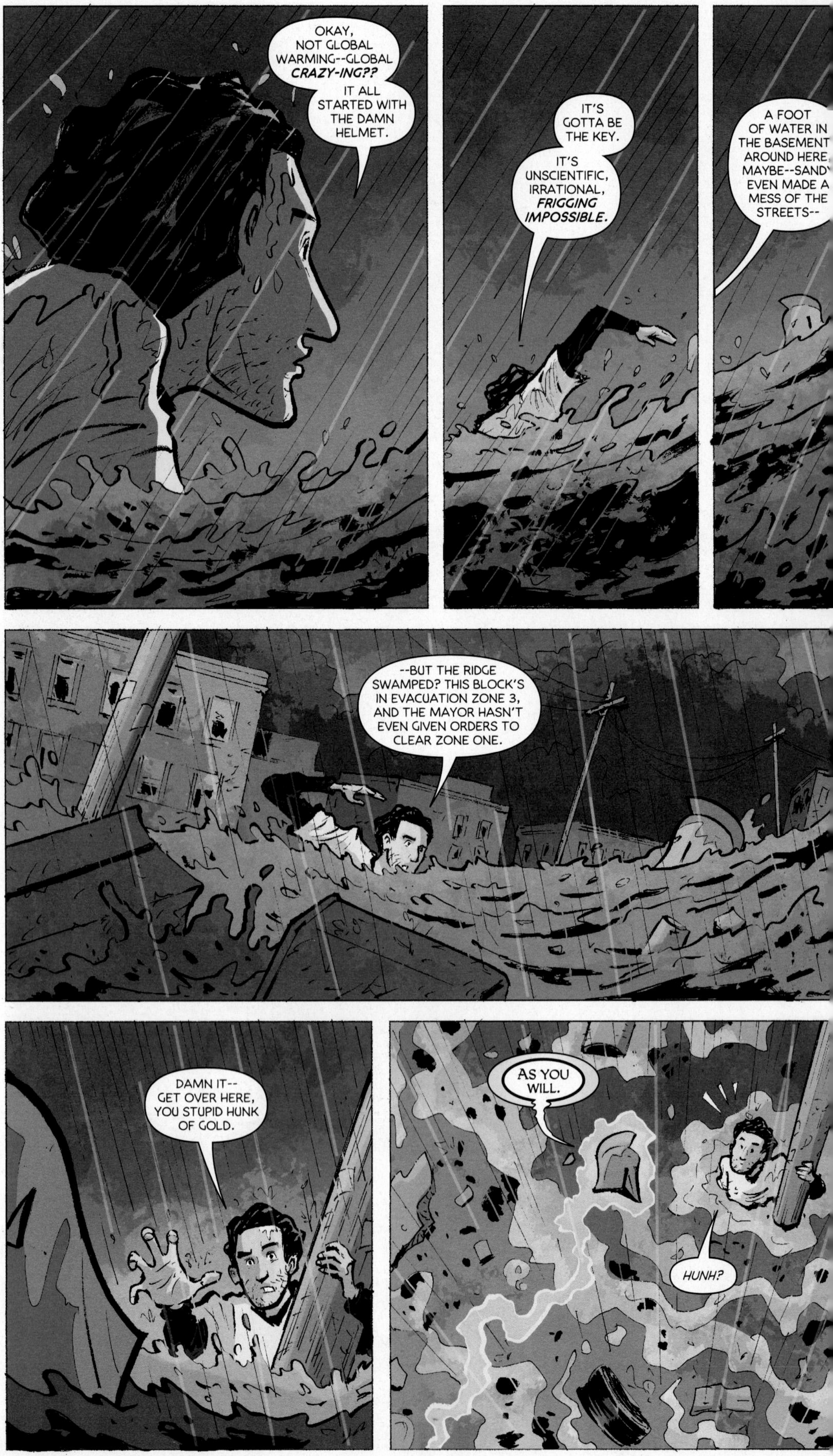
OKAY, NOT GLOBAL WARMING--GLOBAL CRAZY-ING??
IT ALL STARTED WITH THE DAMN HELMET.
IT'S GOTTA BE THE KEY.
IT'S UNSCIENTIFIC, IRRATIONAL, FRIGGING IMPOSSIBLE.
A FOOT OF WATER IN THE BASEMENT AROUND HERE, MAYBE--SANDY EVEN MADE A MESS OF THE STREETS--
--BUT THE RIDGE SWAMPED? THIS BLOCK'S IN EVACUATION ZONE 3, AND THE MAYOR HASN'T EVEN GIVEN ORDERS TO CLEAR ZONE ONE.
DAMN IT-- GET OVER HERE, YOU STUPID HUNK OF GOLD.
AS YOU WILL.
HUNH?

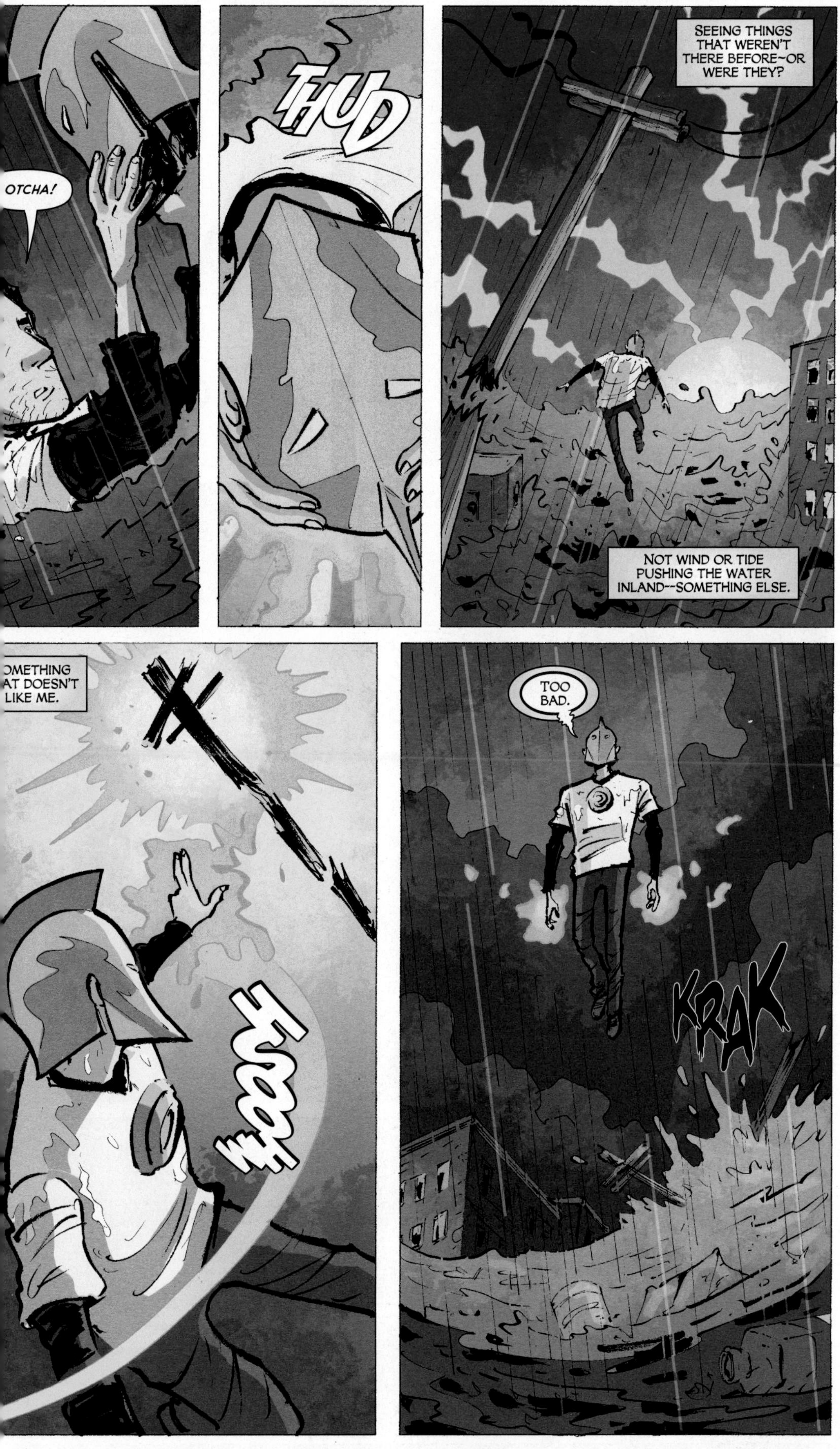
OTCHA!
THUD
SEEING THINGS THAT WEREN'T THERE BEFORE~OR WERE THEY?
NOT WIND OR TIDE PUSHING THE WATER INLAND--SOMETHING ELSE.
OMETHING AT DOESN'T LIKE ME.
WOOSH
TOO BAD.
KRAK

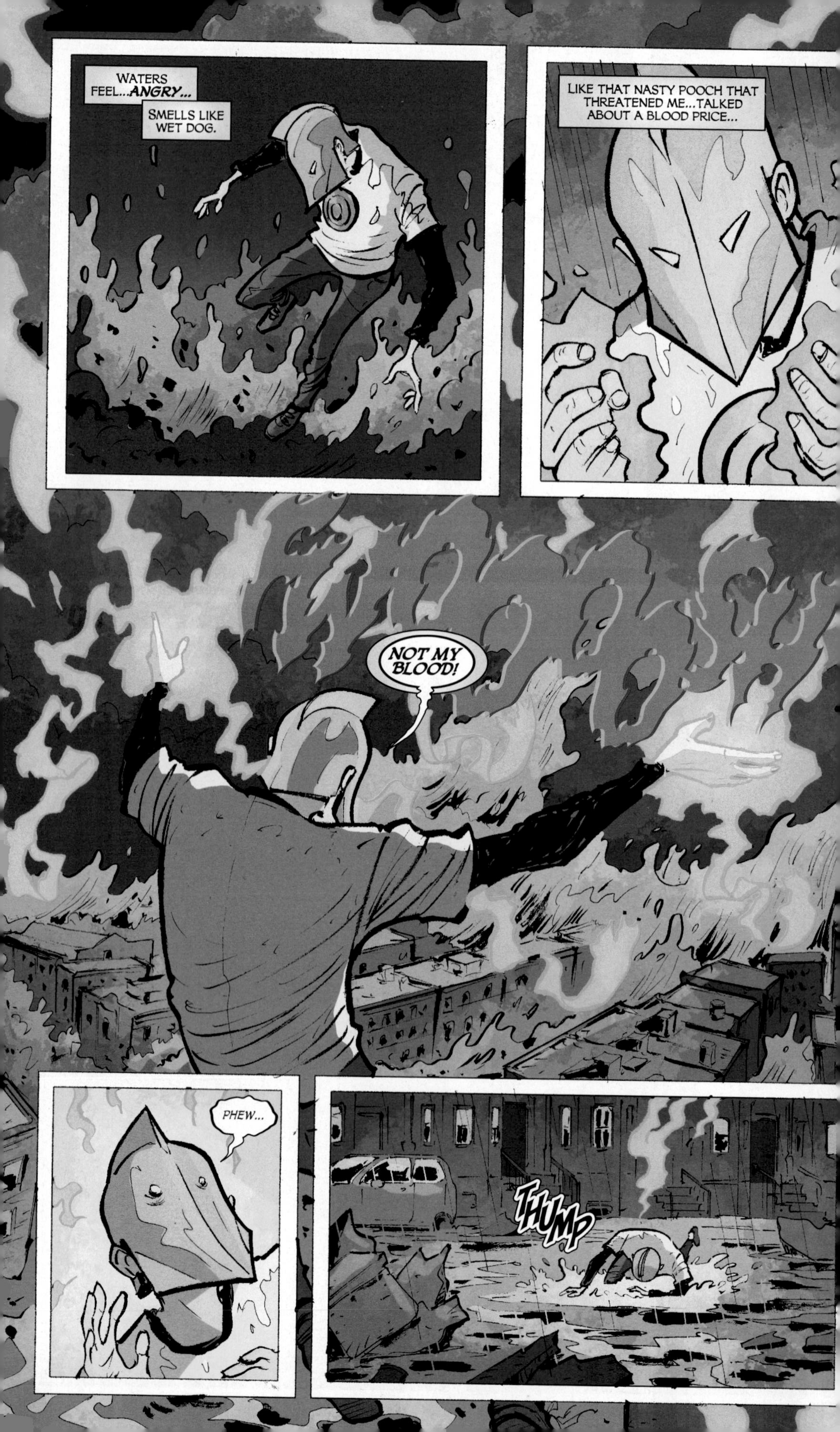
WATERS FEEL...ANGRY...
SMELLS LIKE WET DOG.
LIKE THAT NASTY POOCH THAT THREATENED ME...TALKED ABOUT A BLOOD PRICE...
NOT MY BLOOD!
PHEW...
THUMP

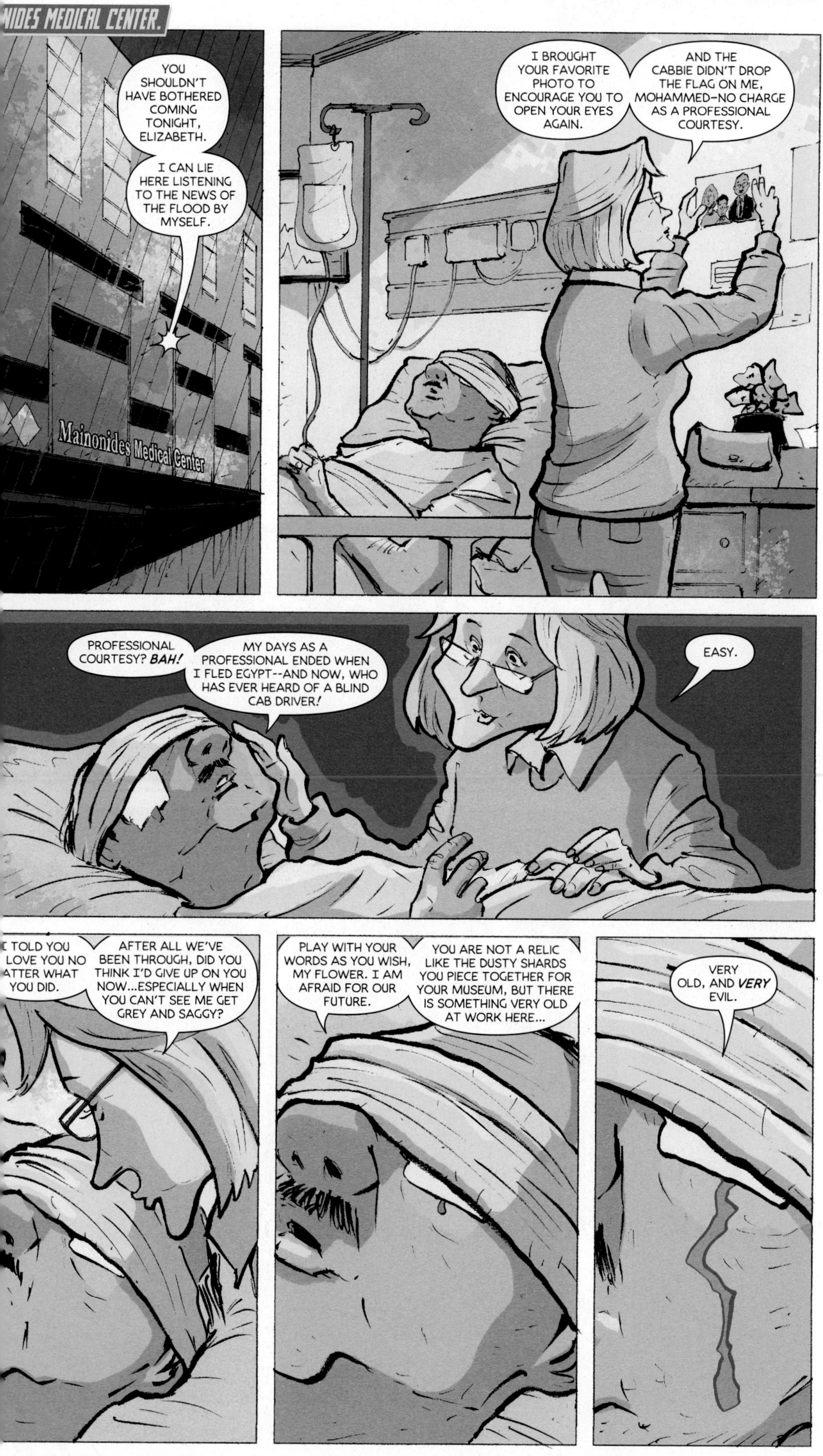

NIDES MEDICAL CENTER.
YOU SHOULDN'T HAVE BOTHERED COMING TONIGHT, ELIZABETH.
I CAN LIE HERE LISTENING TO THE NEWS OF THE FLOOD BY MYSELF.
Mainonides Medical Center
I BROUGHT YOUR FAVORITE PHOTO TO ENCOURAGE YOU TO OPEN YOUR EYES AGAIN.
AND THE CABBIE DIDN'T DROP THE FLAG ON ME, MOHAMMED--NO CHARGE AS A PROFESSIONAL COURTESY.
PROFESSIONAL COURTESY? *BAH!*
MY DAYS AS A PROFESSIONAL ENDED WHEN I FLED EGYPT--AND NOW, WHO HAS EVER HEARD OF A BLIND CAB DRIVER!
EASY.
I TOLD YOU I LOVE YOU NO MATTER WHAT YOU DID.
AFTER ALL WE'VE BEEN THROUGH, DID YOU THINK I'D GIVE UP ON YOU NOW...ESPECIALLY WHEN YOU CAN'T SEE ME GET GREY AND SAGGY?
PLAY WITH YOUR WORDS AS YOU WISH, MY FLOWER. I AM AFRAID FOR OUR FUTURE.
YOU ARE NOT A RELIC LIKE THE DUSTY SHARDS YOU PIECE TOGETHER FOR YOUR MUSEUM, BUT THERE IS SOMETHING VERY OLD AT WORK HERE...
VERY OLD, AND *VERY* EVIL.

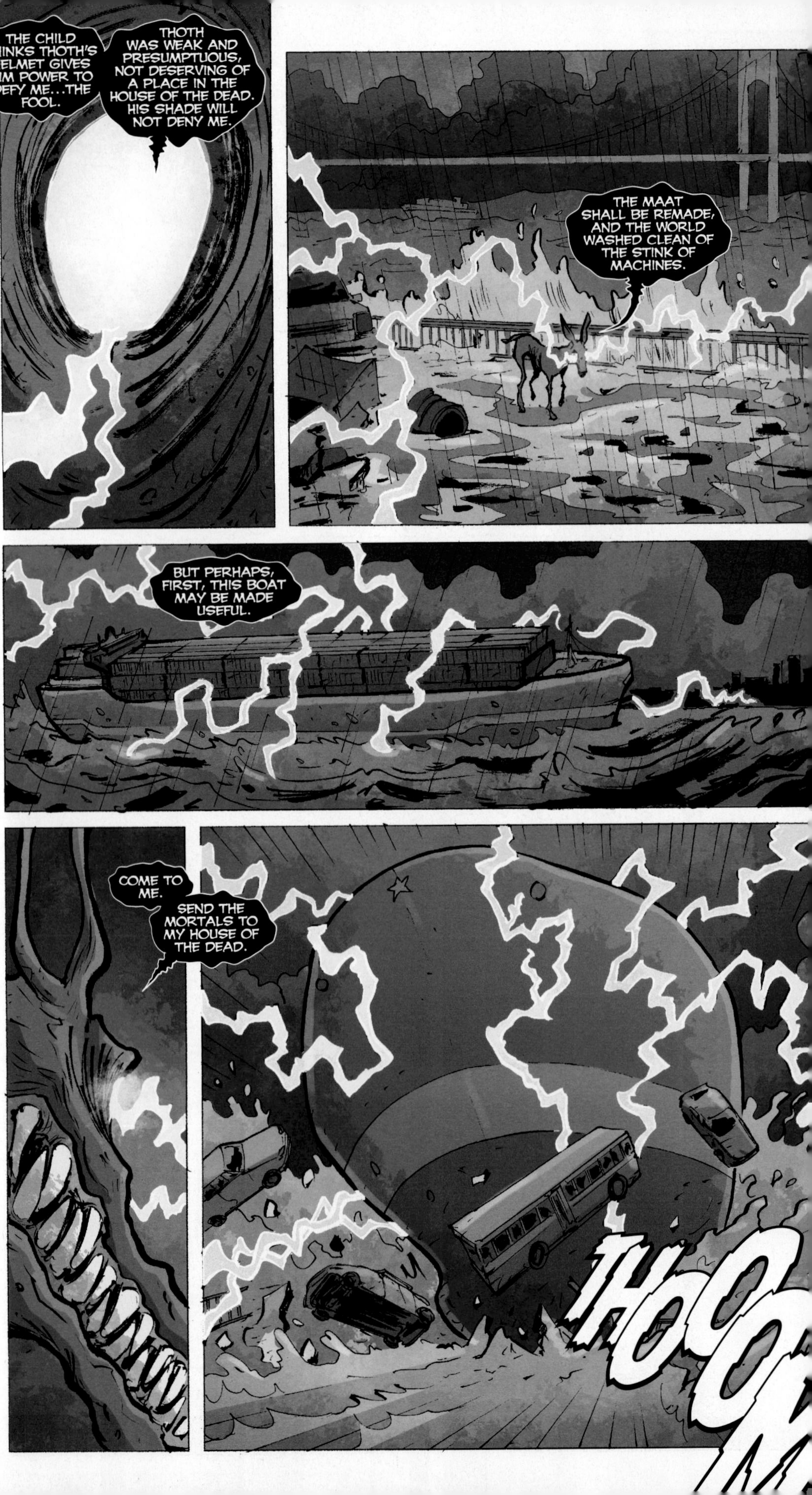

THE CHILD THINKS THOTH'S HELMET GIVES HIM POWER TO DEFY ME...THE FOOL.
THOTH WAS WEAK AND PRESUMPTUOUS, NOT DESERVING OF A PLACE IN THE HOUSE OF THE DEAD. HIS SHADE WILL NOT DENY ME.
THE MAAT SHALL BE REMADE, AND THE WORLD WASHED CLEAN OF THE STINK OF MACHINES.
BUT PERHAPS, FIRST, THIS BOAT MAY BE MADE USEFUL.
COME TO ME.
SEND THE MORTALS TO MY HOUSE OF THE DEAD.
THOO

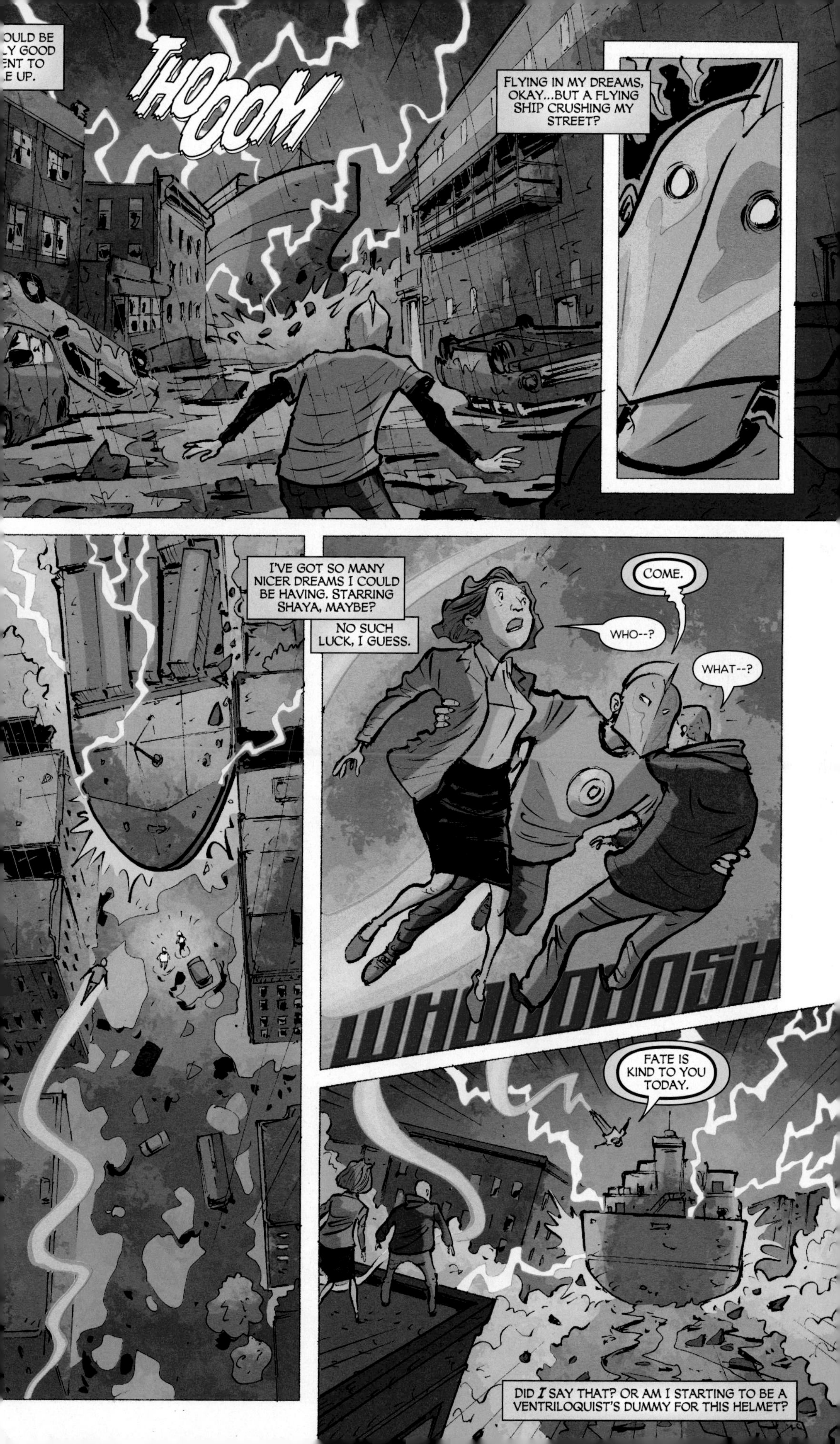
OULD BE
LY GOOD
ENT TO
E UP.
THOOOOM
FLYING IN MY DREAMS, OKAY...BUT A FLYING SHIP CRUSHING MY STREET?
I'VE GOT SO MANY NICER DREAMS I COULD BE HAVING. STARRING SHAYA, MAYBE?
NO SUCH LUCK, I GUESS.
COME.
WHO--?
WHAT--?
WHOOOOOSH
FATE IS KIND TO YOU TODAY.
DID I SAY THAT? OR AM I STARTING TO BE A VENTRILOQUIST'S DUMMY FOR THIS HELMET?

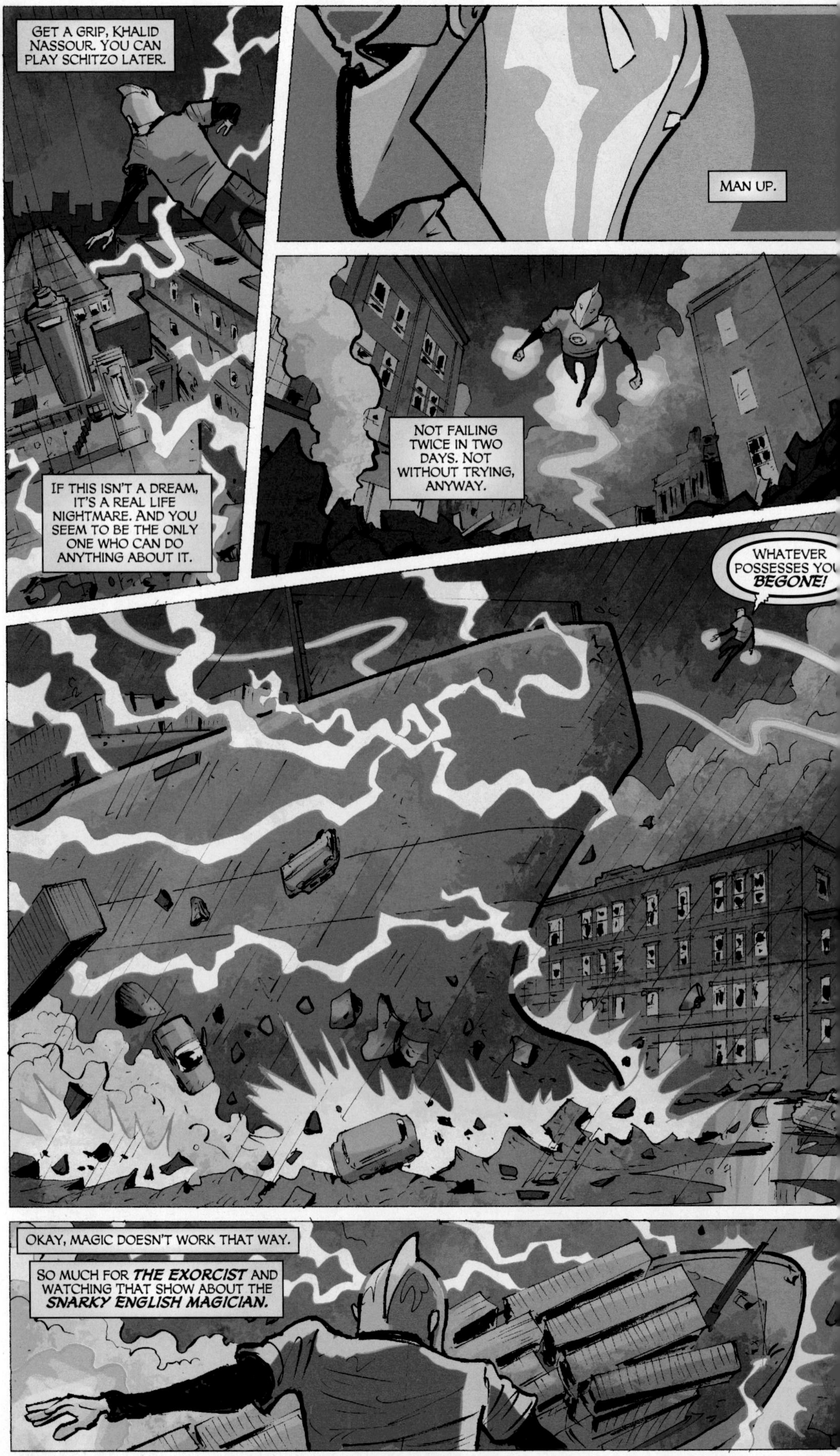
GET A GRIP, KHALID NASSOUR. YOU CAN PLAY SCHITZO LATER.
IF THIS ISN'T A DREAM, IT'S A REAL LIFE NIGHTMARE. AND YOU SEEM TO BE THE ONLY ONE WHO CAN DO ANYTHING ABOUT IT.
MAN UP.
NOT FAILING TWICE IN TWO DAYS. NOT WITHOUT TRYING, ANYWAY.
WHATEVER POSSESSES YO
BEGONE!
OKAY, MAGIC DOESN'T WORK THAT WAY.
SO MUCH FOR THE EXORCIST AND WATCHING THAT SHOW ABOUT THE SNARKY ENGLISH MAGICIAN.

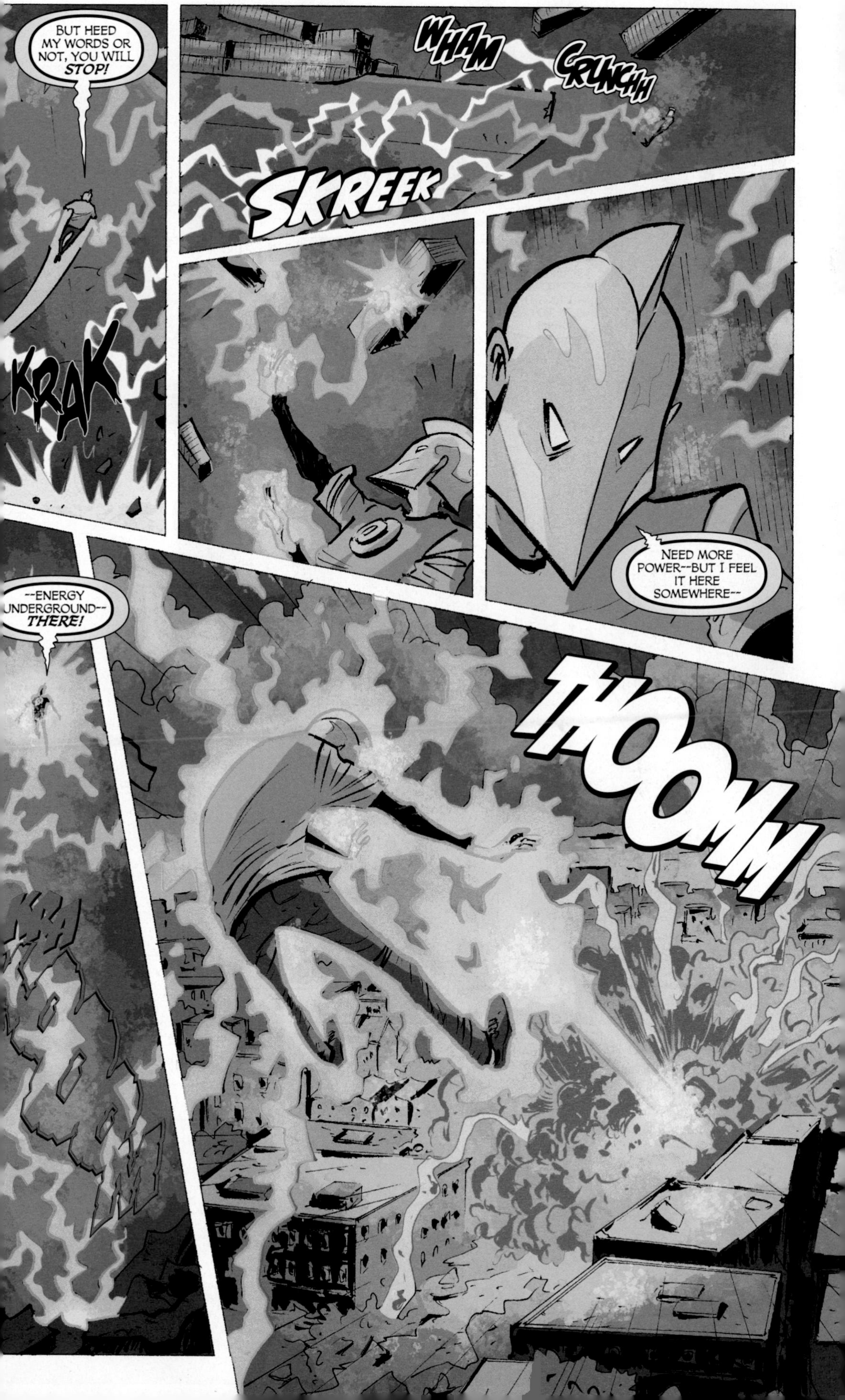
BUT HEED MY WORDS OR NOT, YOU WILL STOP!
WHAM
CRUNCHH
SKREEK
KRAK
NEED MORE POWER--BUT I FEEL IT HERE SOMEWHERE--
--ENERGY UNDERGROUND--THERE!
THOOMM

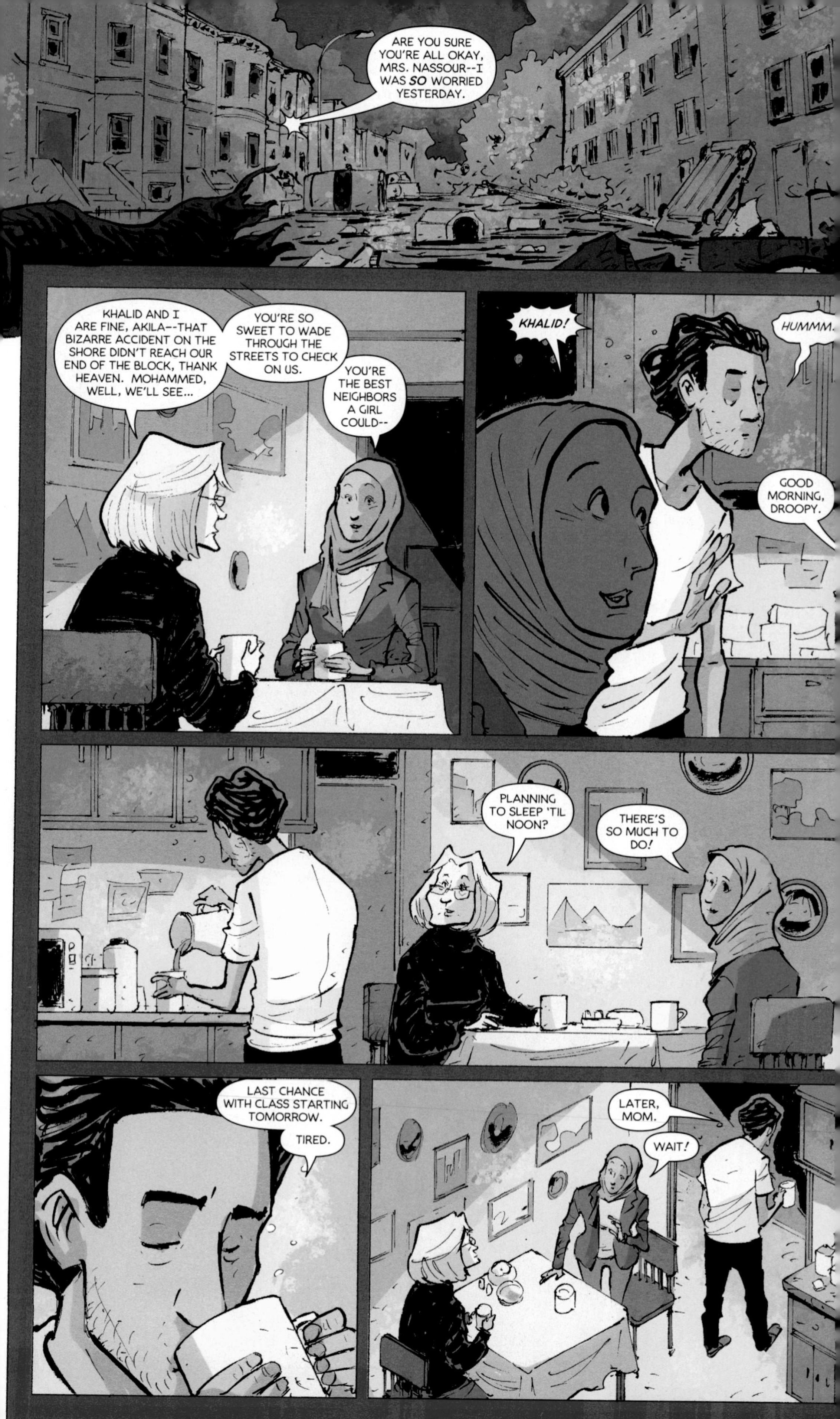
ARE YOU SURE YOU'RE ALL OKAY, MRS. NASSOUR--I WAS **SO** WORRIED YESTERDAY.
KHALID AND I ARE FINE, AKILA--THAT BIZARRE ACCIDENT ON THE SHORE DIDN'T REACH OUR END OF THE BLOCK, THANK HEAVEN. MOHAMMED, WELL, WE'LL SEE...
YOU'RE SO SWEET TO WADE THROUGH THE STREETS TO CHECK ON US.
YOU'RE THE BEST NEIGHBORS A GIRL COULD--
KHALID!
HUMMM.
GOOD MORNING, DROOPY.
PLANNING TO SLEEP 'TIL NOON?
THERE'S SO MUCH TO DO*!*
LAST CHANCE WITH CLASS STARTING TOMORROW.
TIRED.
LATER, MOM.
WAIT*!*

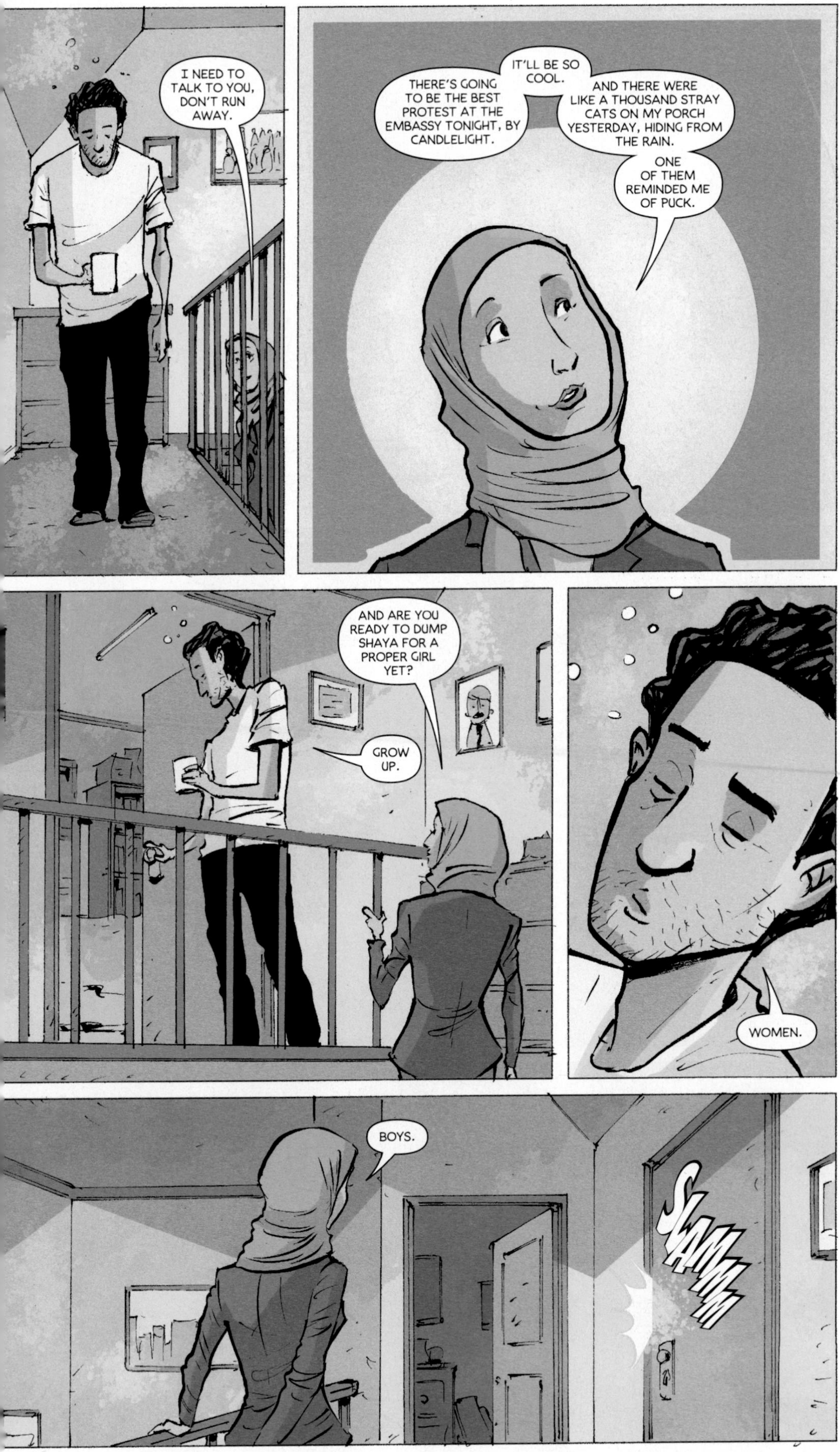
I NEED TO TALK TO YOU, DON'T RUN AWAY.
THERE'S GOING TO BE THE BEST PROTEST AT THE EMBASSY TONIGHT, BY CANDLELIGHT.
IT'LL BE SO COOL.
AND THERE WERE LIKE A THOUSAND STRAY CATS ON MY PORCH YESTERDAY, HIDING FROM THE RAIN.
ONE OF THEM REMINDED ME OF PUCK.
AND ARE YOU READY TO DUMP SHAYA FOR A PROPER GIRL YET?
GROW UP.
WOMEN.
BOYS.
SLAMMM

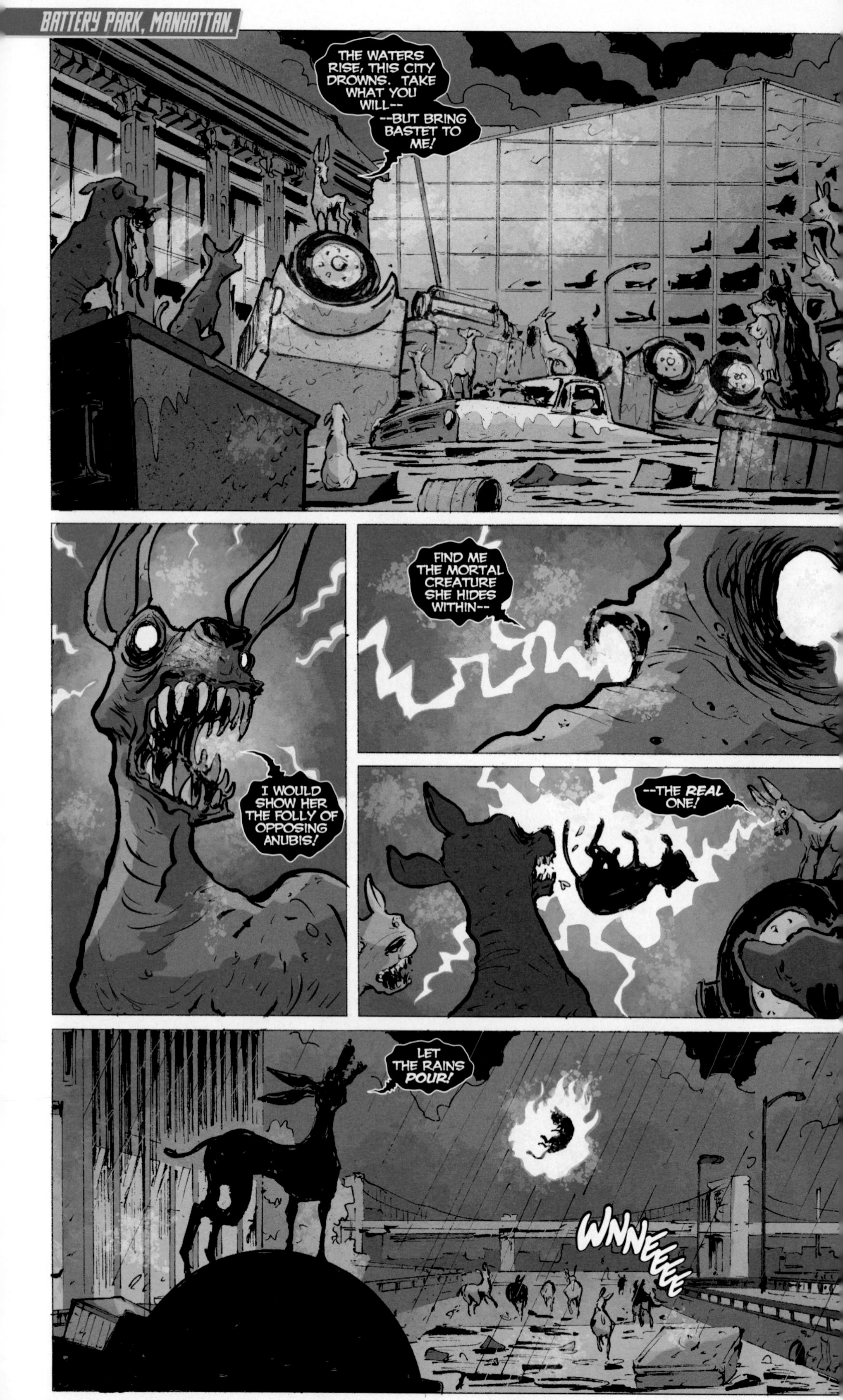
BATTERY PARK, MANHATTAN.
THE WATERS RISE, THIS CITY DROWNS. TAKE WHAT YOU WILL--
--BUT BRING BASTET TO ME!
I WOULD SHOW HER THE FOLLY OF OPPOSING ANUBIS!
FIND ME THE MORTAL CREATURE SHE HIDES WITHIN--
--THE REAL ONE!
LET THE RAINS POUR!
WNNEEEEE

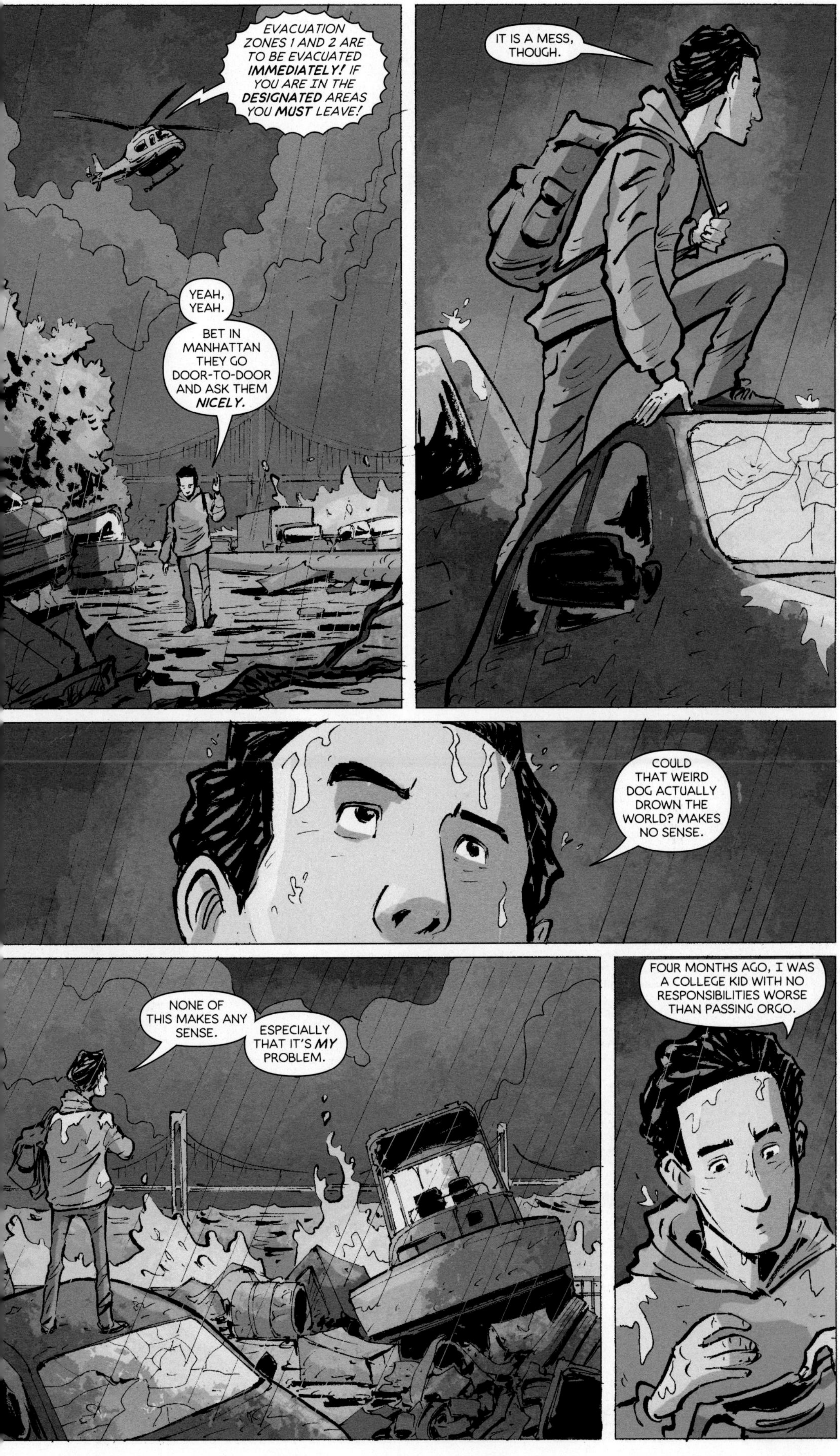
EVACUATION ZONES 1 AND 2 ARE TO BE EVACUATED IMMEDIATELY! IF YOU ARE IN THE DESIGNATED AREAS YOU MUST LEAVE!
YEAH, YEAH.
BET IN MANHATTAN THEY GO DOOR-TO-DOOR AND ASK THEM NICELY.
IT IS A MESS, THOUGH.
COULD THAT WEIRD DOG ACTUALLY DROWN THE WORLD? MAKES NO SENSE.
NONE OF THIS MAKES ANY SENSE.
ESPECIALLY THAT IT'S MY PROBLEM.
FOUR MONTHS AGO, I WAS A COLLEGE KID WITH NO RESPONSIBILITIES WORSE THAN PASSING ORGO.

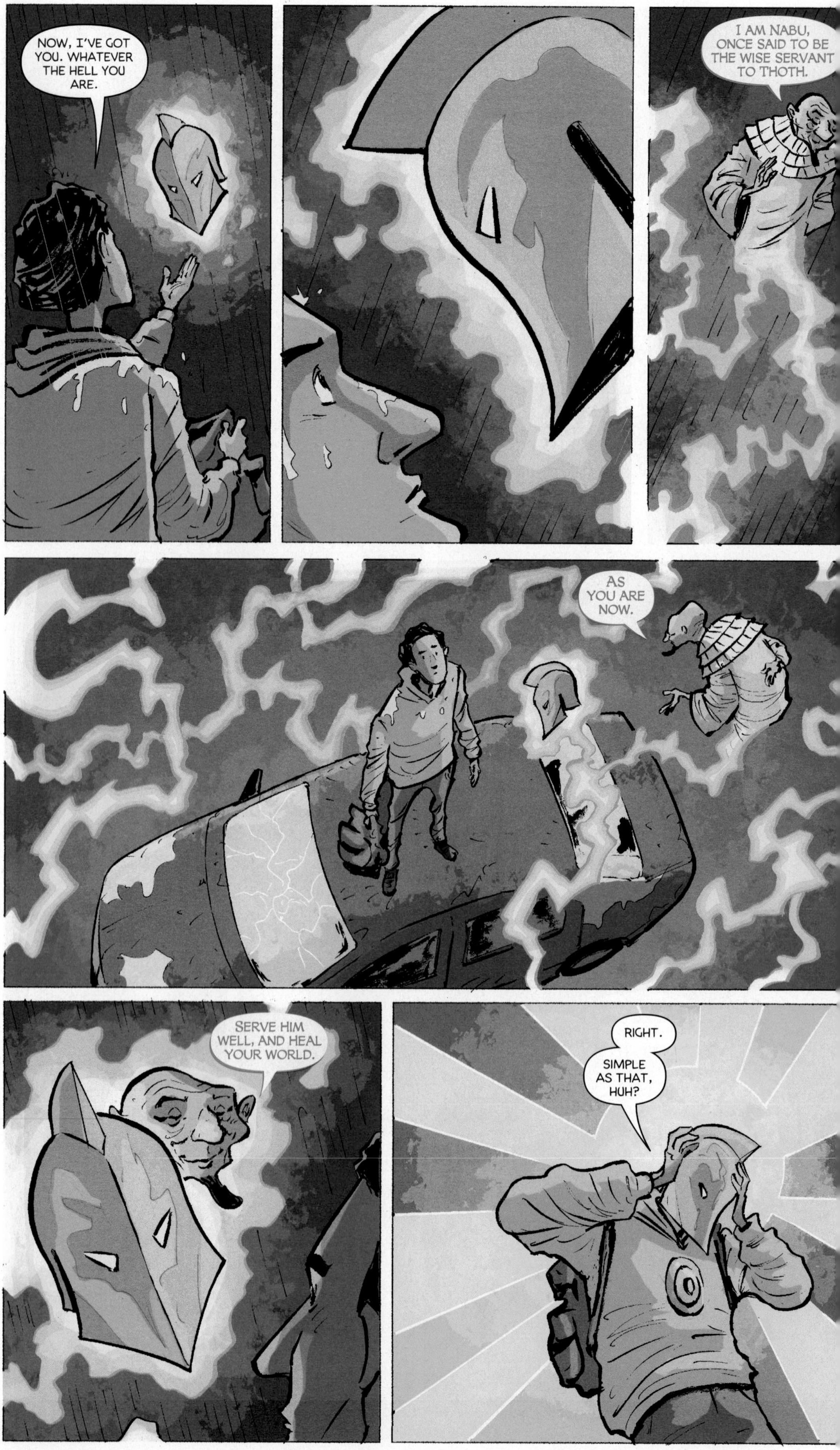
NOW, I'VE GOT YOU. WHATEVER THE HELL YOU ARE.
I AM NABU, ONCE SAID TO BE THE WISE SERVANT TO THOTH.
AS YOU ARE NOW.
SERVE HIM WELL, AND HEAL YOUR WORLD.
RIGHT.
SIMPLE AS THAT, HUH?

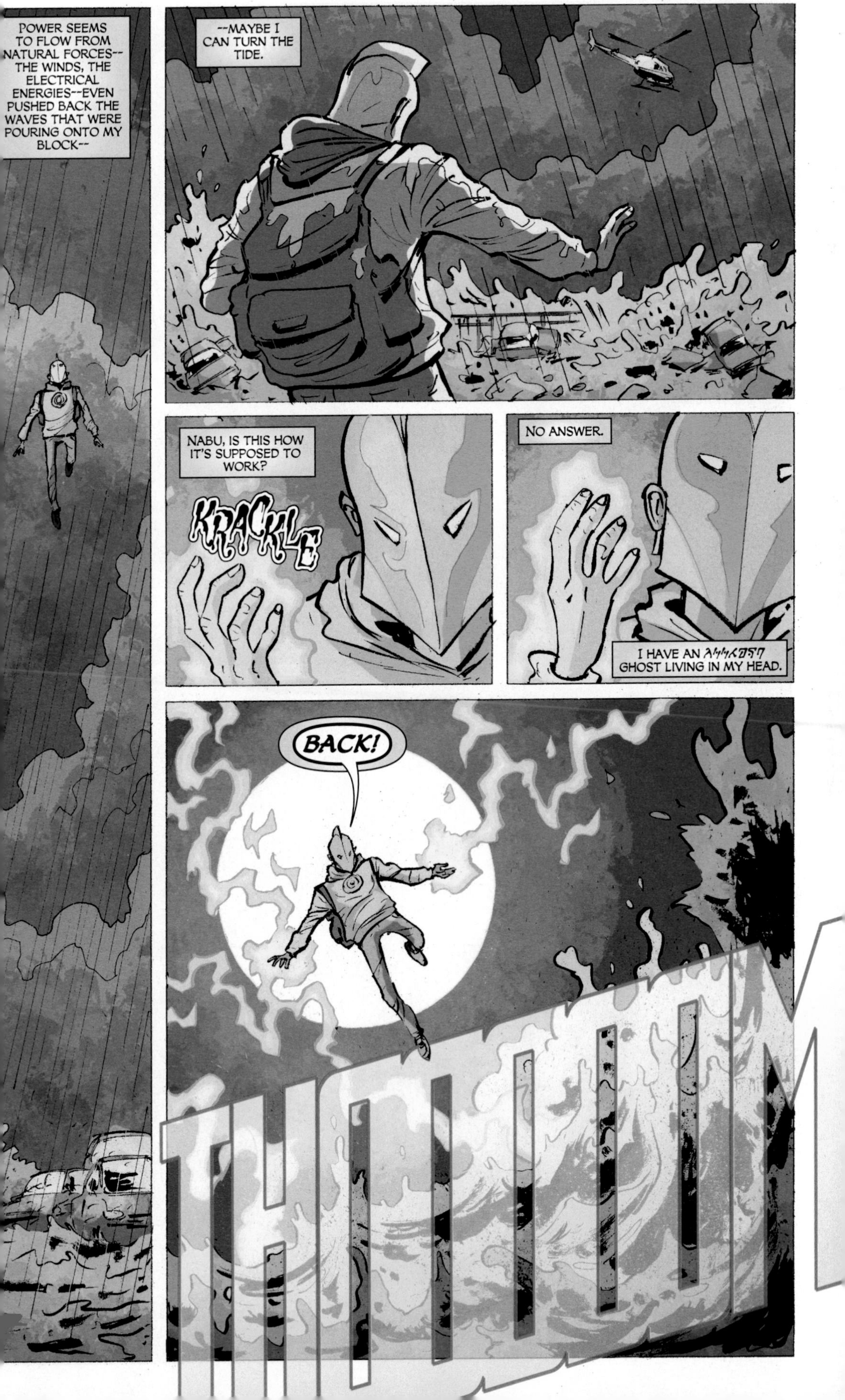
POWER SEEMS TO FLOW FROM NATURAL FORCES-- THE WINDS, THE ELECTRICAL ENERGIES--EVEN PUSHED BACK THE WAVES THAT WERE POURING ONTO MY BLOCK--
--MAYBE I CAN TURN THE TIDE.
NABU, IS THIS HOW IT'S SUPPOSED TO WORK?
KRACKLE
NO ANSWER.
I HAVE AN GHOST LIVING IN MY HEAD.
BACK!

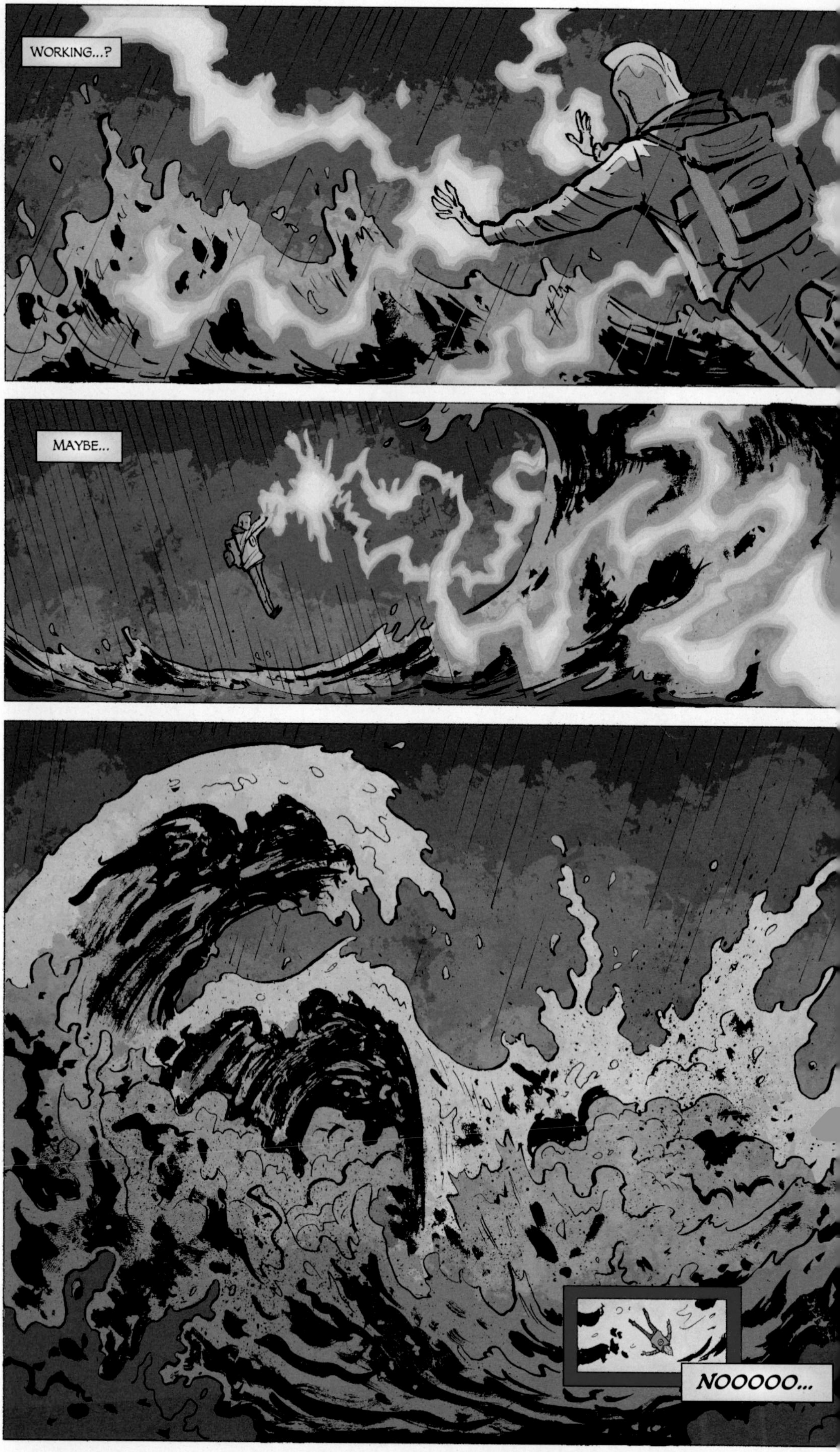
WORKING...?
MAYBE...
NOOOOO...

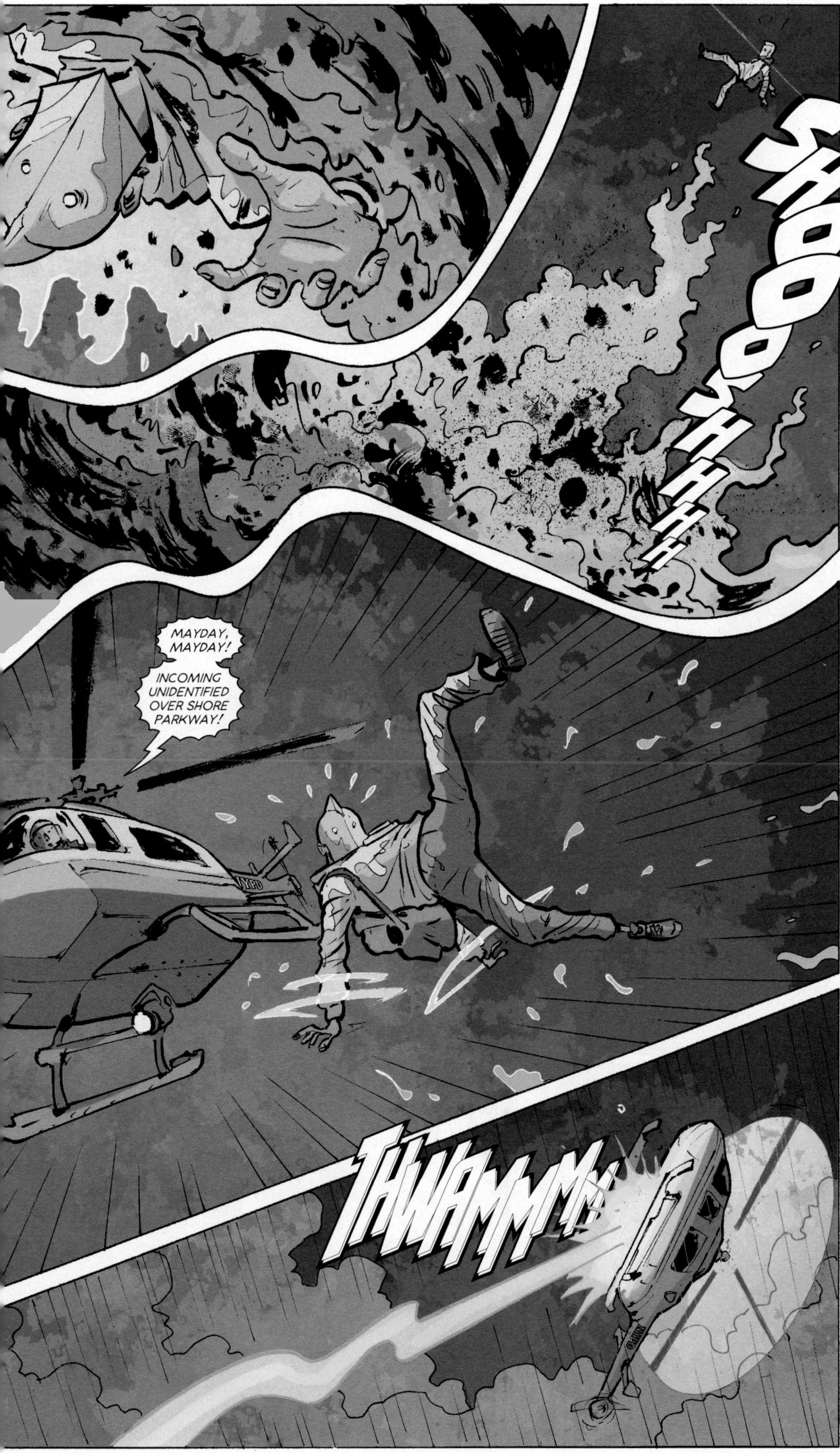
SHOOOSHHHHH
MAYDAY, MAYDAY!
INCOMING UNIDENTIFIED OVER SHORE PARKWAY!
THWAMMM

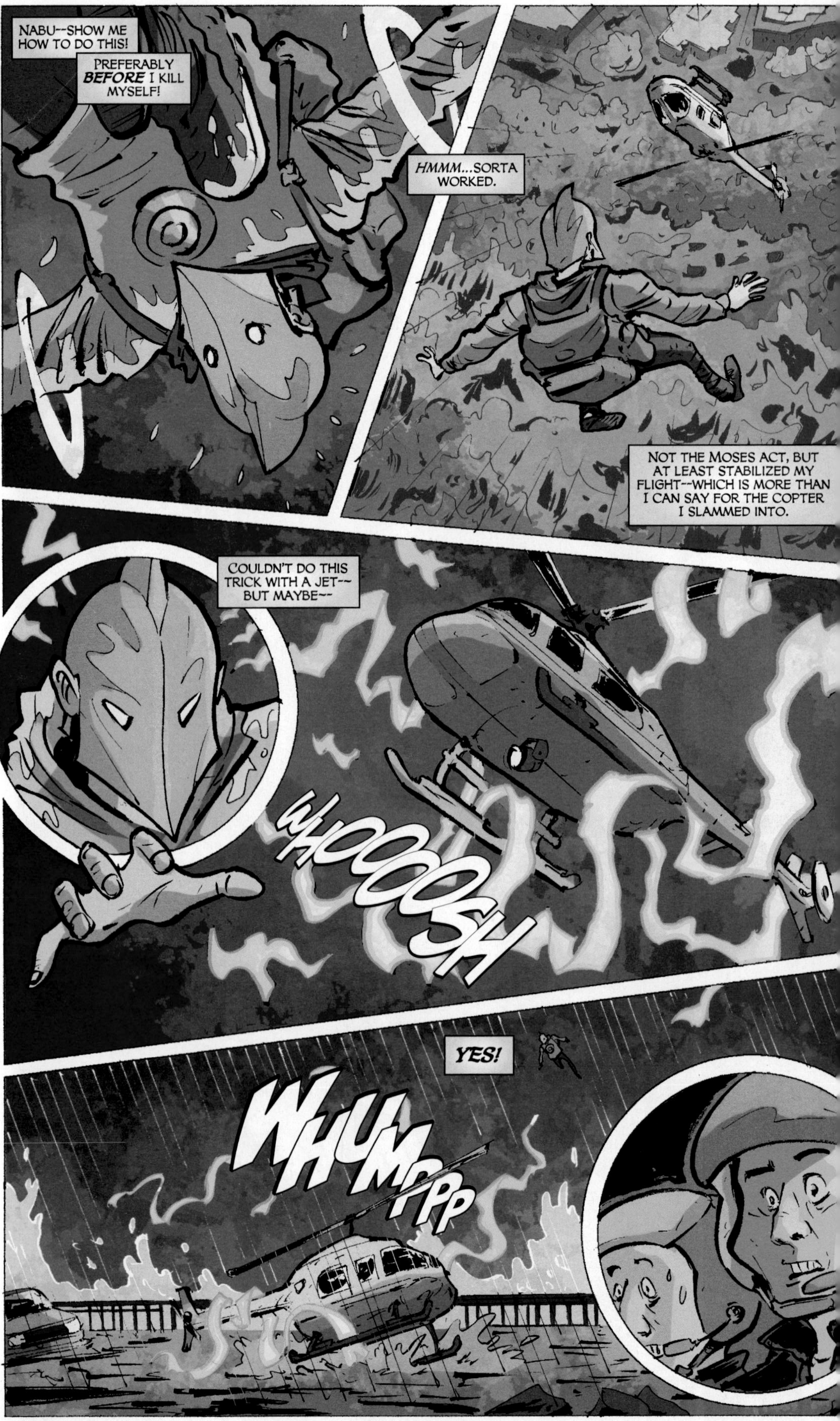

NABU--SHOW ME HOW TO DO THIS!
PREFERABLY *BEFORE* I KILL MYSELF!
HMMM...SORTA WORKED.
NOT THE MOSES ACT, BUT AT LEAST STABILIZED MY FLIGHT--WHICH IS MORE THAN I CAN SAY FOR THE COPTER I SLAMMED INTO.
COULDN'T DO THIS TRICK WITH A JET-- BUT MAYBE--
WHOOOOSH
YES!
WHUMPPP

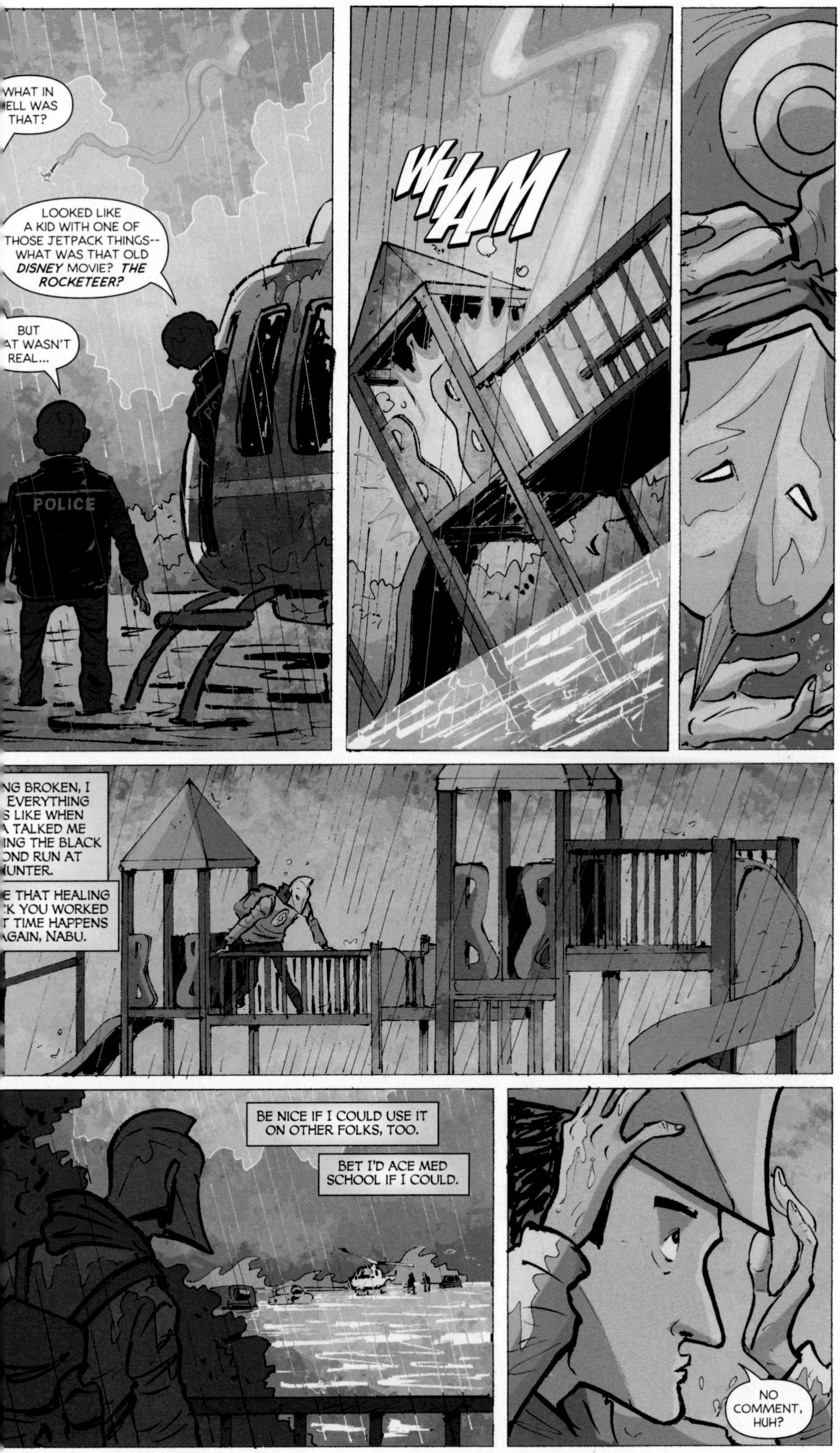
WHAT IN
ELL WAS
THAT?
LOOKED LIKE A KID WITH ONE OF THOSE JETPACK THINGS-- WHAT WAS THAT OLD *DISNEY* MOVIE? *THE ROCKETEER?*
BUT
AT WASN'T
REAL...
POLICE
WHAM
NG BROKEN, I EVERYTHING S LIKE WHEN A TALKED ME ING THE BLACK OND RUN AT HUNTER.
E THAT HEALING K YOU WORKED T TIME HAPPENS AGAIN, NABU.
BE NICE IF I COULD USE IT ON OTHER FOLKS, TOO.
BET I'D ACE MED SCHOOL IF I COULD.
NO COMMENT, HUH?

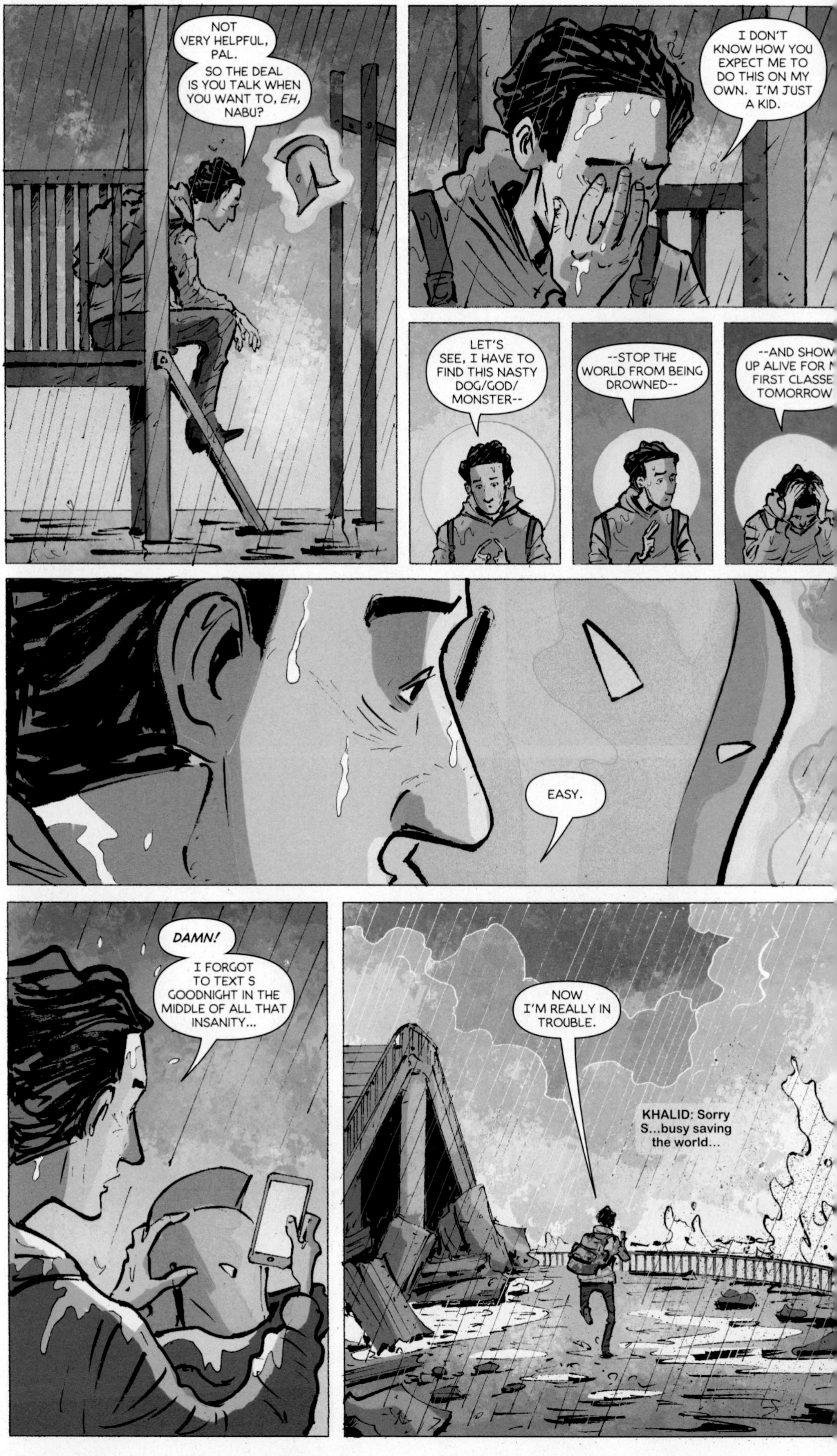
NOT VERY HELPFUL, PAL.
SO THE DEAL IS YOU TALK WHEN YOU WANT TO, *EH,* NABU?
I DON'T KNOW HOW YOU EXPECT ME TO DO THIS ON MY OWN. I'M JUST A KID.
LET'S SEE, I HAVE TO FIND THIS NASTY DOG/GOD/ MONSTER--
--STOP THE WORLD FROM BEING DROWNED--
--AND SHOW UP ALIVE FOR FIRST CLASSE TOMORROW
EASY.
DAMN!
I FORGOT TO TEXT S GOODNIGHT IN THE MIDDLE OF ALL THAT INSANITY...
NOW I'M REALLY IN TROUBLE.
KHALID: Sorry S...busy saving the world...

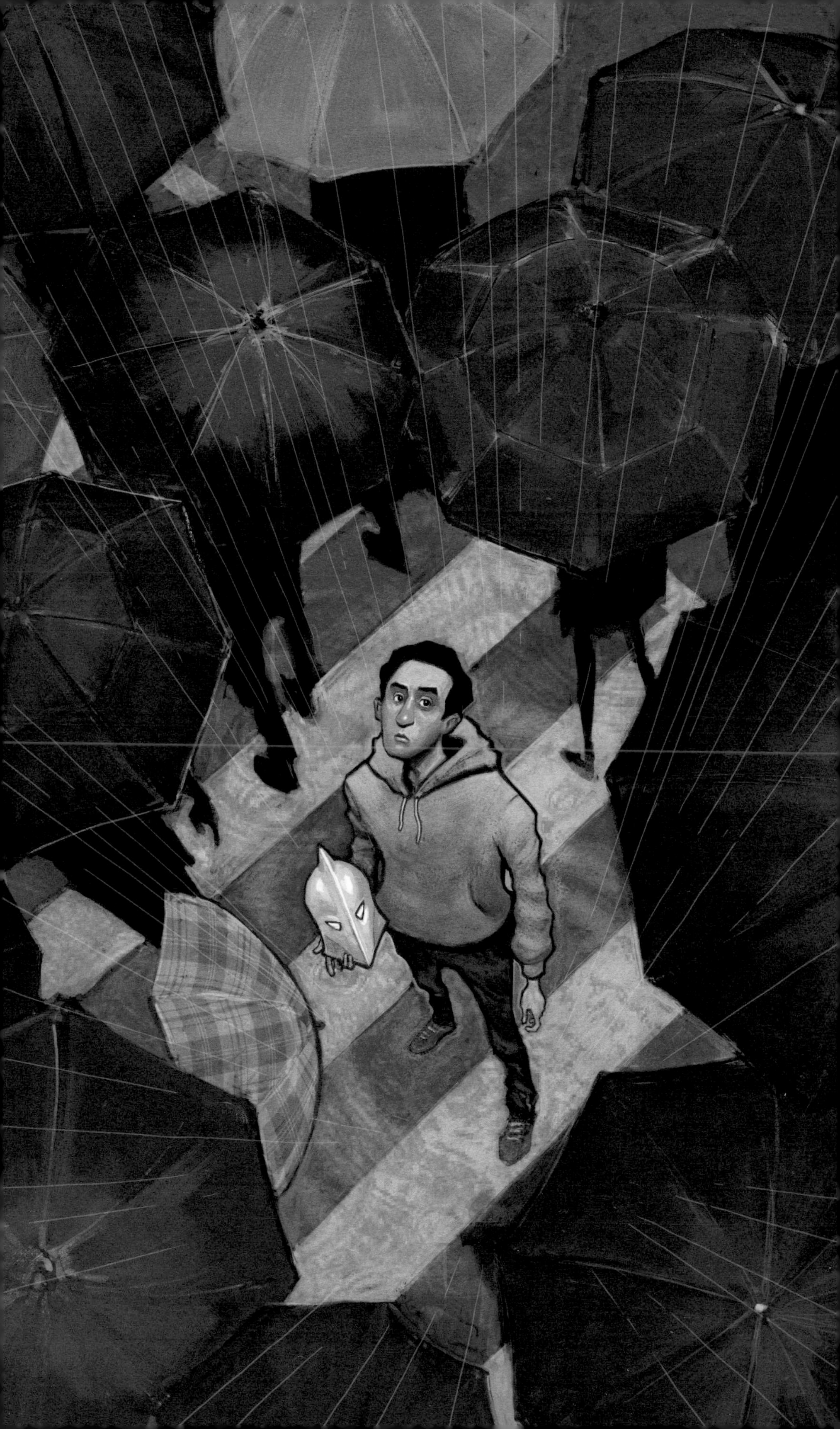

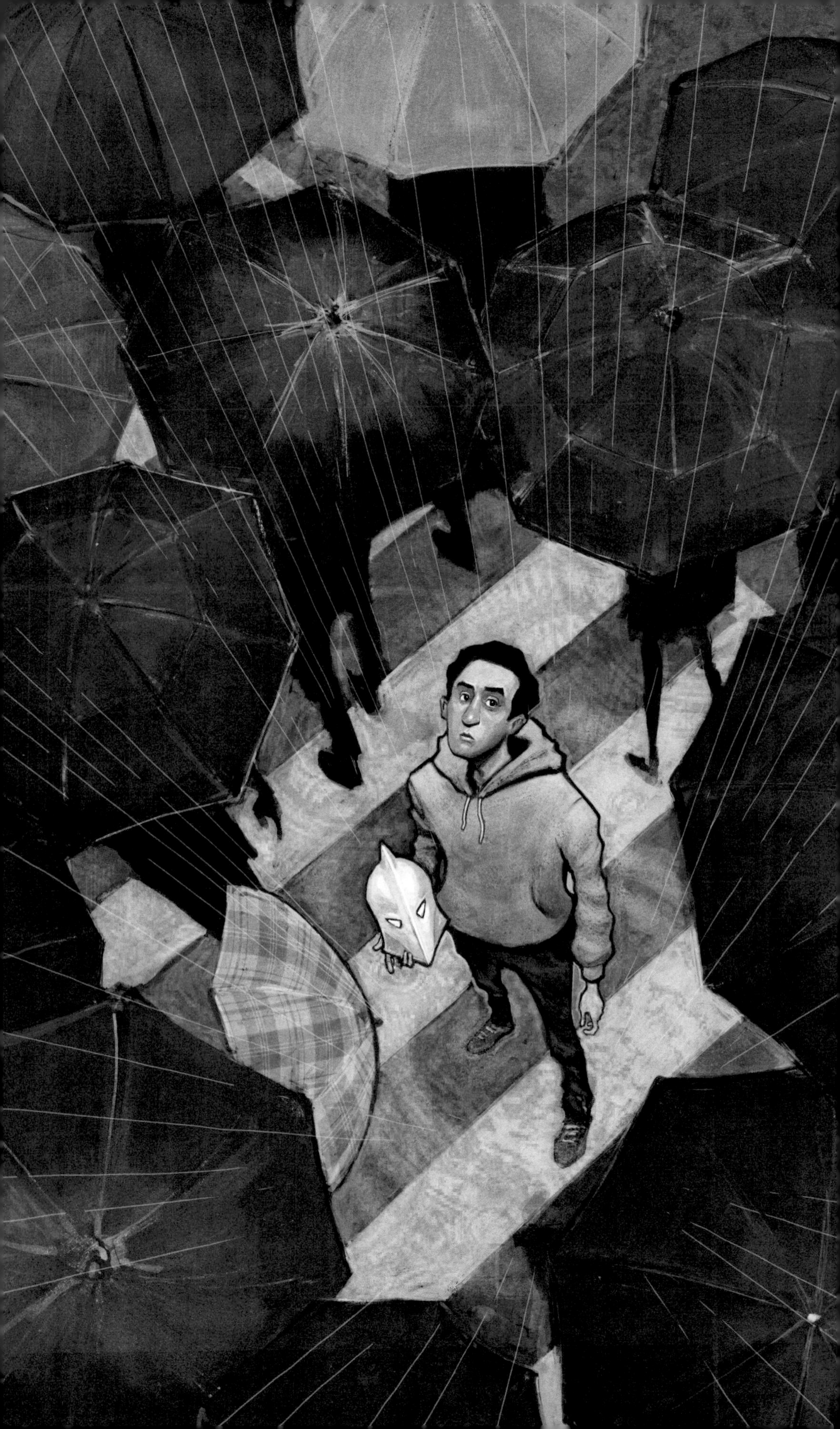

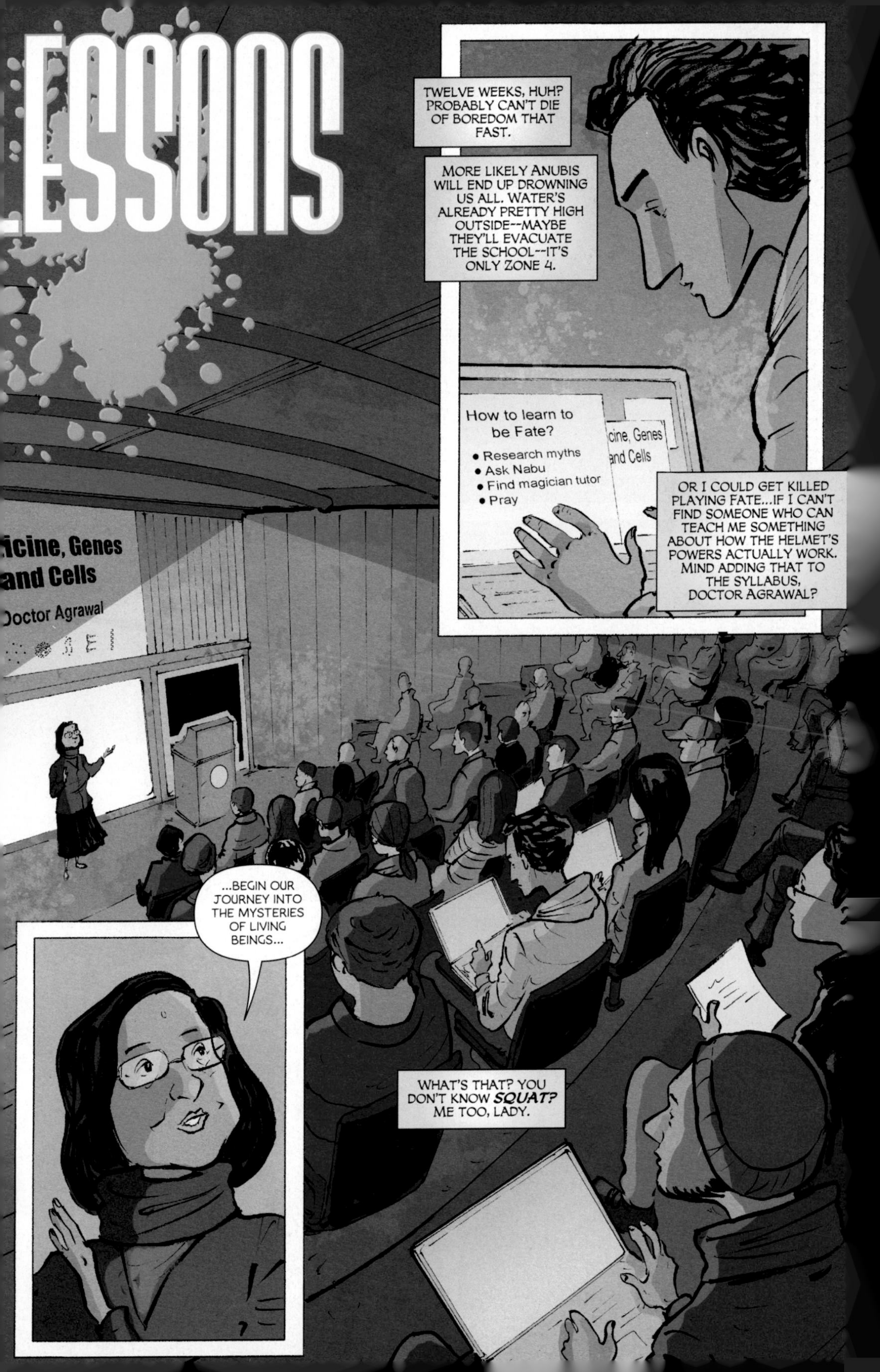
LESSONS
TWELVE WEEKS, HUH? PROBABLY CAN'T DIE OF BOREDOM THAT FAST.
MORE LIKELY ANUBIS WILL END UP DROWNING US ALL. WATER'S ALREADY PRETTY HIGH OUTSIDE--MAYBE THEY'LL EVACUATE THE SCHOOL--IT'S ONLY ZONE 4.
How to learn to be Fate?
• Research myths
• Ask Nabu
• Find magician tutor
• Pray
icine, Genes and Cells
OR I COULD GET KILLED PLAYING FATE...IF I CAN'T FIND SOMEONE WHO CAN TEACH ME SOMETHING ABOUT HOW THE HELMET'S POWERS ACTUALLY WORK. MIND ADDING THAT TO THE SYLLABUS, DOCTOR AGRAWAL?
icine, Genes
and Cells
Doctor Agrawal
...BEGIN OUR JOURNEY INTO THE MYSTERIES OF LIVING BEINGS...
WHAT'S THAT? YOU DON'T KNOW SQUAT? ME TOO, LADY.

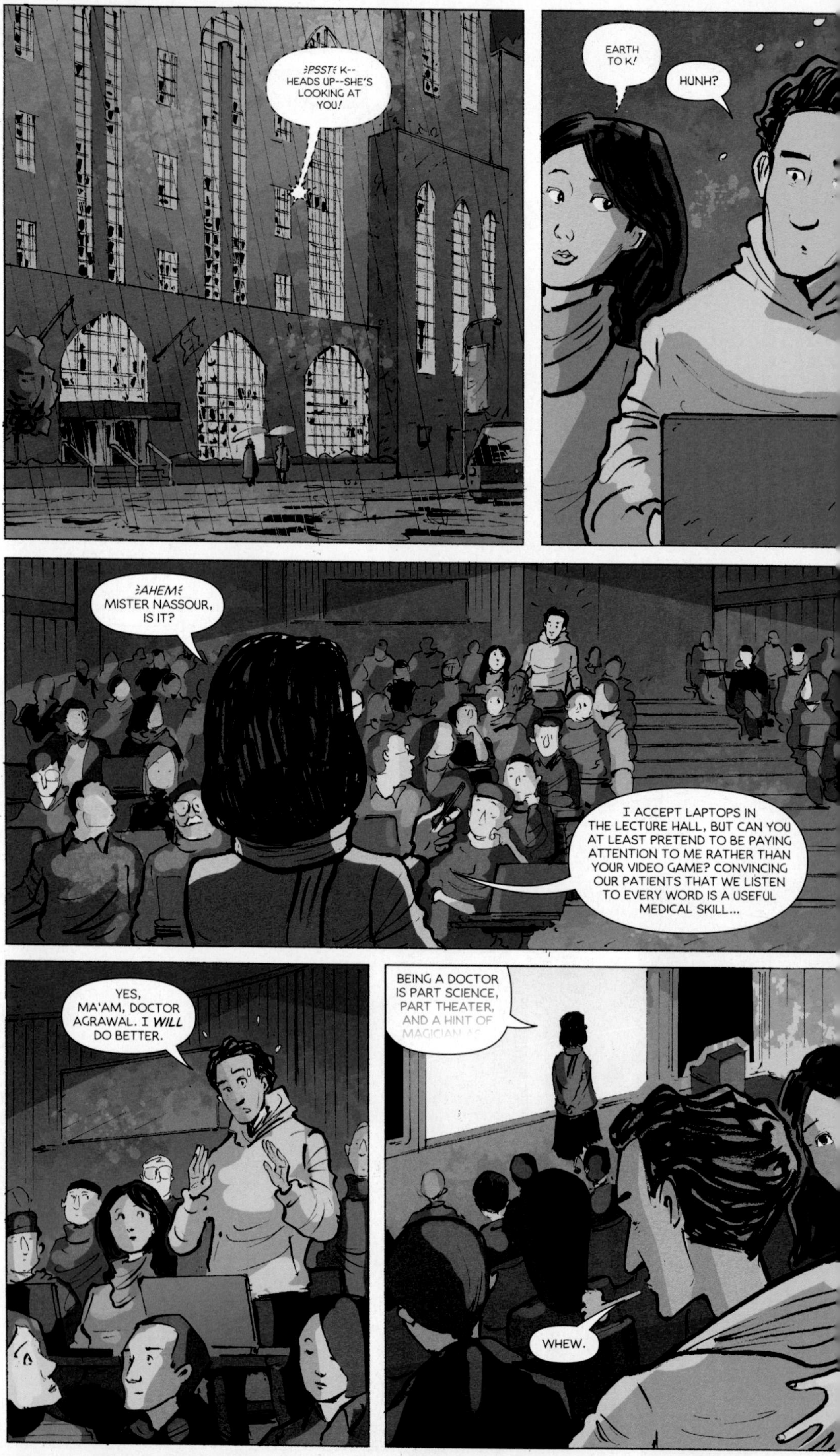
PSST K-- HEADS UP--SHE'S LOOKING AT YOU!
EARTH TO K!
HUNH?
AHEM MISTER NASSOUR, IS IT?
I ACCEPT LAPTOPS IN THE LECTURE HALL, BUT CAN YOU AT LEAST PRETEND TO BE PAYING ATTENTION TO ME RATHER THAN YOUR VIDEO GAME? CONVINCING OUR PATIENTS THAT WE LISTEN TO EVERY WORD IS A USEFUL MEDICAL SKILL...
YES, MA'AM, DOCTOR AGRAWAL. I WILL DO BETTER.
BEING A DOCTOR IS PART SCIENCE, PART THEATER, AND A HINT OF
WHEW.

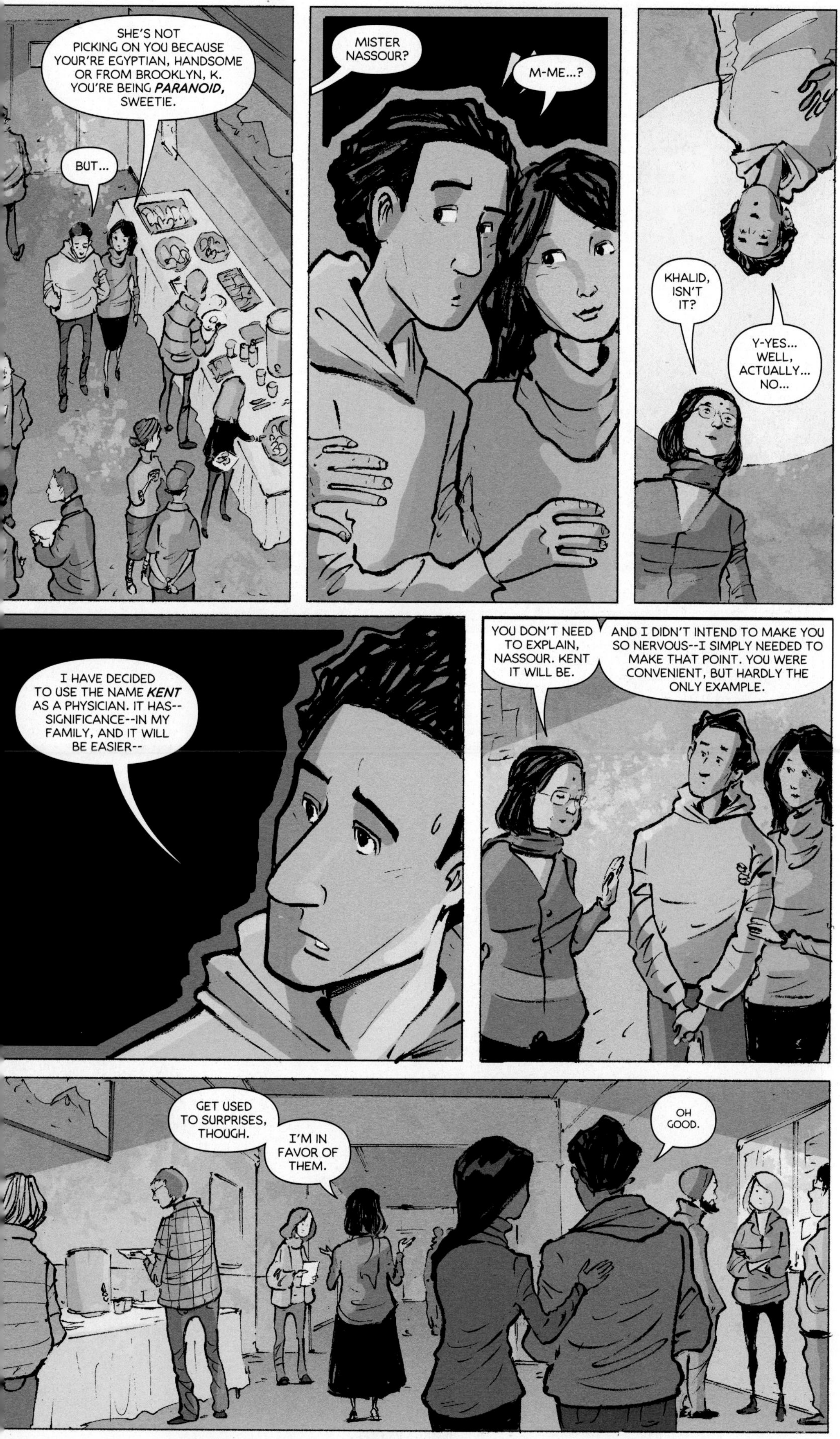
SHE'S NOT PICKING ON YOU BECAUSE YOUR'RE EGYPTIAN, HANDSOME OR FROM BROOKLYN, K. YOU'RE BEING *PARANOID,* SWEETIE.
BUT...
MISTER NASSOUR?
M-ME...?
KHALID, ISN'T IT?
Y-YES... WELL, ACTUALLY... NO...
I HAVE DECIDED TO USE THE NAME *KENT* AS A PHYSICIAN. IT HAS--SIGNIFICANCE--IN MY FAMILY, AND IT WILL BE EASIER--
YOU DON'T NEED TO EXPLAIN, NASSOUR. KENT IT WILL BE.
AND I DIDN'T INTEND TO MAKE YOU SO NERVOUS--I SIMPLY NEEDED TO MAKE THAT POINT. YOU WERE CONVENIENT, BUT HARDLY THE ONLY EXAMPLE.
GET USED TO SURPRISES, THOUGH.
I'M IN FAVOR OF THEM.
OH GOOD.

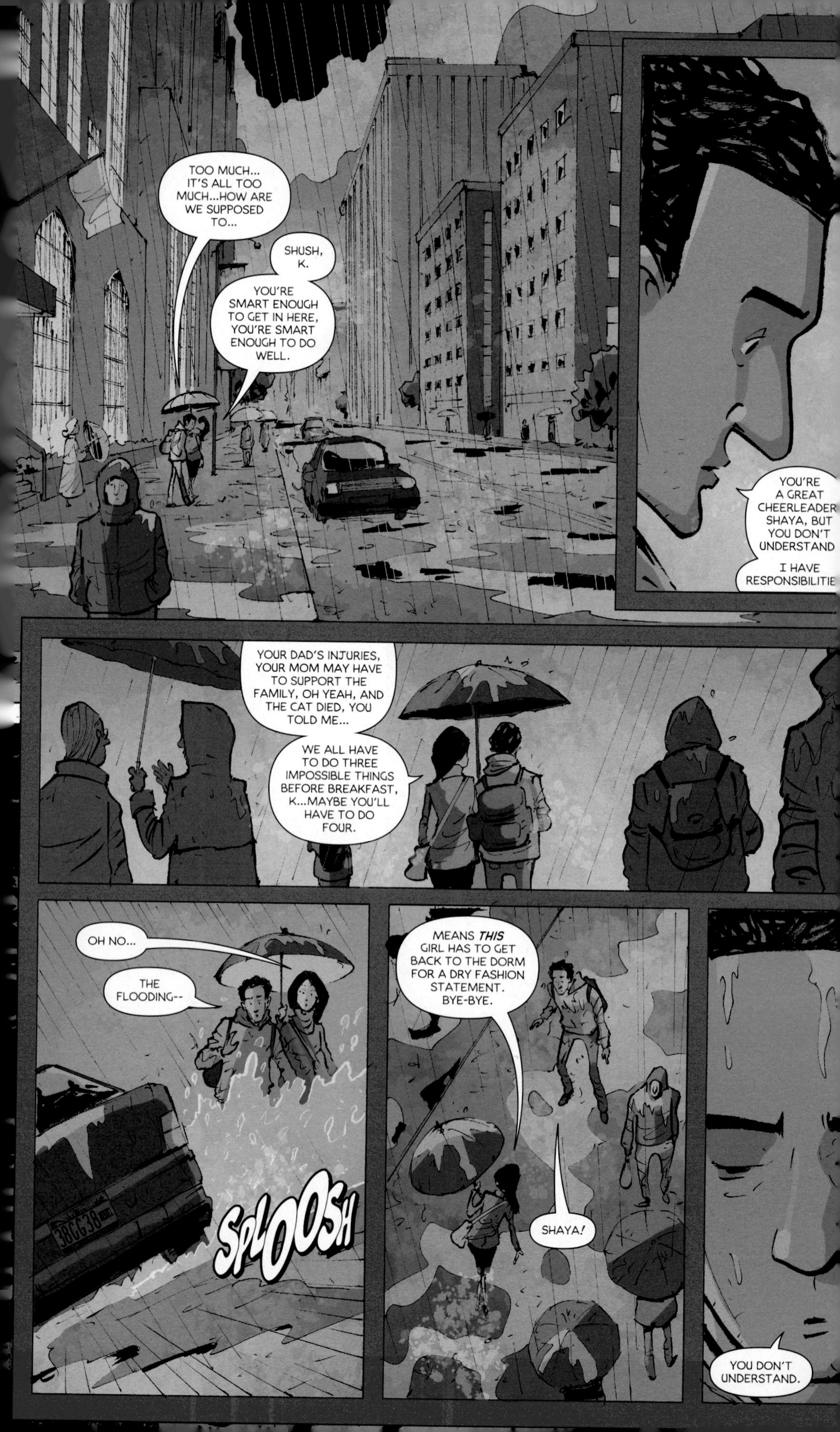
TOO MUCH... IT'S ALL TOO MUCH...HOW ARE WE SUPPOSED TO...
SHUSH, K.
YOU'RE SMART ENOUGH TO GET IN HERE, YOU'RE SMART ENOUGH TO DO WELL.
YOU'RE A GREAT CHEERLEADER SHAYA, BUT YOU DON'T UNDERSTAND
I HAVE RESPONSIBILITIE
YOUR DAD'S INJURIES, YOUR MOM MAY HAVE TO SUPPORT THE FAMILY, OH YEAH, AND THE CAT DIED, YOU TOLD ME...
WE ALL HAVE TO DO THREE IMPOSSIBLE THINGS BEFORE BREAKFAST, K...MAYBE YOU'LL HAVE TO DO FOUR.
OH NO...
THE FLOODING--
SPLOOSH
MEANS *THIS* GIRL HAS TO GET BACK TO THE DORM FOR A DRY FASHION STATEMENT. BYE-BYE.
SHAYA!
YOU DON'T UNDERSTAND.

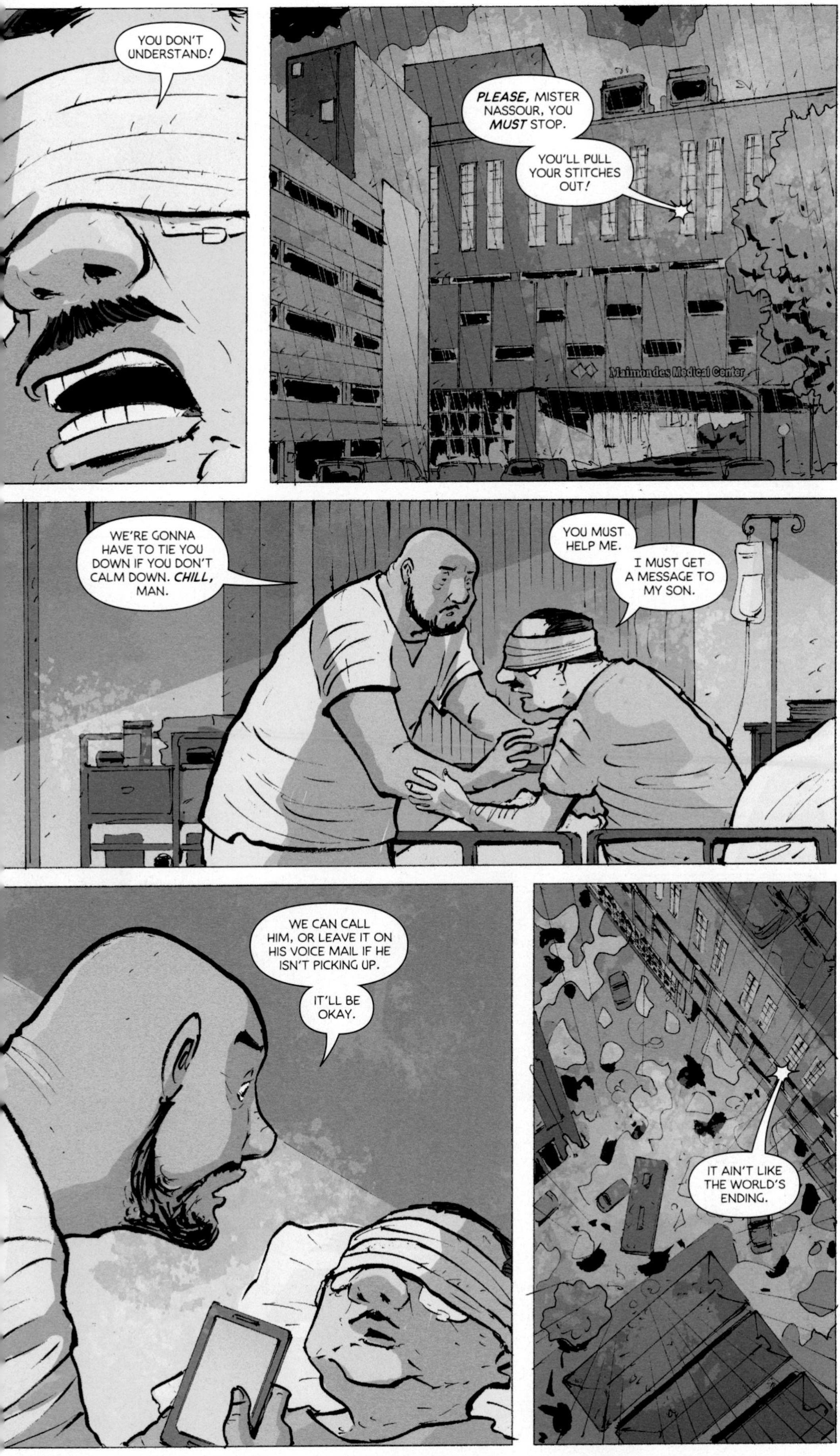
YOU DON'T UNDERSTAND!
PLEASE, MISTER NASSOUR, YOU MUST STOP.
YOU'LL PULL YOUR STITCHES OUT!
Maimondes Medical Center
WE'RE GONNA HAVE TO TIE YOU DOWN IF YOU DON'T CALM DOWN. CHILL, MAN.
YOU MUST HELP ME.
I MUST GET A MESSAGE TO MY SON.
WE CAN CALL HIM, OR LEAVE IT ON HIS VOICE MAIL IF HE ISN'T PICKING UP.
IT'LL BE OKAY.
IT AIN'T LIKE THE WORLD'S ENDING.

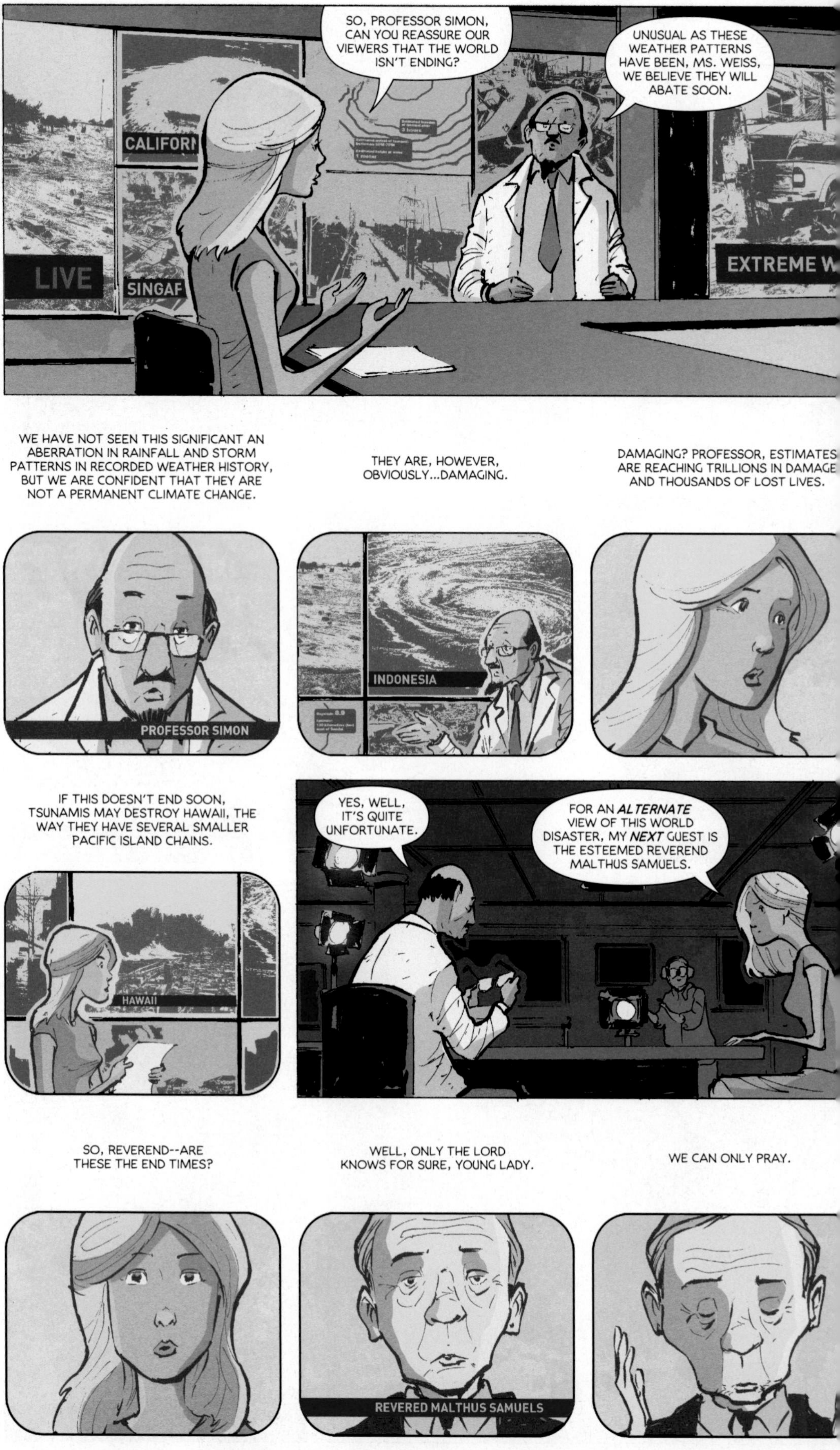
SO, PROFESSOR SIMON, CAN YOU REASSURE OUR VIEWERS THAT THE WORLD ISN'T ENDING?
UNUSUAL AS THESE WEATHER PATTERNS HAVE BEEN, MS. WEISS, WE BELIEVE THEY WILL ABATE SOON.
CALIFORN
LIVE
SINGAP
EXTREME W
WE HAVE NOT SEEN THIS SIGNIFICANT AN ABERRATION IN RAINFALL AND STORM PATTERNS IN RECORDED WEATHER HISTORY, BUT WE ARE CONFIDENT THAT THEY ARE NOT A PERMANENT CLIMATE CHANGE.
PROFESSOR SIMON
THEY ARE, HOWEVER, OBVIOUSLY...DAMAGING.
INDONESIA
DAMAGING? PROFESSOR, ESTIMATES ARE REACHING TRILLIONS IN DAMAGE AND THOUSANDS OF LOST LIVES.
IF THIS DOESN'T END SOON, TSUNAMIS MAY DESTROY HAWAII, THE WAY THEY HAVE SEVERAL SMALLER PACIFIC ISLAND CHAINS.
HAWAII
YES, WELL, IT'S QUITE UNFORTUNATE.
FOR AN *ALTERNATE* VIEW OF THIS WORLD DISASTER, MY *NEXT* GUEST IS THE ESTEEMED REVEREND MALTHUS SAMUELS.
SO, REVEREND--ARE THESE THE END TIMES?
WELL, ONLY THE LORD KNOWS FOR SURE, YOUNG LADY.
REVERED MALTHUS SAMUELS
WE CAN ONLY PRAY.

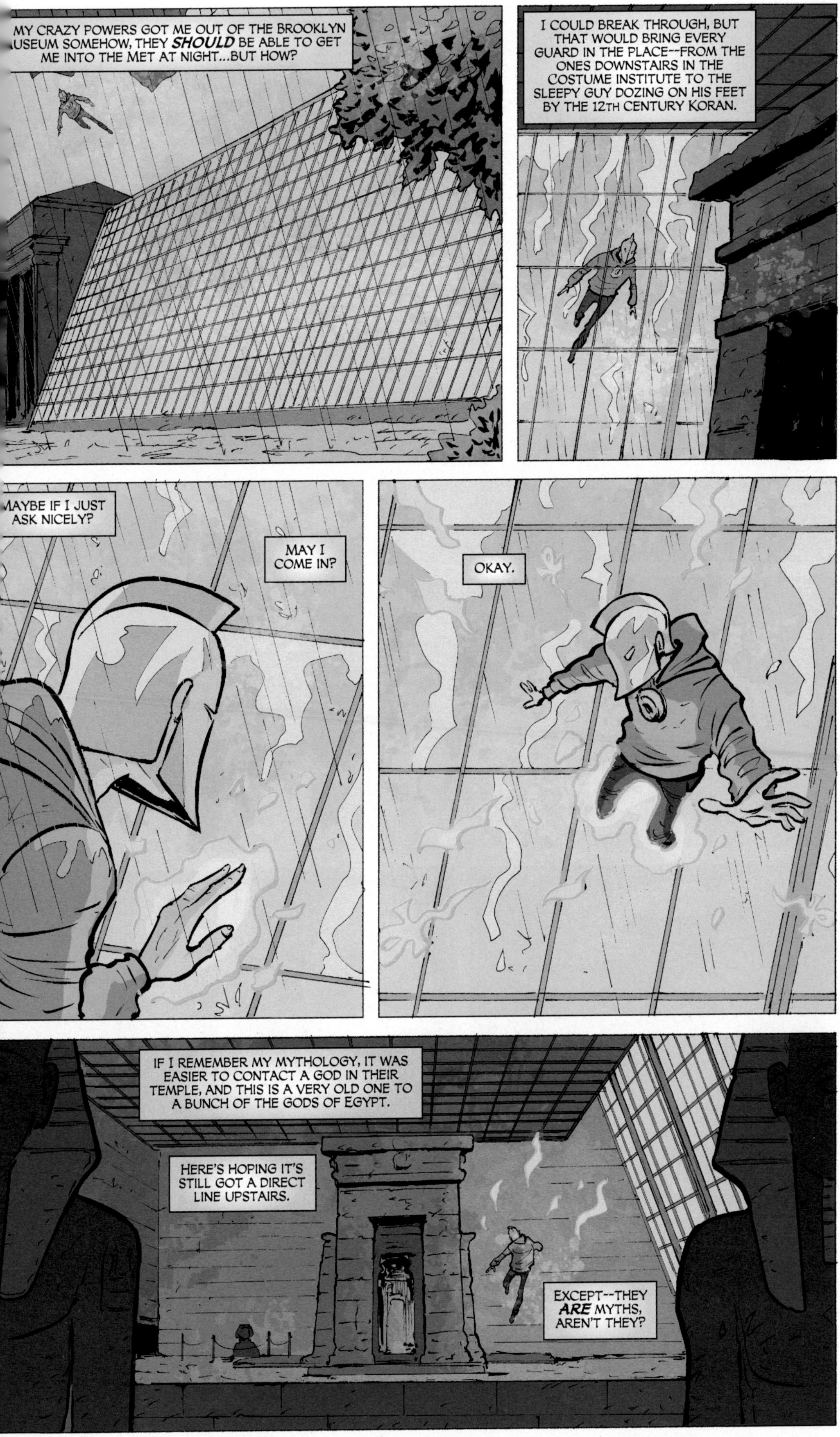
MY CRAZY POWERS GOT ME OUT OF THE BROOKLYN MUSEUM SOMEHOW, THEY SHOULD BE ABLE TO GET ME INTO THE MET AT NIGHT...BUT HOW?
I COULD BREAK THROUGH, BUT THAT WOULD BRING EVERY GUARD IN THE PLACE--FROM THE ONES DOWNSTAIRS IN THE COSTUME INSTITUTE TO THE SLEEPY GUY DOZING ON HIS FEET BY THE 12TH CENTURY KORAN.
MAYBE IF I JUST ASK NICELY?
MAY I COME IN?
OKAY.
IF I REMEMBER MY MYTHOLOGY, IT WAS EASIER TO CONTACT A GOD IN THEIR TEMPLE, AND THIS IS A VERY OLD ONE TO A BUNCH OF THE GODS OF EGYPT.
HERE'S HOPING IT'S STILL GOT A DIRECT LINE UPSTAIRS.
EXCEPT--THEY ARE MYTHS, AREN'T THEY?

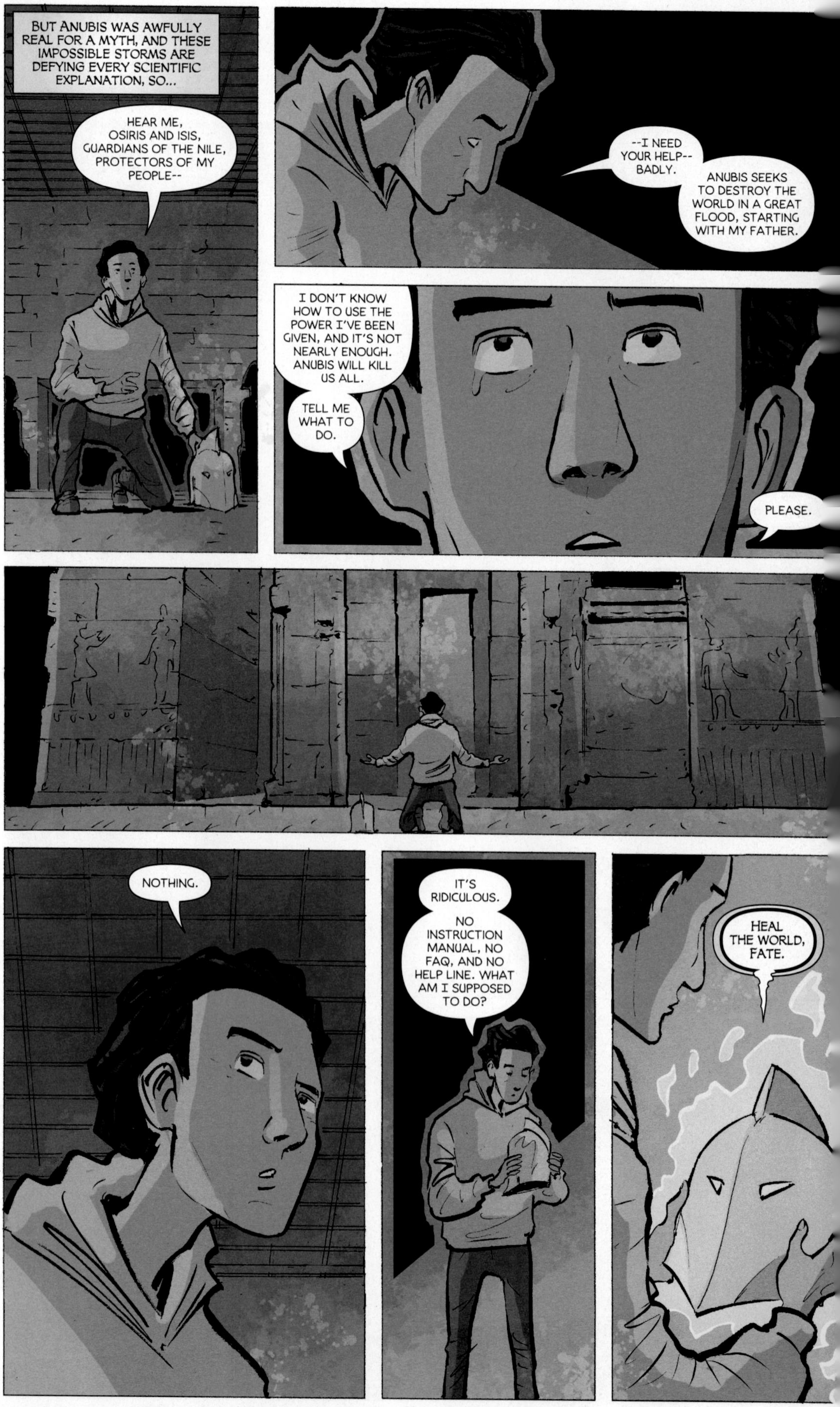

BUT ANUBIS WAS AWFULLY REAL FOR A MYTH, AND THESE IMPOSSIBLE STORMS ARE DEFYING EVERY SCIENTIFIC EXPLANATION, SO...
HEAR ME, OSIRIS AND ISIS, GUARDIANS OF THE NILE, PROTECTORS OF MY PEOPLE--
--I NEED YOUR HELP-- BADLY.
ANUBIS SEEKS TO DESTROY THE WORLD IN A GREAT FLOOD, STARTING WITH MY FATHER.
I DON'T KNOW HOW TO USE THE POWER I'VE BEEN GIVEN, AND IT'S NOT NEARLY ENOUGH. ANUBIS WILL KILL US ALL.
TELL ME WHAT TO DO.
PLEASE.
NOTHING.
IT'S RIDICULOUS.
NO INSTRUCTION MANUAL, NO FAQ, AND NO HELP LINE. WHAT AM I SUPPOSED TO DO?
HEAL THE WORLD, FATE.

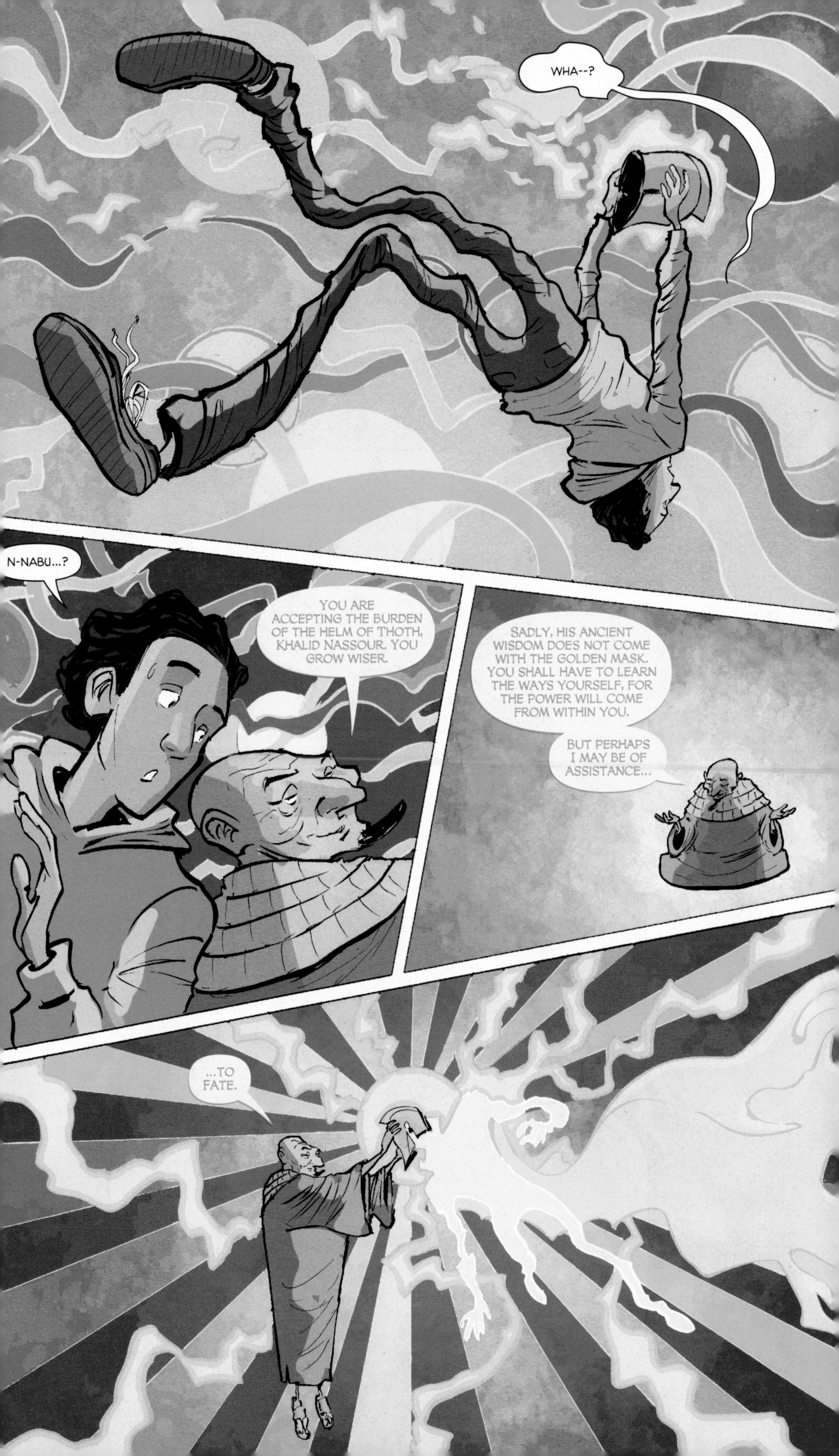
WHA--?
N-NABU...?
YOU ARE ACCEPTING THE BURDEN OF THE HELM OF THOTH, KHALID NASSOUR. YOU GROW WISER.
SADLY, HIS ANCIENT WISDOM DOES NOT COME WITH THE GOLDEN MASK. YOU SHALL HAVE TO LEARN THE WAYS YOURSELF, FOR THE POWER WILL COME FROM WITHIN YOU.
BUT PERHAPS I MAY BE OF ASSISTANCE...
...TO FATE.

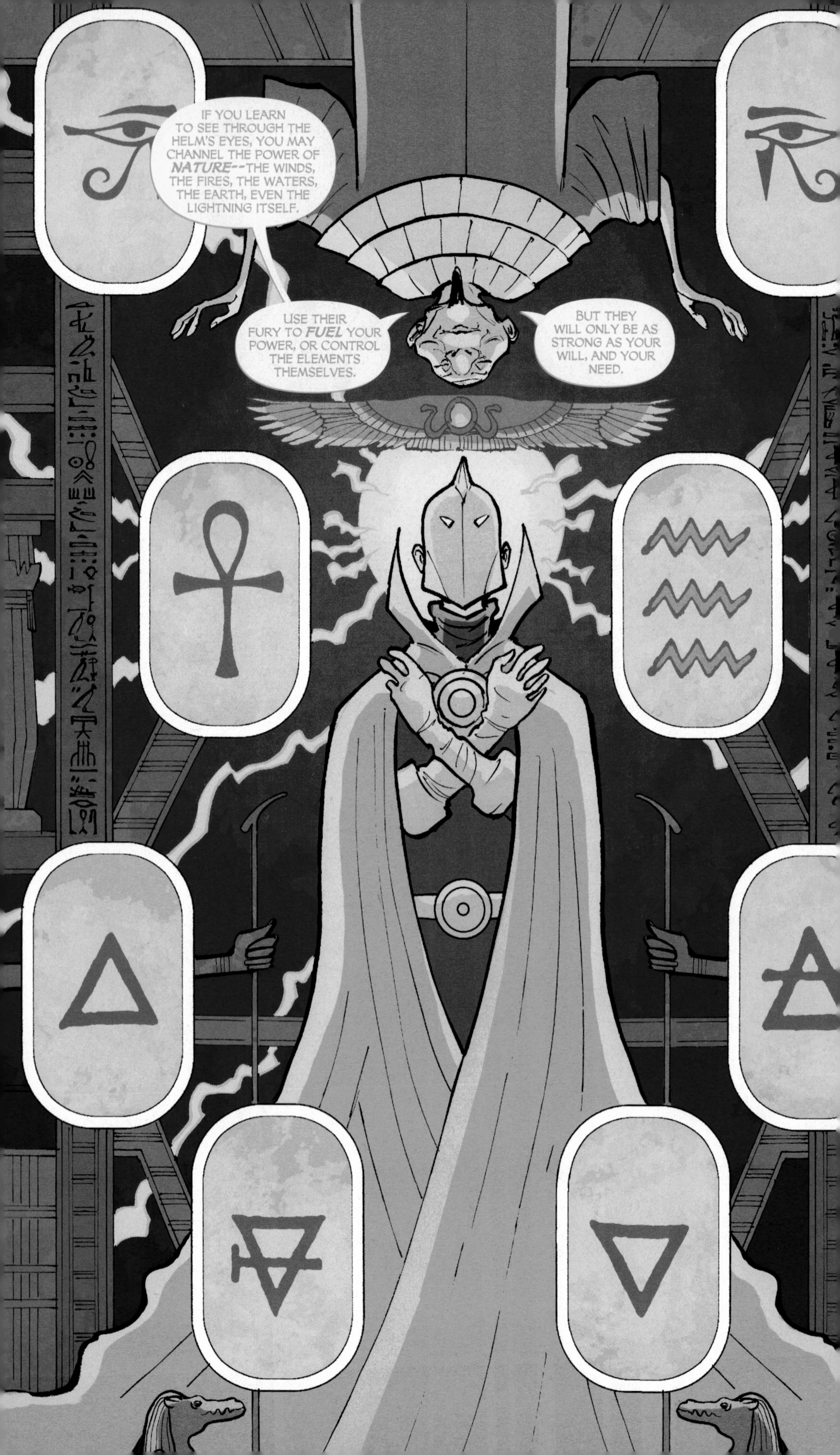
IF YOU LEARN TO SEE THROUGH THE HELM'S EYES, YOU MAY CHANNEL THE POWER OF NATURE--THE WINDS, THE FIRES, THE WATERS, THE EARTH, EVEN THE LIGHTNING ITSELF.
USE THEIR FURY TO FUEL YOUR POWER, OR CONTROL THE ELEMENTS THEMSELVES.
BUT THEY WILL ONLY BE AS STRONG AS YOUR WILL, AND YOUR NEED.

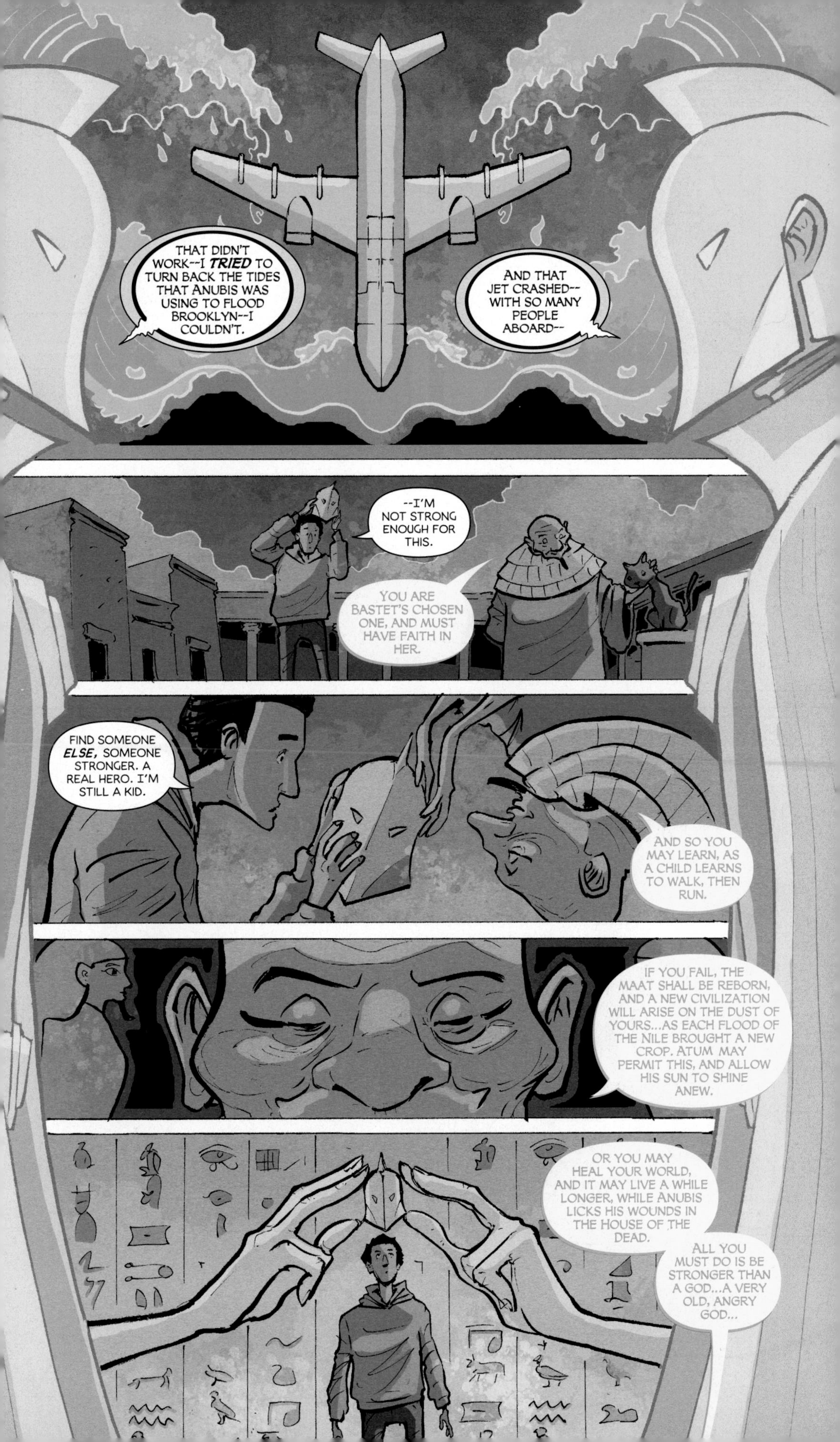
THAT DIDN'T WORK--I TRIED TO TURN BACK THE TIDES THAT ANUBIS WAS USING TO FLOOD BROOKLYN--I COULDN'T.
AND THAT JET CRASHED--WITH SO MANY PEOPLE ABOARD--
--I'M NOT STRONG ENOUGH FOR THIS.
YOU ARE BASTET'S CHOSEN ONE, AND MUST HAVE FAITH IN HER.
FIND SOMEONE ELSE, SOMEONE STRONGER. A REAL HERO. I'M STILL A KID.
AND SO YOU MAY LEARN, AS A CHILD LEARNS TO WALK, THEN RUN.
IF YOU FAIL, THE MAAT SHALL BE REBORN, AND A NEW CIVILIZATION WILL ARISE ON THE DUST OF YOURS...AS EACH FLOOD OF THE NILE BROUGHT A NEW CROP. ATUM MAY PERMIT THIS, AND ALLOW HIS SUN TO SHINE ANEW.
OR YOU MAY HEAL YOUR WORLD, AND IT MAY LIVE A WHILE LONGER, WHILE ANUBIS LICKS HIS WOUNDS IN THE HOUSE OF THE DEAD.
ALL YOU MUST DO IS BE STRONGER THAN A GOD...A VERY OLD, ANGRY GOD...

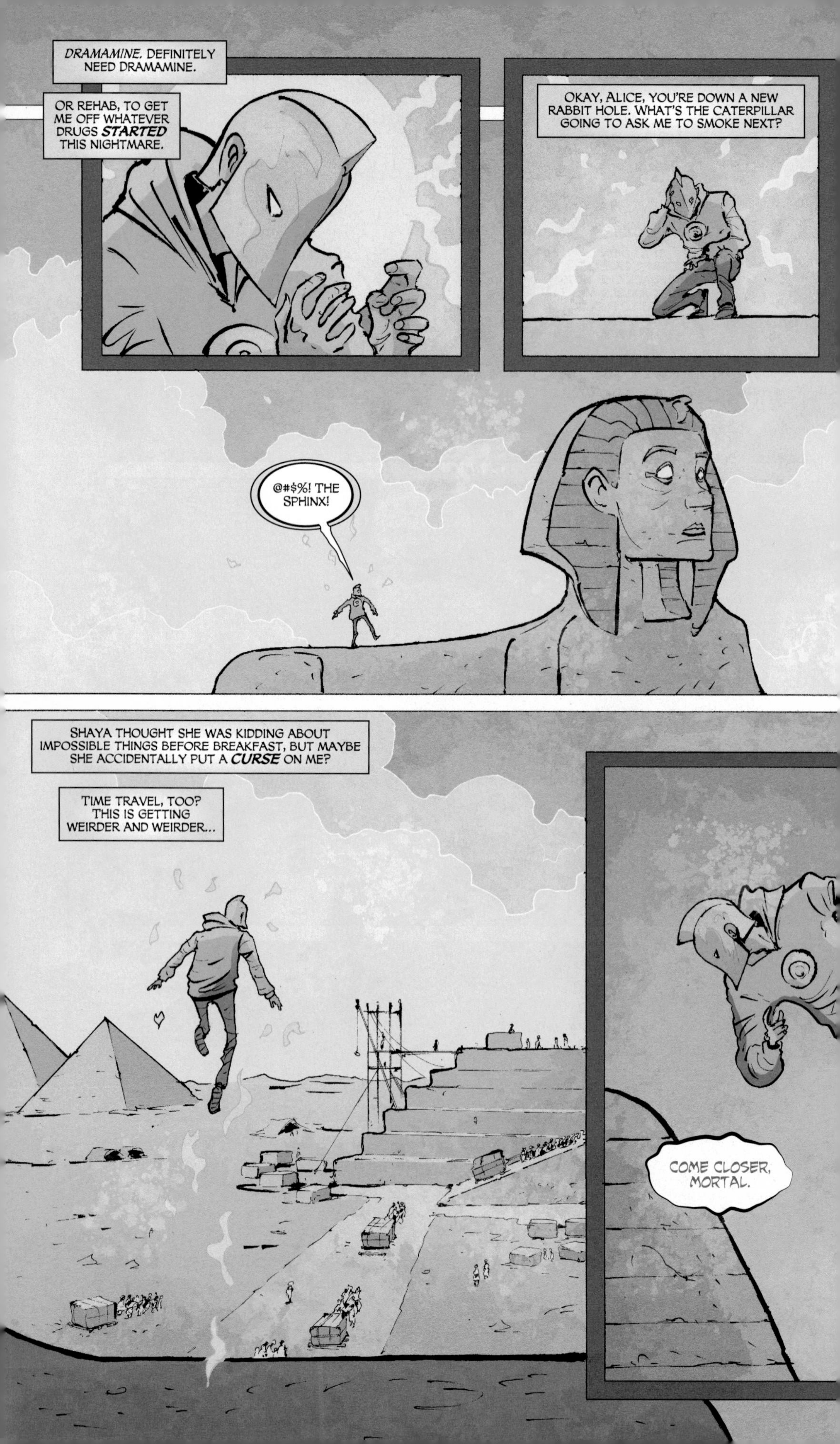
DRAMAMINE. DEFINITELY NEED DRAMAMINE.
OR REHAB, TO GET ME OFF WHATEVER DRUGS STARTED THIS NIGHTMARE.
OKAY, ALICE, YOU'RE DOWN A NEW RABBIT HOLE. WHAT'S THE CATERPILLAR GOING TO ASK ME TO SMOKE NEXT?
@#$%! THE SPHINX!
SHAYA THOUGHT SHE WAS KIDDING ABOUT IMPOSSIBLE THINGS BEFORE BREAKFAST, BUT MAYBE SHE ACCIDENTALLY PUT A CURSE ON ME?
TIME TRAVEL, TOO? THIS IS GETTING WEIRDER AND WEIRDER...
COME CLOSER, MORTAL.

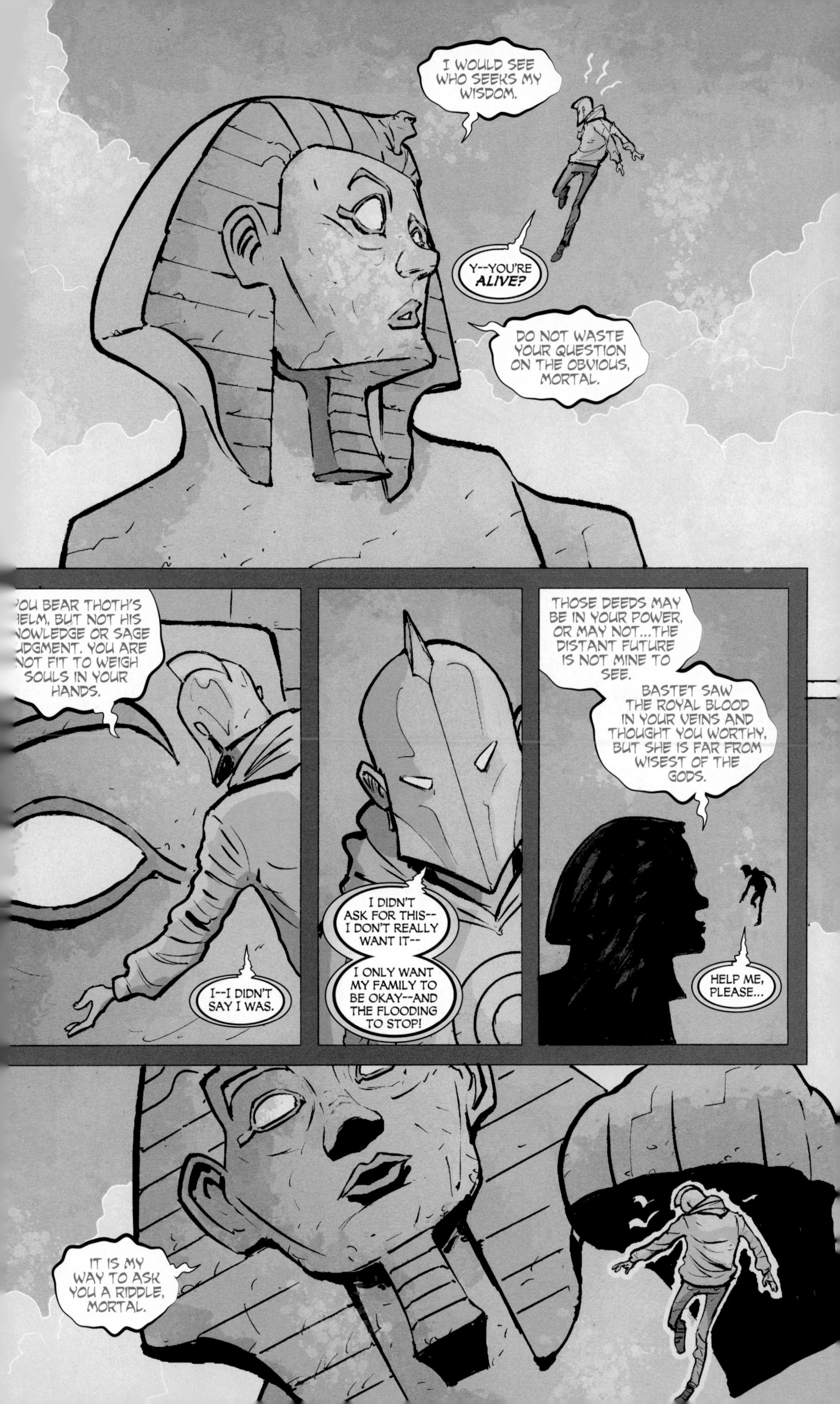
I WOULD SEE WHO SEEKS MY WISDOM.
Y--YOU'RE *ALIVE?*
DO NOT WASTE YOUR QUESTION ON THE OBVIOUS, MORTAL.
YOU BEAR THOTH'S HELM, BUT NOT HIS KNOWLEDGE OR SAGE JUDGMENT. YOU ARE NOT FIT TO WEIGH SOULS IN YOUR HANDS.
I--I DIDN'T SAY I WAS.
I DIDN'T ASK FOR THIS-- I DON'T REALLY WANT IT--
I ONLY WANT MY FAMILY TO BE OKAY--AND THE FLOODING TO STOP!
THOSE DEEDS MAY BE IN YOUR POWER, OR MAY NOT...THE DISTANT FUTURE IS NOT MINE TO SEE.
BASTET SAW THE ROYAL BLOOD IN YOUR VEINS AND THOUGHT YOU WORTHY, BUT SHE IS FAR FROM WISEST OF THE GODS.
HELP ME, PLEASE...
IT IS MY WAY TO ASK YOU A RIDDLE, MORTAL.

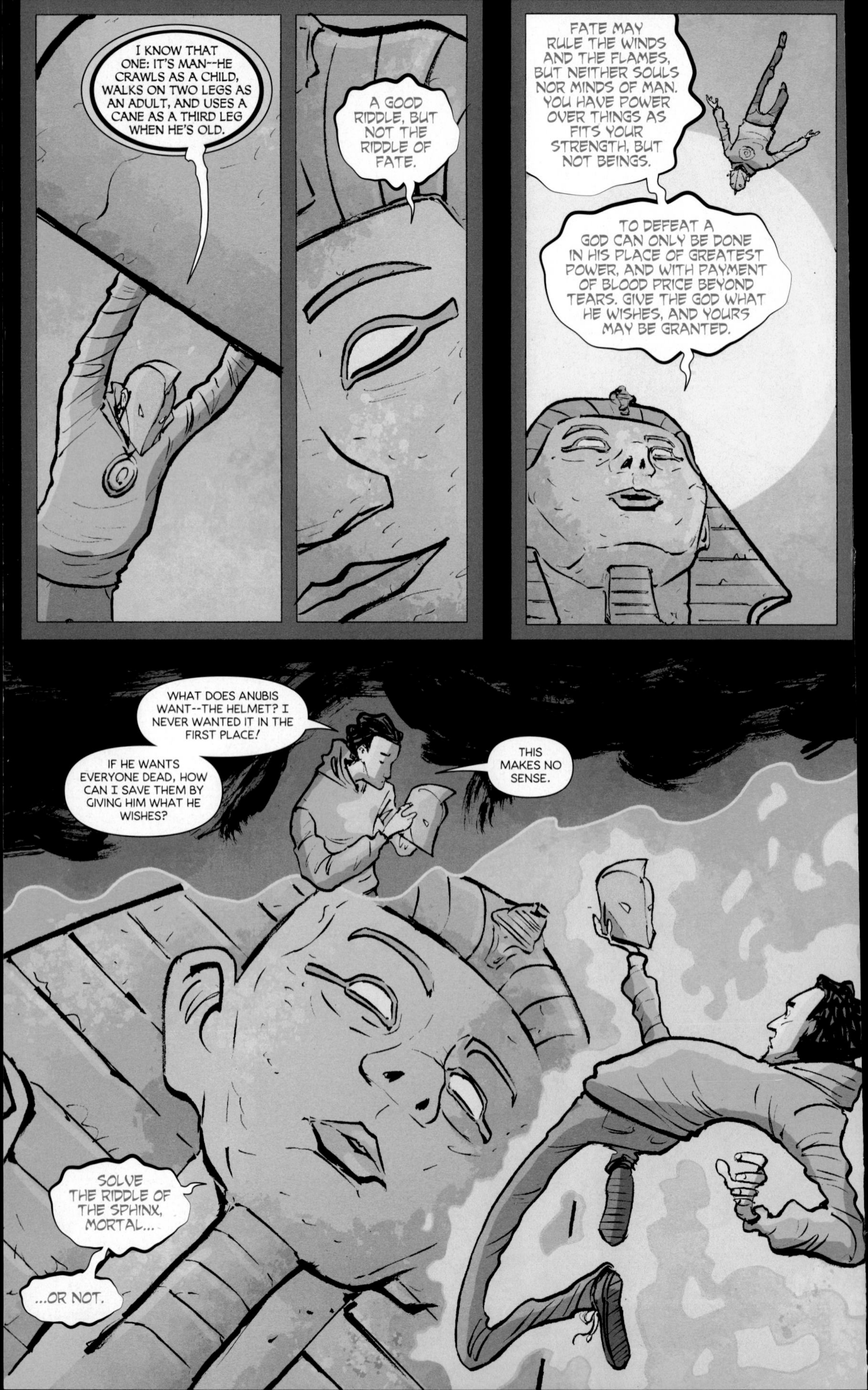
I KNOW THAT ONE: IT'S MAN--HE CRAWLS AS A CHILD, WALKS ON TWO LEGS AS AN ADULT, AND USES A CANE AS A THIRD LEG WHEN HE'S OLD.
A GOOD RIDDLE, BUT NOT THE RIDDLE OF FATE.
FATE MAY RULE THE WINDS AND THE FLAMES, BUT NEITHER SOULS NOR MINDS OF MAN. YOU HAVE POWER OVER THINGS AS FITS YOUR STRENGTH, BUT NOT BEINGS.
TO DEFEAT A GOD CAN ONLY BE DONE IN HIS PLACE OF GREATEST POWER, AND WITH PAYMENT OF BLOOD PRICE BEYOND TEARS. GIVE THE GOD WHAT HE WISHES, AND YOURS MAY BE GRANTED.
WHAT DOES ANUBIS WANT--THE HELMET? I NEVER WANTED IT IN THE FIRST PLACE!
IF HE WANTS EVERYONE DEAD, HOW CAN I SAVE THEM BY GIVING HIM WHAT HE WISHES?
THIS MAKES NO SENSE.
SOLVE THE RIDDLE OF THE SPHINX, MORTAL...
...OR NOT.

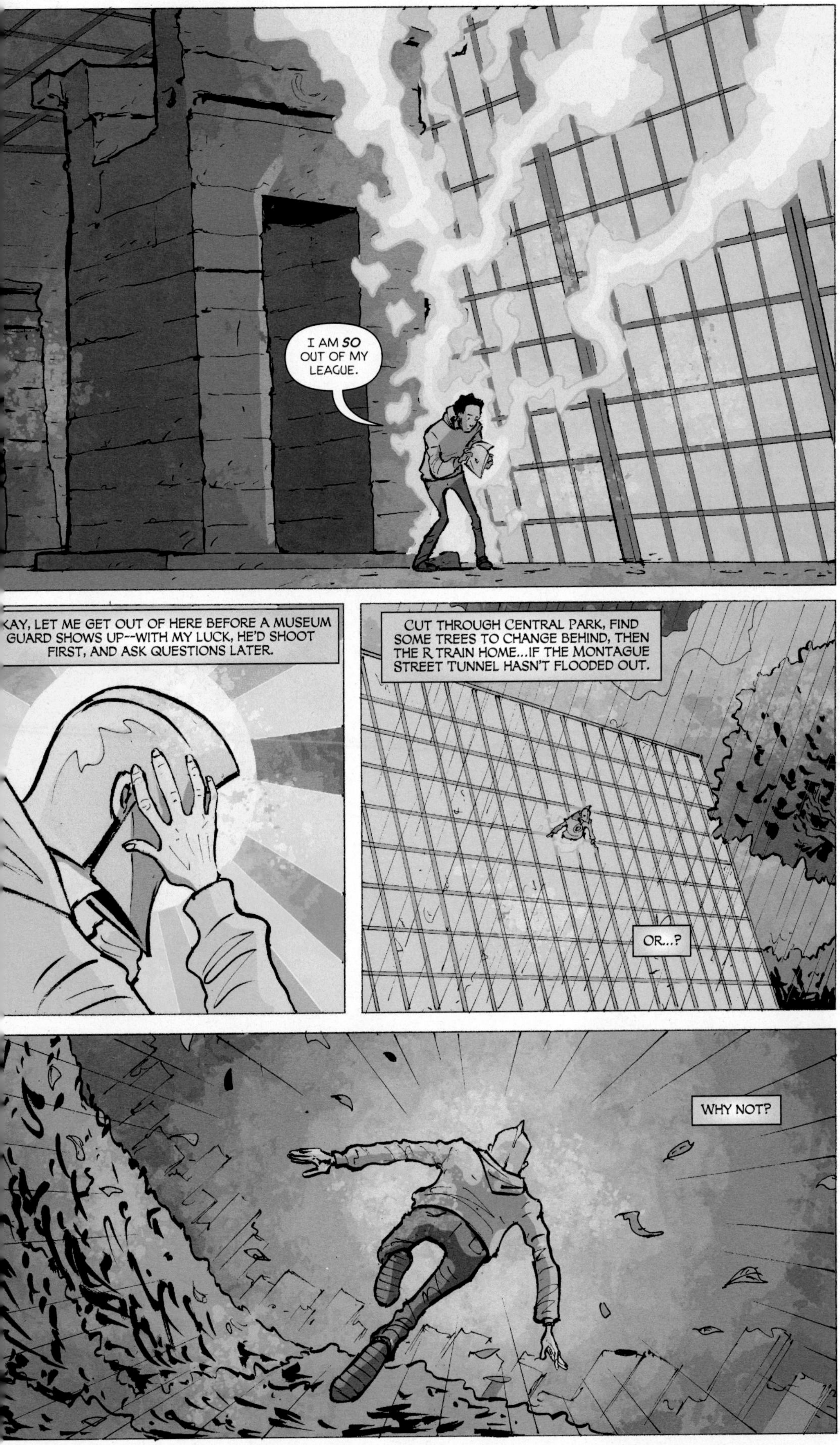
I AM SO OUT OF MY LEAGUE.
KAY, LET ME GET OUT OF HERE BEFORE A MUSEUM GUARD SHOWS UP--WITH MY LUCK, HE'D SHOOT FIRST, AND ASK QUESTIONS LATER.
CUT THROUGH CENTRAL PARK, FIND SOME TREES TO CHANGE BEHIND, THEN THE R TRAIN HOME...IF THE MONTAGUE STREET TUNNEL HASN'T FLOODED OUT.
OR...?
WHY NOT?

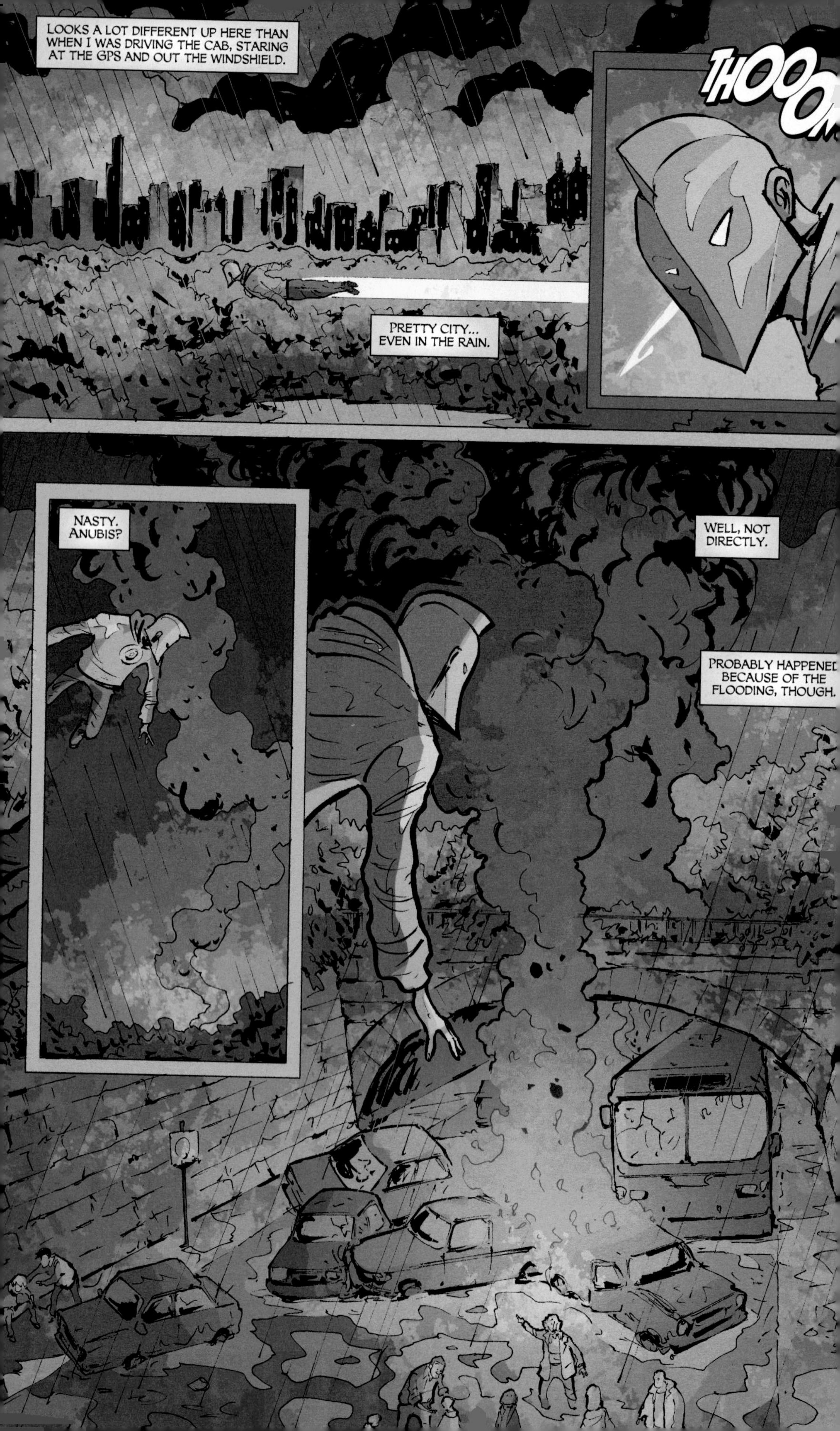
LOOKS A LOT DIFFERENT UP HERE THAN WHEN I WAS DRIVING THE CAB, STARING AT THE GPS AND OUT THE WINDSHIELD.
PRETTY CITY... EVEN IN THE RAIN.
THOOOM
NASTY. ANUBIS?
WELL, NOT DIRECTLY.
PROBABLY HAPPENED BECAUSE OF THE FLOODING, THOUGH.

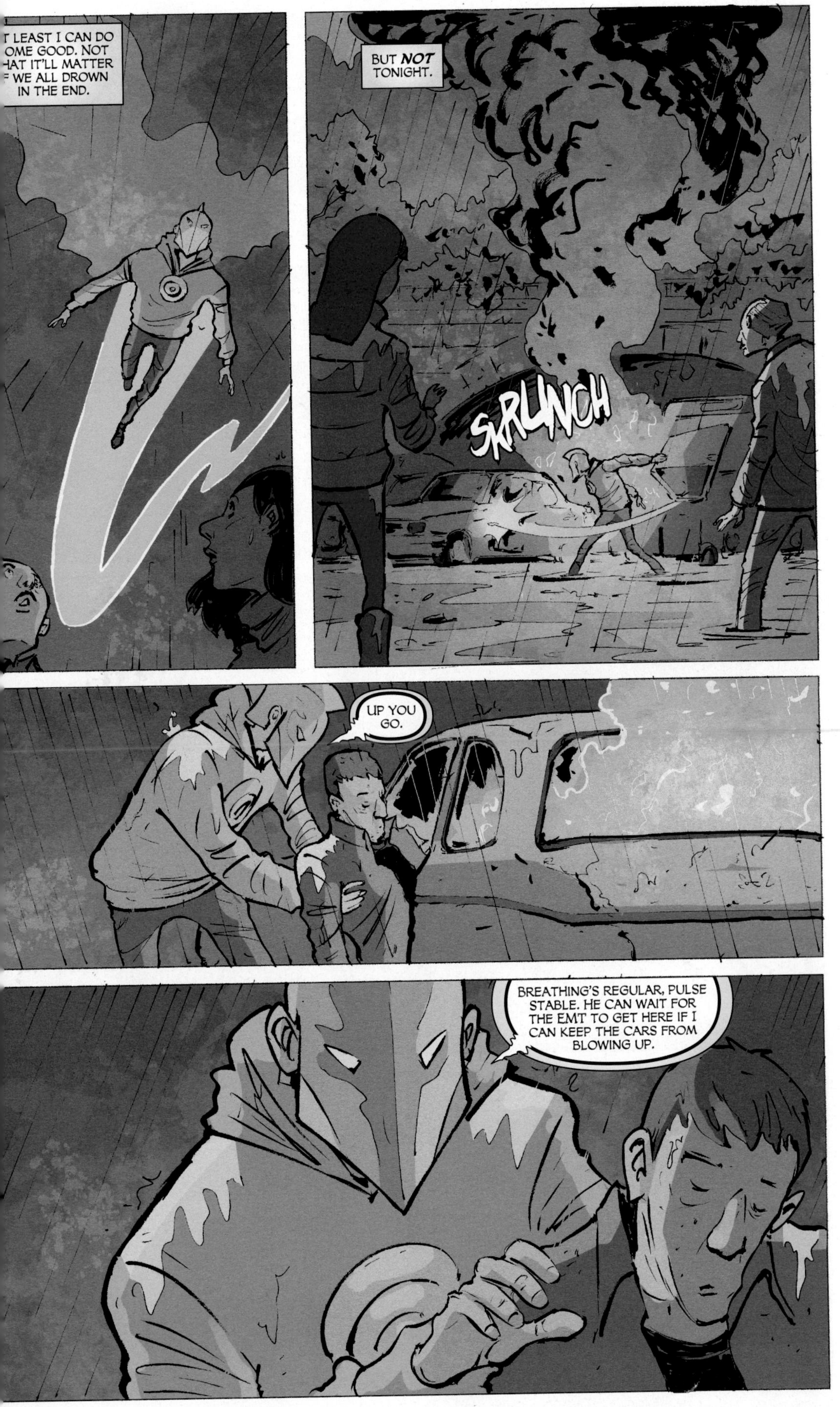
T LEAST I CAN DO OME GOOD. NOT HAT IT'LL MATTER F WE ALL DROWN IN THE END.
BUT NOT TONIGHT.
SKRUNCH
UP YOU GO.
BREATHING'S REGULAR, PULSE STABLE. HE CAN WAIT FOR THE EMT TO GET HERE IF I CAN KEEP THE CARS FROM BLOWING UP.

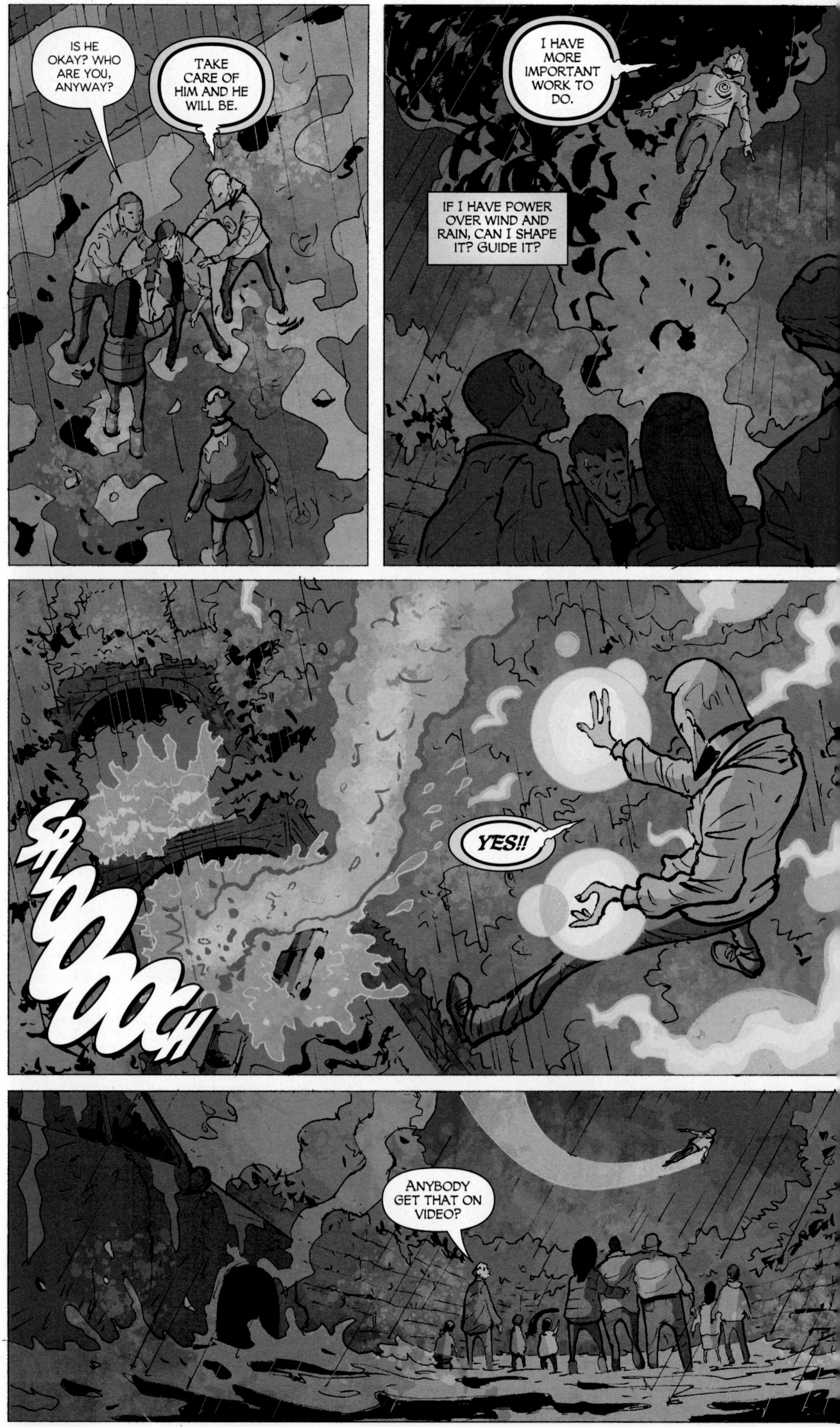
IS HE OKAY? WHO ARE YOU, ANYWAY?
TAKE CARE OF HIM AND HE WILL BE.
I HAVE MORE IMPORTANT WORK TO DO.
IF I HAVE POWER OVER WIND AND RAIN, CAN I SHAPE IT? GUIDE IT?
SPLOOOOCH
YES!!
ANYBODY GET THAT ON VIDEO?

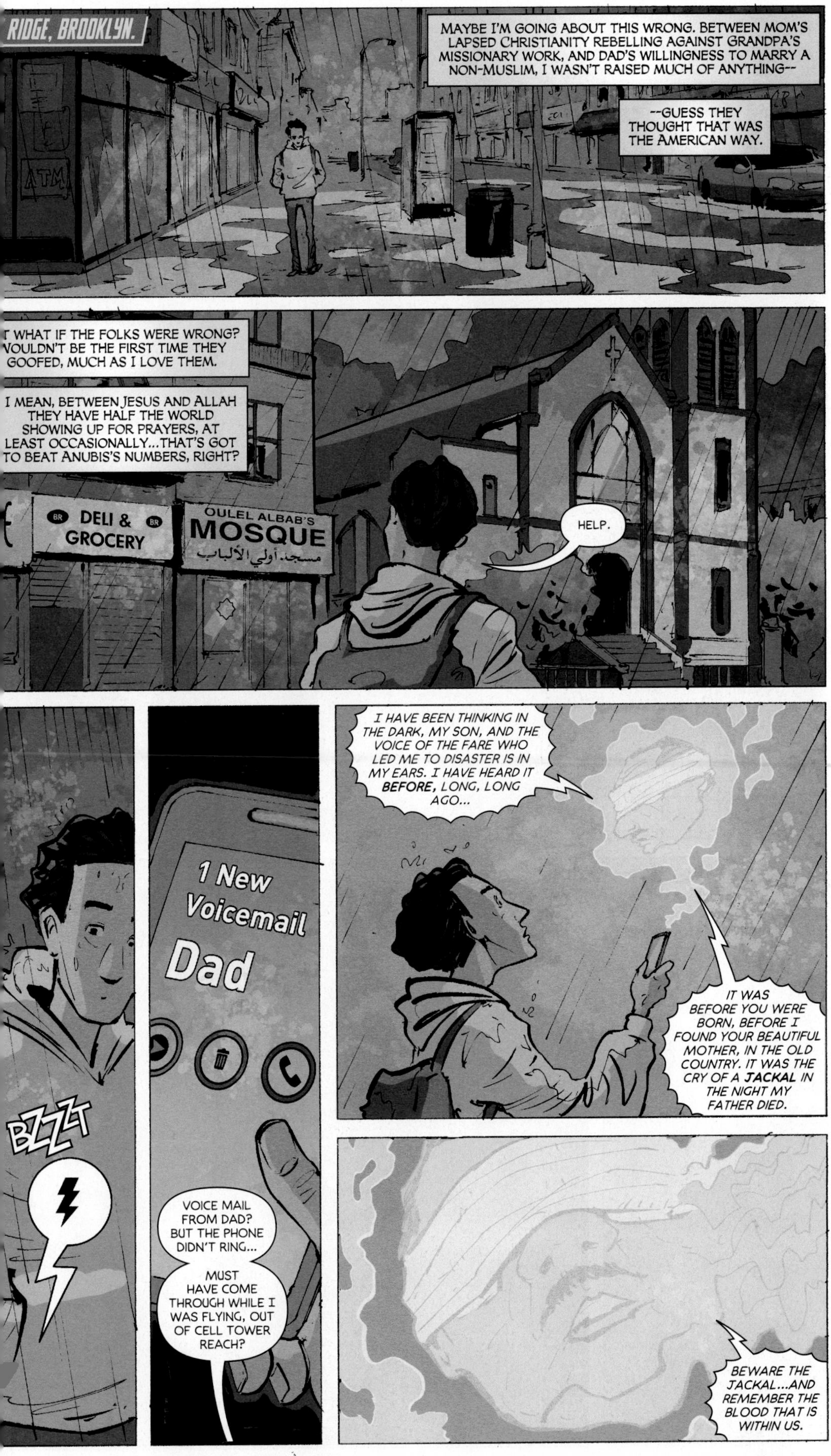
RIDGE, BROOKLYN.
MAYBE I'M GOING ABOUT THIS WRONG. BETWEEN MOM'S LAPSED CHRISTIANITY REBELLING AGAINST GRANDPA'S MISSIONARY WORK, AND DAD'S WILLINGNESS TO MARRY A NON-MUSLIM, I WASN'T RAISED MUCH OF ANYTHING--
--GUESS THEY THOUGHT THAT WAS THE AMERICAN WAY.
T WHAT IF THE FOLKS WERE WRONG? VOULDN'T BE THE FIRST TIME THEY GOOFED, MUCH AS I LOVE THEM.
I MEAN, BETWEEN JESUS AND ALLAH THEY HAVE HALF THE WORLD SHOWING UP FOR PRAYERS, AT LEAST OCCASIONALLY...THAT'S GOT TO BEAT ANUBIS'S NUMBERS, RIGHT?
DELI & GROCERY
OULEL ALBAB'S MOSQUE
مسجد أولي الألباب
HELP.
BZZZT
1 New Voicemail
Dad
VOICE MAIL FROM DAD? BUT THE PHONE DIDN'T RING...
MUST HAVE COME THROUGH WHILE I WAS FLYING, OUT OF CELL TOWER REACH?
I HAVE BEEN THINKING IN THE DARK, MY SON, AND THE VOICE OF THE FARE WHO LED ME TO DISASTER IS IN MY EARS. I HAVE HEARD IT BEFORE, LONG, LONG AGO...
IT WAS BEFORE YOU WERE BORN, BEFORE I FOUND YOUR BEAUTIFUL MOTHER, IN THE OLD COUNTRY. IT WAS THE CRY OF A JACKAL IN THE NIGHT MY FATHER DIED.
BEWARE THE JACKAL...AND REMEMBER THE BLOOD THAT IS WITHIN US.

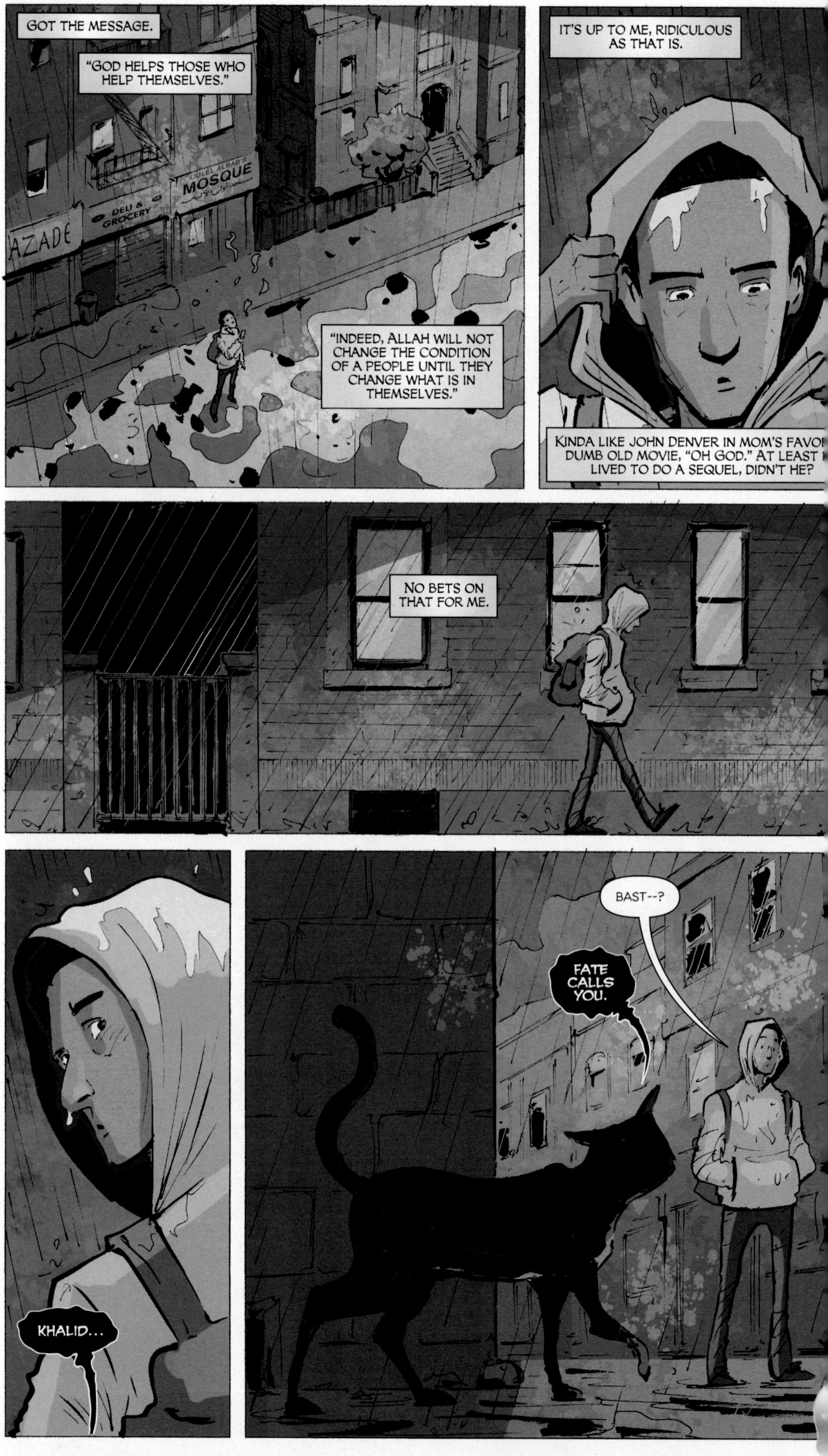
GOT THE MESSAGE.
"GOD HELPS THOSE WHO HELP THEMSELVES."
OULEL ALBAB'S MOSQUE
DELI & GROCERY
AZADE
"INDEED, ALLAH WILL NOT CHANGE THE CONDITION OF A PEOPLE UNTIL THEY CHANGE WHAT IS IN THEMSELVES."
IT'S UP TO ME, RIDICULOUS AS THAT IS.
KINDA LIKE JOHN DENVER IN MOM'S FAVO DUMB OLD MOVIE, "OH GOD." AT LEAST LIVED TO DO A SEQUEL, DIDN'T HE?
NO BETS ON THAT FOR ME.
KHALID...
BAST--?
FATE CALLS YOU.

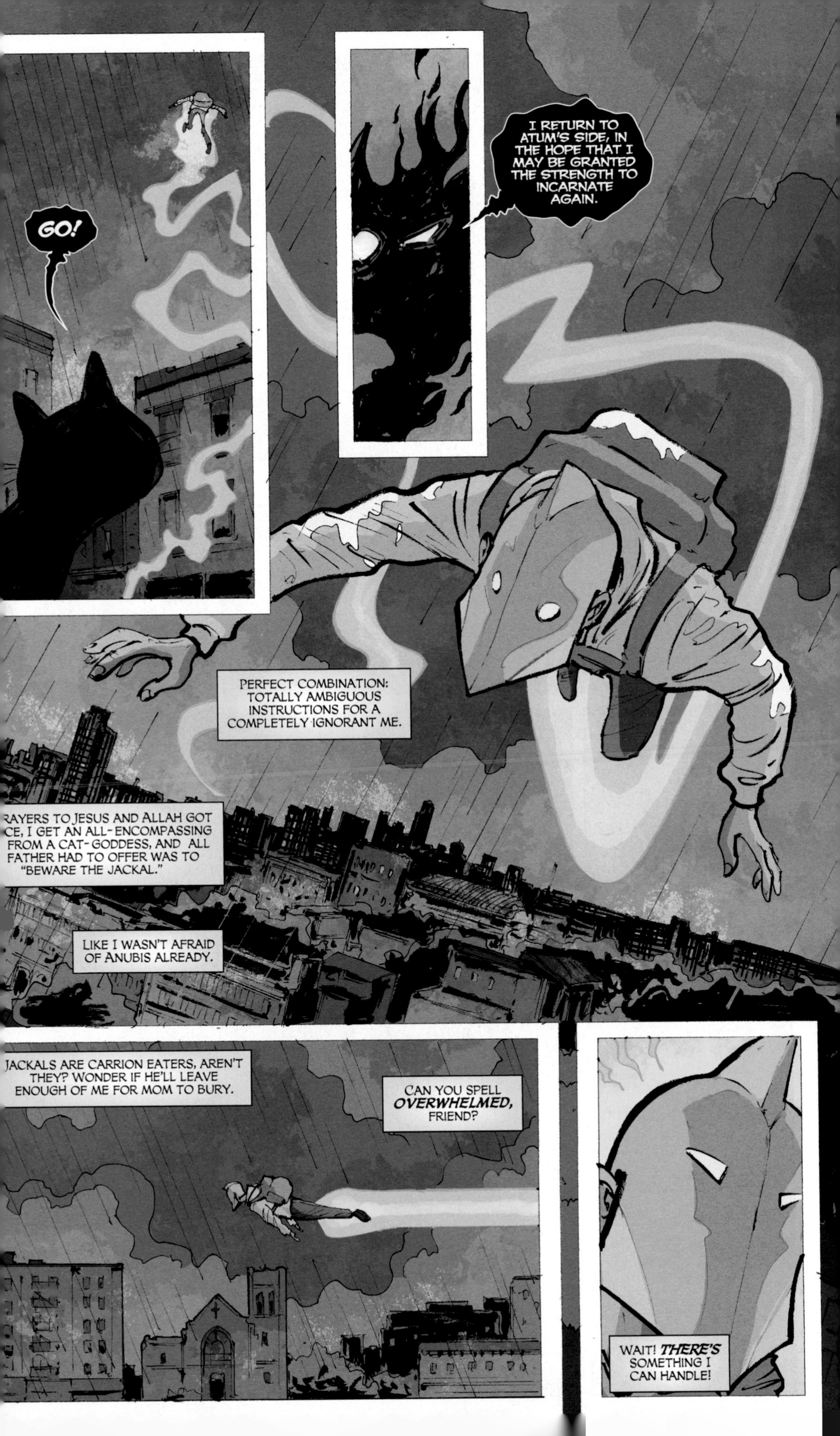
GO!
I RETURN TO ATUM'S SIDE, IN THE HOPE THAT I MAY BE GRANTED THE STRENGTH TO INCARNATE AGAIN.
PERFECT COMBINATION: TOTALLY AMBIGUOUS INSTRUCTIONS FOR A COMPLETELY IGNORANT ME.
RAYERS TO JESUS AND ALLAH GOT CE, I GET AN ALL-ENCOMPASSING FROM A CAT-GODDESS, AND ALL FATHER HAD TO OFFER WAS TO "BEWARE THE JACKAL."
LIKE I WASN'T AFRAID OF ANUBIS ALREADY.
JACKALS ARE CARRION EATERS, AREN'T THEY? WONDER IF HE'LL LEAVE ENOUGH OF ME FOR MOM TO BURY.
CAN YOU SPELL *OVERWHELMED,* FRIEND?
WAIT! ***THERE'S*** SOMETHING I CAN HANDLE!

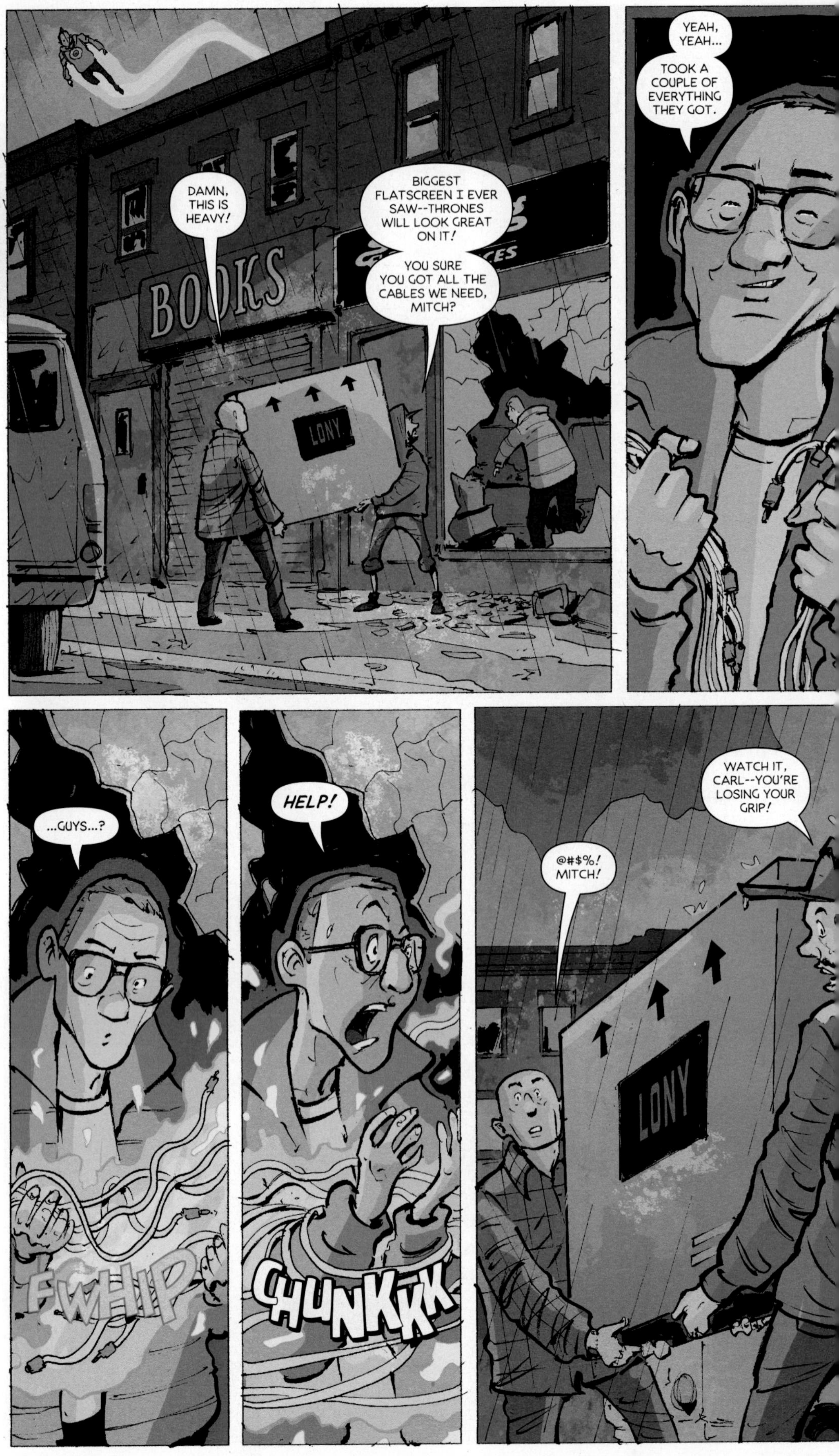
DAMN, THIS IS HEAVY!
BIGGEST FLATSCREEN I EVER SAW--THRONES WILL LOOK GREAT ON IT!
YOU SURE YOU GOT ALL THE CABLES WE NEED, MITCH?
BOOKS
LONY
YEAH, YEAH...
TOOK A COUPLE OF EVERYTHING THEY GOT.
...GUYS...?
FWHIP
HELP!
CHUNKKK
WATCH IT, CARL--YOU'RE LOSING YOUR GRIP!
@#$%! MITCH!
LONY

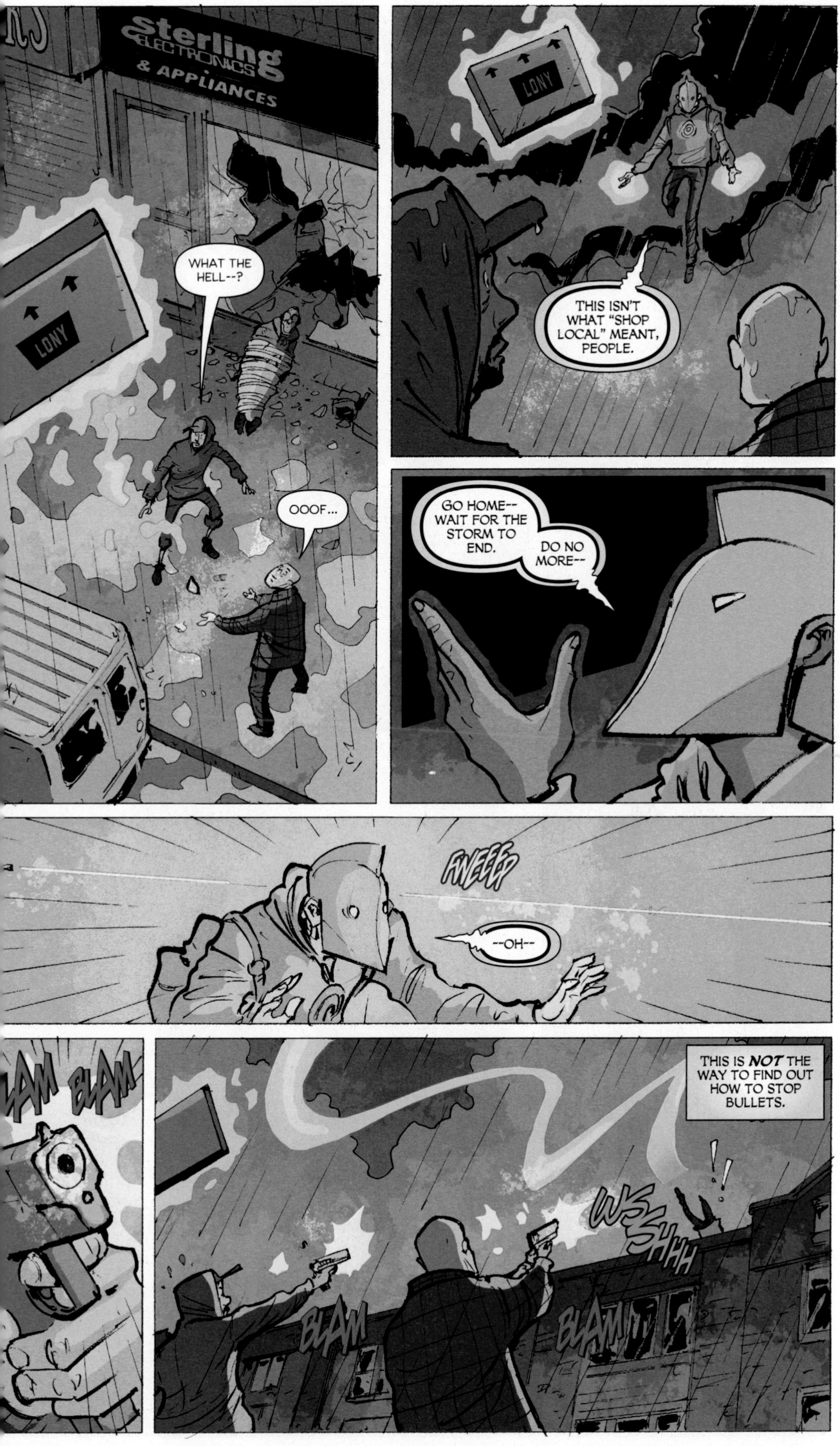
Sterling
ELECTRONICS
& APPLIANCES
LONY
WHAT THE HELL--?
OOOF...
LONY
THIS ISN'T WHAT "SHOP LOCAL" MEANT, PEOPLE.
GO HOME-- WAIT FOR THE STORM TO END.
DO NO MORE--
FWEEEP
--OH--
BLAM BLAM
THIS IS **NOT** THE WAY TO FIND OUT HOW TO STOP BULLETS.
!!
WSSHHH
BLAM
BLAM

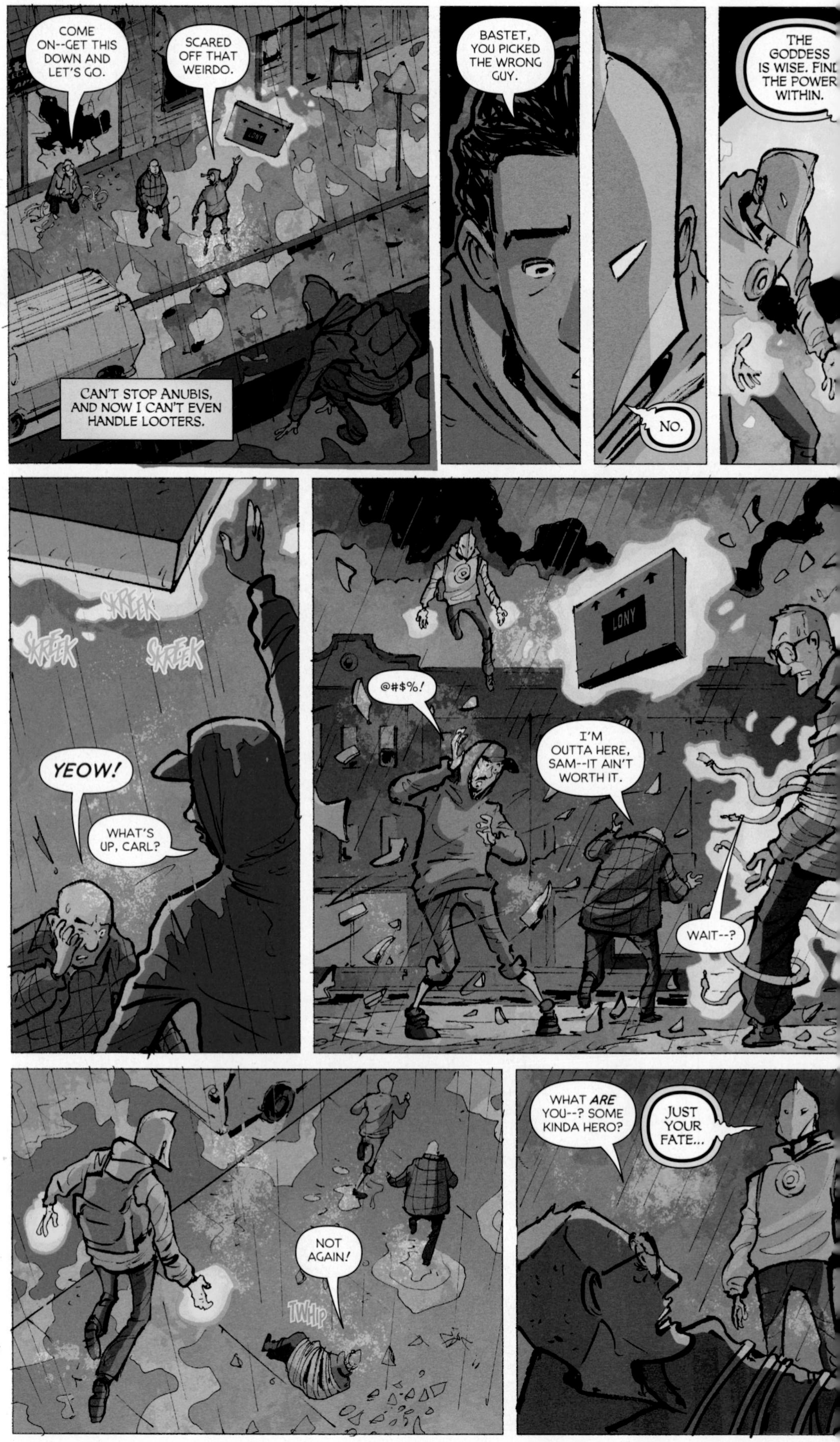
COME ON--GET THIS DOWN AND LET'S GO.
SCARED OFF THAT WEIRDO.
LONY
CAN'T STOP ANUBIS, AND NOW I CAN'T EVEN HANDLE LOOTERS.
BASTET, YOU PICKED THE WRONG GUY.
NO.
THE GODDESS IS WISE. FIND THE POWER WITHIN.
SKREEK
SKREEK
SKREEK
YEOW!
WHAT'S UP, CARL?
LONY
@#$%!
I'M OUTTA HERE, SAM--IT AIN'T WORTH IT.
WAIT--?
NOT AGAIN!
TWHIP
WHAT *ARE* YOU--? SOME KINDA HERO?
JUST YOUR FATE...

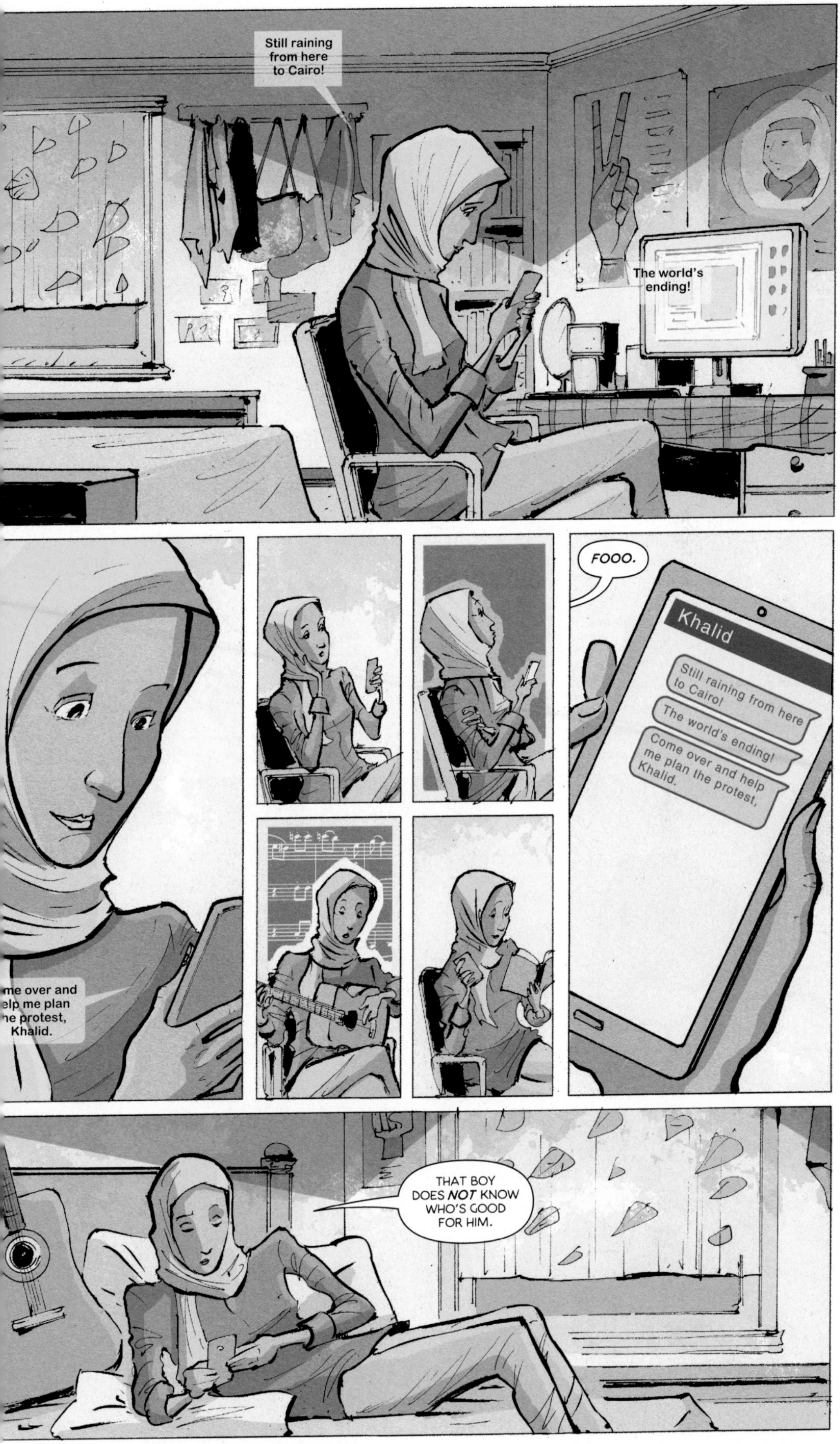
Still raining from here to Cairo!
The world's ending!
FOOO.
Khalid
Still raining from here to Cairo!
The world's ending!
Come over and help me plan the protest, Khalid.
me over and elp me plan he protest, Khalid.
THAT BOY DOES NOT KNOW WHO'S GOOD FOR HIM.

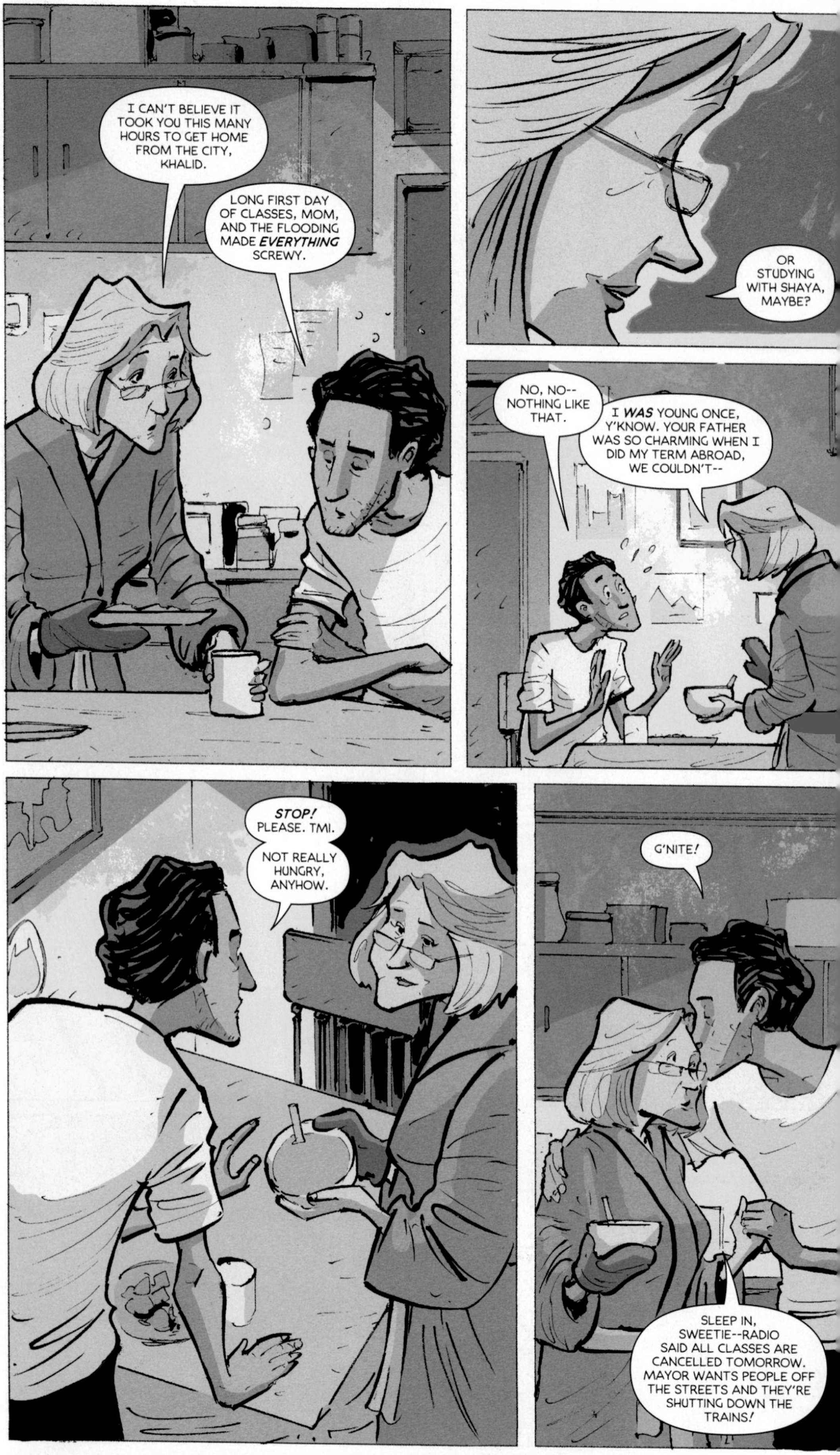
I CAN'T BELIEVE IT TOOK YOU THIS MANY HOURS TO GET HOME FROM THE CITY, KHALID.
LONG FIRST DAY OF CLASSES, MOM, AND THE FLOODING MADE ***EVERYTHING*** SCREWY.
OR STUDYING WITH SHAYA, MAYBE?
NO, NO-- NOTHING LIKE THAT.
I ***WAS*** YOUNG ONCE, Y'KNOW. YOUR FATHER WAS SO CHARMING WHEN I DID MY TERM ABROAD, WE COULDN'T--
STOP! PLEASE. TMI.
NOT REALLY HUNGRY, ANYHOW.
G'NITE!
SLEEP IN, SWEETIE--RADIO SAID ALL CLASSES ARE CANCELLED TOMORROW. MAYOR WANTS PEOPLE OFF THE STREETS AND THEY'RE SHUTTING DOWN THE TRAINS!

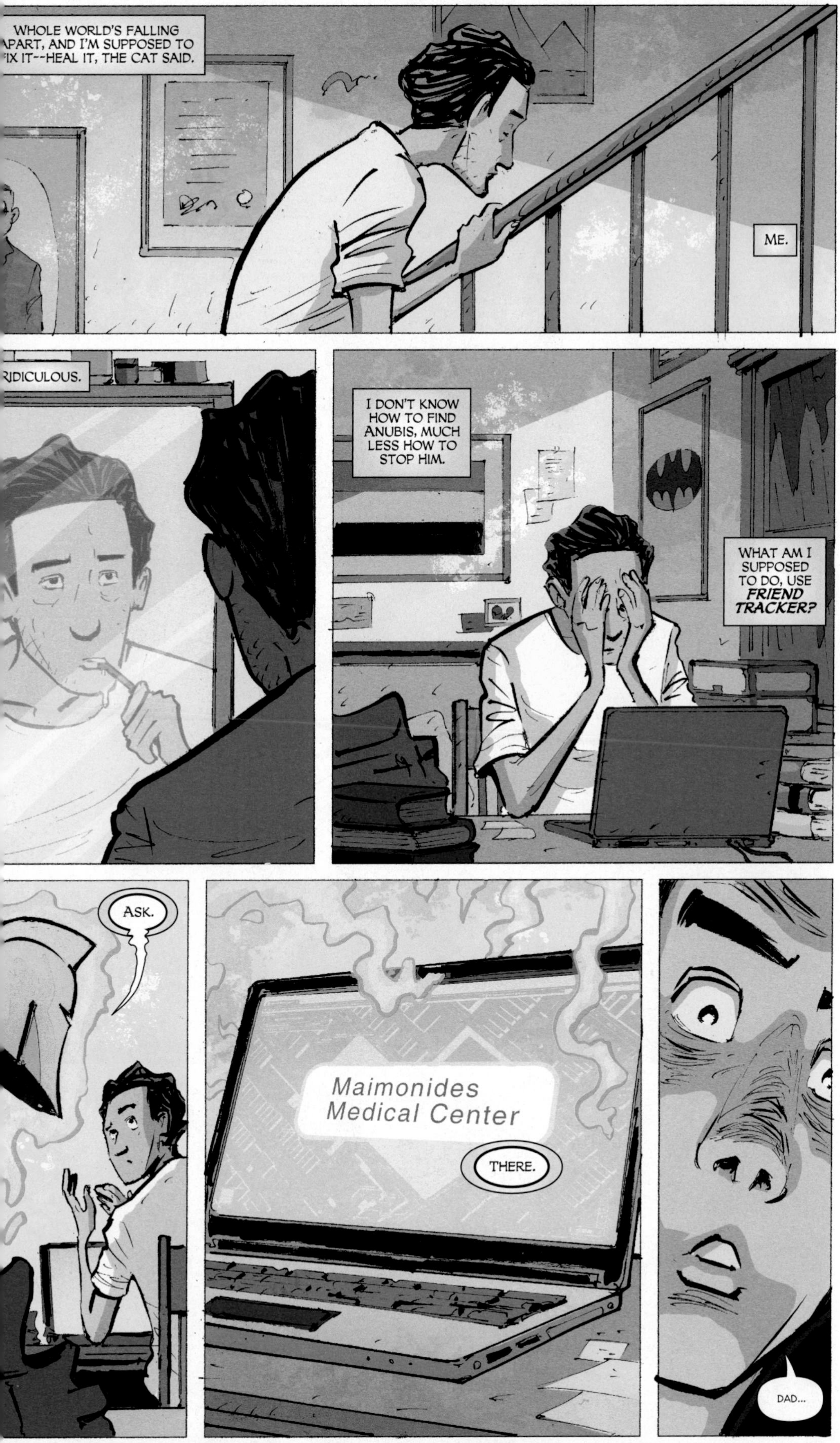
WHOLE WORLD'S FALLING APART, AND I'M SUPPOSED TO FIX IT--HEAL IT, THE CAT SAID.
ME.
RIDICULOUS.
I DON'T KNOW HOW TO FIND ANUBIS, MUCH LESS HOW TO STOP HIM.
WHAT AM I SUPPOSED TO DO, USE *FRIEND TRACKER?*
ASK.
Maimonides Medical Center
THERE.
DAD...

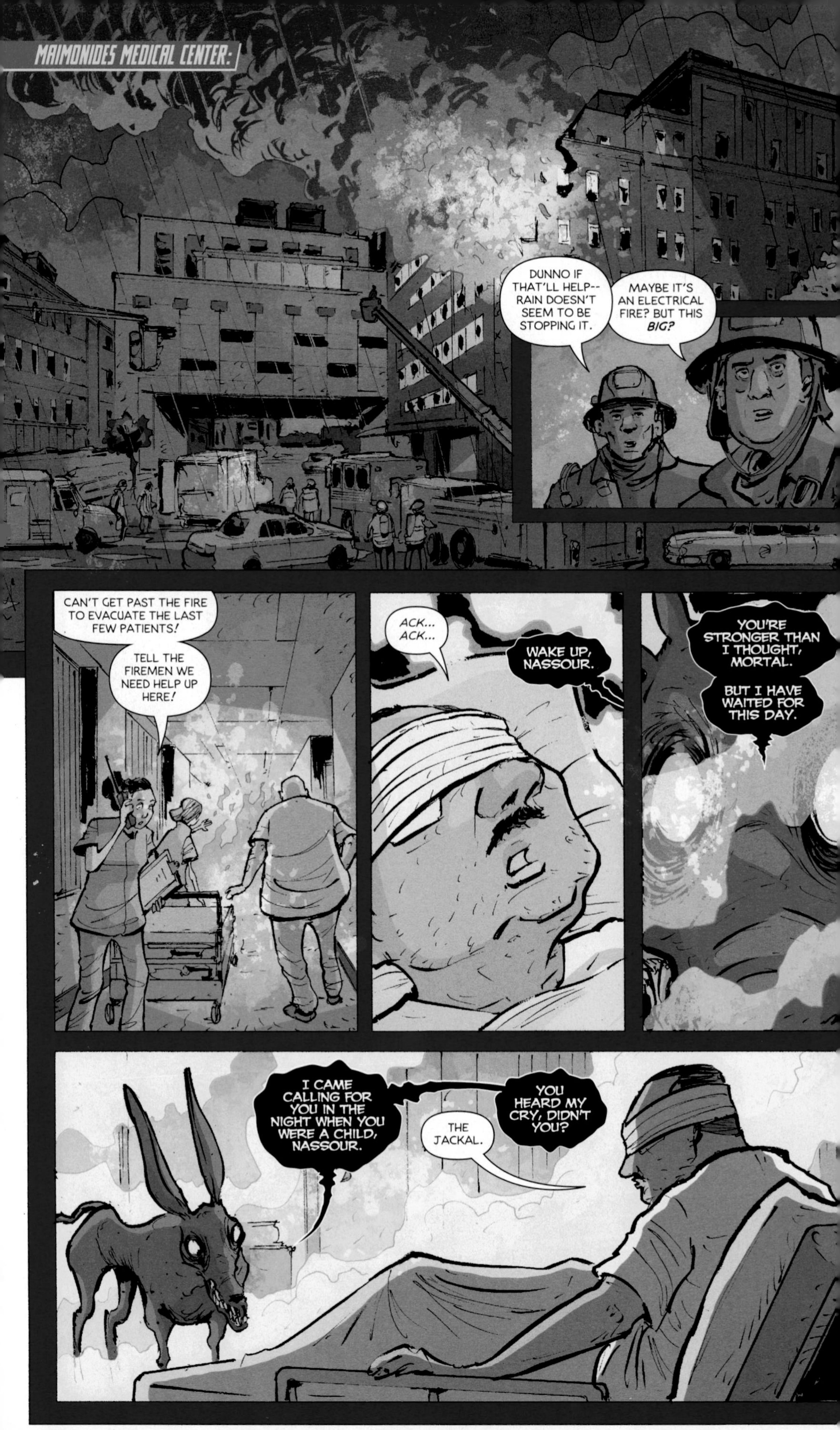
MAIMONIDES MEDICAL CENTER:
DUNNO IF THAT'LL HELP-- RAIN DOESN'T SEEM TO BE STOPPING IT.
MAYBE IT'S AN ELECTRICAL FIRE? BUT THIS BIG?
CAN'T GET PAST THE FIRE TO EVACUATE THE LAST FEW PATIENTS!
TELL THE FIREMEN WE NEED HELP UP HERE!
ACK... ACK...
WAKE UP, NASSOUR.
YOU'RE STRONGER THAN I THOUGHT, MORTAL.
BUT I HAVE WAITED FOR THIS DAY.
I CAME CALLING FOR YOU IN THE NIGHT WHEN YOU WERE A CHILD, NASSOUR.
YOU HEARD MY CRY, DIDN'T YOU?
THE JACKAL.

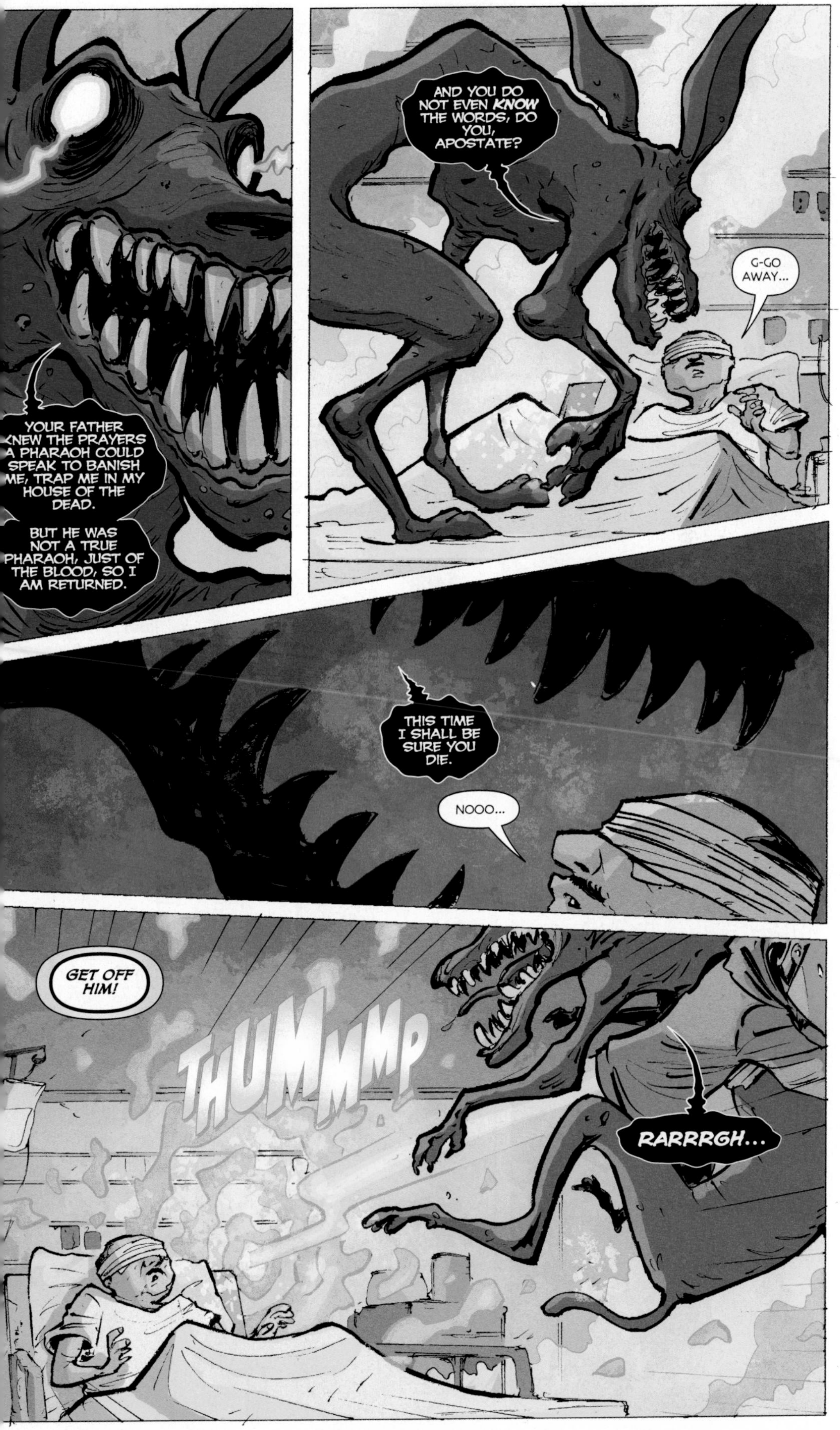
YOUR FATHER KNEW THE PRAYERS A PHARAOH COULD SPEAK TO BANISH ME, TRAP ME IN MY HOUSE OF THE DEAD.
BUT HE WAS NOT A TRUE PHARAOH, JUST OF THE BLOOD, SO I AM RETURNED.
AND YOU DO NOT EVEN KNOW THE WORDS, DO YOU, APOSTATE?
G-GO AWAY...
THIS TIME I SHALL BE SURE YOU DIE.
NOOO...
GET OFF HIM!
THUMMMP
RARRRGH...

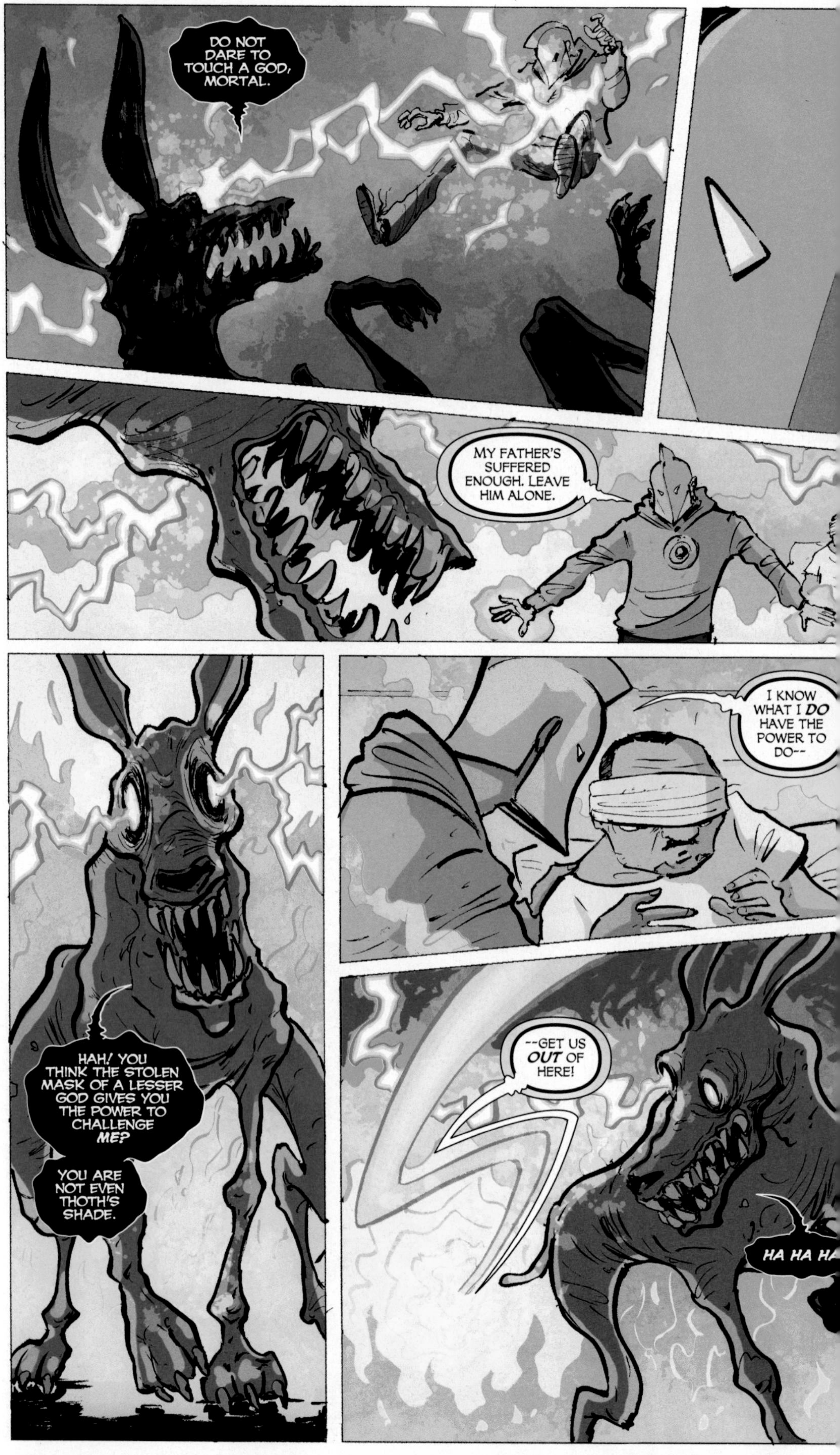
DO NOT DARE TO TOUCH A GOD, MORTAL.
MY FATHER'S SUFFERED ENOUGH. LEAVE HIM ALONE.
HAH! YOU THINK THE STOLEN MASK OF A LESSER GOD GIVES YOU THE POWER TO CHALLENGE ME?
YOU ARE NOT EVEN THOTH'S SHADE.
I KNOW WHAT I DO HAVE THE POWER TO DO--
--GET US OUT OF HERE!
HA HA HA

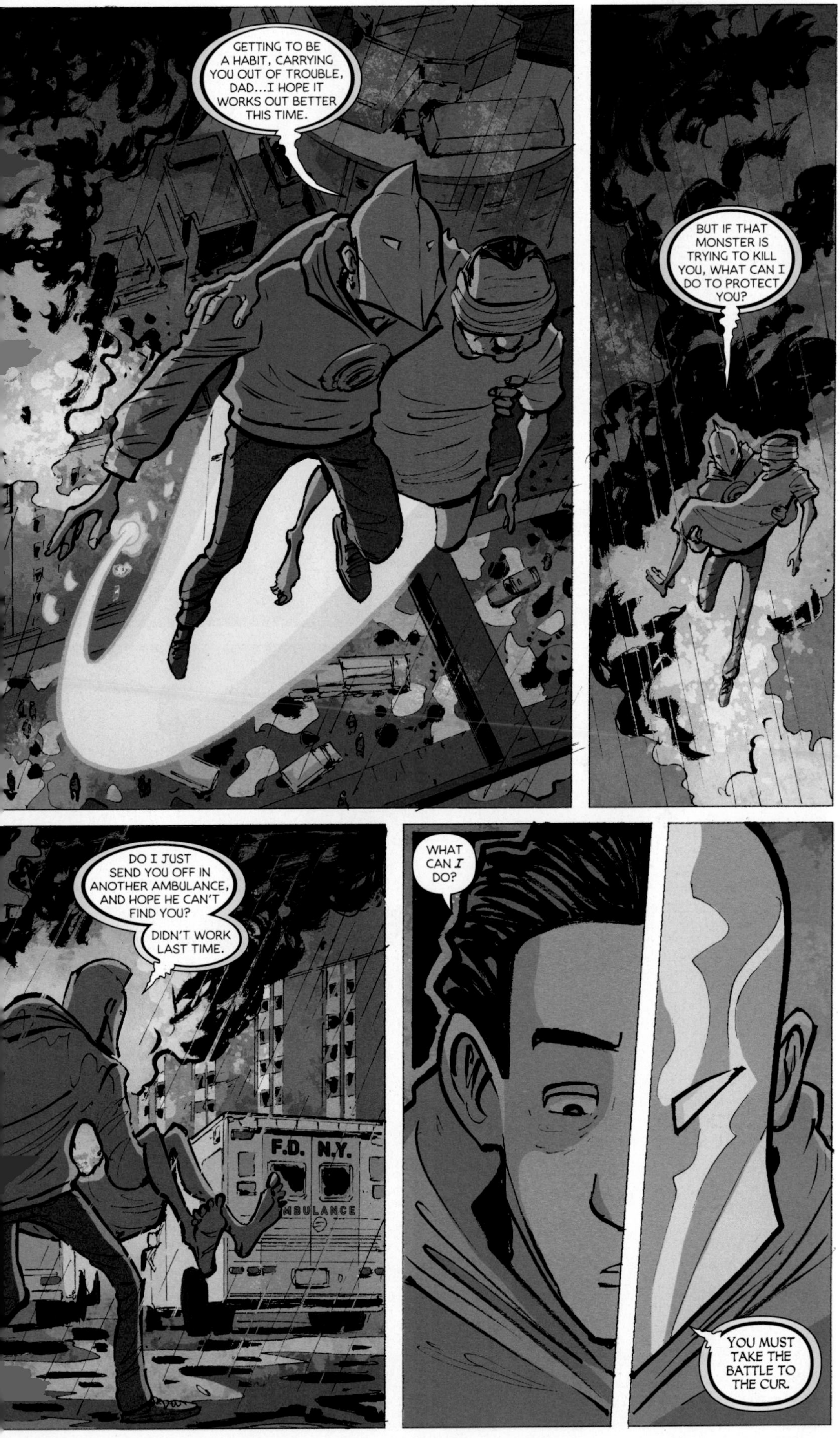
GETTING TO BE A HABIT, CARRYING YOU OUT OF TROUBLE, DAD...I HOPE IT WORKS OUT BETTER THIS TIME.
BUT IF THAT MONSTER IS TRYING TO KILL YOU, WHAT CAN I DO TO PROTECT YOU?
DO I JUST SEND YOU OFF IN ANOTHER AMBULANCE, AND HOPE HE CAN'T FIND YOU?
DIDN'T WORK LAST TIME.
F.D. N.Y.
AMBULANCE
WHAT CAN *I* DO?
YOU MUST TAKE THE BATTLE TO THE CUR.

NOT SURE IF I'M TALKING TO MYSELF, OR FIGHTING OFF BEING POSSESSED.

NOTE TO SELF: LOOK UP SCHIZOPHRENIA IN THE DSM-5...AND THE ADDRESS OF A GOOD EXORCIST!

KRRRUMBLLL

BUT NOT RIGHT NOW.

SORRY, DAD--YOU'LL HAVE TO COME ALONG FOR THE RIDE.

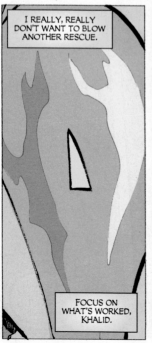

I REALLY, REALLY DON'T WANT TO BLOW ANOTHER RESCUE.

FOCUS ON WHAT'S WORKED, KHALID.

FWOOOOOSH!

DID IT

LIKE BLOWING OUT A BIRTHDAY CAKE CANDLE--EXCEPT I'M MAKING SURE THE GLASS ALL GOES INSIDE, NOT ON THE PEOPLE BELOW.

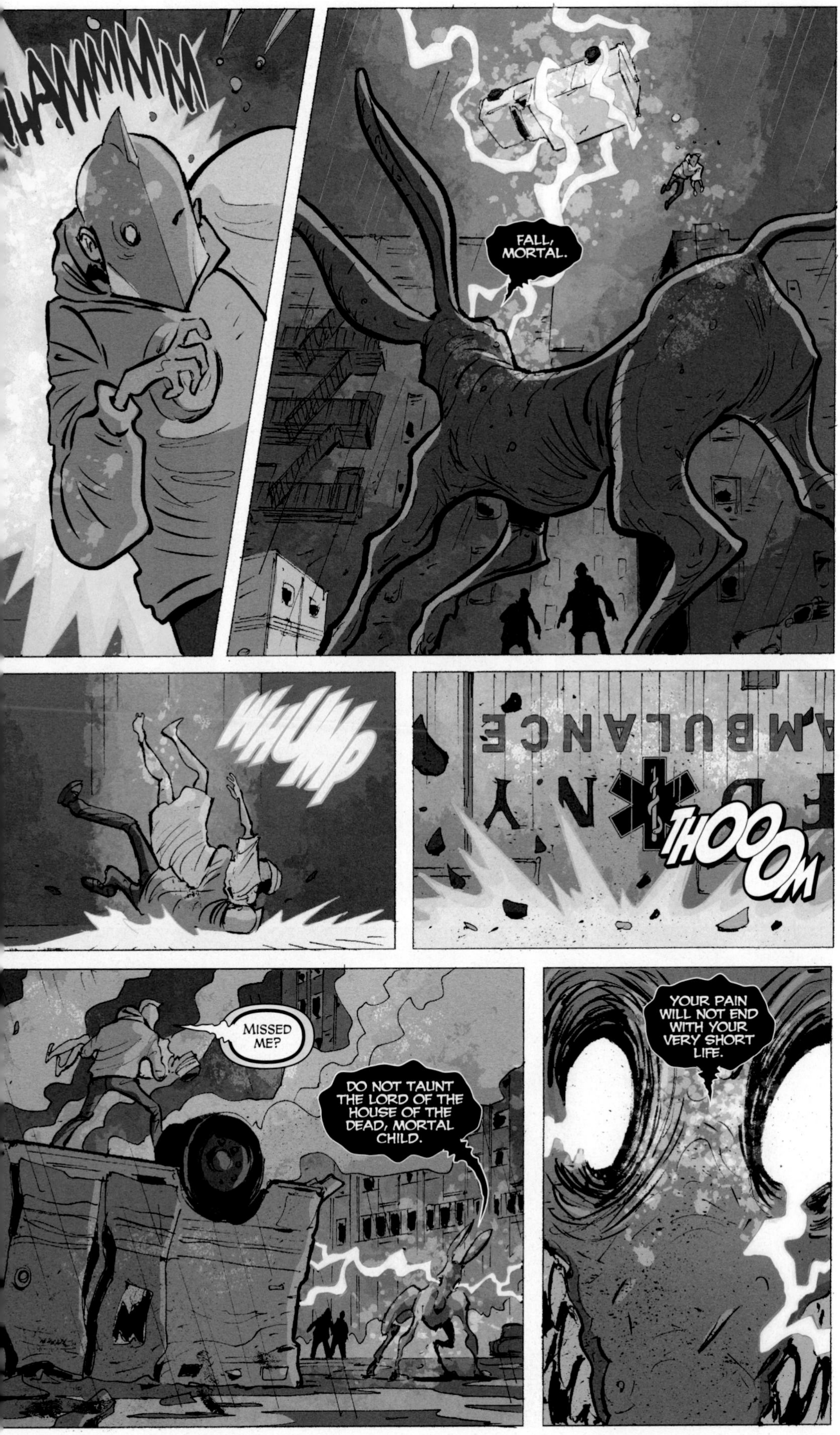
HAMMMMM
FALL, MORTAL.
WHUMP
AMBULANCE
THOOOM
MISSED ME?
DO NOT TAUNT THE LORD OF THE HOUSE OF THE DEAD, MORTAL CHILD.
YOUR PAIN WILL NOT END WITH YOUR VERY SHORT LIFE.

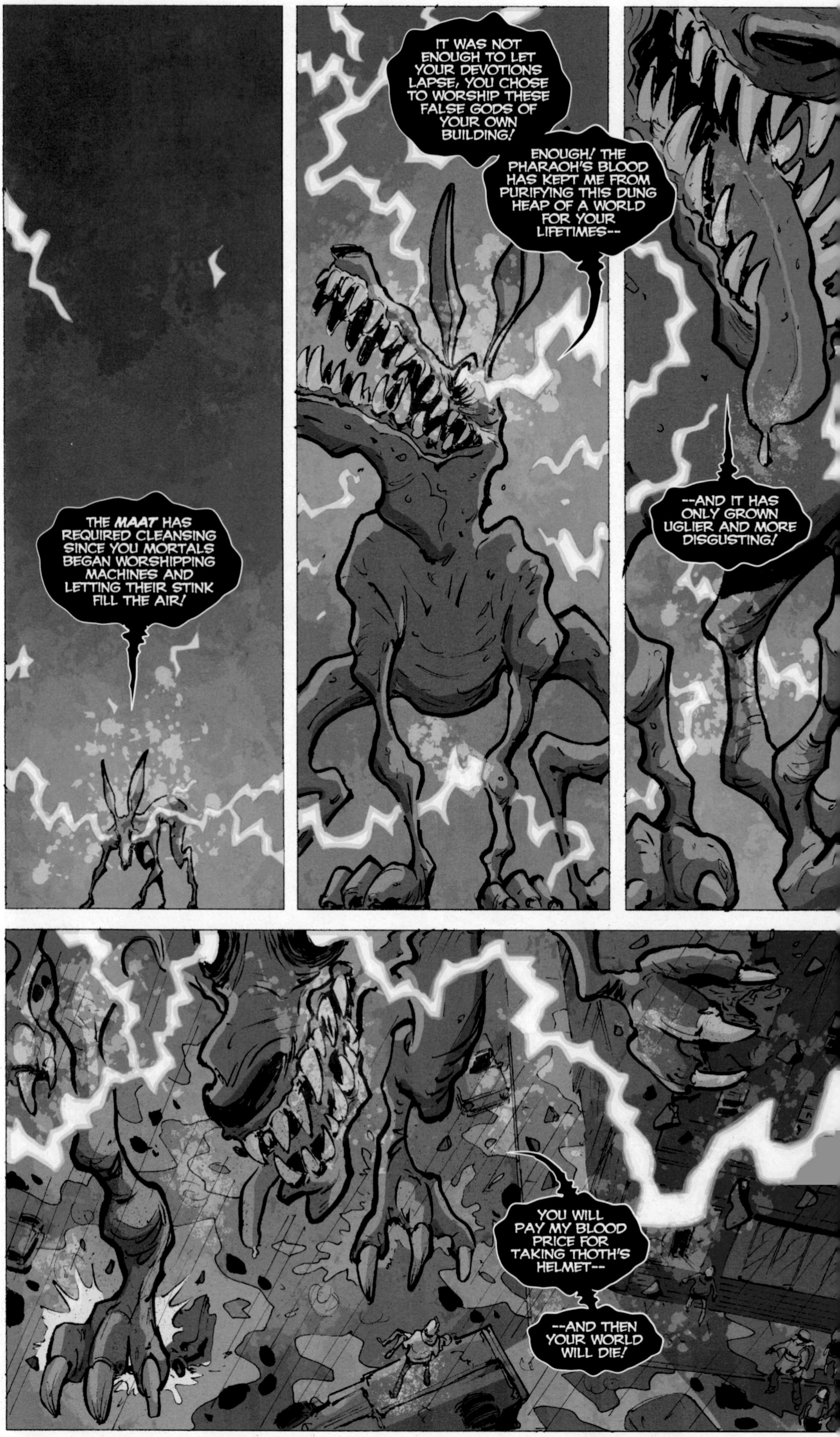
THE *MAAT* HAS REQUIRED CLEANSING SINCE YOU MORTALS BEGAN WORSHIPPING MACHINES AND LETTING THEIR STINK FILL THE AIR!
IT WAS NOT ENOUGH TO LET YOUR DEVOTIONS LAPSE, YOU CHOSE TO WORSHIP THESE FALSE GODS OF YOUR OWN BUILDING!
ENOUGH! THE PHARAOH'S BLOOD HAS KEPT ME FROM PURIFYING THIS DUNG HEAP OF A WORLD FOR YOUR LIFETIMES--
--AND IT HAS ONLY GROWN UGLIER AND MORE DISGUSTING!
YOU WILL PAY MY BLOOD PRICE FOR TAKING THOTH'S HELMET--
--AND THEN YOUR WORLD WILL DIE!

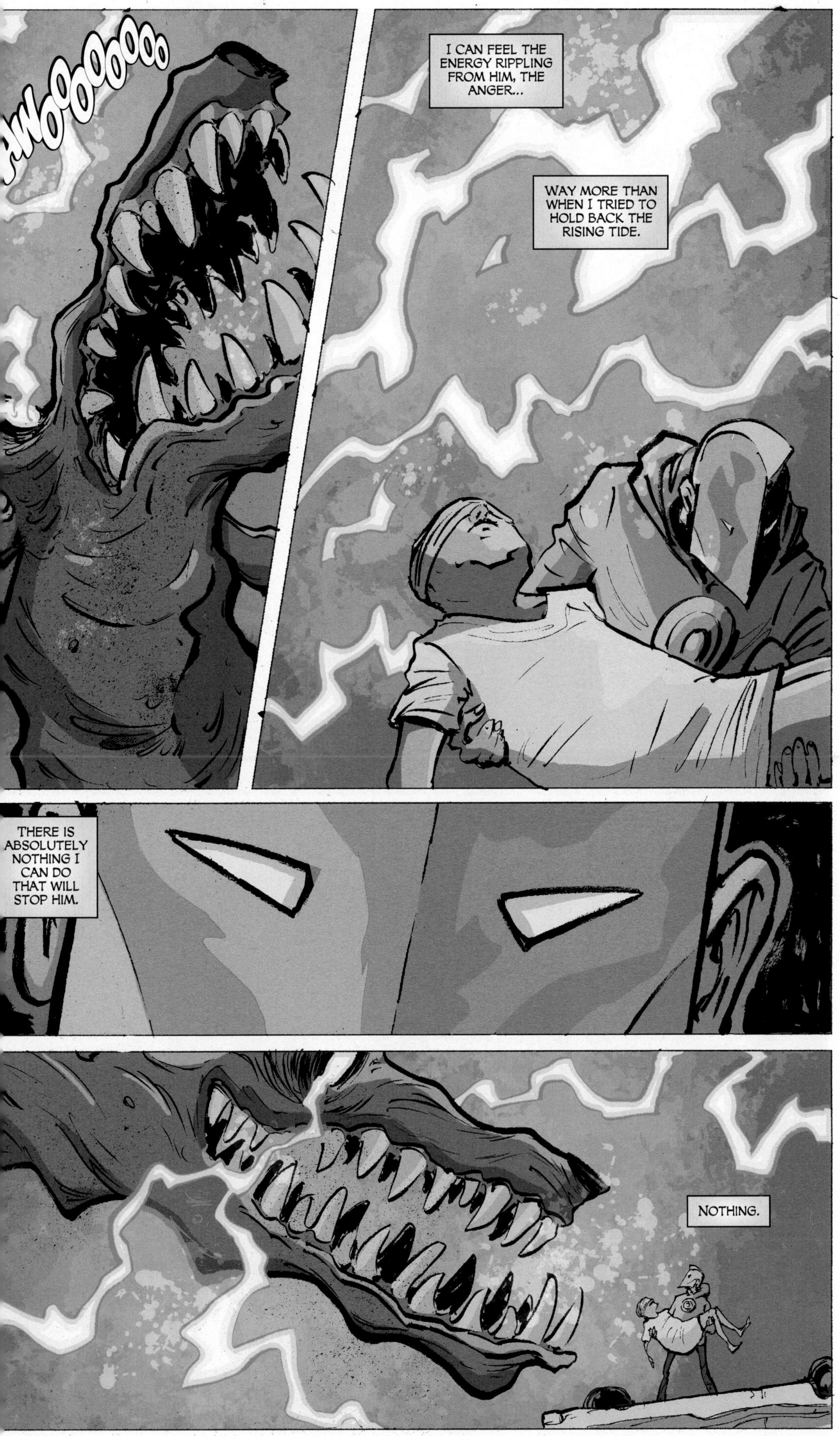
AWOOOOOOOO
I CAN FEEL THE ENERGY RIPPLING FROM HIM, THE ANGER...
WAY MORE THAN WHEN I TRIED TO HOLD BACK THE RISING TIDE.
THERE IS ABSOLUTELY NOTHING I CAN DO THAT WILL STOP HIM.
NOTHING.

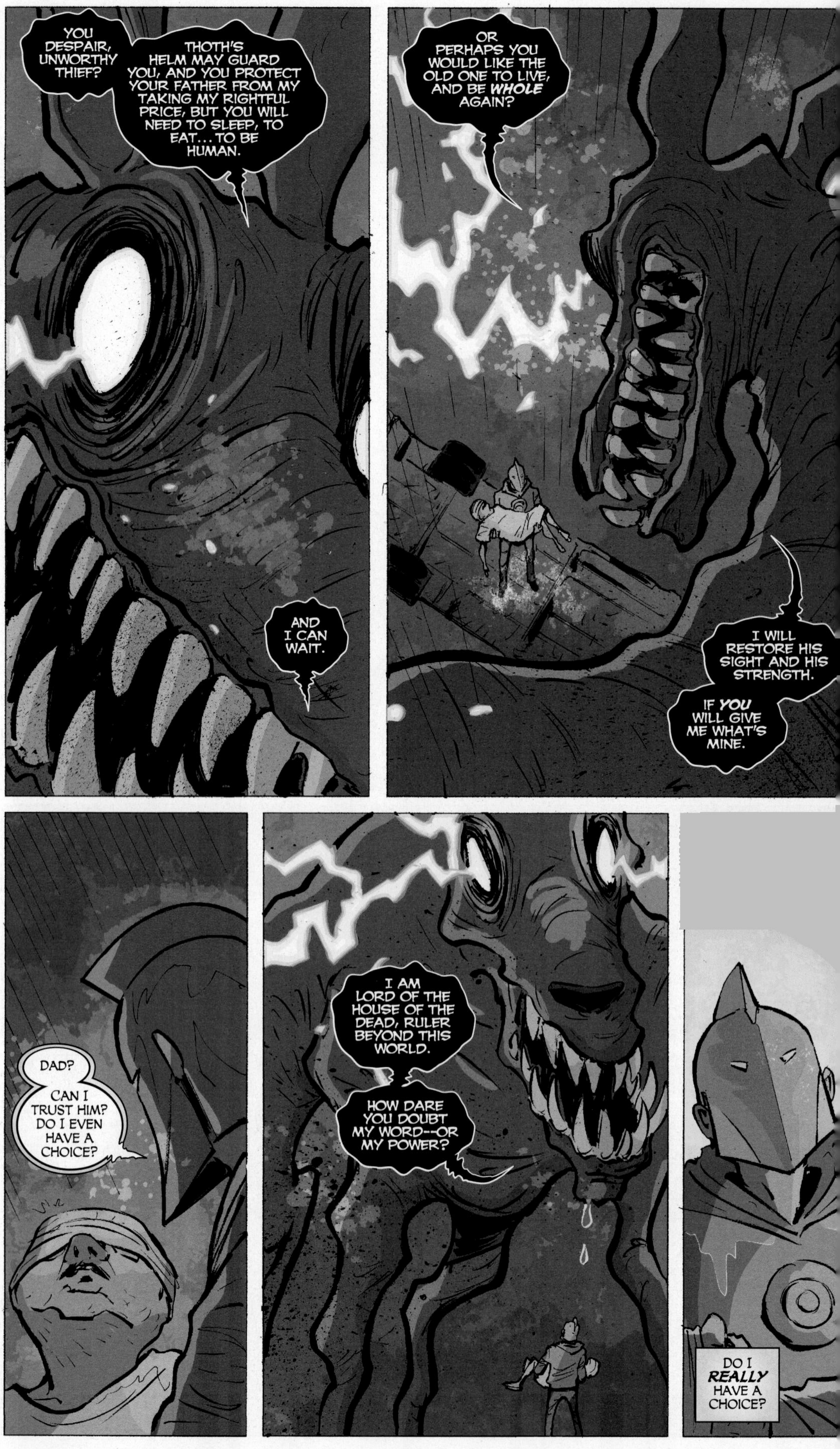

YOU DESPAIR, UNWORTHY THIEF?
THOTH'S HELM MAY GUARD YOU, AND YOU PROTECT YOUR FATHER FROM MY TAKING MY RIGHTFUL PRICE, BUT YOU WILL NEED TO SLEEP, TO EAT... TO BE HUMAN.
AND I CAN WAIT.
OR PERHAPS YOU WOULD LIKE THE OLD ONE TO LIVE, AND BE *WHOLE* AGAIN?
I WILL RESTORE HIS SIGHT AND HIS STRENGTH.
IF *YOU* WILL GIVE ME WHAT'S MINE.
DAD?
CAN I TRUST HIM? DO I EVEN HAVE A CHOICE?
I AM LORD OF THE HOUSE OF THE DEAD, RULER BEYOND THIS WORLD.
HOW DARE YOU DOUBT MY WORD--OR MY POWER?
DO I *REALLY* HAVE A CHOICE?

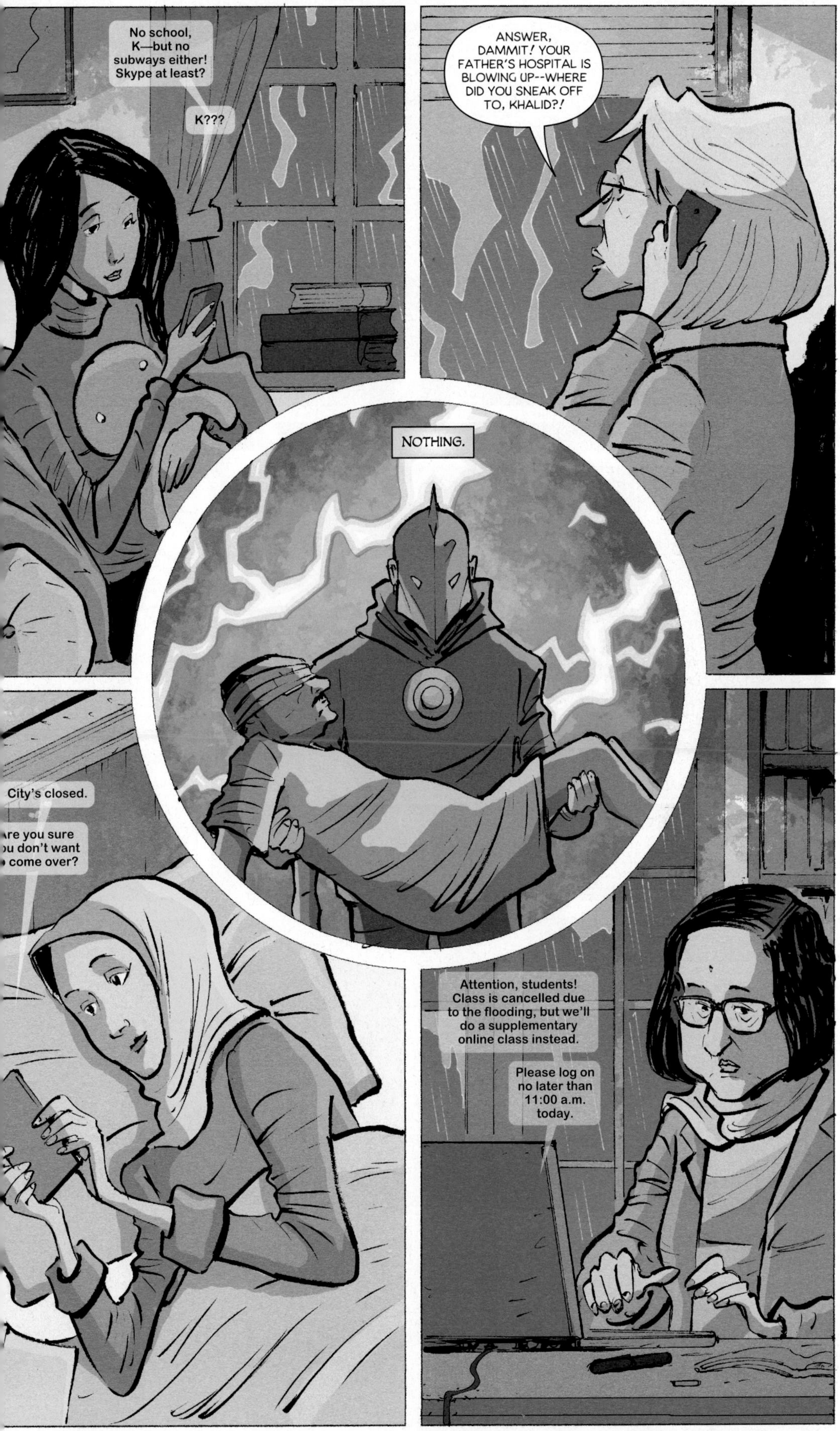
No school, K—but no subways either! Skype at least?
K???
ANSWER, DAMMIT! YOUR FATHER'S HOSPITAL IS BLOWING UP--WHERE DID YOU SNEAK OFF TO, KHALID?!
NOTHING.
City's closed.
Attention, students! Class is cancelled due to the flooding, but we'll do a supplementary online class instead.
Please log on no later than 11:00 a.m. today.

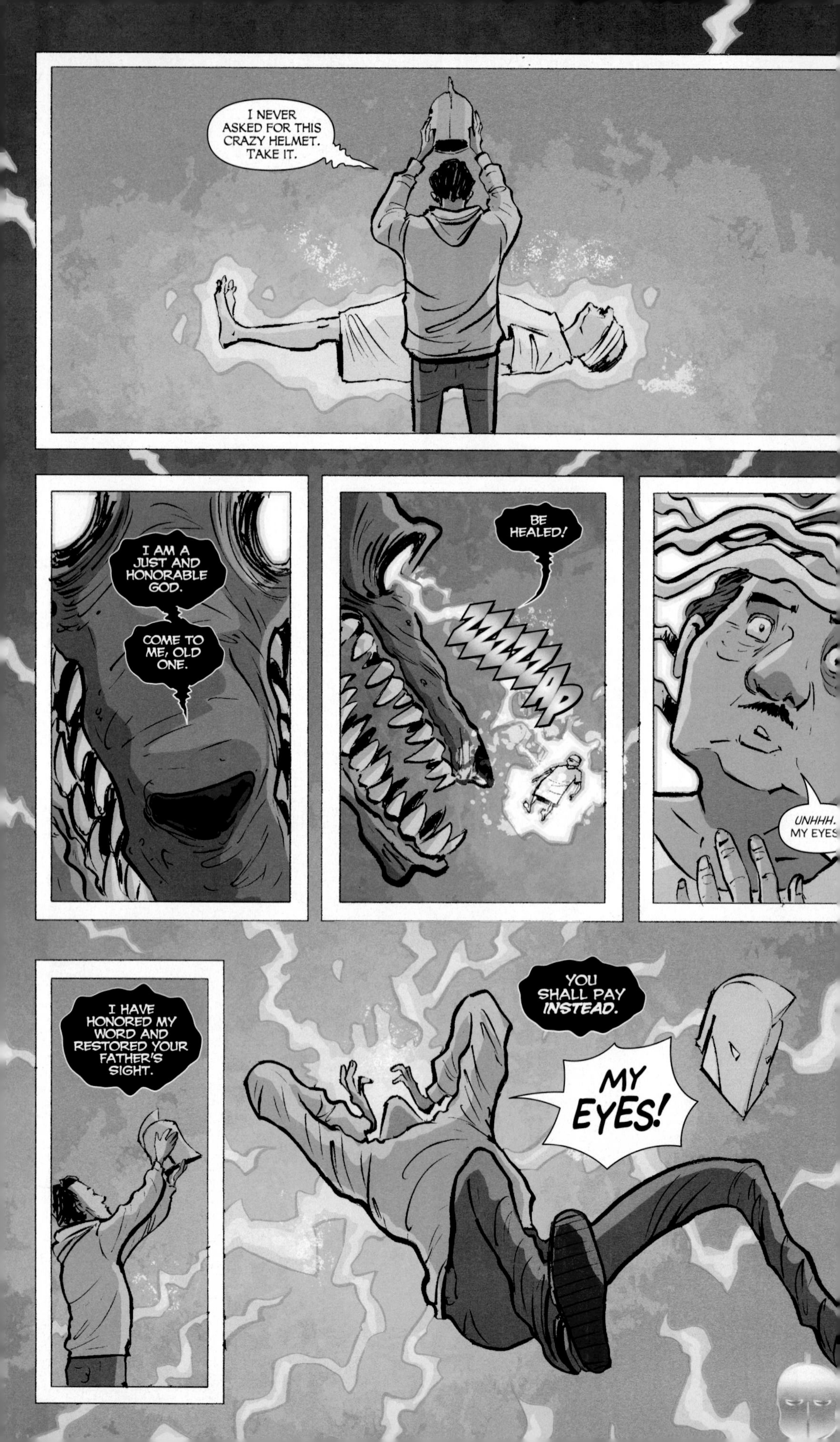
I NEVER ASKED FOR THIS CRAZY HELMET. TAKE IT.
I AM A JUST AND HONORABLE GOD.
COME TO ME, OLD ONE.
BE HEALED!
ZZZZZAP
UNHHH. MY EYES
I HAVE HONORED MY WORD AND RESTORED YOUR FATHER'S SIGHT.
YOU SHALL PAY INSTEAD.
MY EYES!

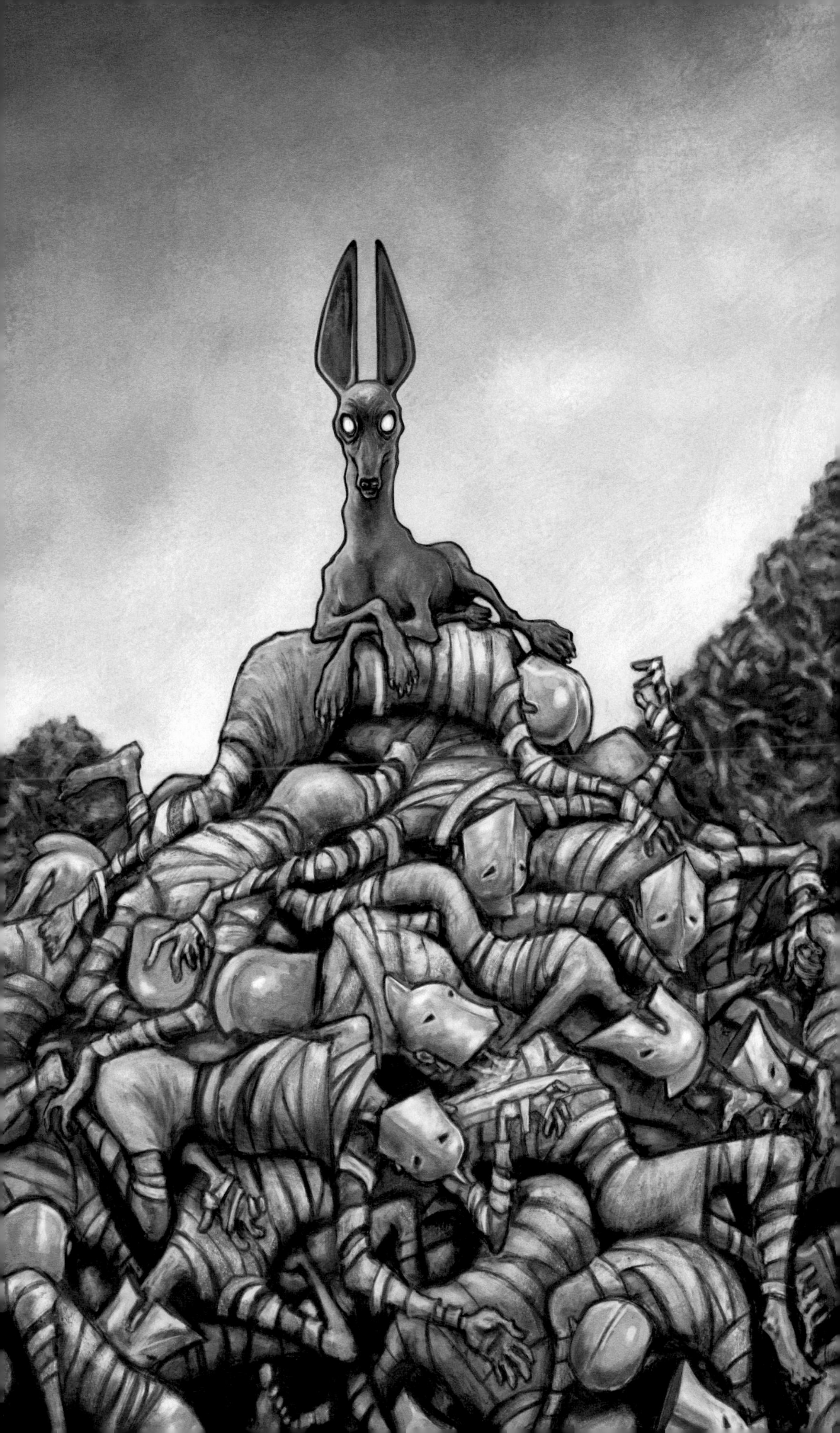

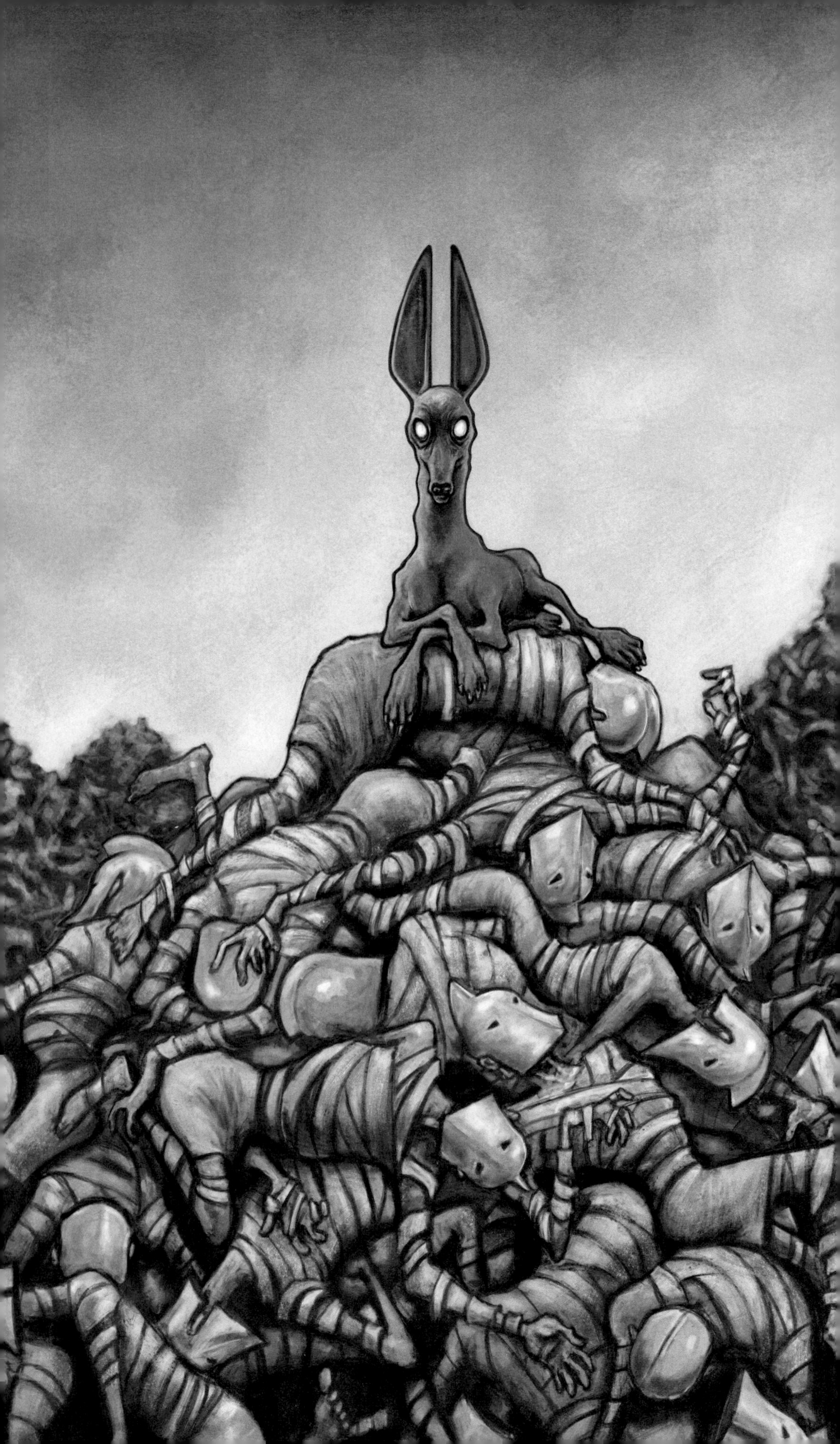

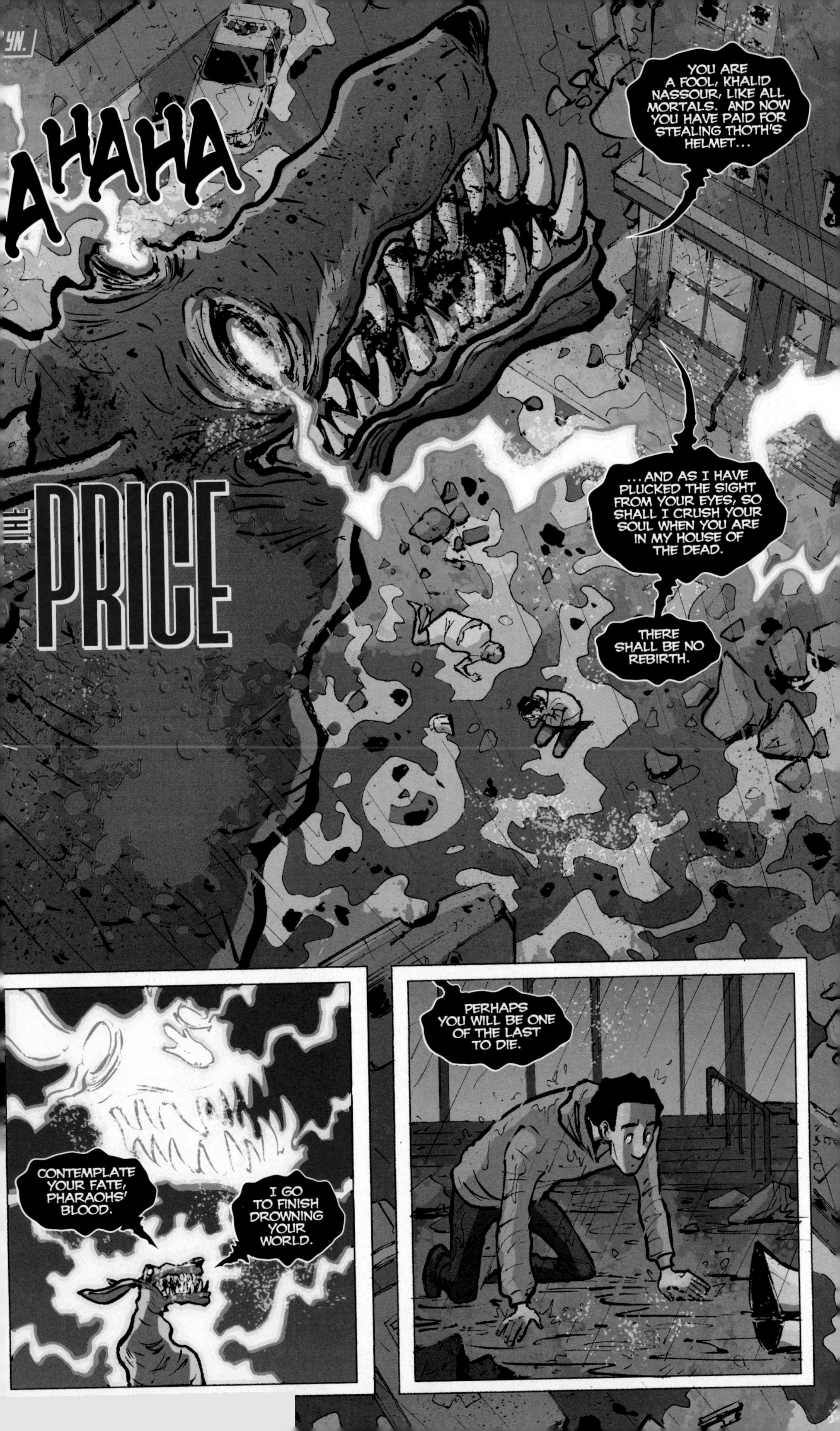
AHAHA
YOU ARE A FOOL, KHALID NASSOUR, LIKE ALL MORTALS. AND NOW YOU HAVE PAID FOR STEALING THOTH'S HELMET...
...AND AS I HAVE PLUCKED THE SIGHT FROM YOUR EYES, SO SHALL I CRUSH YOUR SOUL WHEN YOU ARE IN MY HOUSE OF THE DEAD.
THERE SHALL BE NO REBIRTH.
THE PRICE
CONTEMPLATE YOUR FATE, PHARAOHS' BLOOD.
I GO TO FINISH DROWNING YOUR WORLD.
PERHAPS YOU WILL BE ONE OF THE LAST TO DIE.

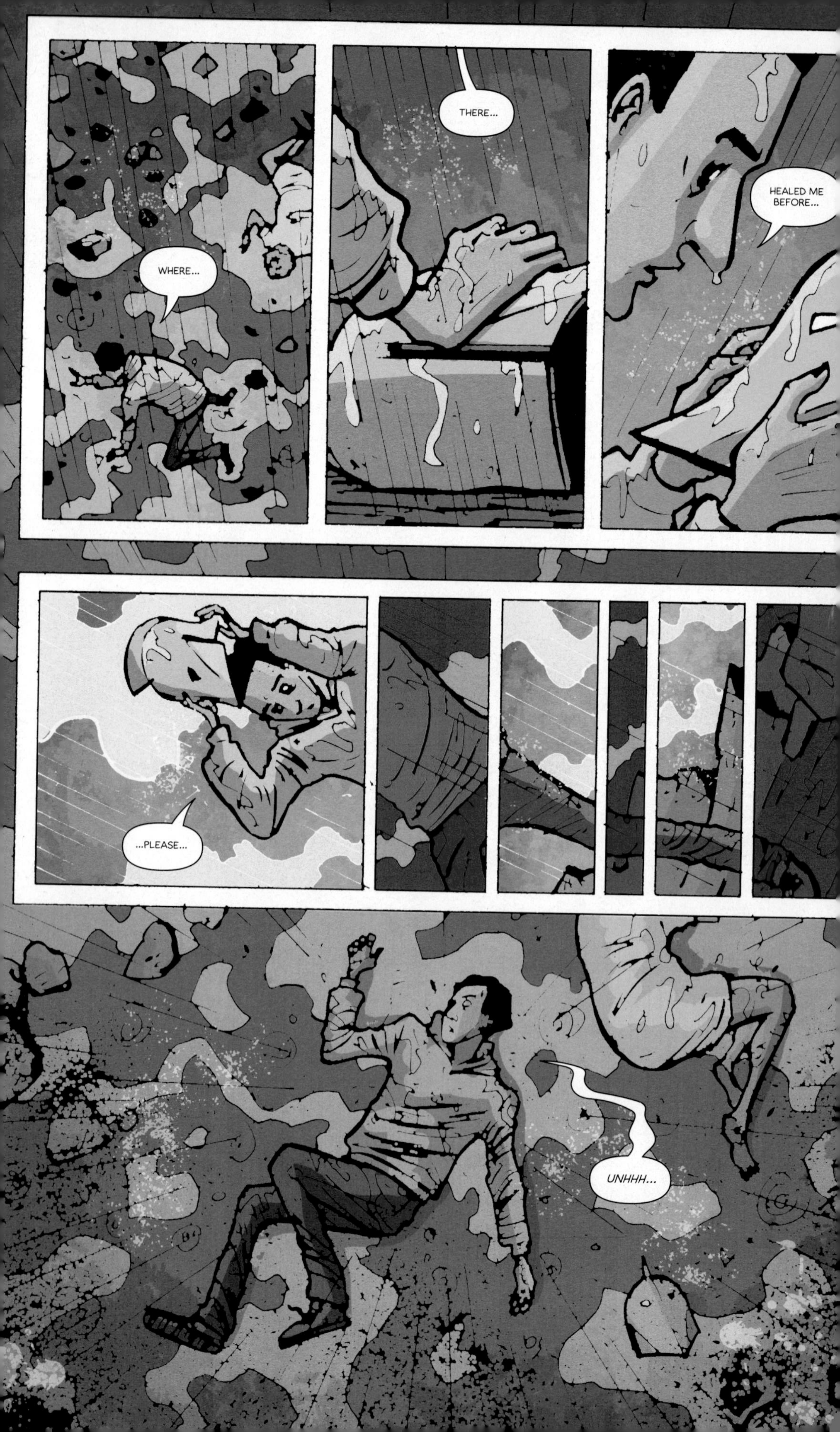
WHERE...
THERE...
HEALED ME BEFORE...
...PLEASE...
UNHHH...

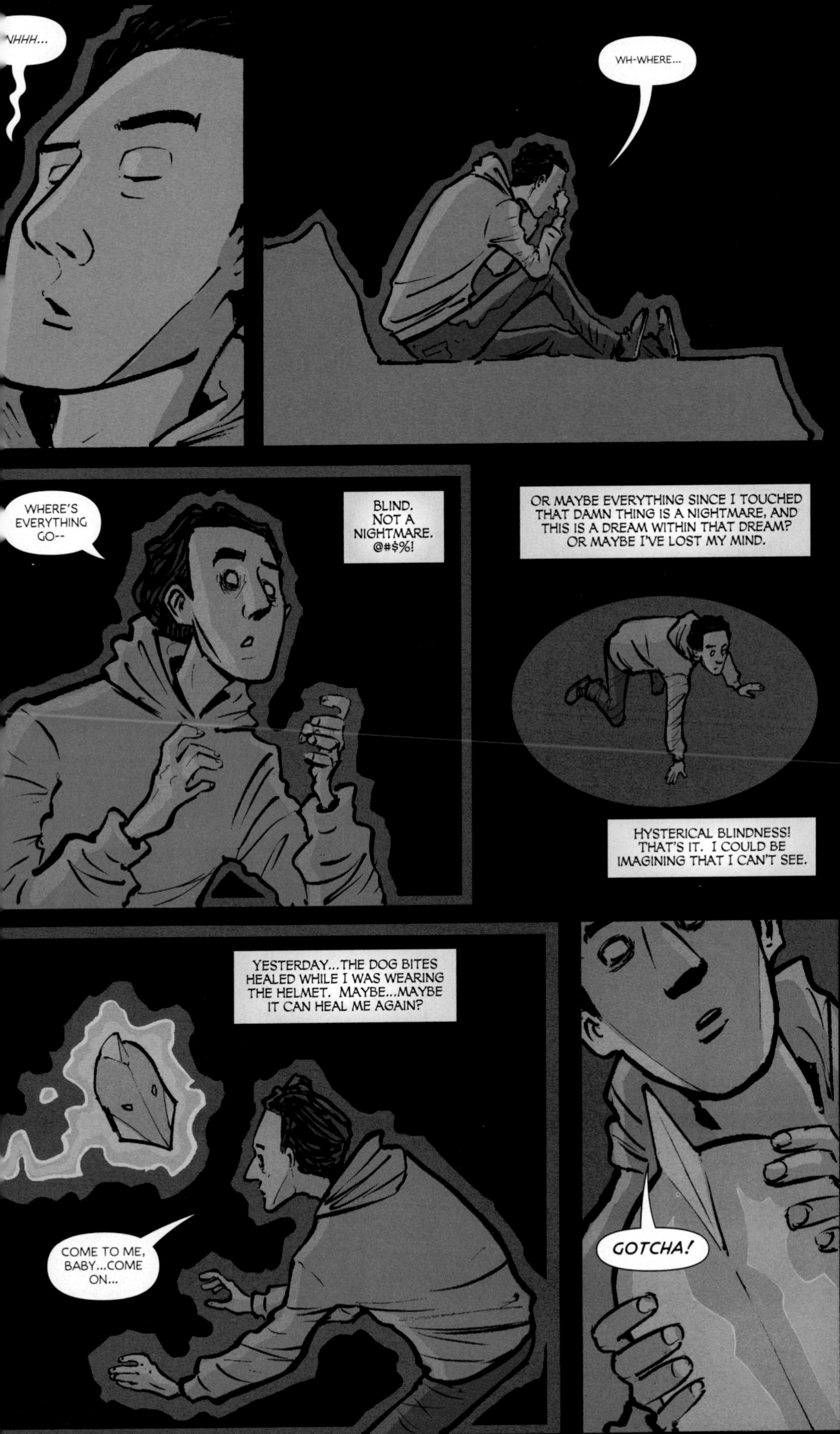
NHHH...
WH-WHERE...
WHERE'S EVERYTHING GO--
BLIND. NOT A NIGHTMARE. @#$%!
OR MAYBE EVERYTHING SINCE I TOUCHED THAT DAMN THING IS A NIGHTMARE, AND THIS IS A DREAM WITHIN THAT DREAM? OR MAYBE I'VE LOST MY MIND.
HYSTERICAL BLINDNESS! THAT'S IT. I COULD BE IMAGINING THAT I CAN'T SEE.
YESTERDAY...THE DOG BITES HEALED WHILE I WAS WEARING THE HELMET. MAYBE...MAYBE IT CAN HEAL ME AGAIN?
COME TO ME, BABY...COME ON...
GOTCHA!

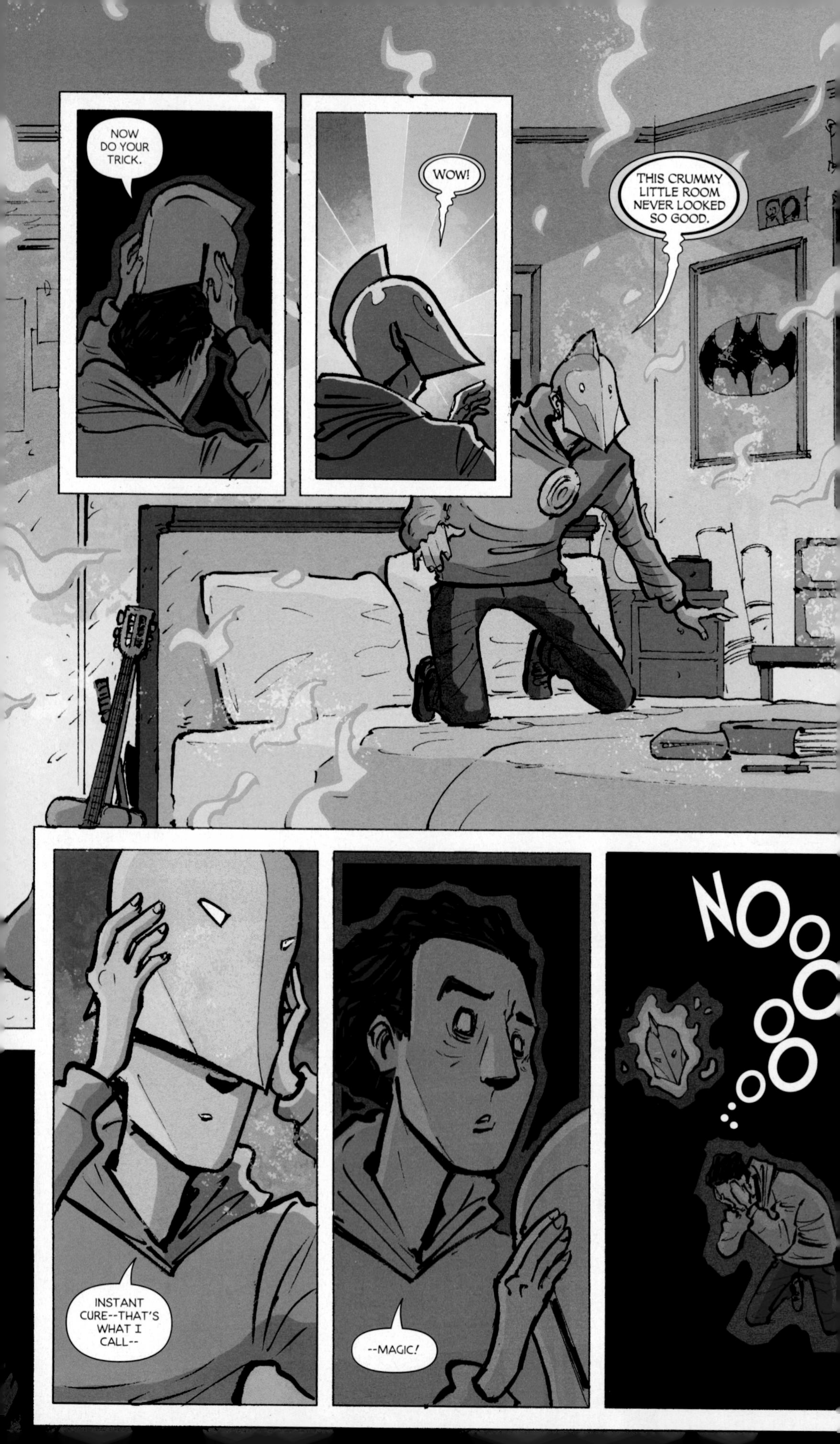
NOW DO YOUR TRICK.
WOW!
THIS CRUMMY LITTLE ROOM NEVER LOOKED SO GOOD.
INSTANT CURE--THAT'S WHAT I CALL--
--MAGIC!
NOOOOOOO

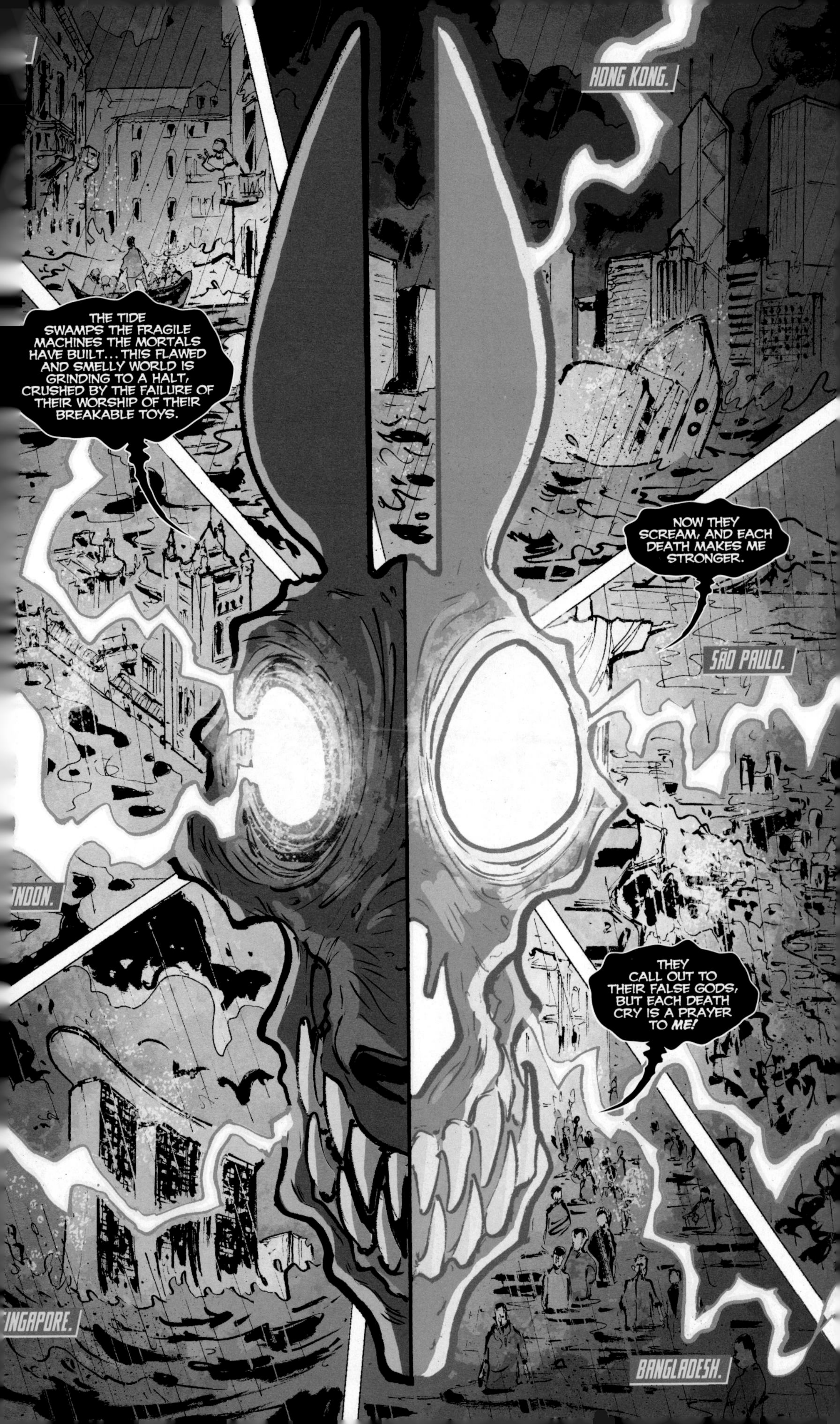
THE TIDE SWAMPS THE FRAGILE MACHINES THE MORTALS HAVE BUILT... THIS FLAWED AND SMELLY WORLD IS GRINDING TO A HALT, CRUSHED BY THE FAILURE OF THEIR WORSHIP OF THEIR BREAKABLE TOYS.
HONG KONG.
NOW THEY SCREAM, AND EACH DEATH MAKES ME STRONGER.
SÃO PAULO.
NDON.
THEY CALL OUT TO THEIR FALSE GODS, BUT EACH DEATH CRY IS A PRAYER TO *ME!*
INGAPORE.
BANGLADESH.

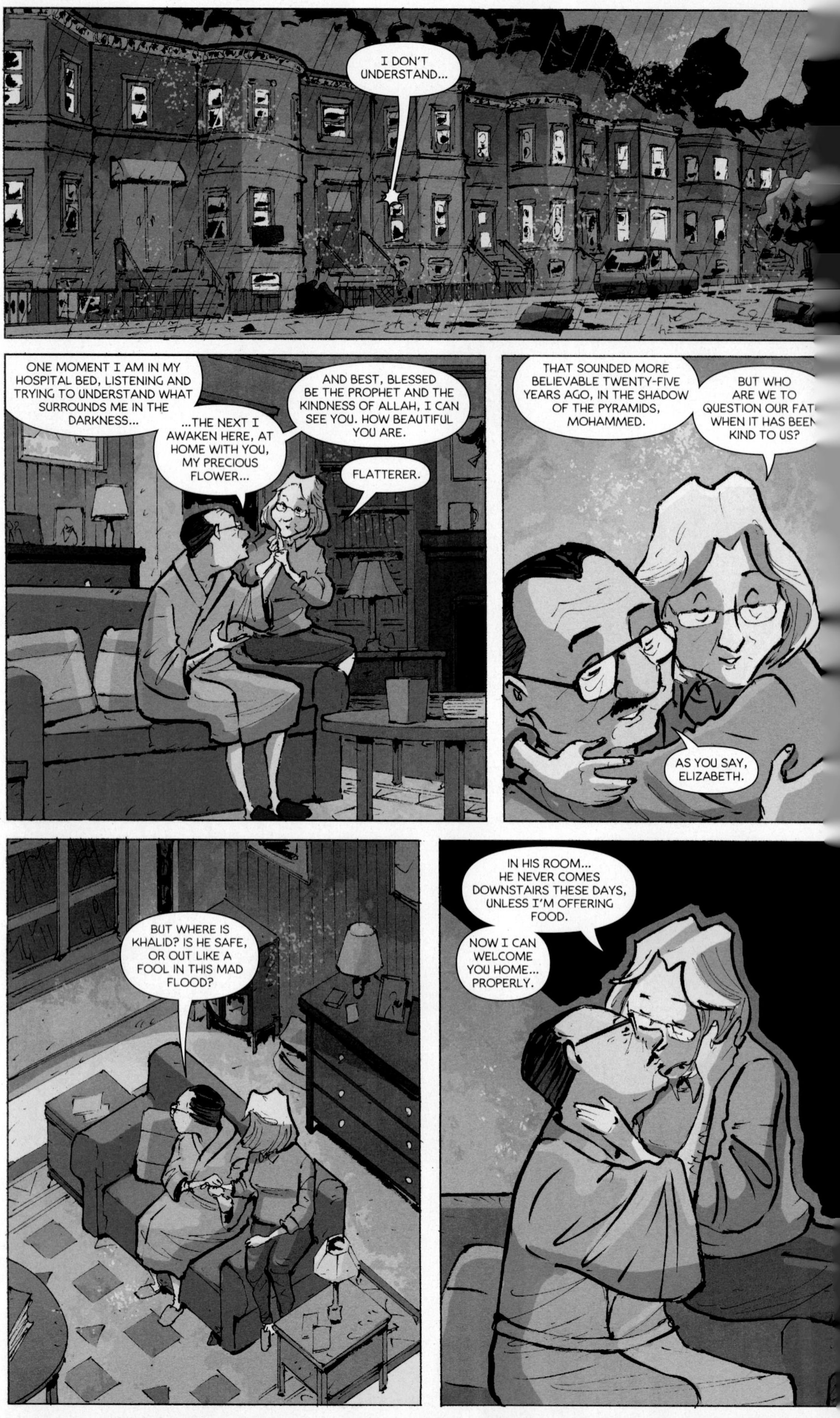
I DON'T UNDERSTAND...
ONE MOMENT I AM IN MY HOSPITAL BED, LISTENING AND TRYING TO UNDERSTAND WHAT SURROUNDS ME IN THE DARKNESS...
...THE NEXT I AWAKEN HERE, AT HOME WITH YOU, MY PRECIOUS FLOWER...
AND BEST, BLESSED BE THE PROPHET AND THE KINDNESS OF ALLAH, I CAN SEE YOU. HOW BEAUTIFUL YOU ARE.
FLATTERER.
THAT SOUNDED MORE BELIEVABLE TWENTY-FIVE YEARS AGO, IN THE SHADOW OF THE PYRAMIDS, MOHAMMED.
BUT WHO ARE WE TO QUESTION OUR FAT WHEN IT HAS BEEN KIND TO US?
AS YOU SAY, ELIZABETH.
BUT WHERE IS KHALID? IS HE SAFE, OR OUT LIKE A FOOL IN THIS MAD FLOOD?
IN HIS ROOM... HE NEVER COMES DOWNSTAIRS THESE DAYS, UNLESS I'M OFFERING FOOD.
NOW I CAN WELCOME YOU HOME... PROPERLY.

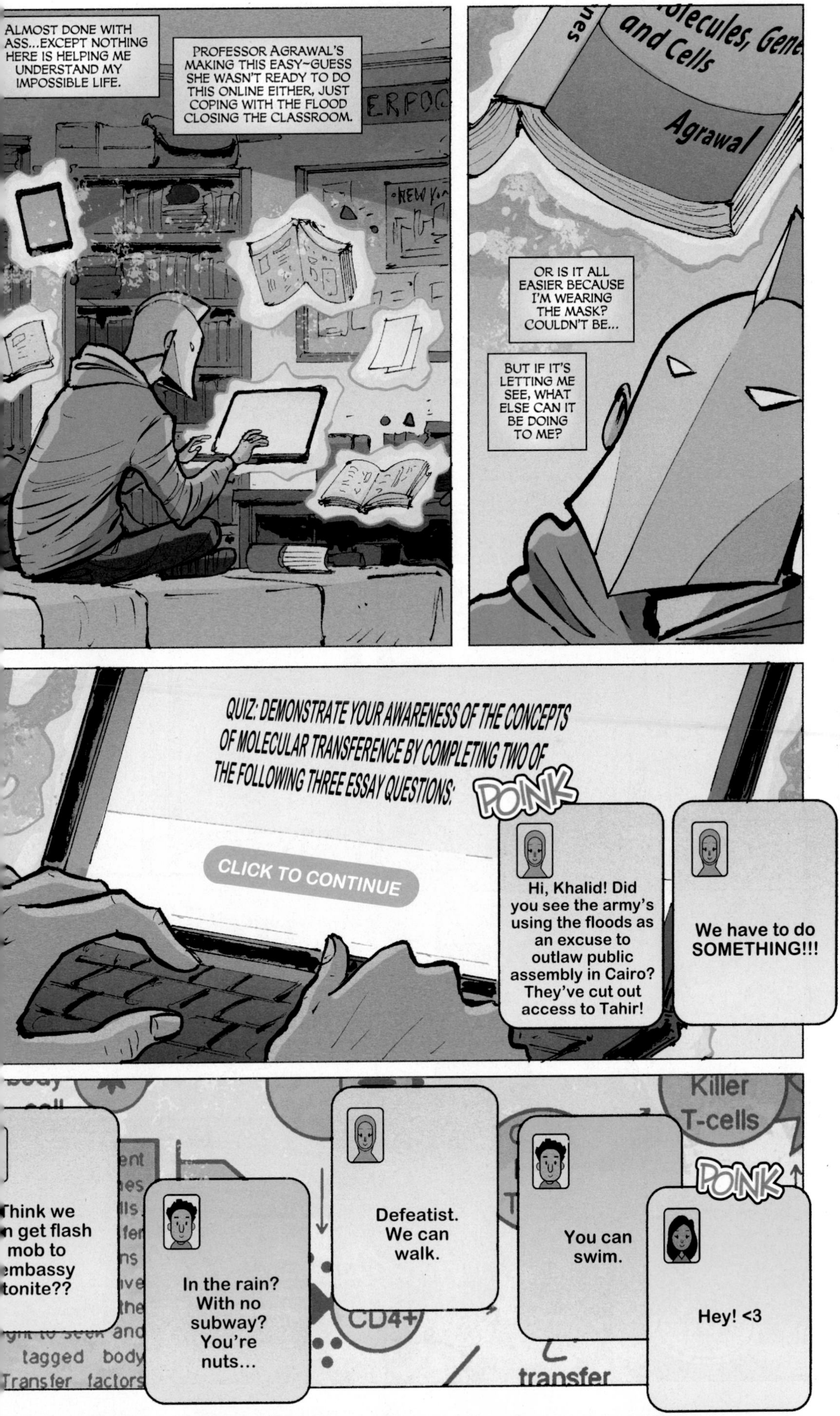
ALMOST DONE WITH ASS...EXCEPT NOTHING HERE IS HELPING ME UNDERSTAND MY IMPOSSIBLE LIFE.
PROFESSOR AGRAWAL'S MAKING THIS EASY~GUESS SHE WASN'T READY TO DO THIS ONLINE EITHER, JUST COPING WITH THE FLOOD CLOSING THE CLASSROOM.
and Cells
Agrawal
OR IS IT ALL EASIER BECAUSE I'M WEARING THE MASK? COULDN'T BE...
BUT IF IT'S LETTING ME SEE, WHAT ELSE CAN IT BE DOING TO ME?
QUIZ: DEMONSTRATE YOUR AWARENESS OF THE CONCEPTS OF MOLECULAR TRANSFERENCE BY COMPLETING TWO OF THE FOLLOWING THREE ESSAY QUESTIONS:
CLICK TO CONTINUE
POINK
Hi, Khalid! Did you see the army's using the floods as an excuse to outlaw public assembly in Cairo? They've cut out access to Tahir!
We have to do SOMETHING!!!
Killer T-cells
CD4+
transfer
Think we n get flash mob to embassy tonite??
In the rain? With no subway? You're nuts...
Defeatist. We can walk.
You can swim.
POINK
Hey! <3

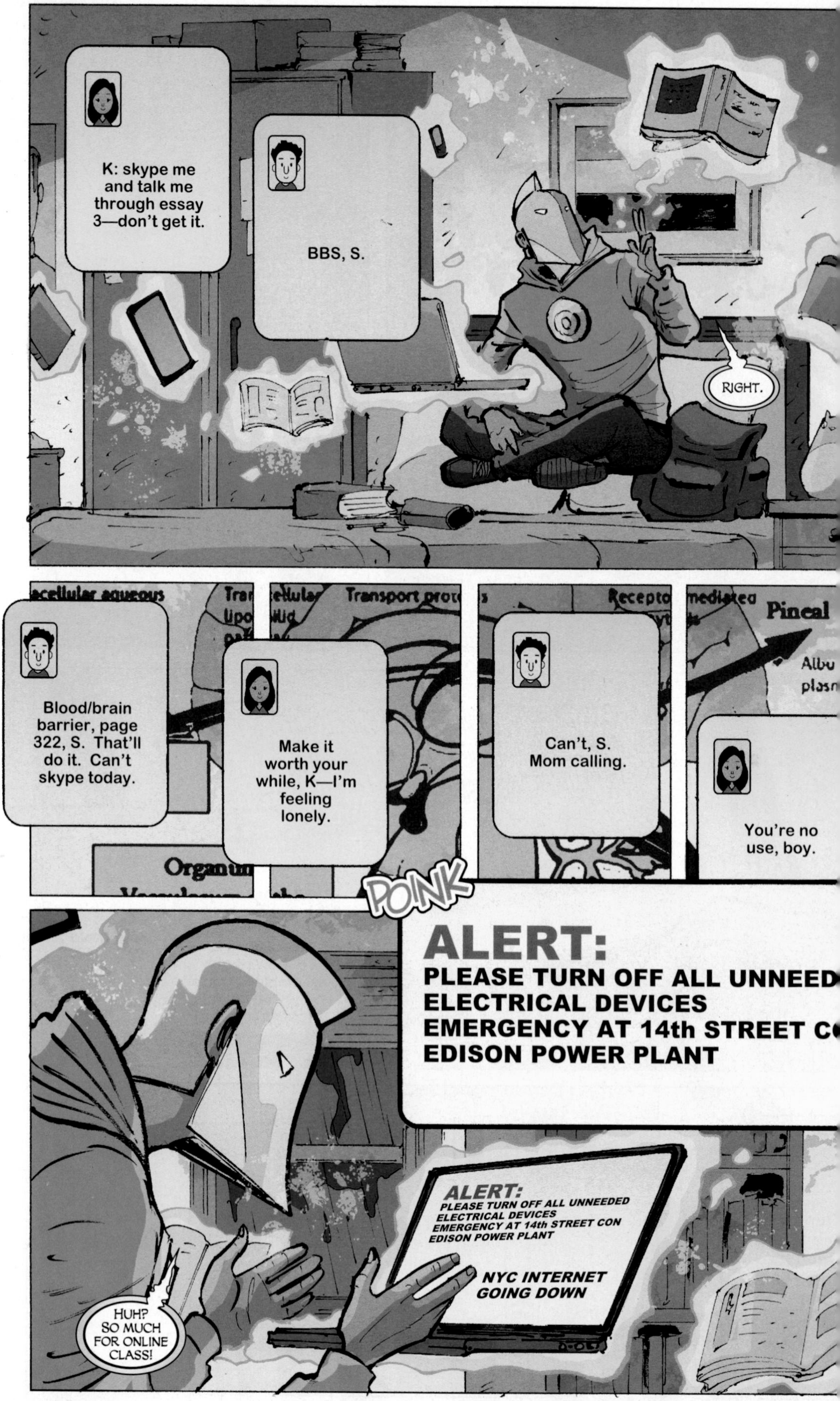
K: skype me and talk me through essay 3—don't get it.
BBS, S.
RIGHT.
Blood/brain barrier, page 322, S. That'll do it. Can't skype today.
Make it worth your while, K—I'm feeling lonely.
Can't, S. Mom calling.
You're no use, boy.
POINK
ALERT:
PLEASE TURN OFF ALL UNNEED
ELECTRICAL DEVICES
EMERGENCY AT 14th STREET C
EDISON POWER PLANT
ALERT:
PLEASE TURN OFF ALL UNNEEDED
ELECTRICAL DEVICES
EMERGENCY AT 14th STREET CON
EDISON POWER PLANT
NYC INTERNET GOING DOWN
HUH? SO MUCH FOR ONLINE CLASS!

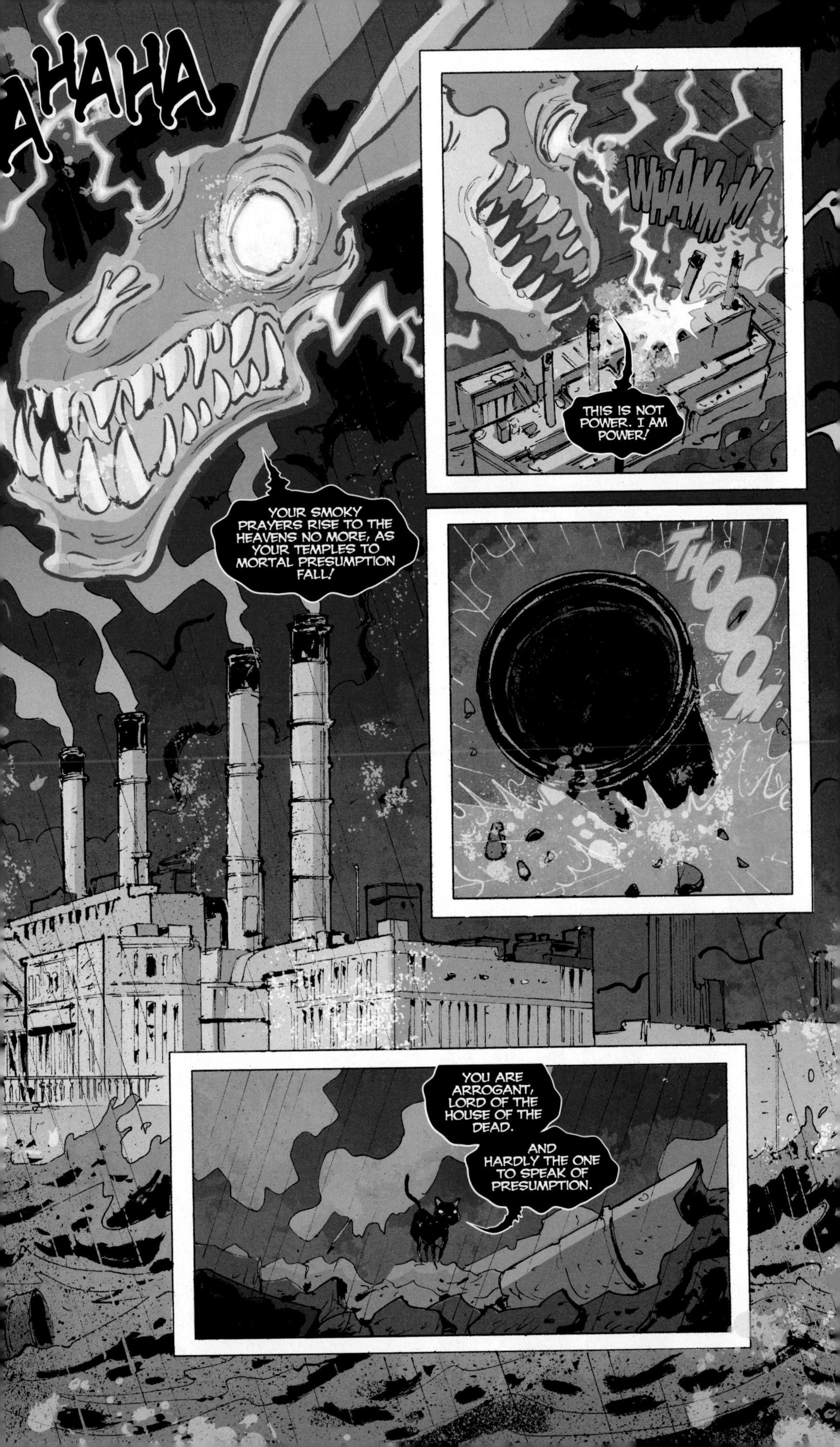
AHAHA
YOUR SMOKY PRAYERS RISE TO THE HEAVENS NO MORE, AS YOUR TEMPLES TO MORTAL PRESUMPTION FALL!
WHAMMM
THIS IS NOT POWER. I AM POWER!
THOOOOM
YOU ARE ARROGANT, LORD OF THE HOUSE OF THE DEAD.
AND HARDLY THE ONE TO SPEAK OF PRESUMPTION.

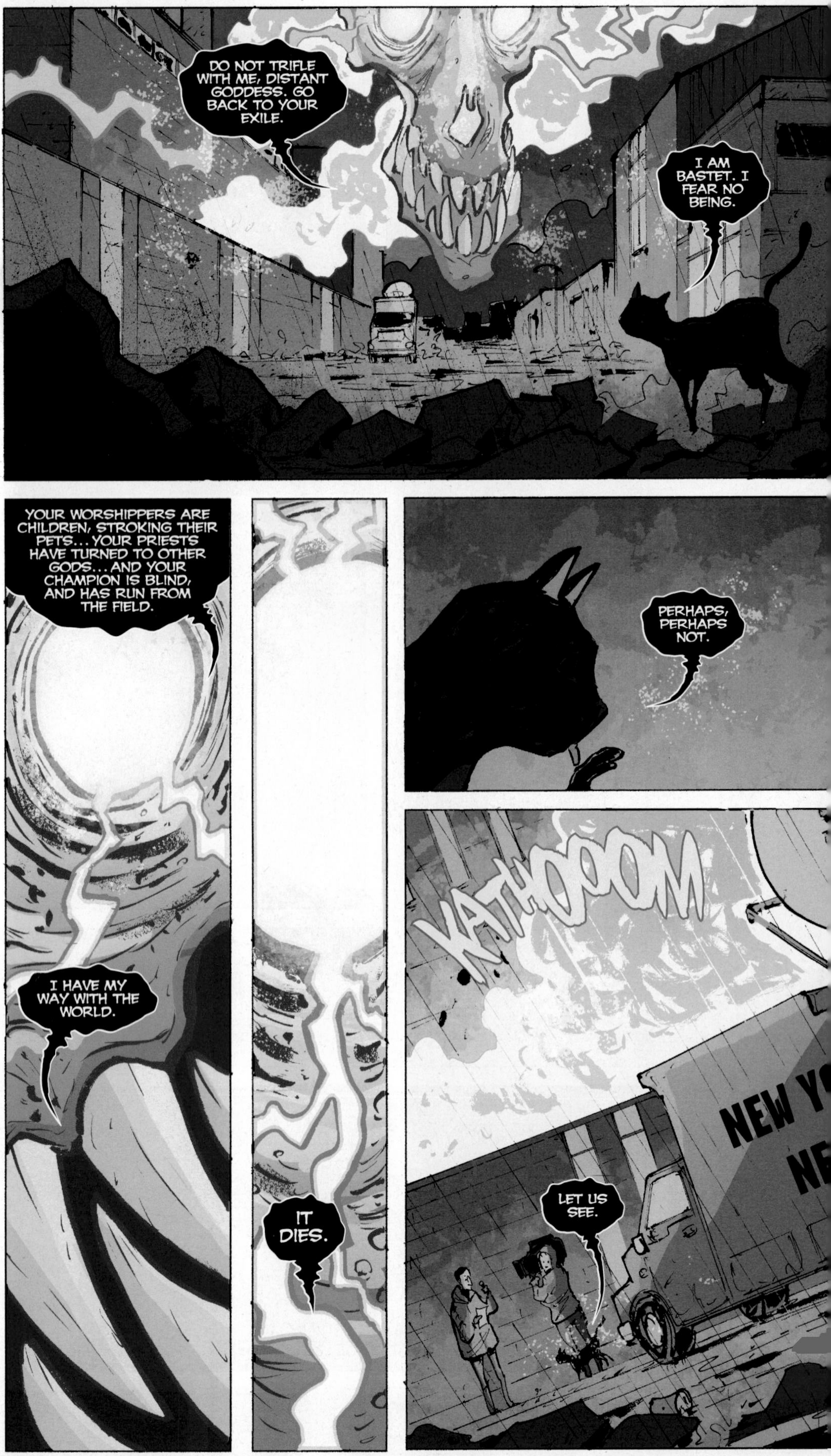
DO NOT TRIFLE WITH ME, DISTANT GODDESS. GO BACK TO YOUR EXILE.
I AM BASTET. I FEAR NO BEING.
YOUR WORSHIPPERS ARE CHILDREN, STROKING THEIR PETS... YOUR PRIESTS HAVE TURNED TO OTHER GODS... AND YOUR CHAMPION IS BLIND, AND HAS RUN FROM THE FIELD.
PERHAPS, PERHAPS NOT.
I HAVE MY WAY WITH THE WORLD.
IT DIES.
KATHOOOM
LET US SEE.

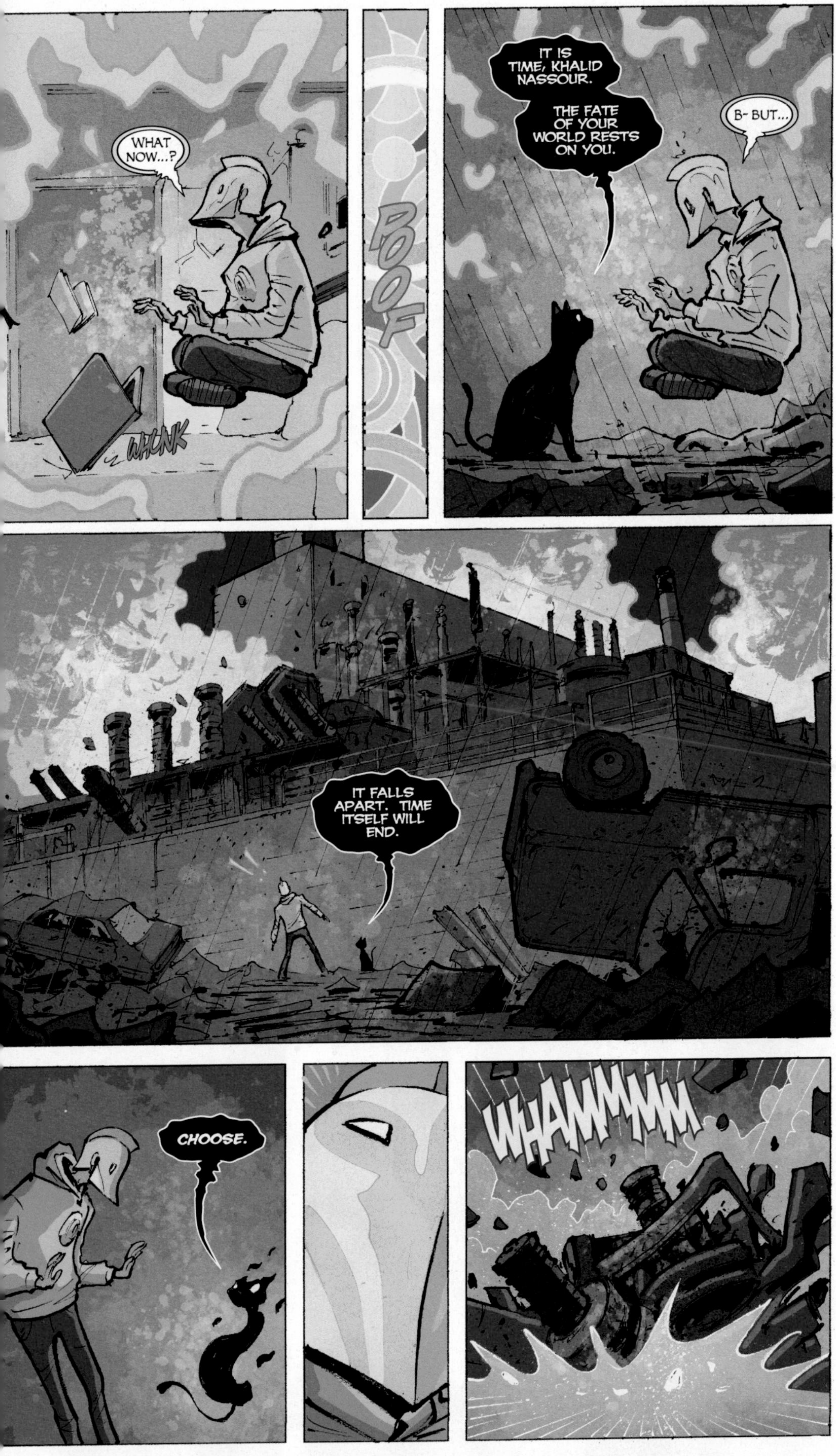
WHAT NOW...?
WHUNK
POOOF
IT IS TIME, KHALID NASSOUR.
THE FATE OF YOUR WORLD RESTS ON YOU.
B- BUT...
IT FALLS APART. TIME ITSELF WILL END.
CHOOSE.
WHAMMMM

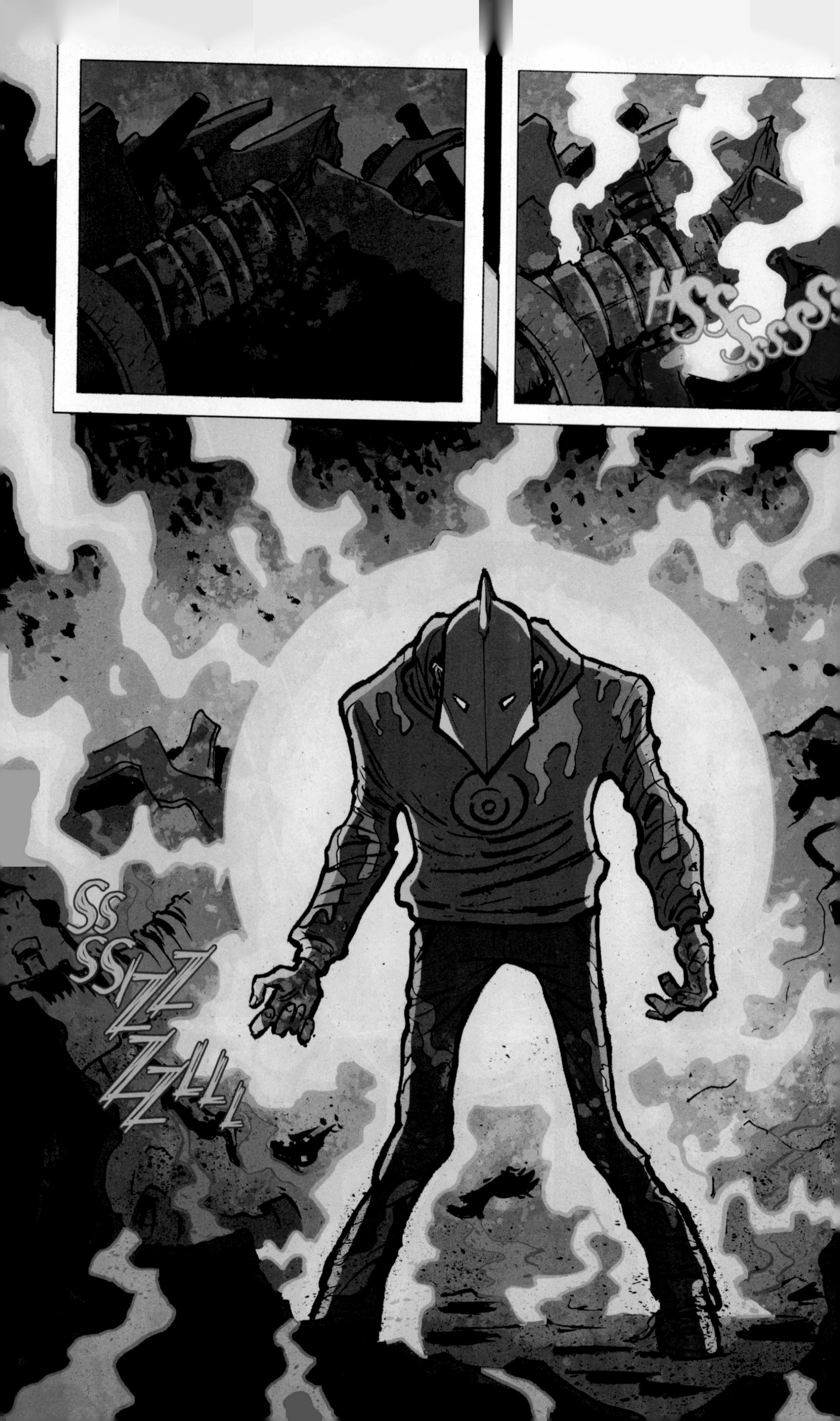
HSSSSSSSS
SSSSSZZZZLLLL

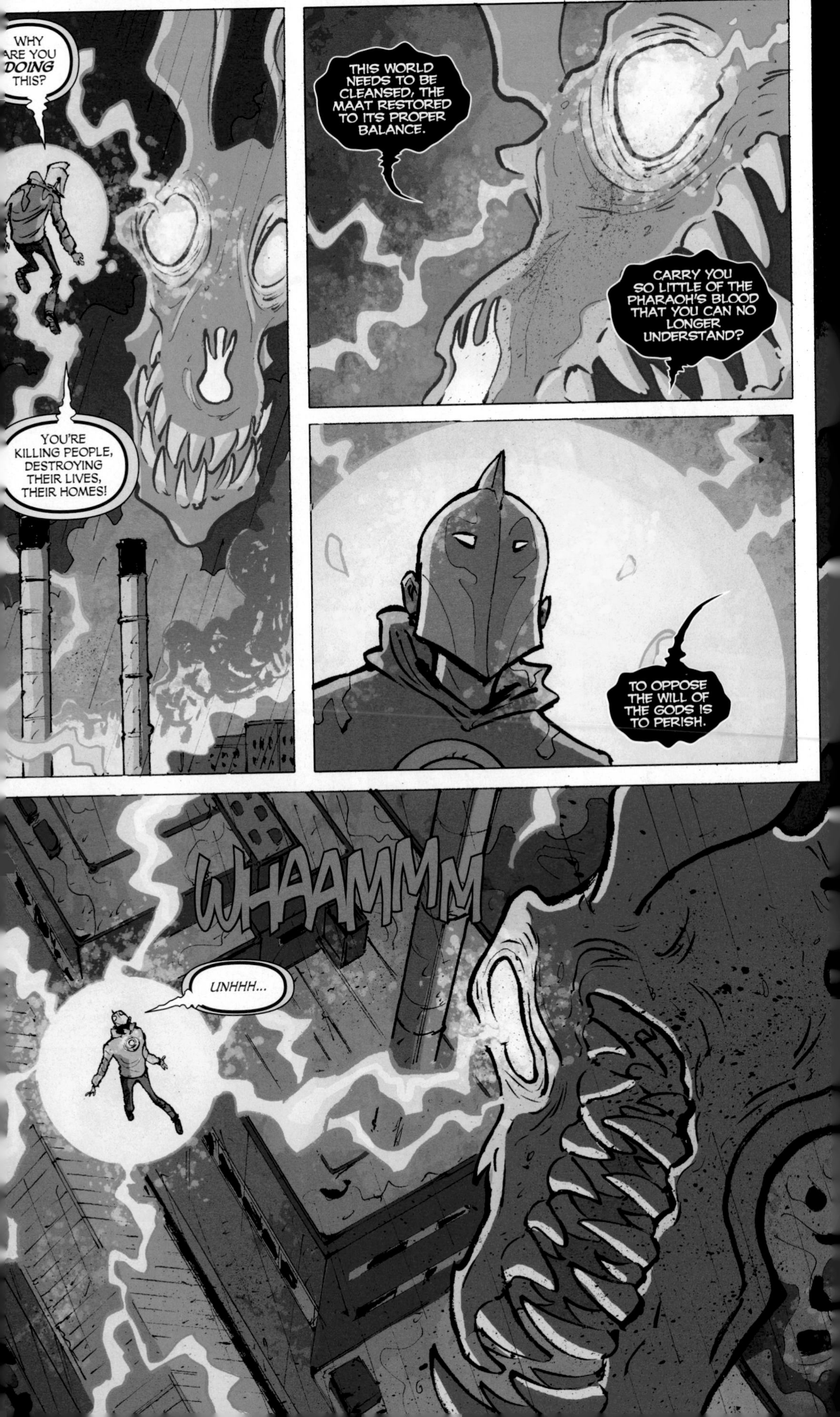

WHY ARE YOU *DOING* THIS?
YOU'RE KILLING PEOPLE, DESTROYING THEIR LIVES, THEIR HOMES!
THIS WORLD NEEDS TO BE CLEANSED, THE MAAT RESTORED TO ITS PROPER BALANCE.
CARRY YOU SO LITTLE OF THE PHARAOH'S BLOOD THAT YOU CAN NO LONGER UNDERSTAND?
TO OPPOSE THE WILL OF THE GODS IS TO PERISH.
WHAAMMM
UNHHH...

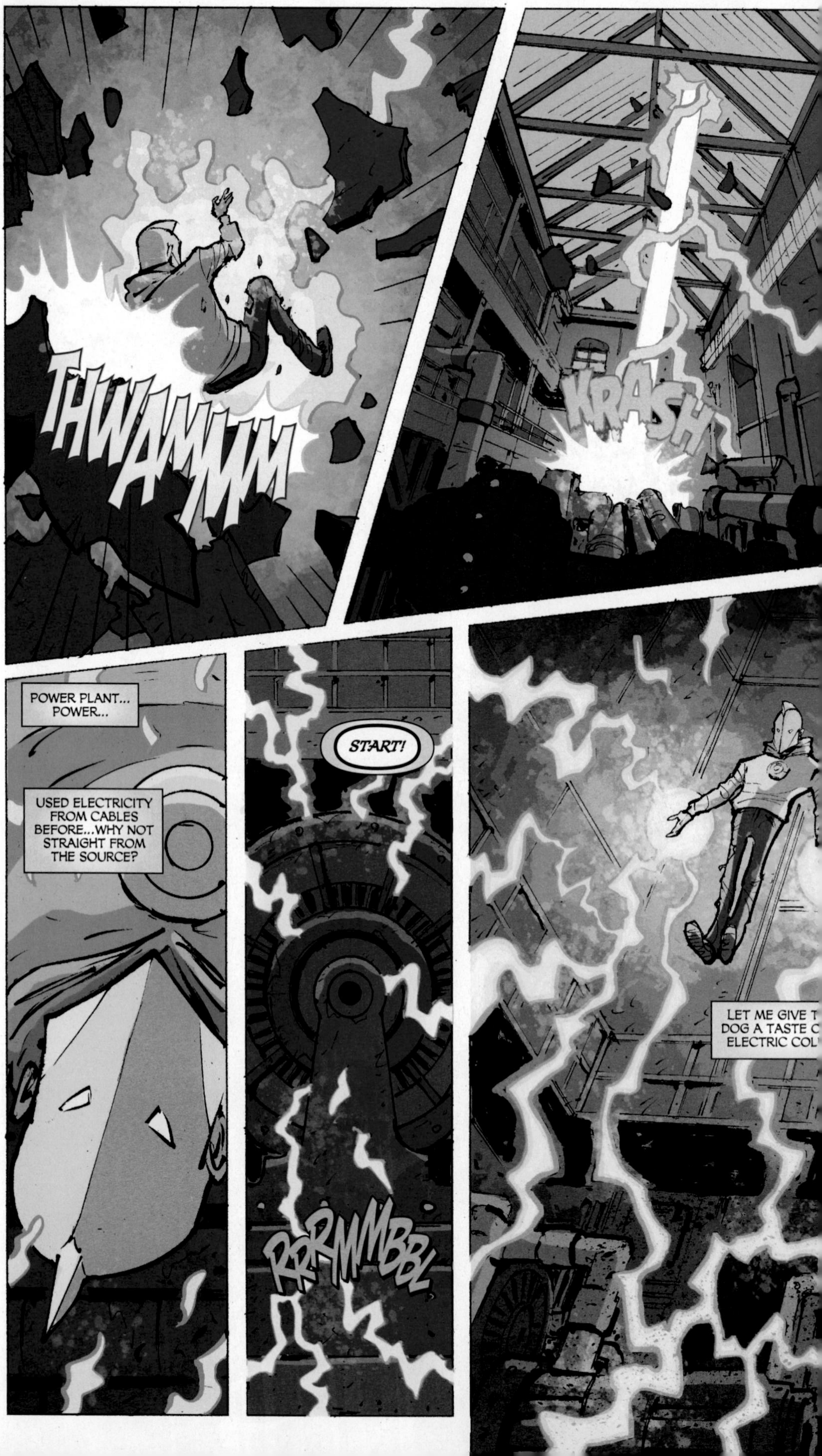
THWAMMM
KRASH
POWER PLANT... POWER...
USED ELECTRICITY FROM CABLES BEFORE...WHY NOT STRAIGHT FROM THE SOURCE?
START!
RRRMMBBL
LET ME GIVE T
DOG A TASTE O
ELECTRIC COL

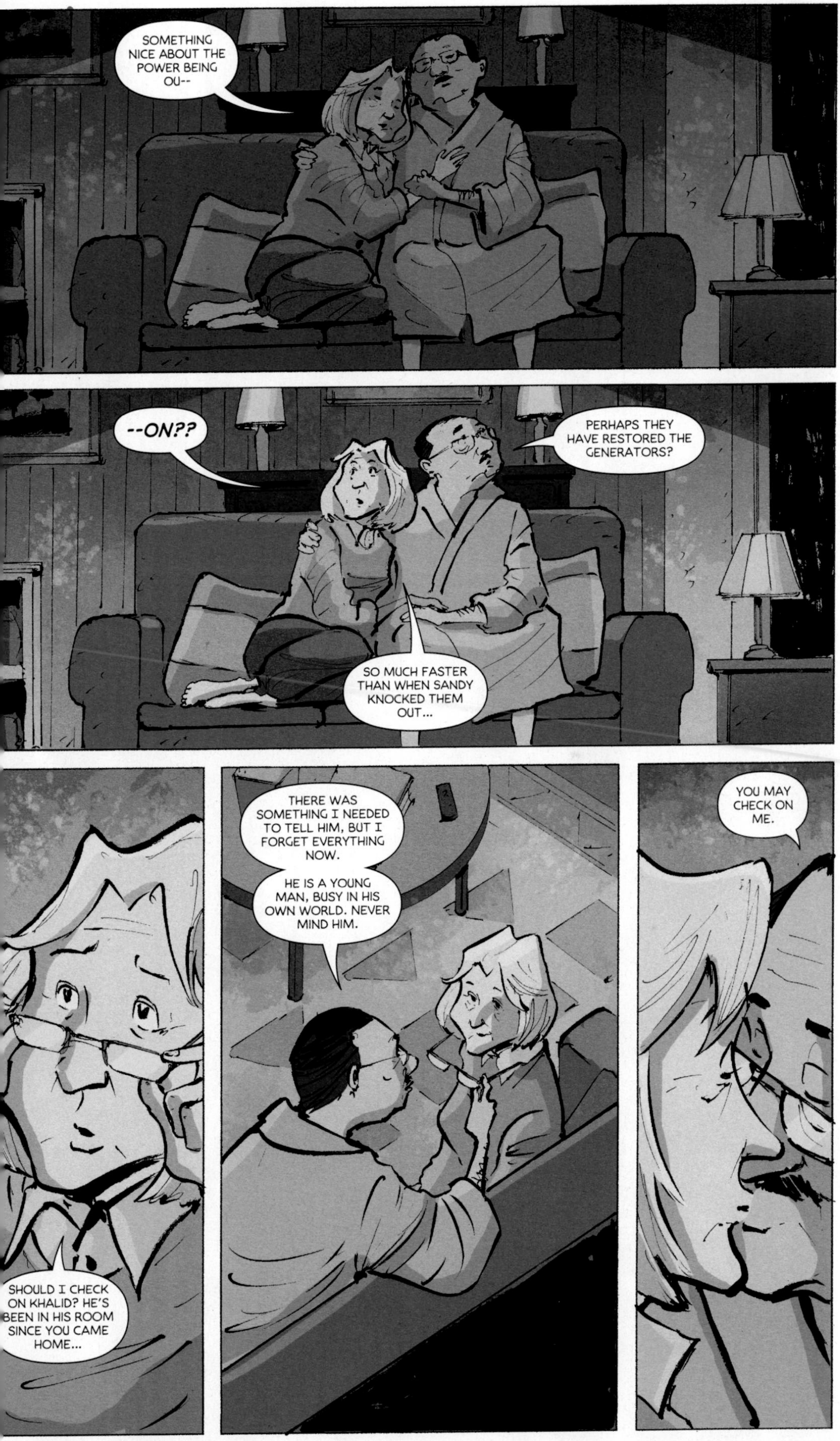
SOMETHING NICE ABOUT THE POWER BEING OU--
--ON??
PERHAPS THEY HAVE RESTORED THE GENERATORS?
SO MUCH FASTER THAN WHEN SANDY KNOCKED THEM OUT...
SHOULD I CHECK ON KHALID? HE'S BEEN IN HIS ROOM SINCE YOU CAME HOME...
THERE WAS SOMETHING I NEEDED TO TELL HIM, BUT I FORGET EVERYTHING NOW.
HE IS A YOUNG MAN, BUSY IN HIS OWN WORLD. NEVER MIND HIM.
YOU MAY CHECK ON ME.

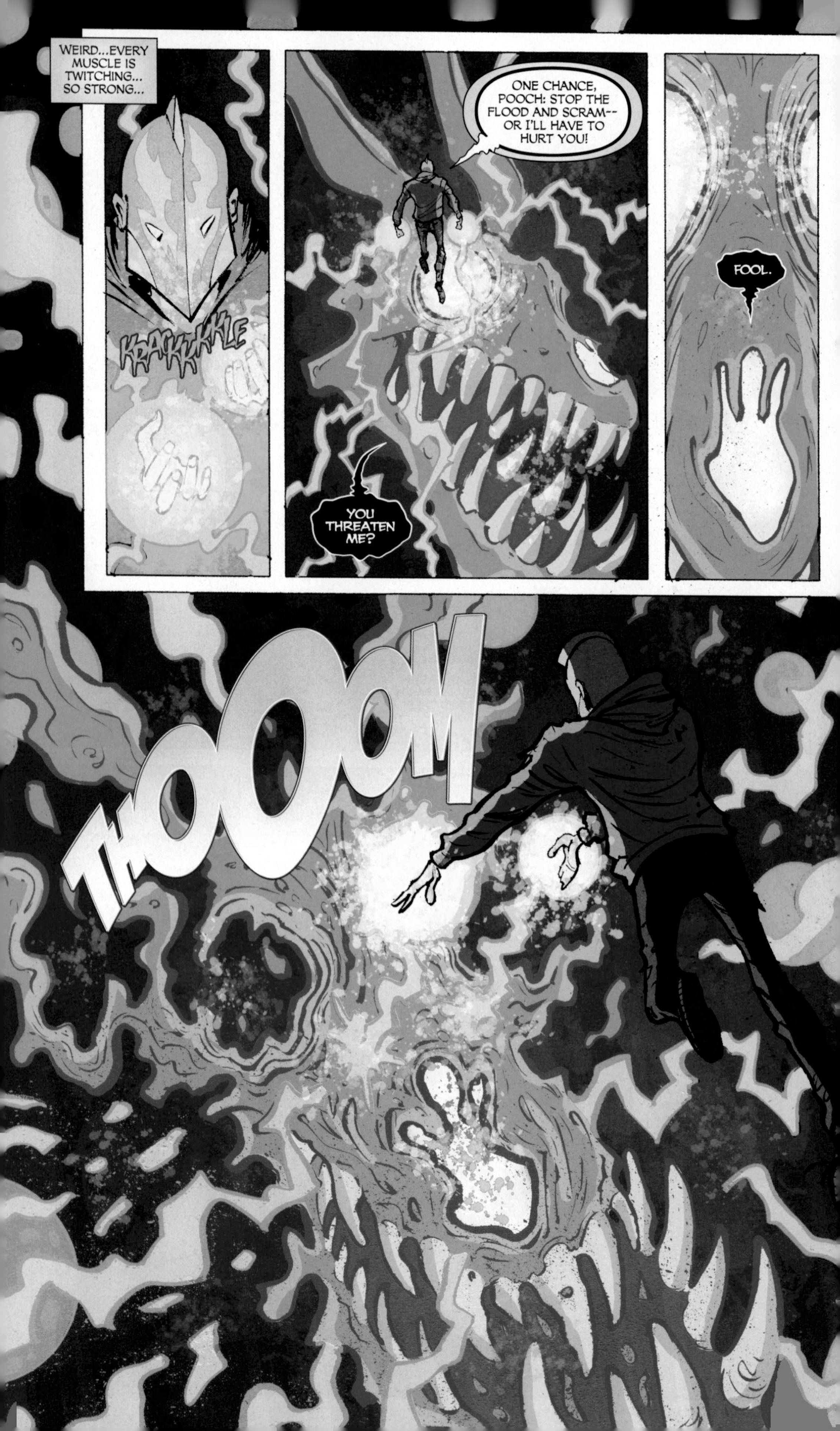
WEIRD...EVERY MUSCLE IS TWITCHING... SO STRONG...
KRACKKKKLE
ONE CHANCE, POOCH: STOP THE FLOOD AND SCRAM-- OR I'LL HAVE TO HURT YOU!
YOU THREATEN ME?
FOOL.
THOOOOM

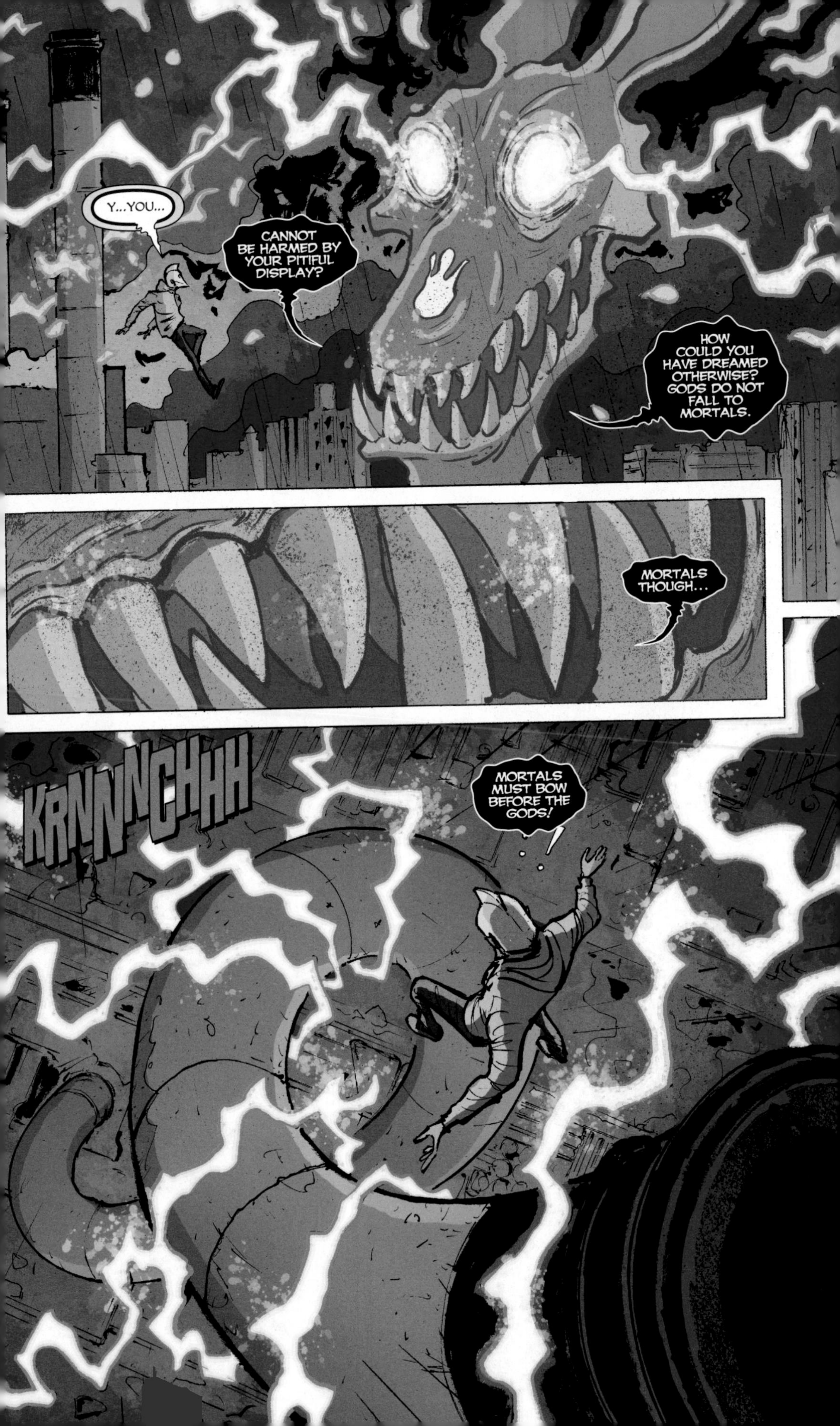

Y...YOU...
CANNOT BE HARMED BY YOUR PITIFUL DISPLAY?
HOW COULD YOU HAVE DREAMED OTHERWISE? GODS DO NOT FALL TO MORTALS.
MORTALS THOUGH...
KRNNNCHHH
MORTALS MUST BOW BEFORE THE GODS!

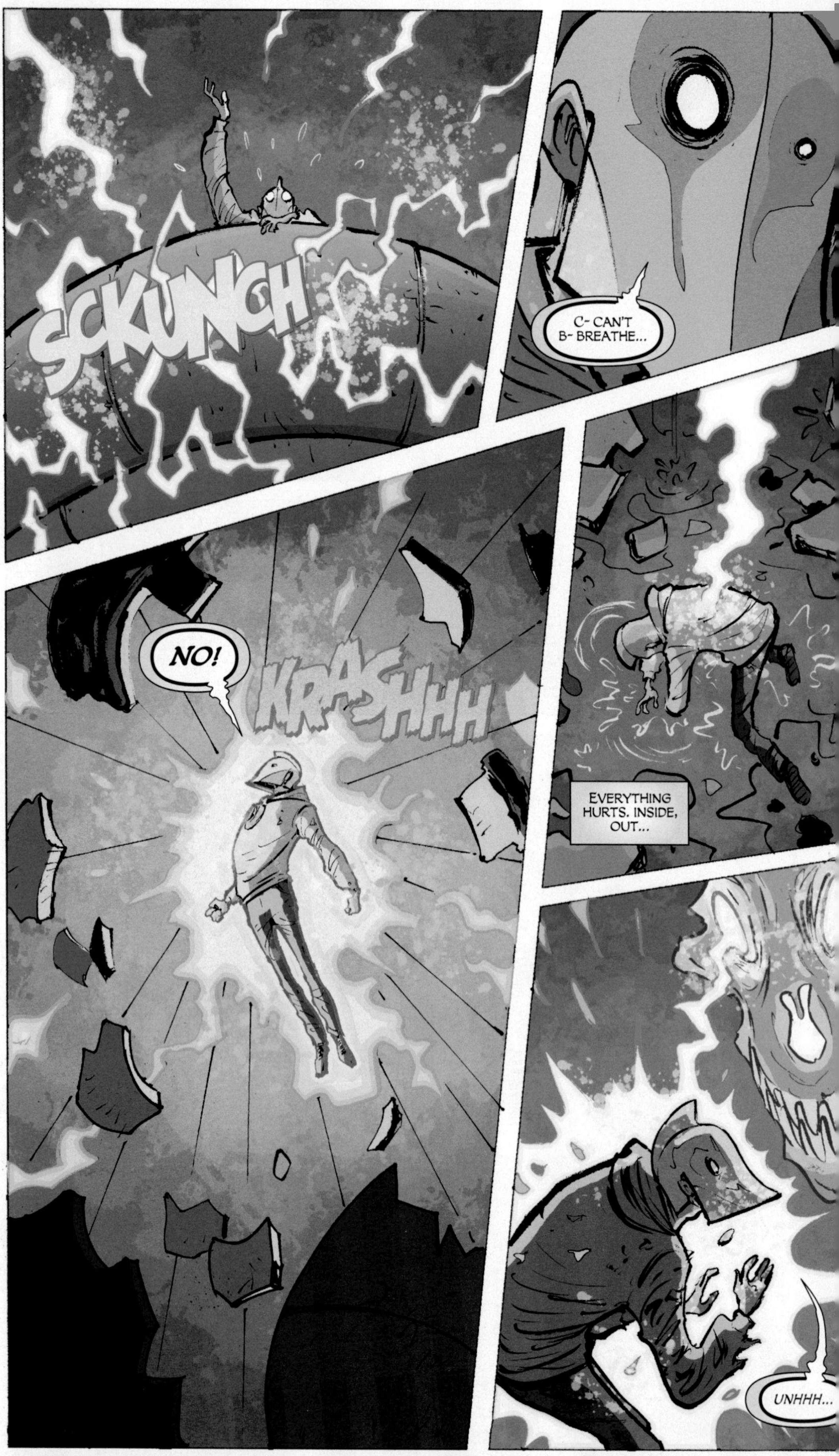
SCKUNCH
C- CAN'T
B- BREATHE...
NO!
KRASHHH
EVERYTHING HURTS. INSIDE, OUT...
UNHHH...

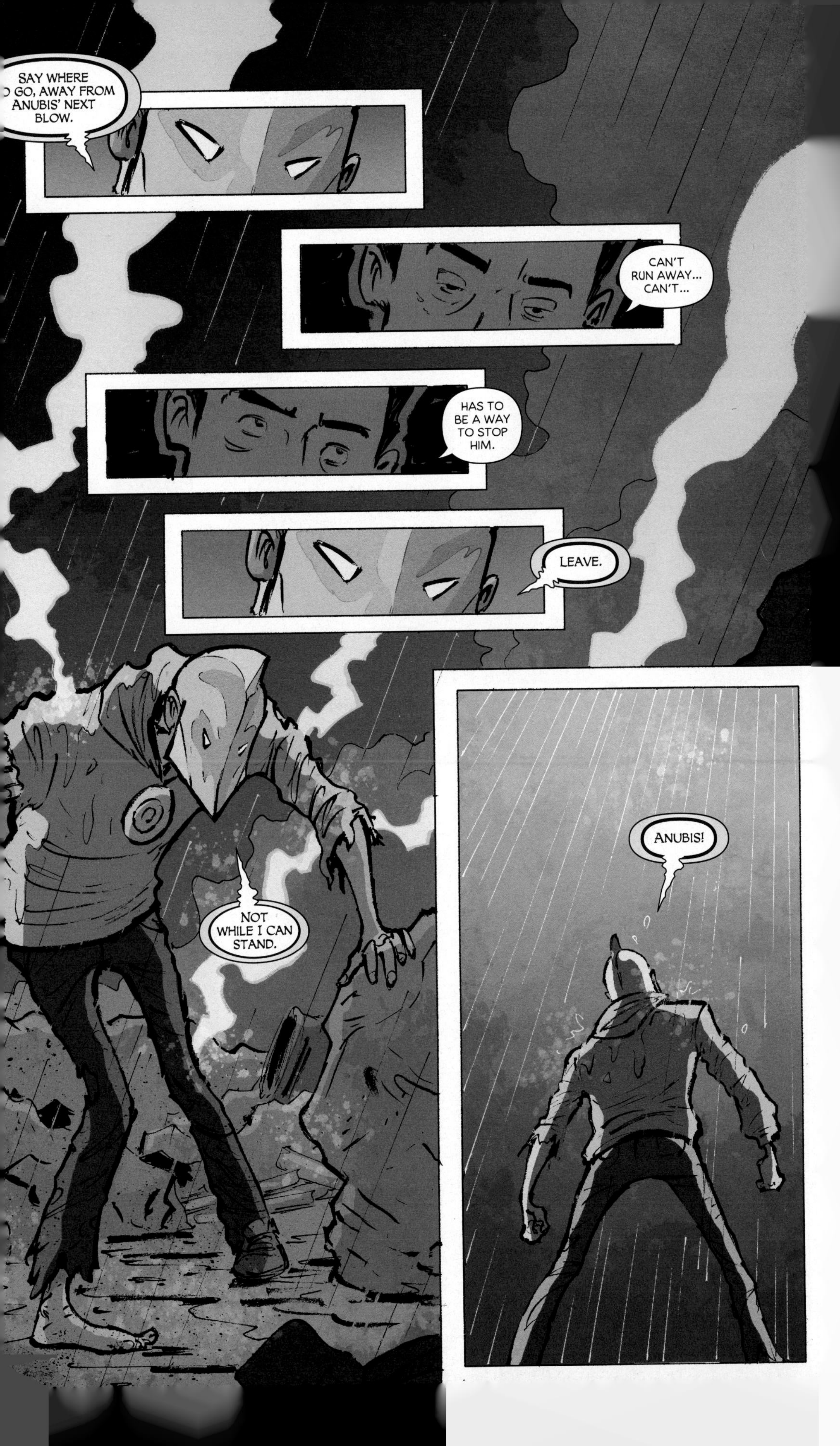
SAY WHERE
O GO, AWAY FROM
ANUBIS' NEXT
BLOW.
CAN'T
RUN AWAY...
CAN'T...
HAS TO
BE A WAY
TO STOP
HIM.
LEAVE.
NOT
WHILE I CAN
STAND.
ANUBIS!

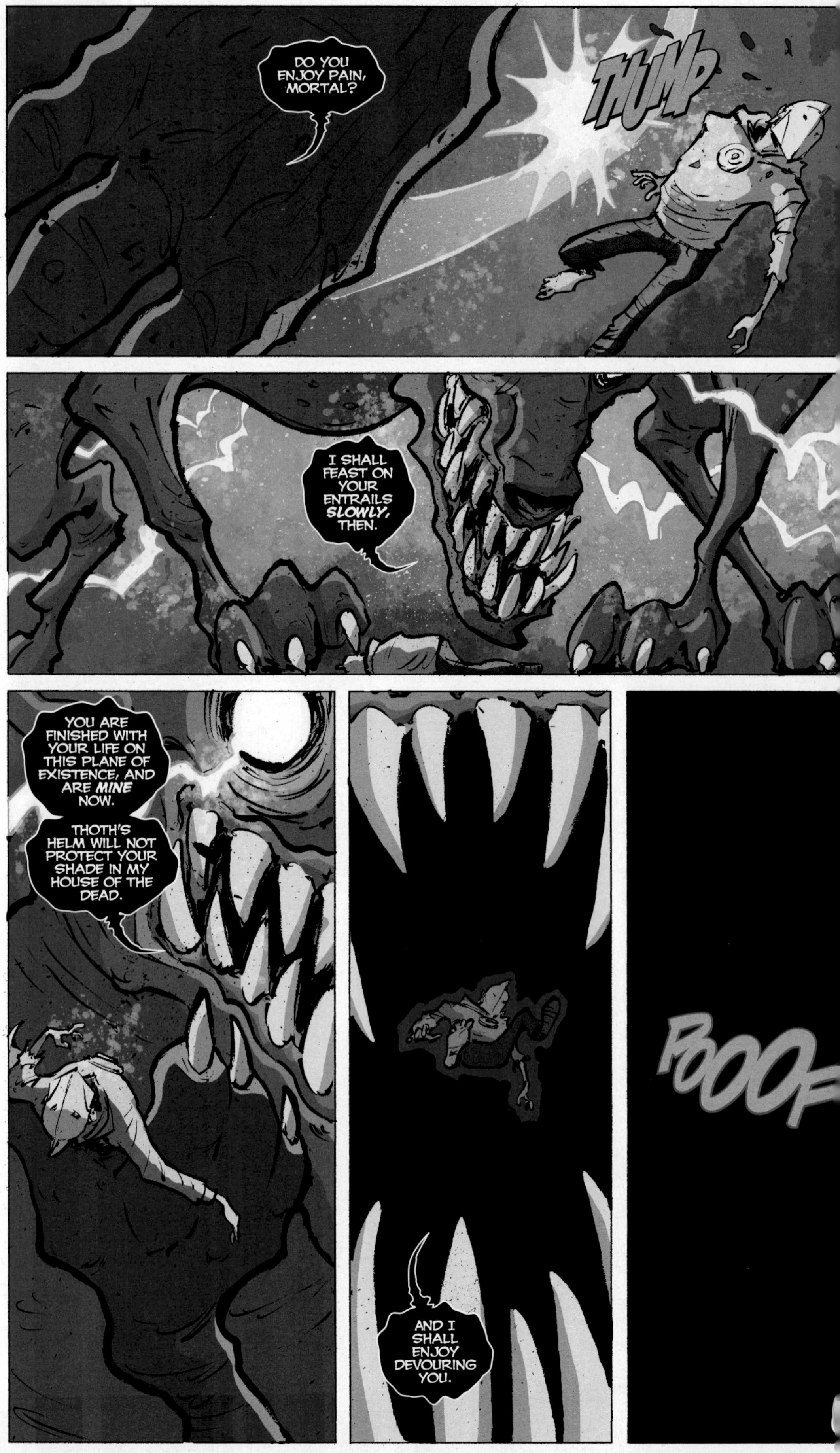
DO YOU ENJOY PAIN, MORTAL?
THUMP
I SHALL FEAST ON YOUR ENTRAILS SLOWLY, THEN.
YOU ARE FINISHED WITH YOUR LIFE ON THIS PLANE OF EXISTENCE, AND ARE MINE NOW.
THOTH'S HELM WILL NOT PROTECT YOUR SHADE IN MY HOUSE OF THE DEAD.
AND I SHALL ENJOY DEVOURING YOU.
POOOF

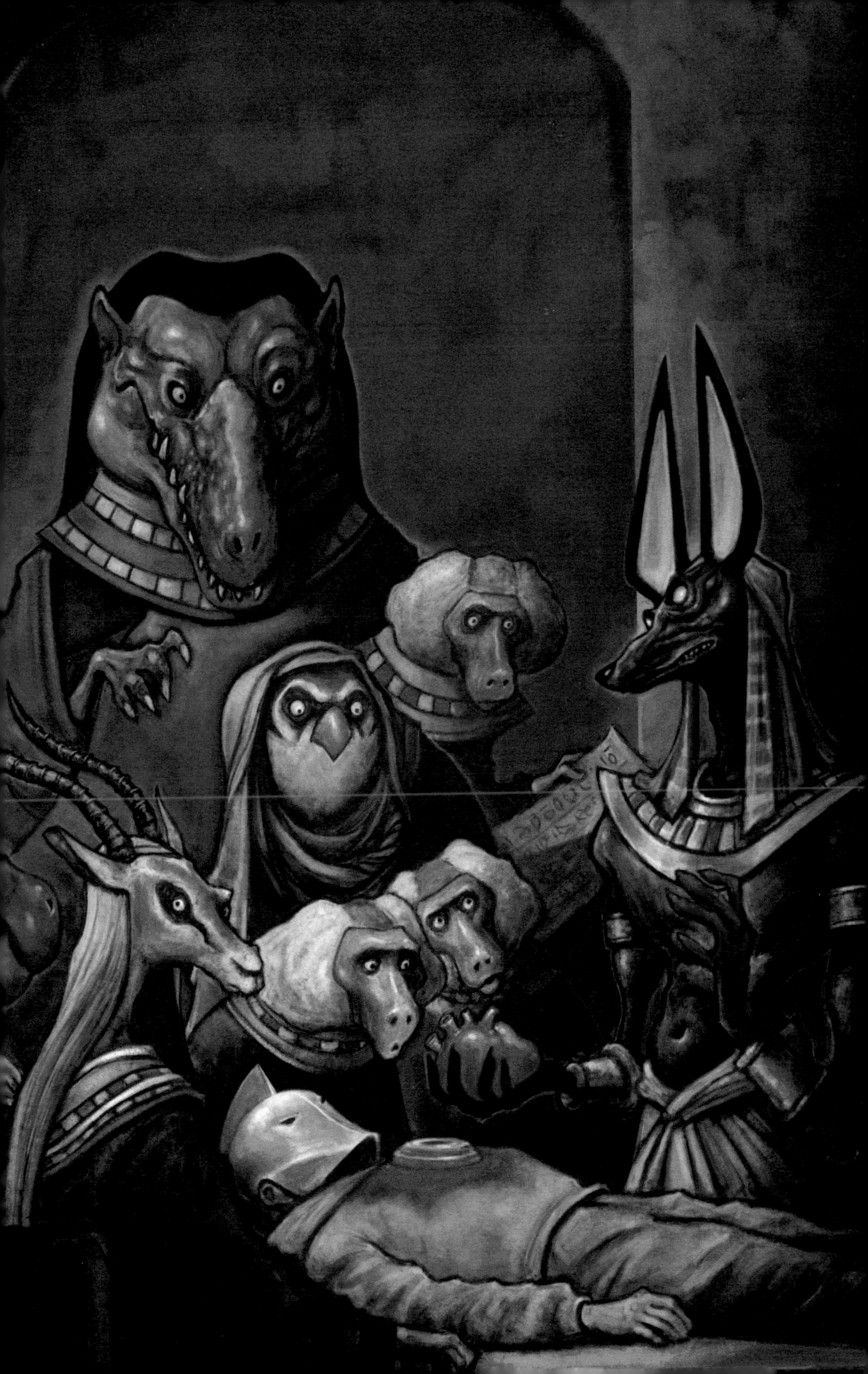

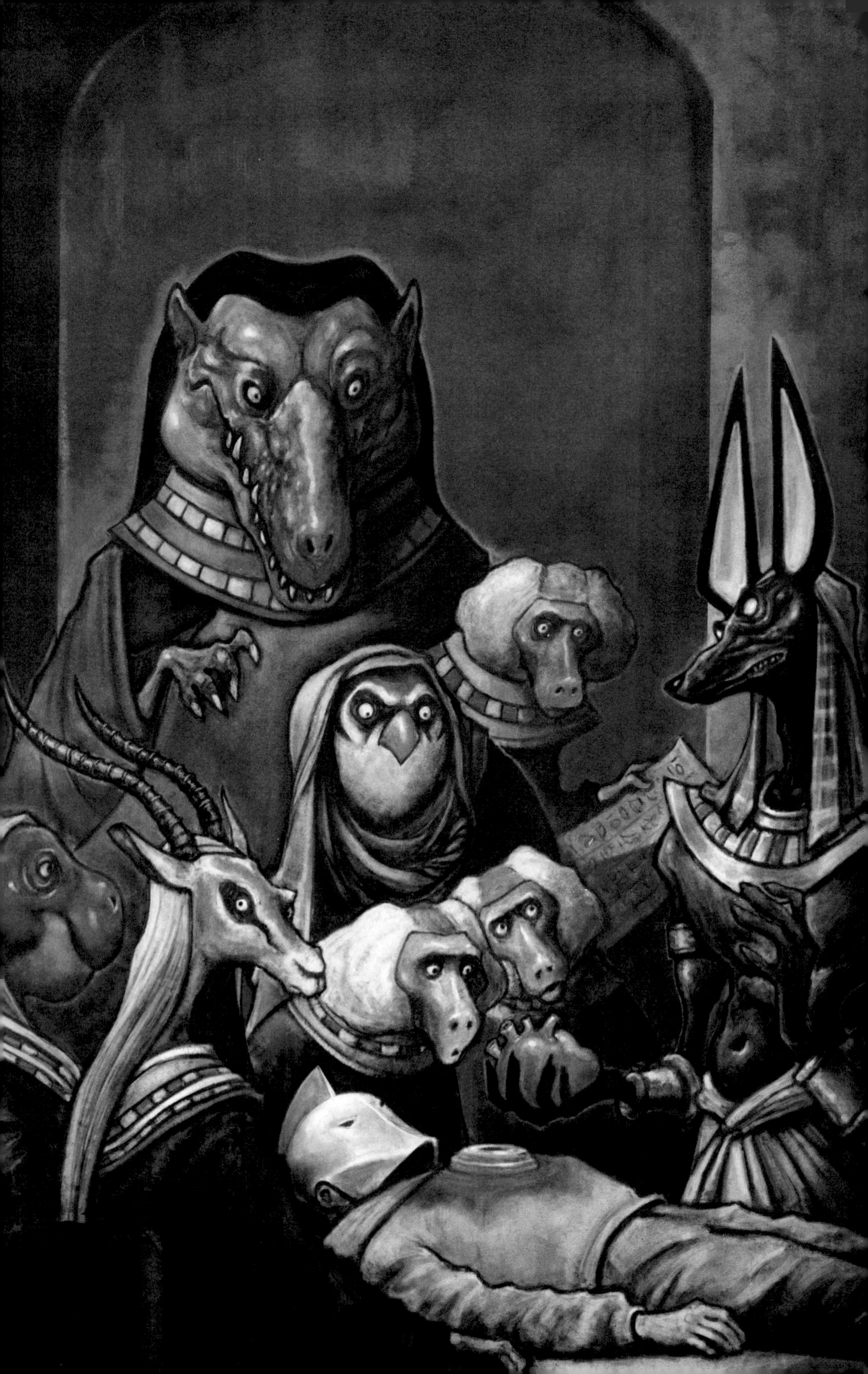

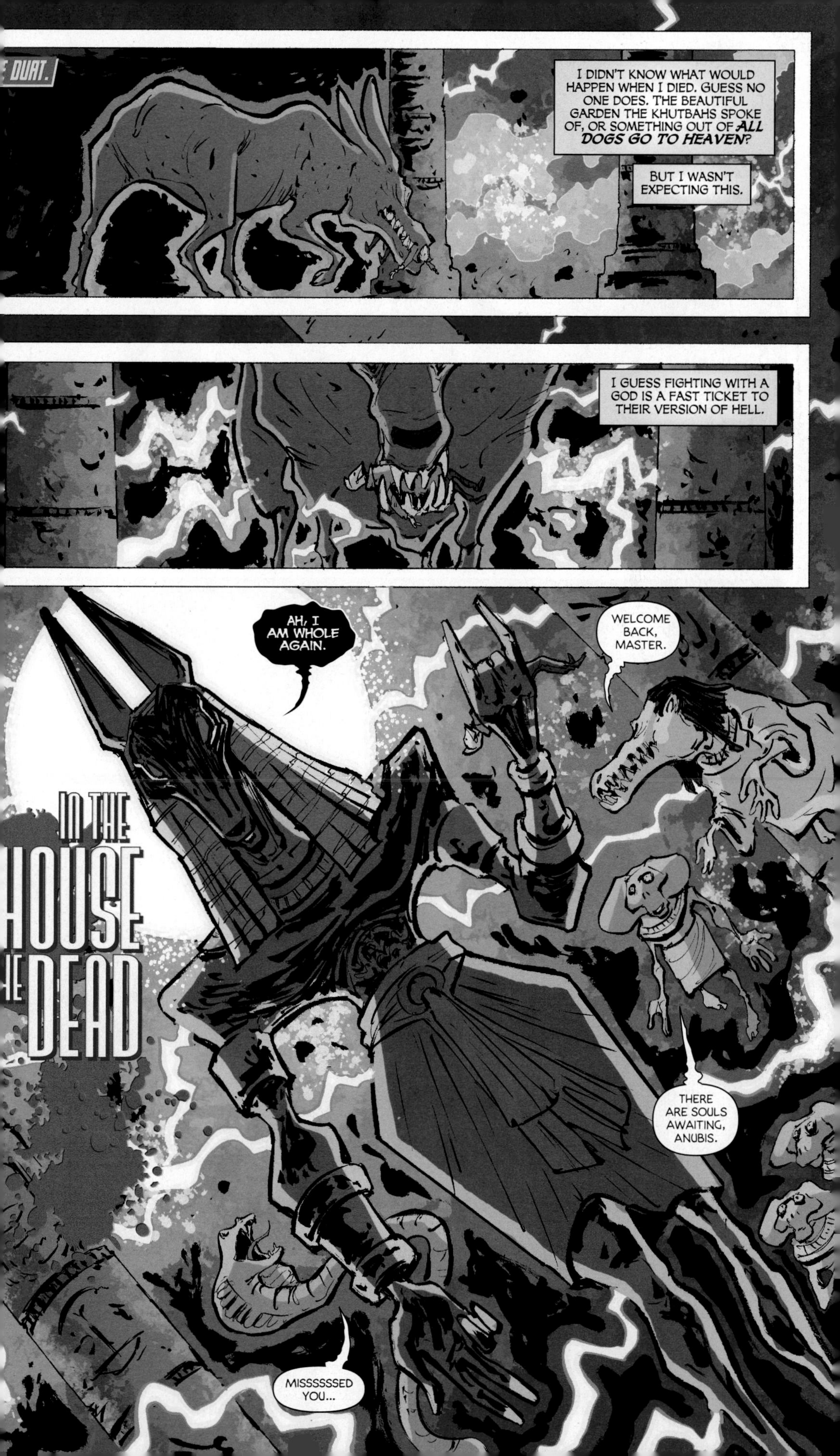

DUAT.
I DIDN'T KNOW WHAT WOULD HAPPEN WHEN I DIED. GUESS NO ONE DOES. THE BEAUTIFUL GARDEN THE KHUTBAHS SPOKE OF, OR SOMETHING OUT OF ALL DOGS GO TO HEAVEN?
BUT I WASN'T EXPECTING THIS.
I GUESS FIGHTING WITH A GOD IS A FAST TICKET TO THEIR VERSION OF HELL.
AH, I AM WHOLE AGAIN.
WELCOME BACK, MASTER.
IN THE HOUSE OF THE DEAD
THERE ARE SOULS AWAITING, ANUBIS.
MISSSSSSED YOU...

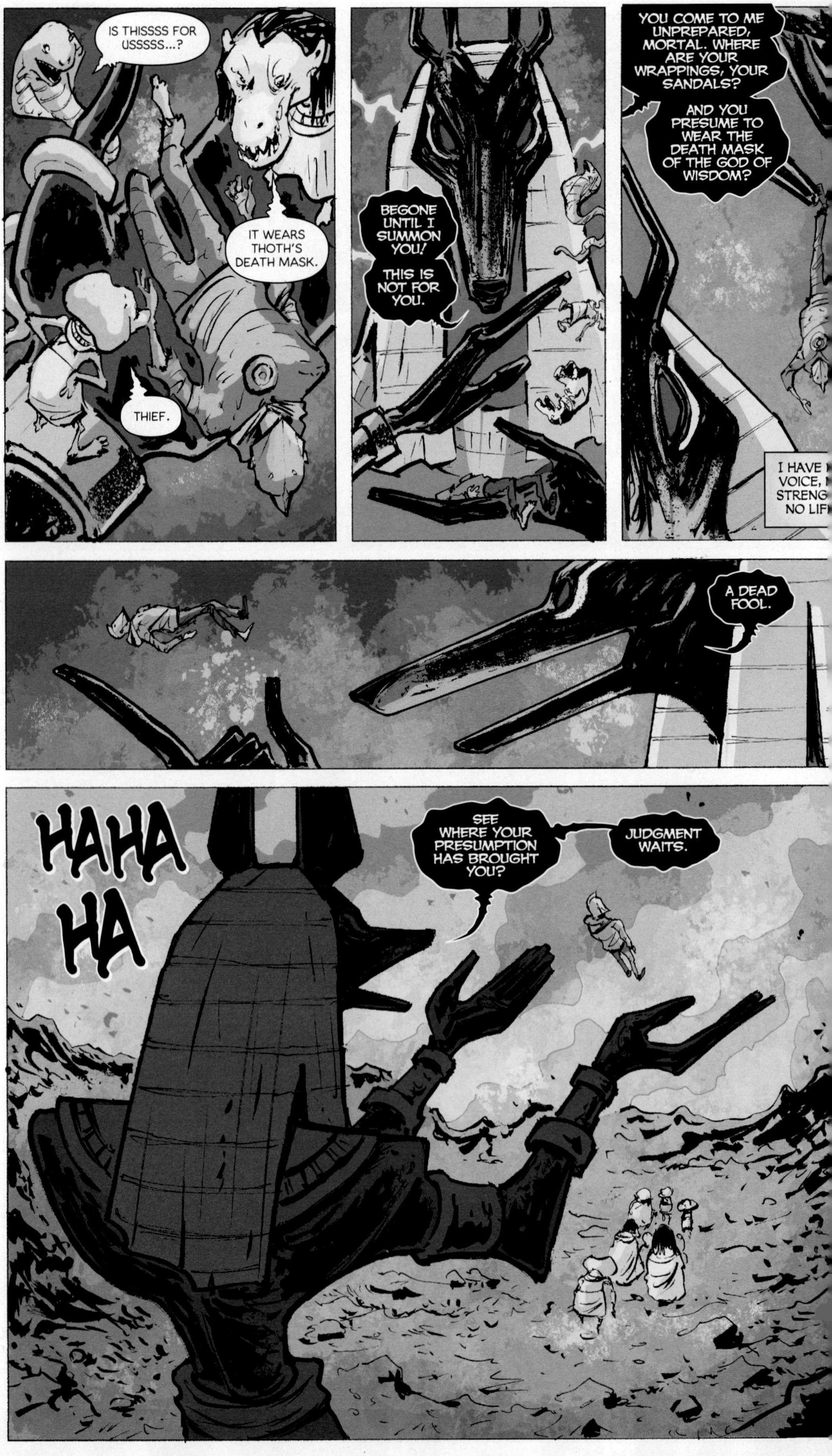

IS THISSSS FOR USSSSS...?
IT WEARS THOTH'S DEATH MASK.
THIEF.
BEGONE UNTIL I SUMMON YOU!
THIS IS NOT FOR YOU.
YOU COME TO ME UNPREPARED, MORTAL. WHERE ARE YOUR WRAPPINGS, YOUR SANDALS?
AND YOU PRESUME TO WEAR THE DEATH MASK OF THE GOD OF WISDOM?
I HAVE
A DEAD FOOL.
HAHA HA
SEE WHERE YOUR PRESUMPTION HAS BROUGHT YOU?
JUDGMENT WAITS.

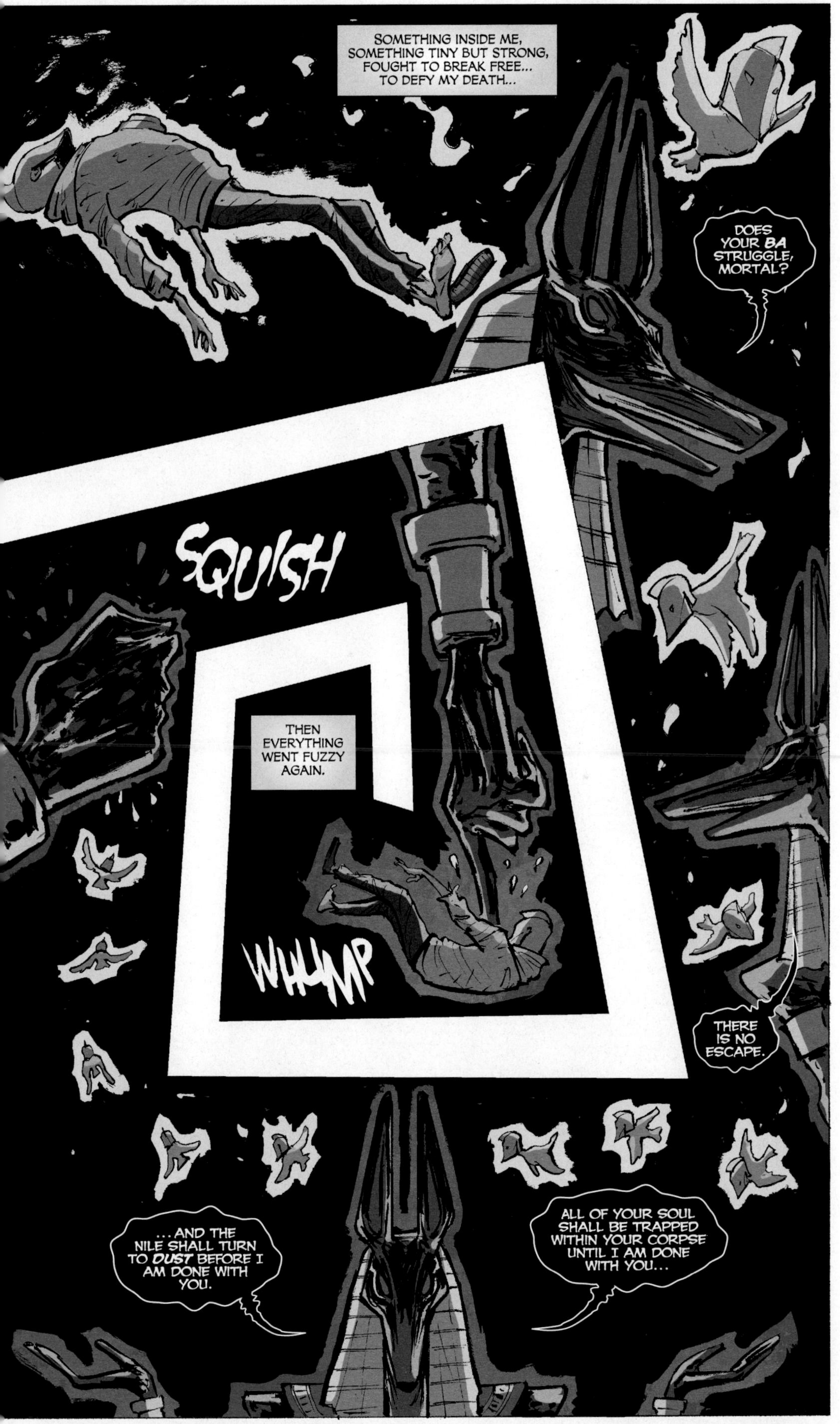
SOMETHING INSIDE ME, SOMETHING TINY BUT STRONG, FOUGHT TO BREAK FREE... TO DEFY MY DEATH...
DOES YOUR BA STRUGGLE, MORTAL?
SQUISH
THEN EVERYTHING WENT FUZZY AGAIN.
WHUMP
THERE IS NO ESCAPE.
ALL OF YOUR SOUL SHALL BE TRAPPED WITHIN YOUR CORPSE UNTIL I AM DONE WITH YOU...
...AND THE NILE SHALL TURN TO DUST BEFORE I AM DONE WITH YOU.

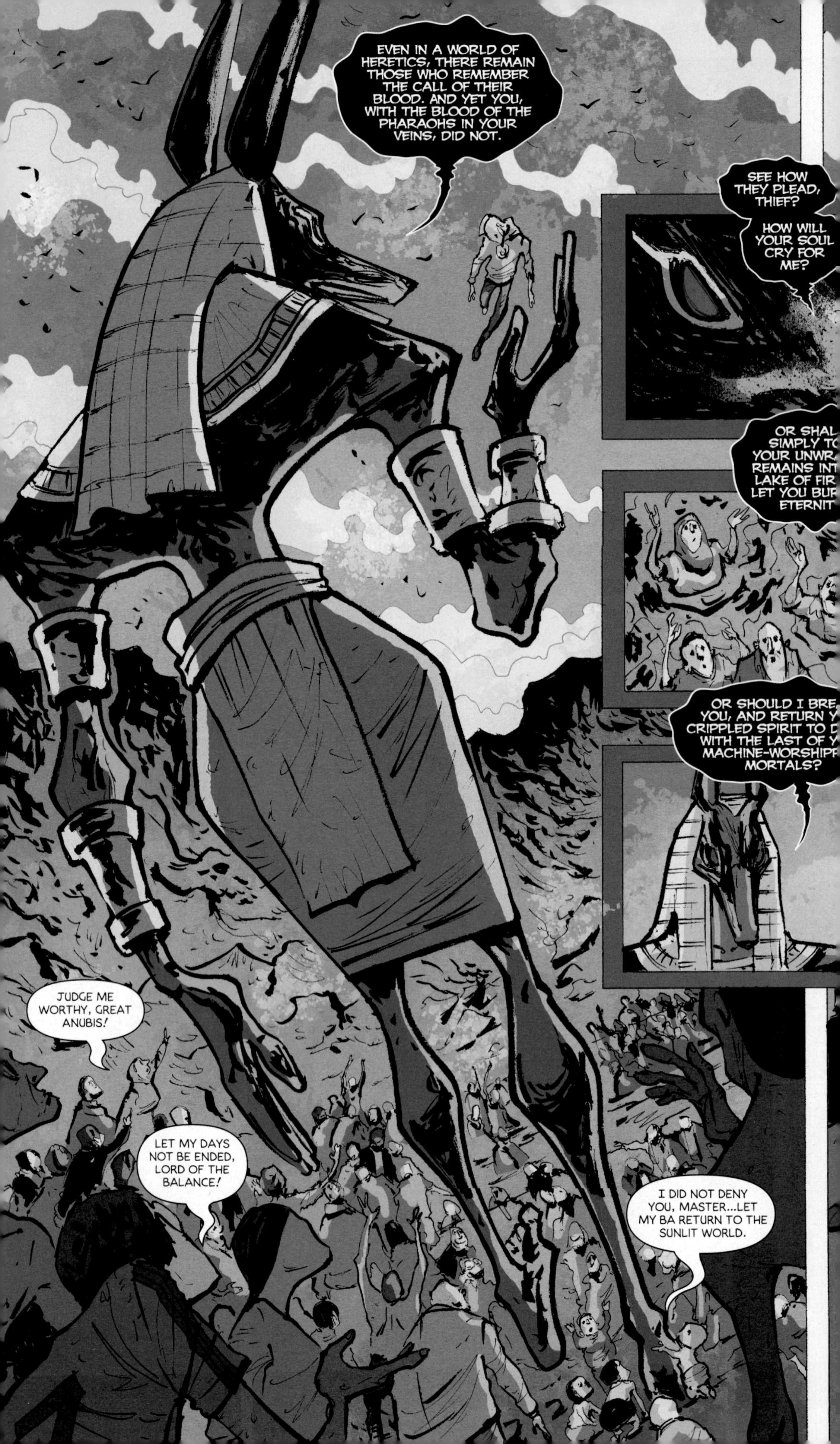
EVEN IN A WORLD OF HERETICS, THERE REMAIN THOSE WHO REMEMBER THE CALL OF THEIR BLOOD. AND YET YOU, WITH THE BLOOD OF THE PHARAOHS IN YOUR VEINS, DID NOT.
SEE HOW THEY PLEAD, THIEF?
HOW WILL YOUR SOUL CRY FOR ME?
OR SHAL SIMPLY TO YOUR UNWR REMAINS INT LAKE OF FIR LET YOU BUR ETERNIT
OR SHOULD I BRE YOU, AND RETURN Y CRIPPLED SPIRIT TO D WITH THE LAST OF Y MACHINE-WORSHIPP MORTALS?
JUDGE ME WORTHY, GREAT ANUBIS!
LET MY DAYS NOT BE ENDED, LORD OF THE BALANCE!
I DID NOT DENY YOU, MASTER...LET MY BA RETURN TO THE SUNLIT WORLD.

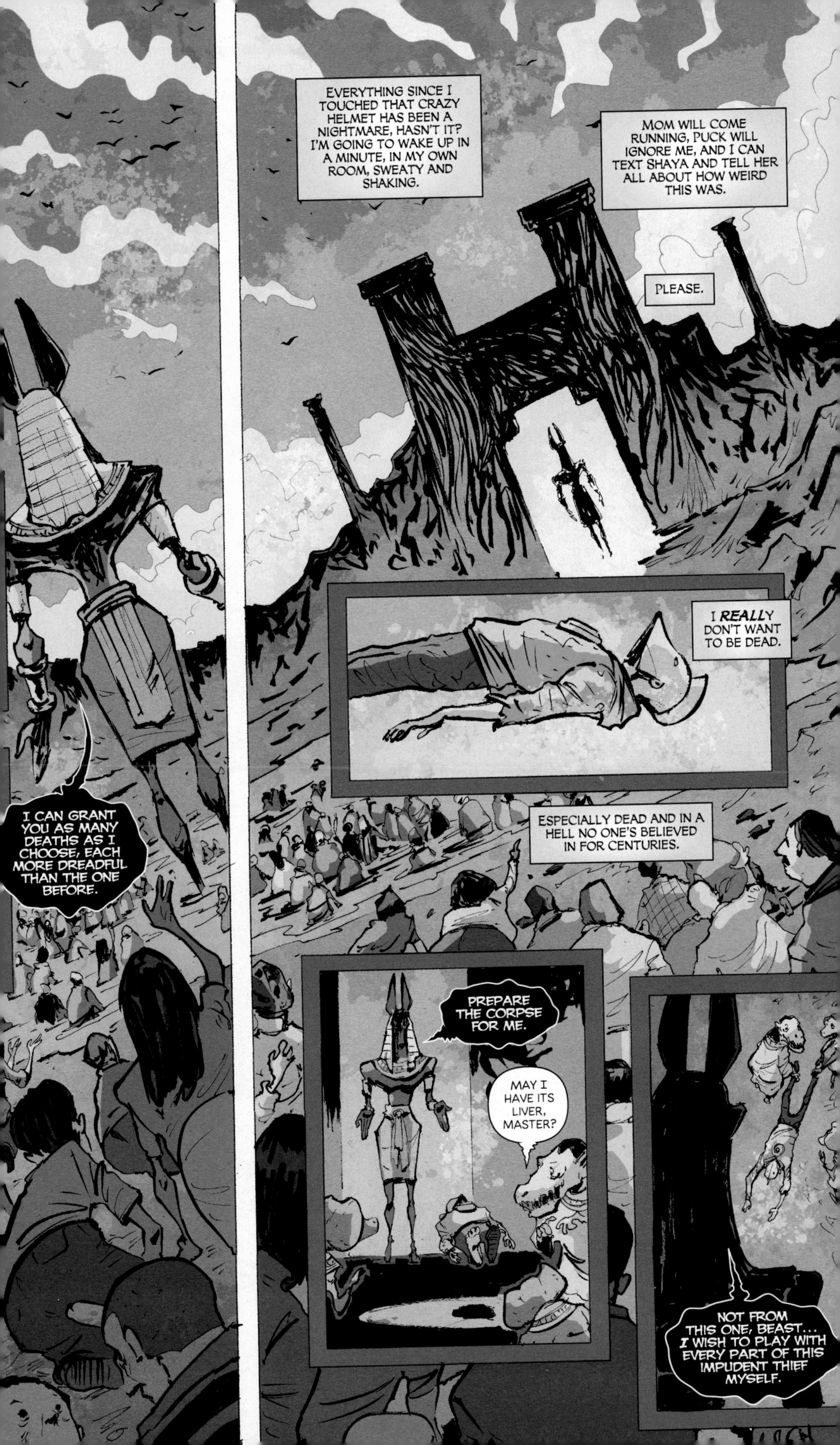
I CAN GRANT YOU AS MANY DEATHS AS I CHOOSE, EACH MORE DREADFUL THAN THE ONE BEFORE.
EVERYTHING SINCE I TOUCHED THAT CRAZY HELMET HAS BEEN A NIGHTMARE, HASN'T IT? I'M GOING TO WAKE UP IN A MINUTE, IN MY OWN ROOM, SWEATY AND SHAKING.
MOM WILL COME RUNNING, PUCK WILL IGNORE ME, AND I CAN TEXT SHAYA AND TELL HER ALL ABOUT HOW WEIRD THIS WAS.
PLEASE.
I ***REALL***Y DON'T WANT TO BE DEAD.
ESPECIALLY DEAD AND IN A HELL NO ONE'S BELIEVED IN FOR CENTURIES.
PREPARE THE CORPSE FOR ME.
MAY I HAVE ITS LIVER, MASTER?
NOT FROM THIS ONE, BEAST... ***I*** WISH TO PLAY WITH EVERY PART OF THIS IMPUDENT THIEF MYSELF.

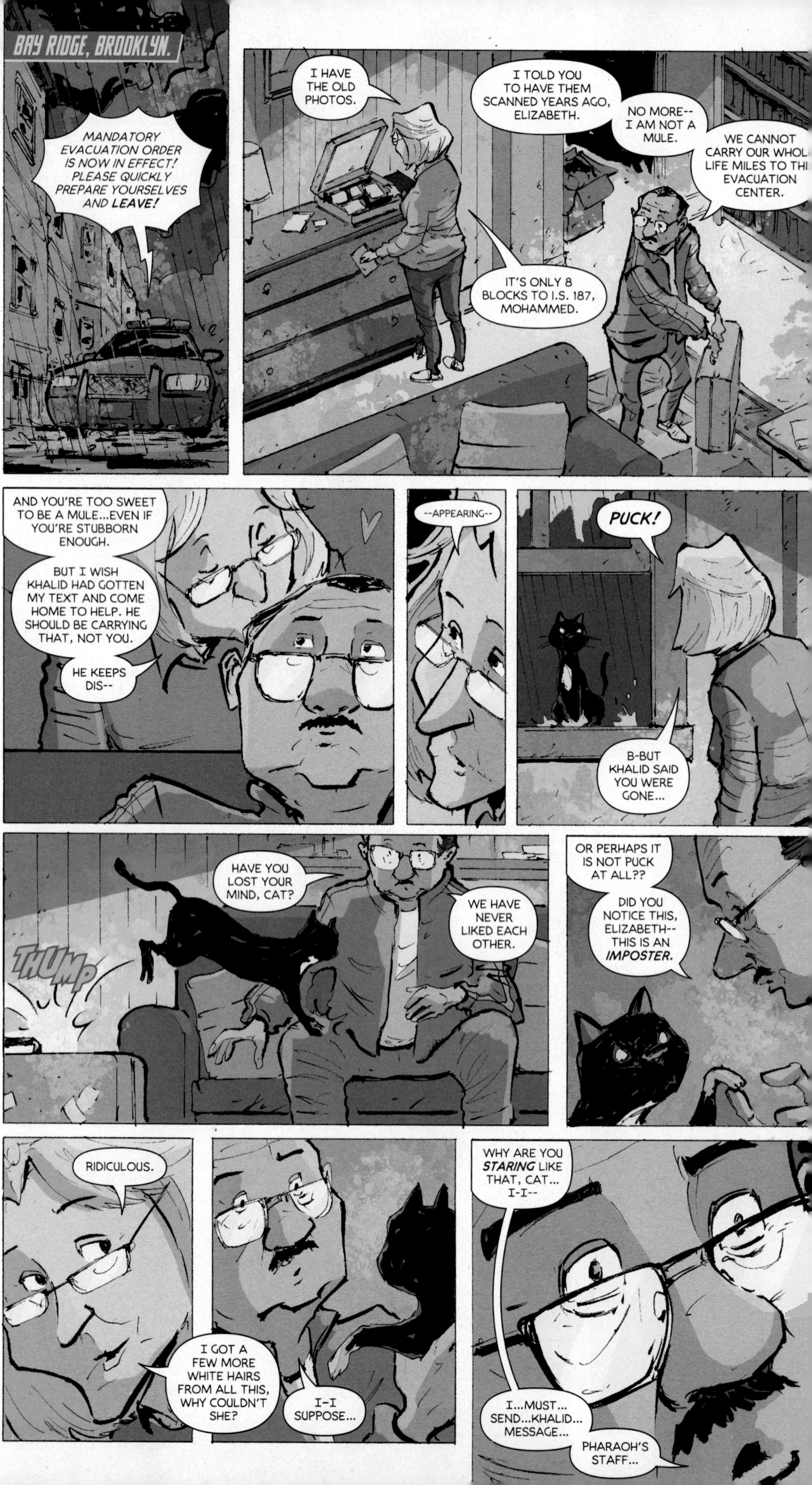
BAY RIDGE, BROOKLYN.
MANDATORY EVACUATION ORDER IS NOW IN EFFECT! PLEASE QUICKLY PREPARE YOURSELVES AND LEAVE!
I HAVE THE OLD PHOTOS.
I TOLD YOU TO HAVE THEM SCANNED YEARS AGO, ELIZABETH.
NO MORE-- I AM NOT A MULE.
WE CANNOT CARRY OUR WHOL LIFE MILES TO THI EVACUATION CENTER.
IT'S ONLY 8 BLOCKS TO I.S. 187, MOHAMMED.
AND YOU'RE TOO SWEET TO BE A MULE...EVEN IF YOU'RE STUBBORN ENOUGH.
BUT I WISH KHALID HAD GOTTEN MY TEXT AND COME HOME TO HELP. HE SHOULD BE CARRYING THAT, NOT YOU.
HE KEEPS DIS--
--APPEARING--
PUCK!
B-BUT KHALID SAID YOU WERE GONE...
THUMP
HAVE YOU LOST YOUR MIND, CAT?
WE HAVE NEVER LIKED EACH OTHER.
OR PERHAPS IT IS NOT PUCK AT ALL??
DID YOU NOTICE THIS, ELIZABETH-- THIS IS AN IMPOSTER.
RIDICULOUS.
I GOT A FEW MORE WHITE HAIRS FROM ALL THIS, WHY COULDN'T SHE?
I-I SUPPOSE...
WHY ARE YOU STARING LIKE THAT, CAT... I-I--
I...MUST... SEND...KHALID... MESSAGE...
PHARAOH'S STAFF...

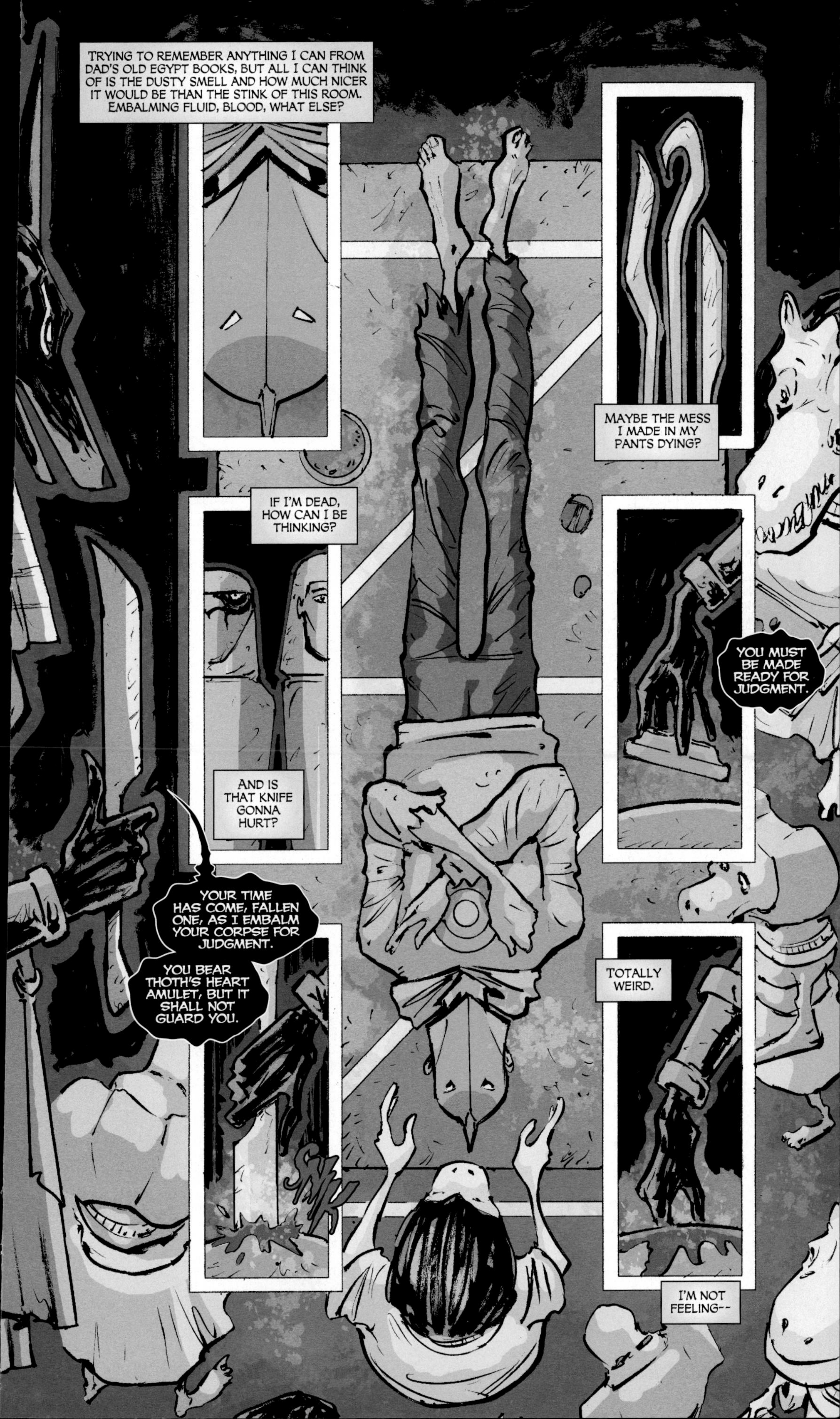
TRYING TO REMEMBER ANYTHING I CAN FROM DAD'S OLD EGYPT BOOKS, BUT ALL I CAN THINK OF IS THE DUSTY SMELL AND HOW MUCH NICER IT WOULD BE THAN THE STINK OF THIS ROOM. EMBALMING FLUID, BLOOD, WHAT ELSE?
MAYBE THE MESS I MADE IN MY PANTS DYING?
IF I'M DEAD, HOW CAN I BE THINKING?
AND IS THAT KNIFE GONNA HURT?
YOU MUST BE MADE READY FOR JUDGMENT.
YOUR TIME HAS COME, FALLEN ONE, AS I EMBALM YOUR CORPSE FOR JUDGMENT.
YOU BEAR THOTH'S HEART AMULET, BUT IT SHALL NOT GUARD YOU.
TOTALLY WEIRD.
SNIK
I'M NOT FEELING--

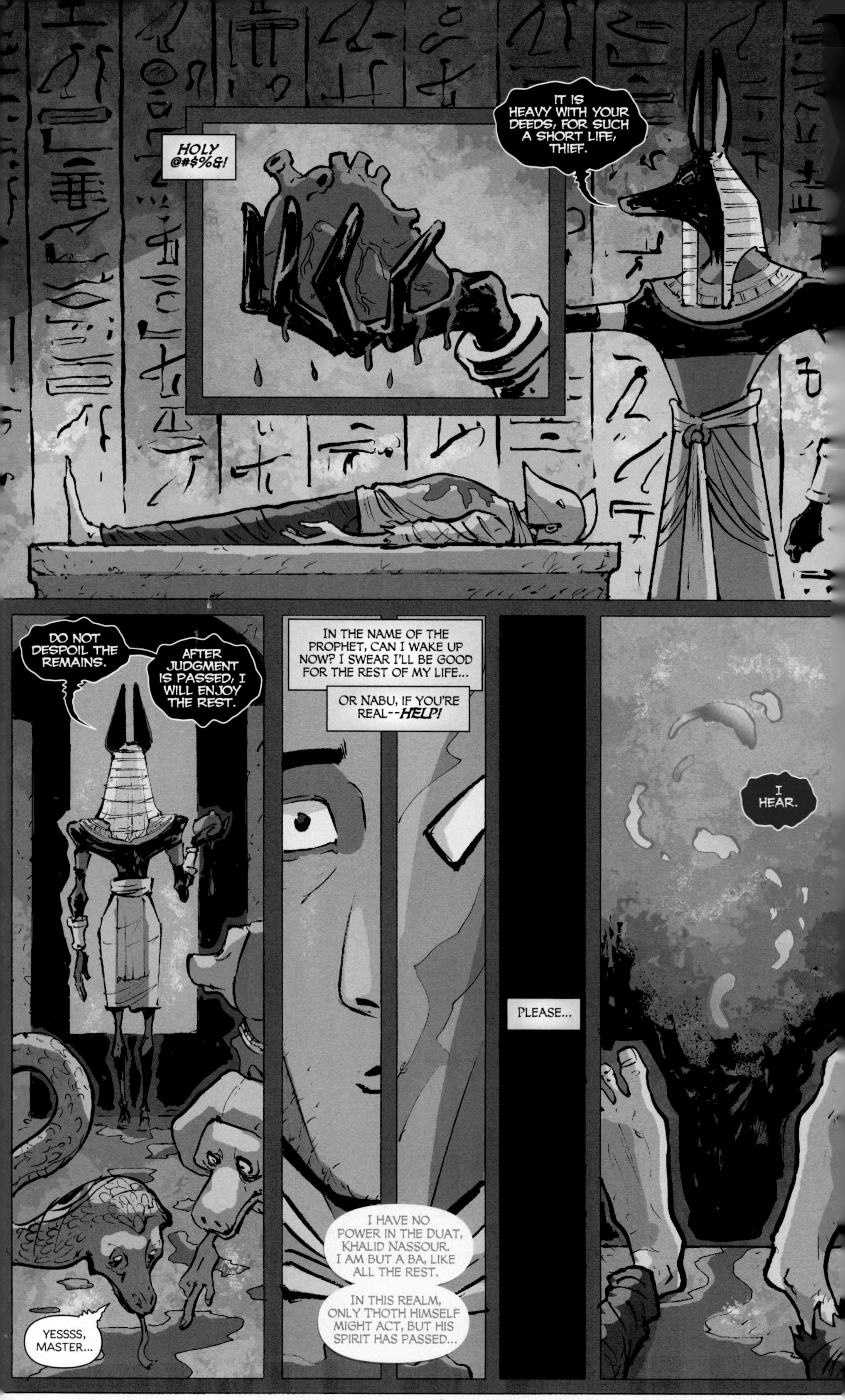
HOLY @#$%&!
IT IS HEAVY WITH YOUR DEEDS, FOR SUCH A SHORT LIFE, THIEF.
DO NOT DESPOIL THE REMAINS.
AFTER JUDGMENT IS PASSED, I WILL ENJOY THE REST.
YESSSS, MASTER...
IN THE NAME OF THE PROPHET, CAN I WAKE UP NOW? I SWEAR I'LL BE GOOD FOR THE REST OF MY LIFE...
OR NABU, IF YOU'RE REAL--HELP!
I HAVE NO POWER IN THE DUAT, KHALID NASSOUR. I AM BUT A BA, LIKE ALL THE REST.
IN THIS REALM, ONLY THOTH HIMSELF MIGHT ACT, BUT HIS SPIRIT HAS PASSED...
PLEASE...
I HEAR.

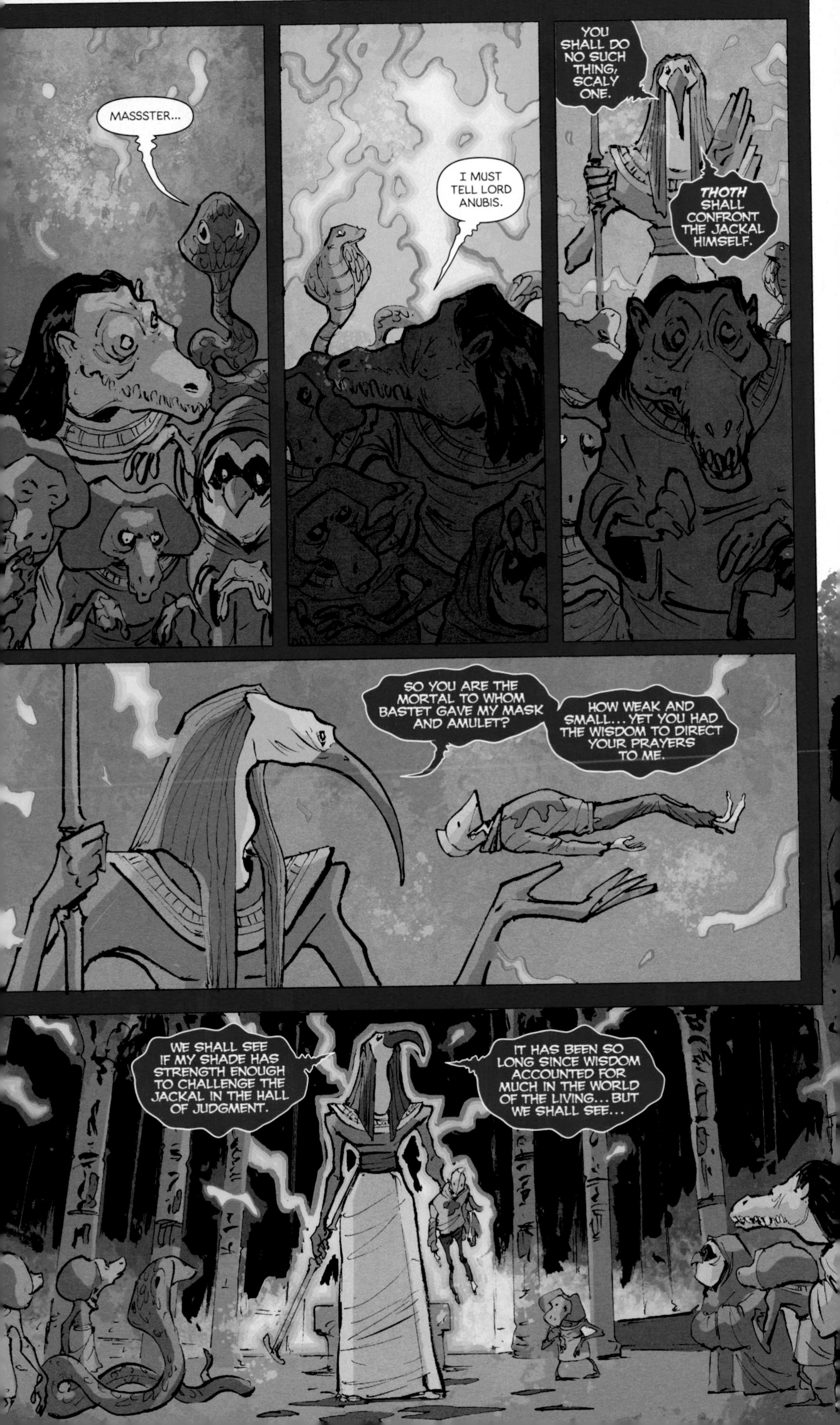

MASSSTER...
I MUST TELL LORD ANUBIS.
YOU SHALL DO NO SUCH THING, SCALY ONE.
THOTH SHALL CONFRONT THE JACKAL HIMSELF.
SO YOU ARE THE MORTAL TO WHOM BASTET GAVE MY MASK AND AMULET?
HOW WEAK AND SMALL... YET YOU HAD THE WISDOM TO DIRECT YOUR PRAYERS TO ME.
WE SHALL SEE IF MY SHADE HAS STRENGTH ENOUGH TO CHALLENGE THE JACKAL IN THE HALL OF JUDGMENT.
IT HAS BEEN SO LONG SINCE WISDOM ACCOUNTED FOR MUCH IN THE WORLD OF THE LIVING... BUT WE SHALL SEE...

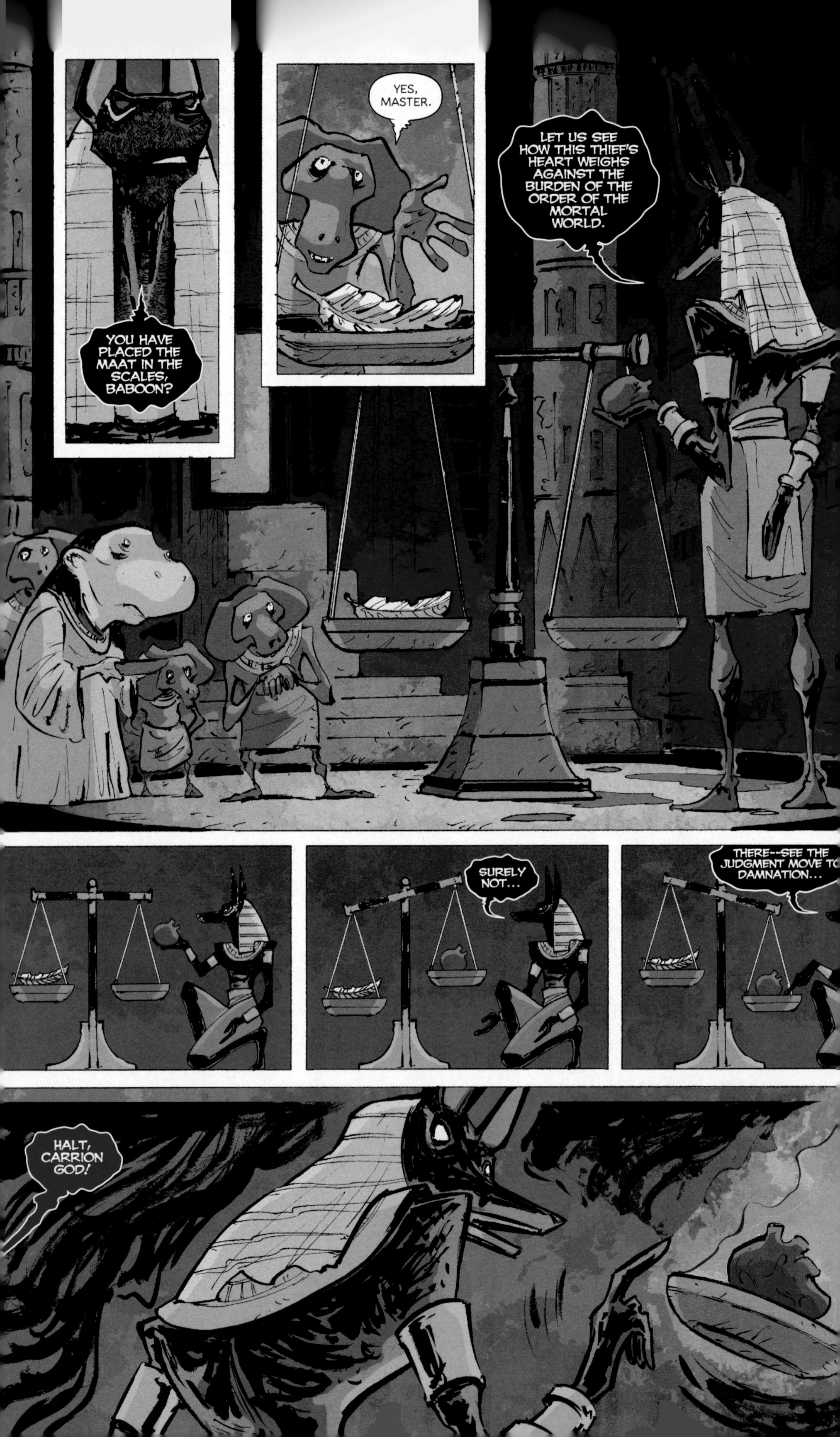
YOU HAVE PLACED THE MAAT IN THE SCALES, BABOON?
YES, MASTER.
LET US SEE HOW THIS THIEF'S HEART WEIGHS AGAINST THE BURDEN OF THE ORDER OF THE MORTAL WORLD.
SURELY NOT...
THERE--SEE THE JUDGMENT MOVE TO DAMNATION...
HALT, CARRION GOD!

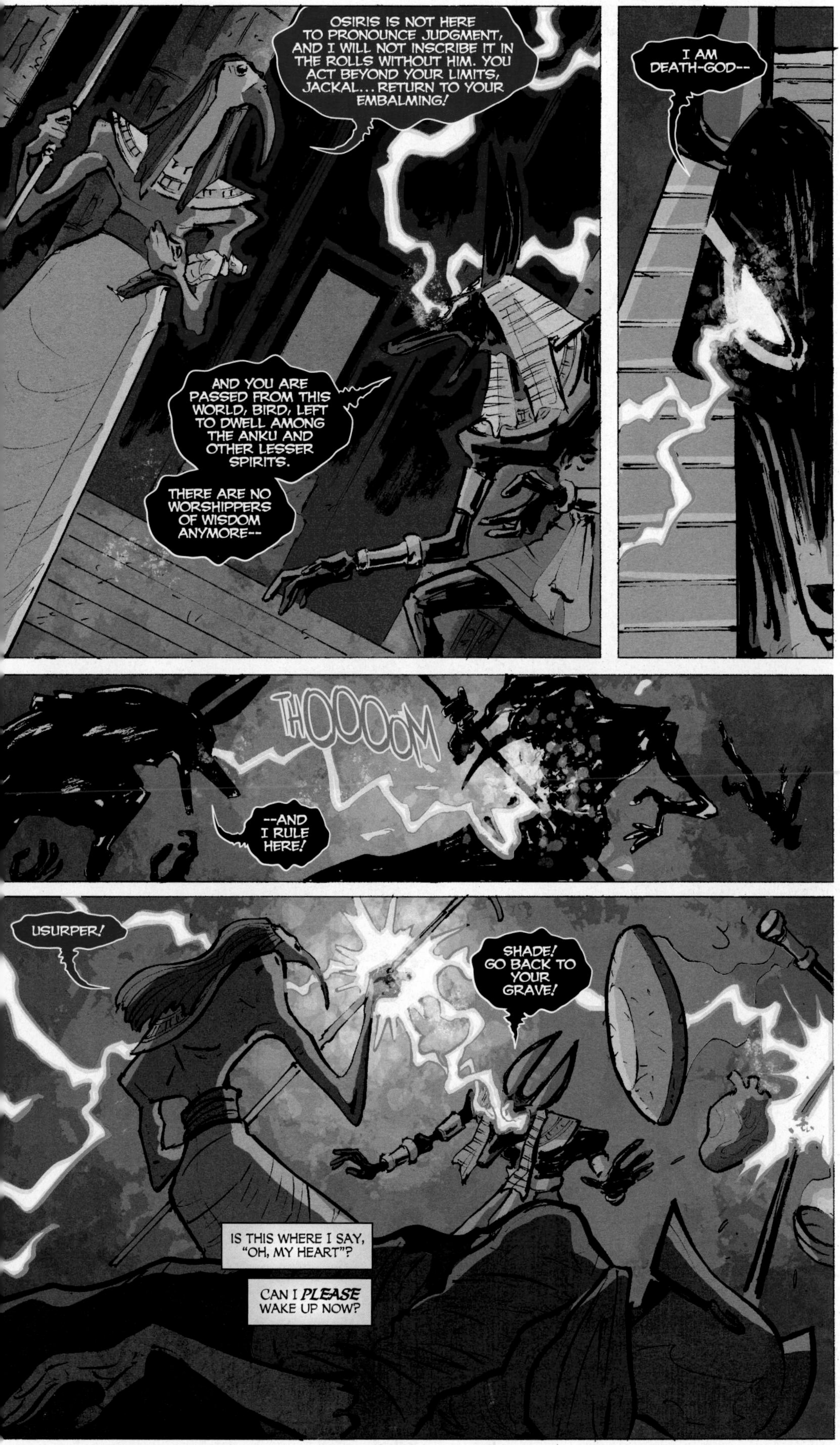
OSIRIS IS NOT HERE TO PRONOUNCE JUDGMENT, AND I WILL NOT INSCRIBE IT IN THE ROLLS WITHOUT HIM. YOU ACT BEYOND YOUR LIMITS, JACKAL...RETURN TO YOUR EMBALMING!
AND YOU ARE PASSED FROM THIS WORLD, BIRD, LEFT TO DWELL AMONG THE ANKU AND OTHER LESSER SPIRITS.
THERE ARE NO WORSHIPPERS OF WISDOM ANYMORE--
I AM DEATH-GOD--
THOOOOOM
--AND I RULE HERE!
USURPER!
SHADE! GO BACK TO YOUR GRAVE!
IS THIS WHERE I SAY, "OH, MY HEART"?
CAN I *PLEASE* WAKE UP NOW?

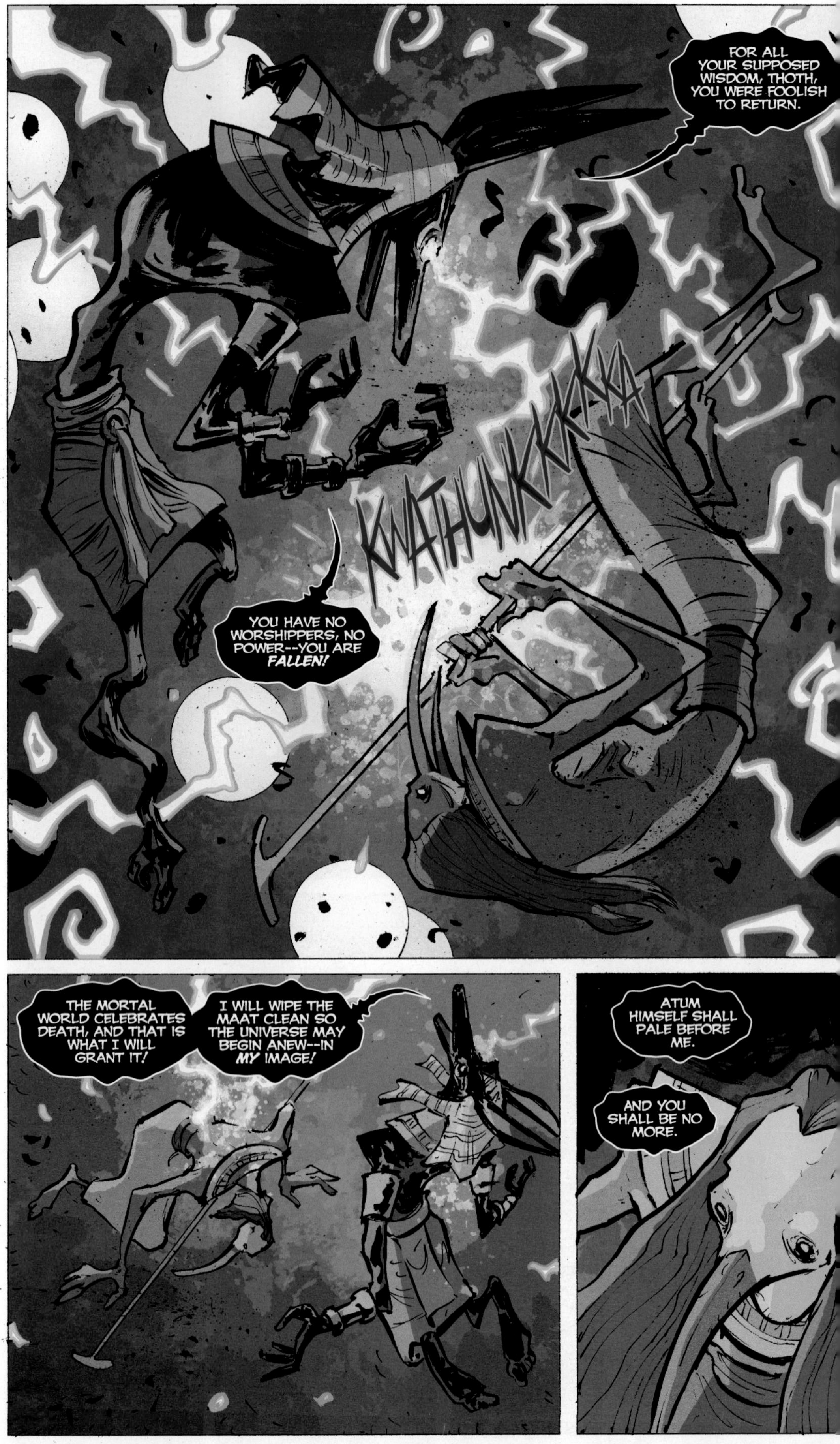

FOR ALL YOUR SUPPOSED WISDOM, THOTH, YOU WERE FOOLISH TO RETURN.
KWATHUNKKKKKA
YOU HAVE NO WORSHIPPERS, NO POWER--YOU ARE *FALLEN!*
THE MORTAL WORLD CELEBRATES DEATH, AND THAT IS WHAT I WILL GRANT IT!
I WILL WIPE THE MAAT CLEAN SO THE UNIVERSE MAY BEGIN ANEW--IN *MY* IMAGE!
ATUM HIMSELF SHALL PALE BEFORE ME.
AND YOU SHALL BE NO MORE.

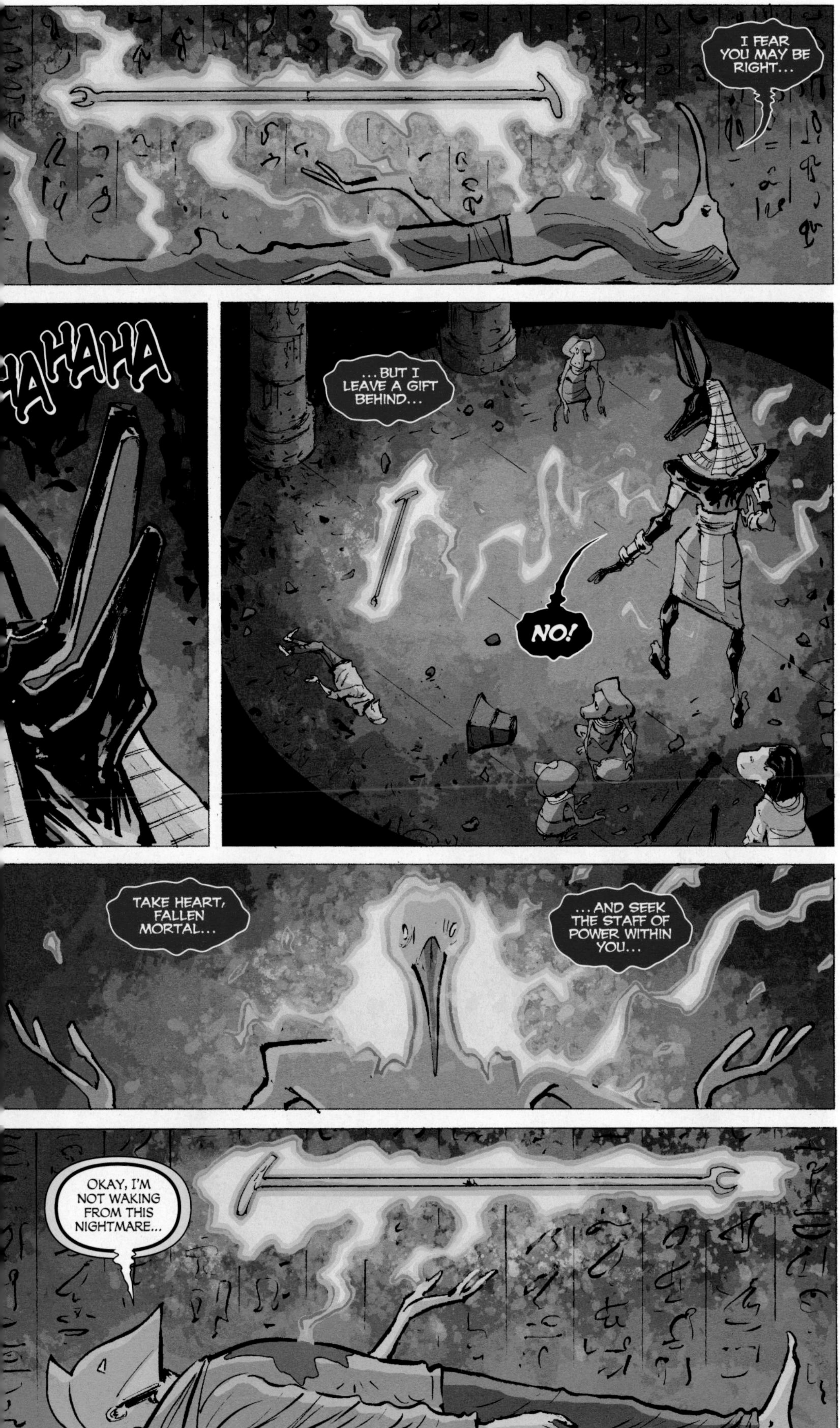
I FEAR YOU MAY BE RIGHT...
HAHAHA
...BUT I LEAVE A GIFT BEHIND...
NO!
TAKE HEART, FALLEN MORTAL...
...AND SEEK THE STAFF OF POWER WITHIN YOU...
OKAY, I'M NOT WAKING FROM THIS NIGHTMARE...

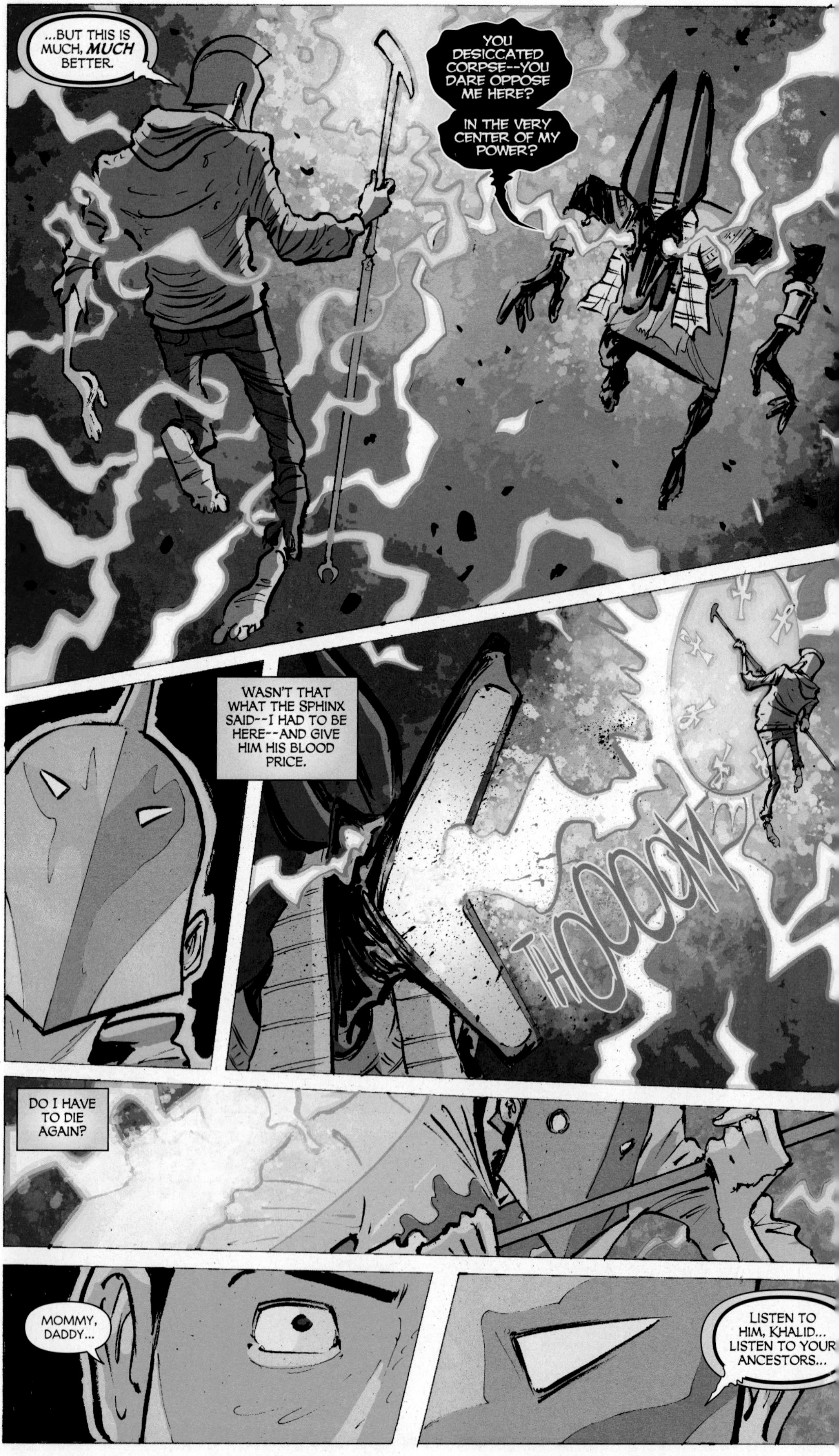
...BUT THIS IS MUCH, ***MUCH*** BETTER.
YOU DESICCATED CORPSE--YOU DARE OPPOSE ME HERE?
IN THE VERY CENTER OF MY POWER?
WASN'T THAT WHAT THE SPHINX SAID--I HAD TO BE HERE--AND GIVE HIM HIS BLOOD PRICE.
THOOOOM
DO I HAVE TO DIE AGAIN?
MOMMY, DADDY...
LISTEN TO HIM, KHALID... LISTEN TO YOUR ANCESTORS...

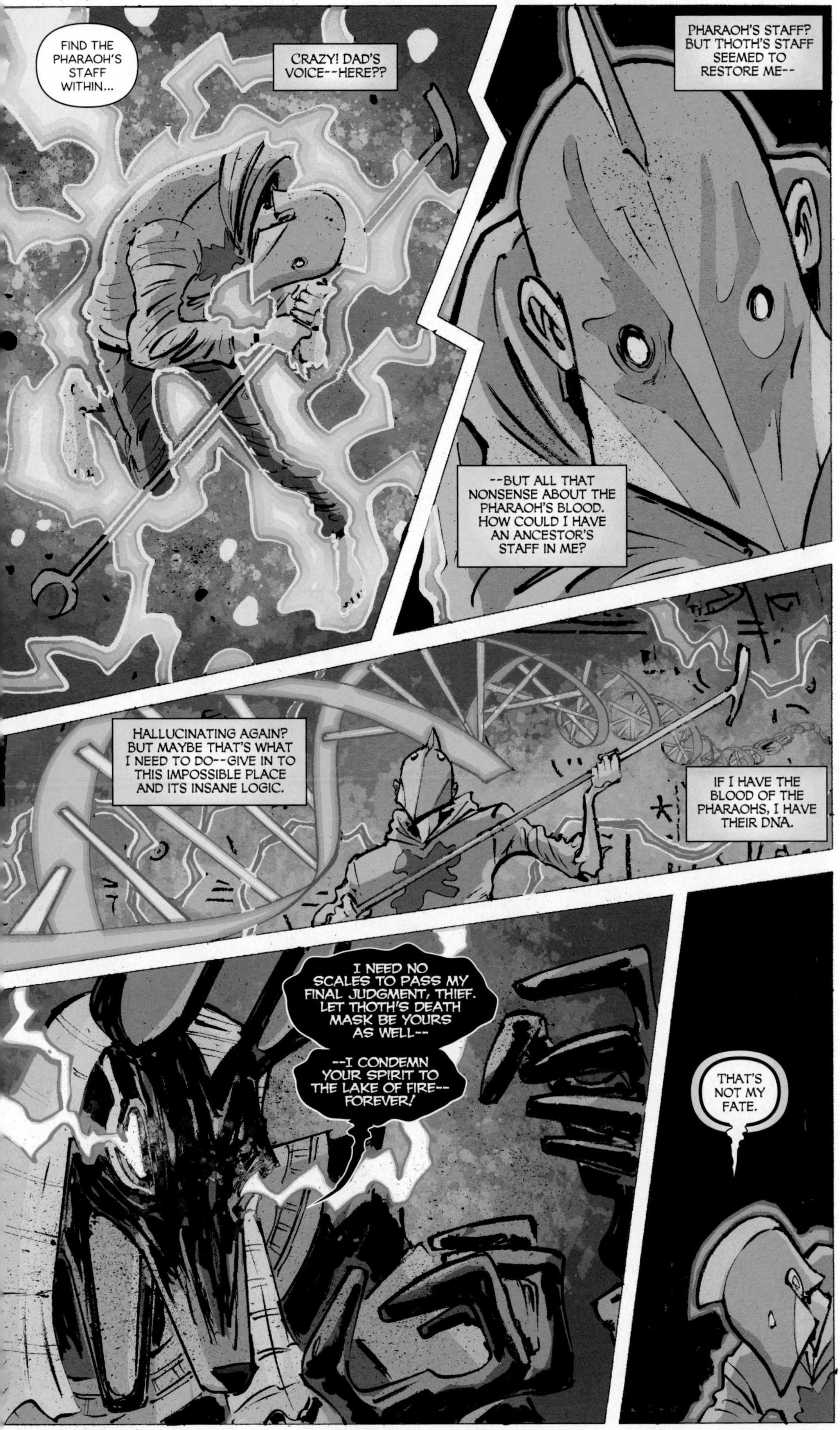

FIND THE PHARAOH'S STAFF WITHIN...
CRAZY! DAD'S VOICE--HERE??
PHARAOH'S STAFF? BUT THOTH'S STAFF SEEMED TO RESTORE ME--
--BUT ALL THAT NONSENSE ABOUT THE PHARAOH'S BLOOD. HOW COULD I HAVE AN ANCESTOR'S STAFF IN ME?
HALLUCINATING AGAIN? BUT MAYBE THAT'S WHAT I NEED TO DO--GIVE IN TO THIS IMPOSSIBLE PLACE AND ITS INSANE LOGIC.
IF I HAVE THE BLOOD OF THE PHARAOHS, I HAVE THEIR DNA.
I NEED NO SCALES TO PASS MY FINAL JUDGMENT, THIEF. LET THOTH'S DEATH MASK BE YOURS AS WELL--
--I CONDEMN YOUR SPIRIT TO THE LAKE OF FIRE--FOREVER!
THAT'S NOT MY FATE.

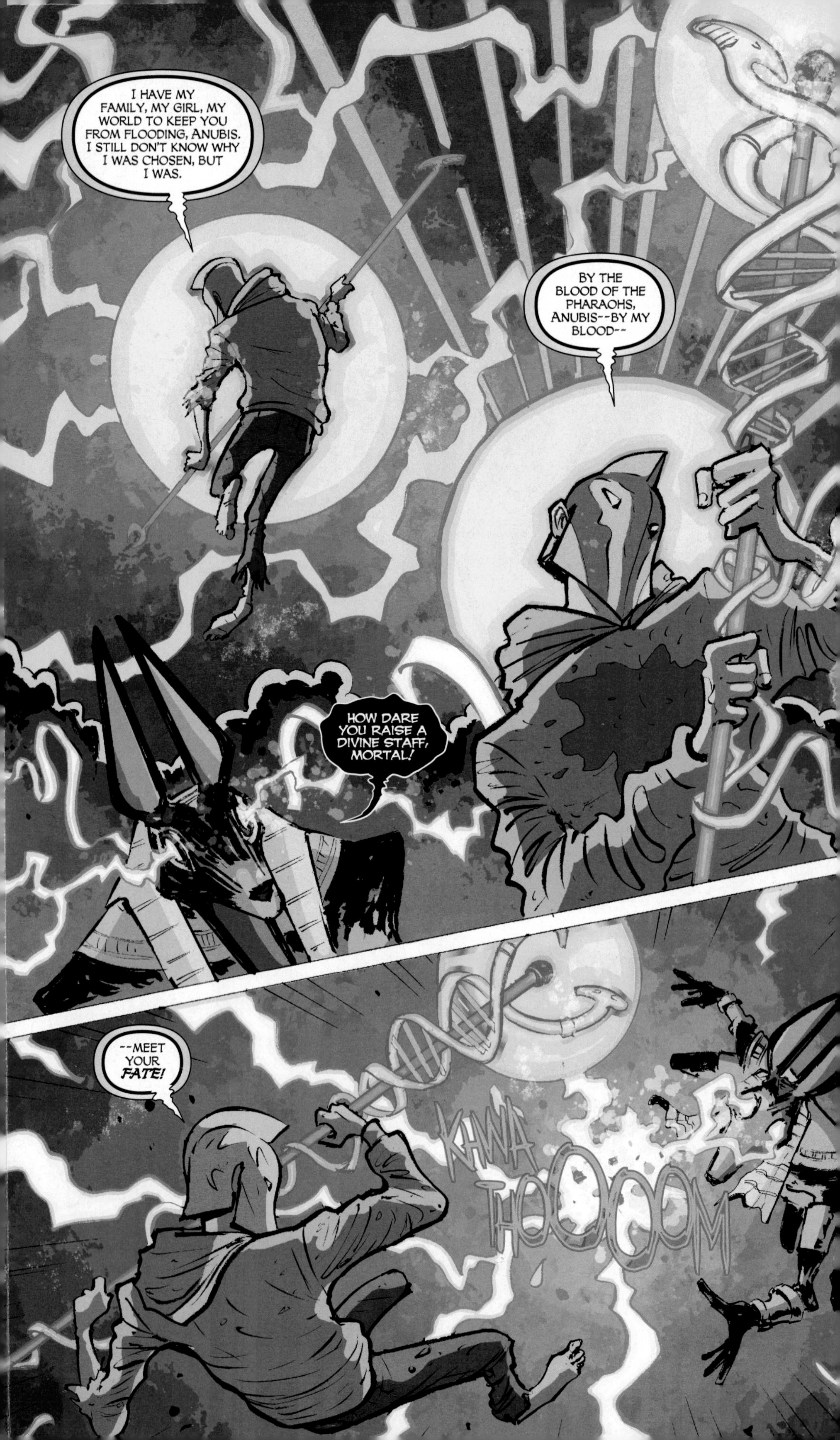
I HAVE MY FAMILY, MY GIRL, MY WORLD TO KEEP YOU FROM FLOODING, ANUBIS. I STILL DON'T KNOW WHY I WAS CHOSEN, BUT I WAS.
BY THE BLOOD OF THE PHARAOHS, ANUBIS--BY MY BLOOD--
HOW DARE YOU RAISE A DIVINE STAFF, MORTAL!
--MEET YOUR FATE!
KWA THOOOOOM

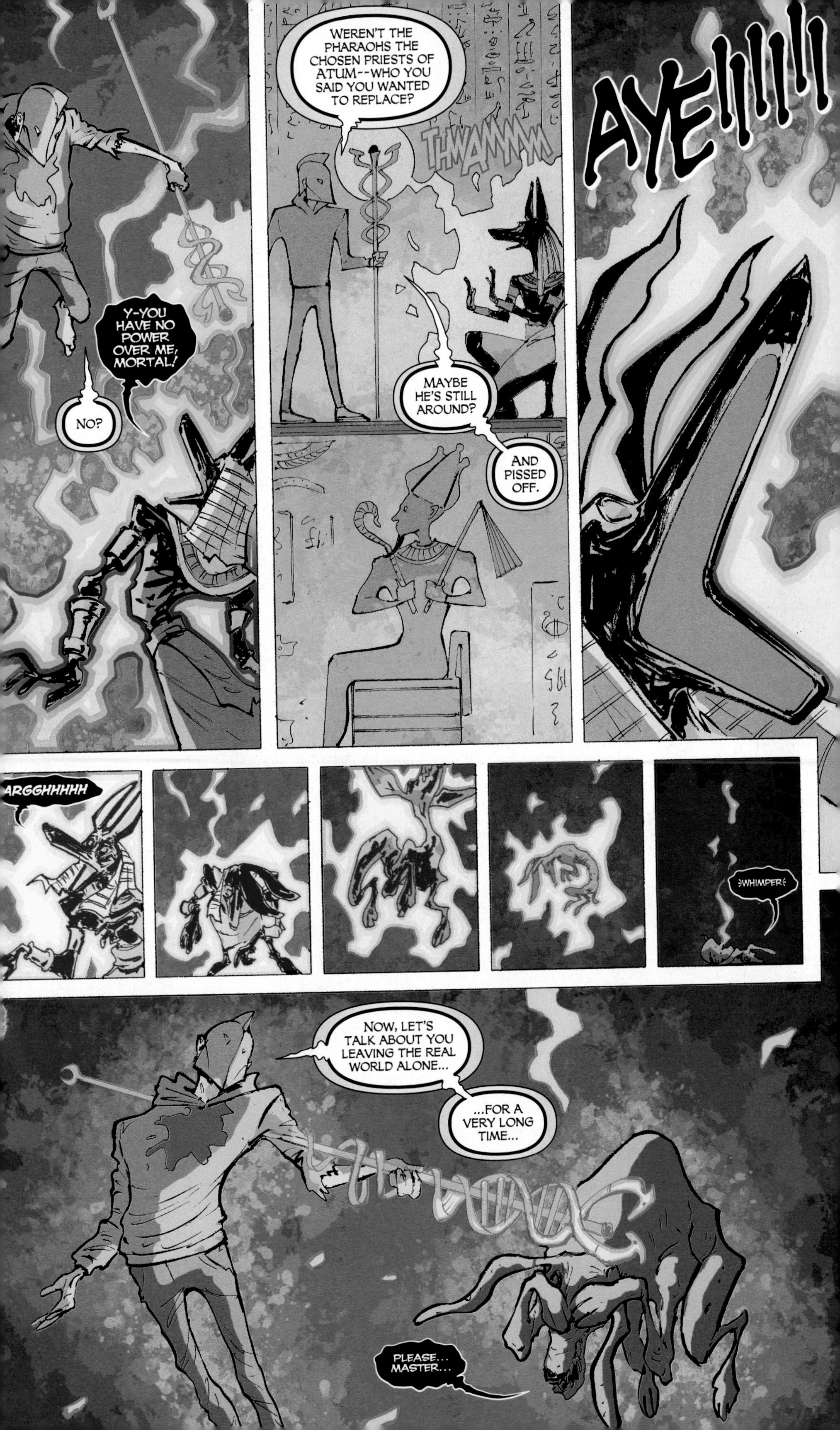
Y-YOU HAVE NO POWER OVER ME, MORTAL!
NO?
WEREN'T THE PHARAOHS THE CHOSEN PRIESTS OF ATUM--WHO YOU SAID YOU WANTED TO REPLACE?
THWAMMM
MAYBE HE'S STILL AROUND?
AND PISSED OFF.
AYE!!!!!!
ARGGHHHHH
WHIMPER
NOW, LET'S TALK ABOUT YOU LEAVING THE REAL WORLD ALONE...
...FOR A VERY LONG TIME...
PLEASE... MASTER...

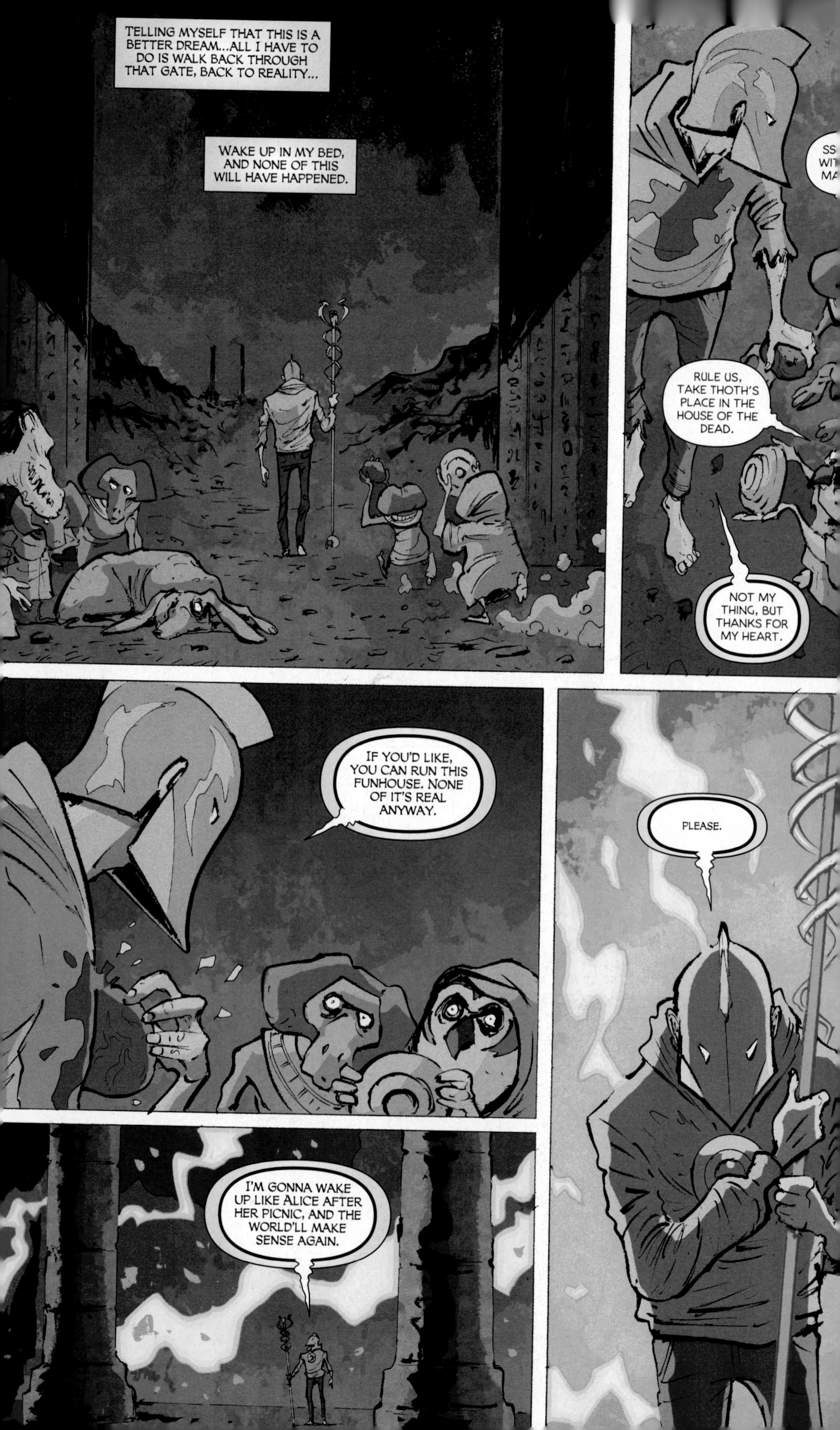
TELLING MYSELF THAT THIS IS A BETTER DREAM...ALL I HAVE TO DO IS WALK BACK THROUGH THAT GATE, BACK TO REALITY...
WAKE UP IN MY BED, AND NONE OF THIS WILL HAVE HAPPENED.
RULE US, TAKE THOTH'S PLACE IN THE HOUSE OF THE DEAD.
NOT MY THING, BUT THANKS FOR MY HEART.
IF YOU'D LIKE, YOU CAN RUN THIS FUNHOUSE. NONE OF IT'S REAL ANYWAY.
I'M GONNA WAKE UP LIKE ALICE AFTER HER PICNIC, AND THE WORLD'LL MAKE SENSE AGAIN.
PLEASE.

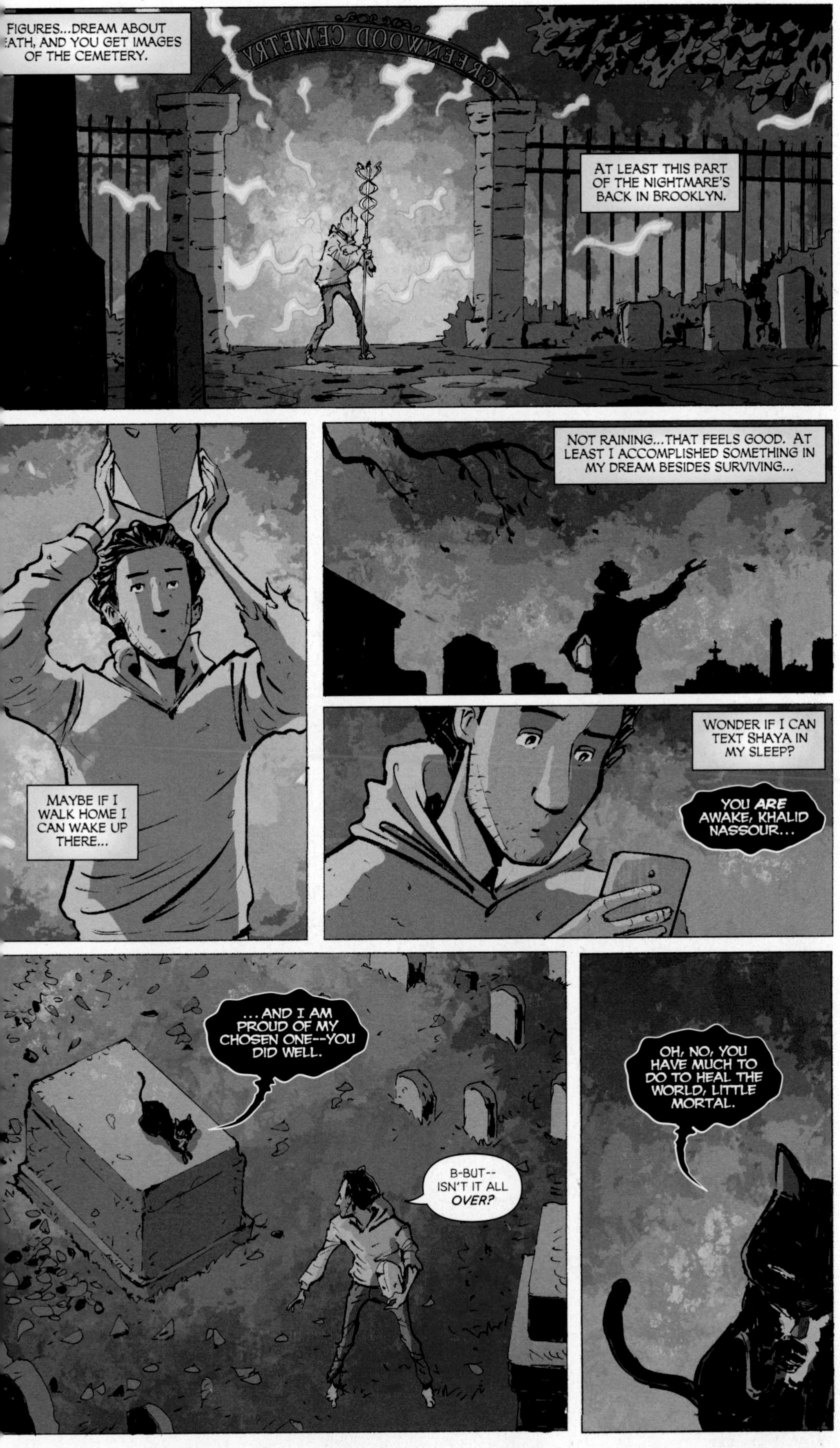

FIGURES...DREAM ABOUT
EATH, AND YOU GET IMAGES
OF THE CEMETERY.
GREENWOOD CEMETERY
AT LEAST THIS PART
OF THE NIGHTMARE'S
BACK IN BROOKLYN.
MAYBE IF I
WALK HOME I
CAN WAKE UP
THERE...
NOT RAINING...THAT FEELS GOOD. AT
LEAST I ACCOMPLISHED SOMETHING IN
MY DREAM BESIDES SURVIVING...
WONDER IF I CAN
TEXT SHAYA IN
MY SLEEP?
YOU ARE
AWAKE, KHALID
NASSOUR...
...AND I AM
PROUD OF MY
CHOSEN ONE--YOU
DID WELL.
B-BUT--
ISN'T IT ALL
OVER?
OH, NO, YOU
HAVE MUCH TO
DO TO HEAL THE
WORLD, LITTLE
MORTAL.

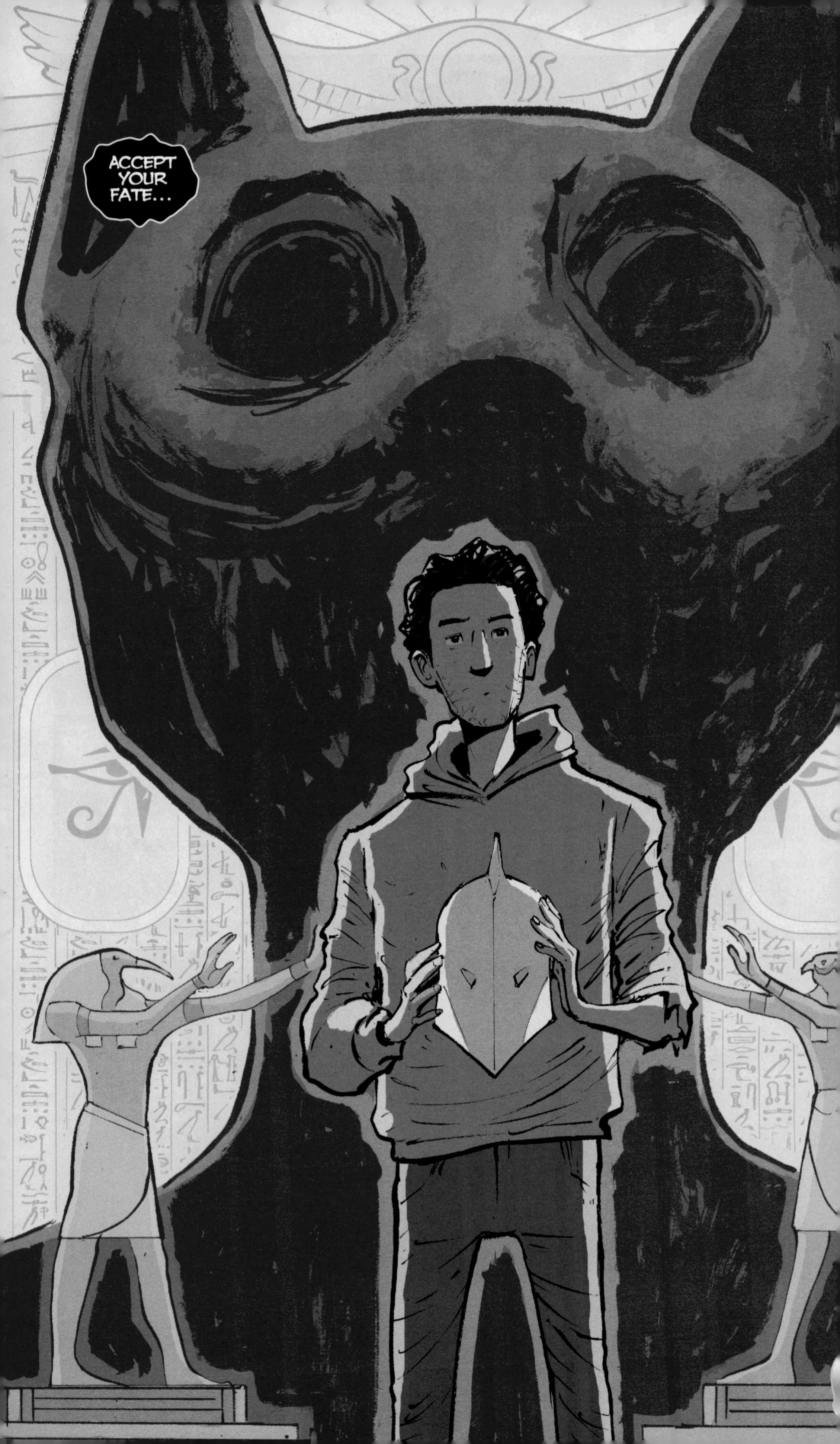
ACCEPT YOUR FATE...